D0869808

Thank you for picking up *Haikyu!!* volume 24! I've finally started running out of ideas about what to draw for the little self-portraits! ➡️ This time I decided to draw Kindaichi because his silhouette is somewhat similar to mine.

HARUICHI FURUDATE began his manga career when he was 25 years old with the one-shot *Ousama Kid* (King Kid), which won an honorable mention for the 14th Jump Treasure Newcomer Manga Prize. His first series, *Kiben Gakuha, Yotsuya Sensei no Kaidan* (Philosophy School, Yotsuya Sensei's Ghost Stories), was serialized in Weekly Shonen Jump in 2010. In 2012, he began serializing *Haikyu!!* in Weekly Shonen Jump, where it became his most popular work to date.

HAIKYU!!
VOLUME 24
SHONEN JUMP Manga Edition

Story and Art by
HARUICHI FURUDATE

Translation **1 ADRIENNE BECK**
Touch-Up Art & Lettering **2 ERIKA TERRIQUEZ**
Design **3 JULIAN [JR] ROBINSON**
Editor **4 MARLENE FIRST**

HAIKYU!! © 2012 by Haruichi Furudate
All rights reserved.
First published in Japan in 2012 by SHUEISHA Inc., Tokyo.
English translation rights arranged by SHUEISHA Inc.

The stories, characters and incidents mentioned
in this publication are entirely fictional.

Printed in the U.S.A.

Published by VIZ Media, LLC
P.O. Box 77010
San Francisco, CA 94107

10 9 8 7 6 5 4 3 2
First printing, June 2018
Second printing, February 2021

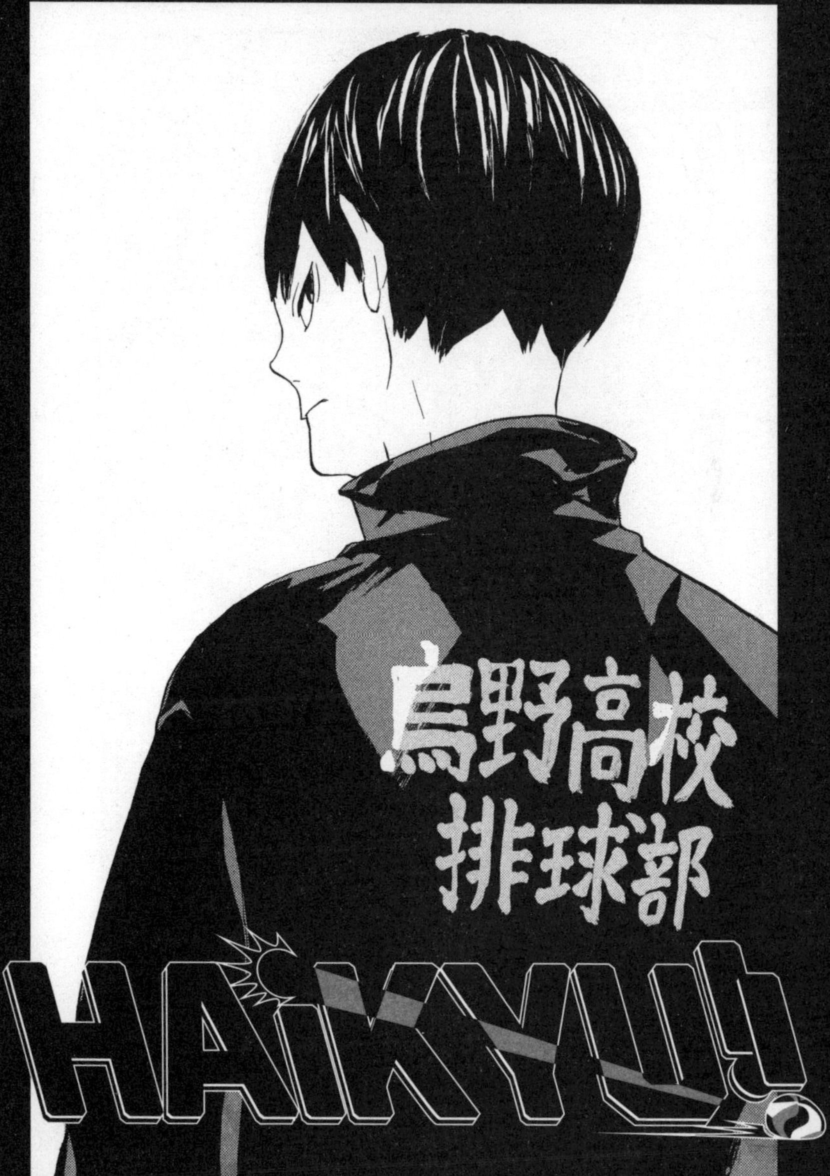
烏野高校
排球部
HAIKYU!!

HARUICHI
FURUDATE

FIRST SNOW 24

SHOYO HINATA

1ST YEAR / MIDDLE BLOCKER

Even though he doesn't have the best body type for volleyball, he is super athletic. Gets nervous easily.

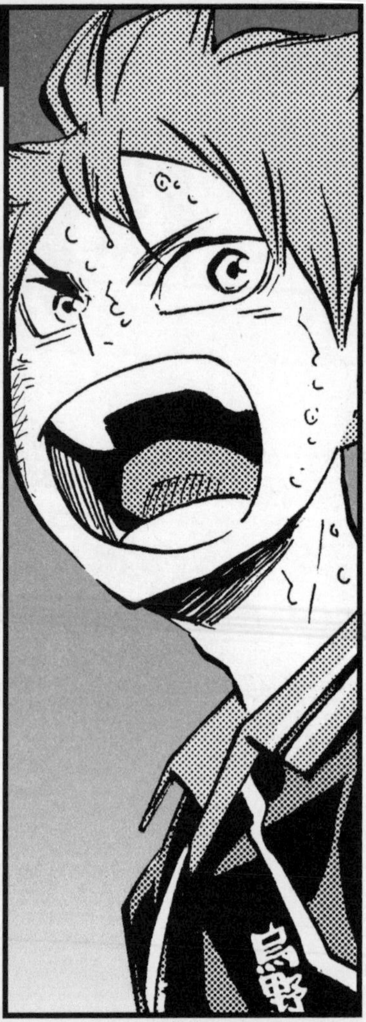

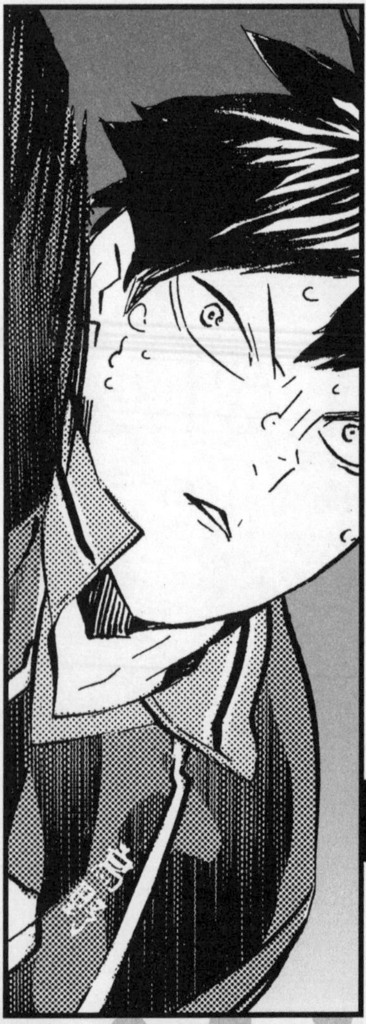

TOBIO KAGEYAMA

1ST YEAR / SETTER

His instincts and athletic talent are so good that he's like a "king" who rules the court. Demanding and egocentric.

CHARACTERS

Karasuno High School Volleyball Club

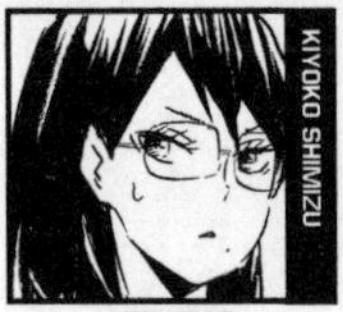
KIYOKO SHIMIZU
3RD YEAR
MANAGER

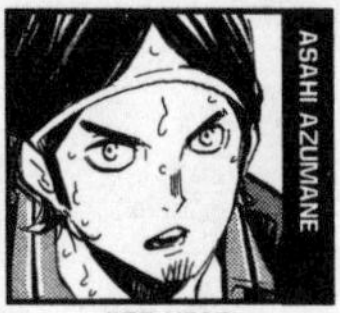
ASAHI AZUMANE
3RD YEAR
WING SPIKER

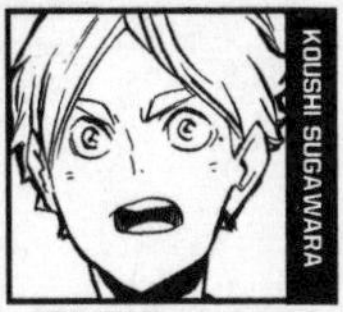
KOUSHI SUGAWARA
3RD YEAR (VICE CAPTAIN)
SETTER

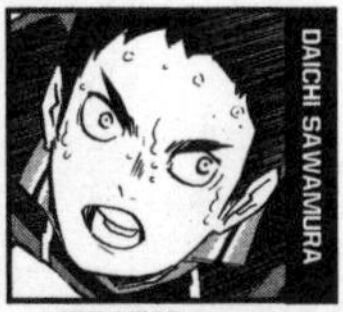
DAICHI SAWAMURA
3RD YEAR (CAPTAIN)
WING SPIKER

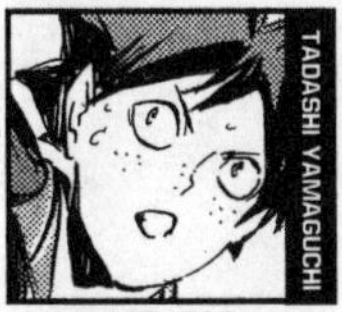
TADASHI YAMAGUCHI
1ST YEAR
MIDDLE BLOCKER

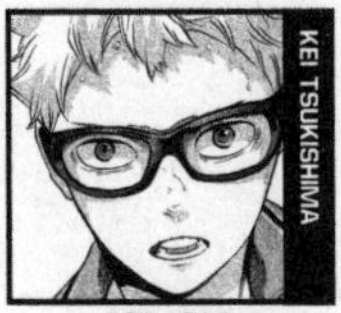
KEI TSUKISHIMA
1ST YEAR
MIDDLE BLOCKER

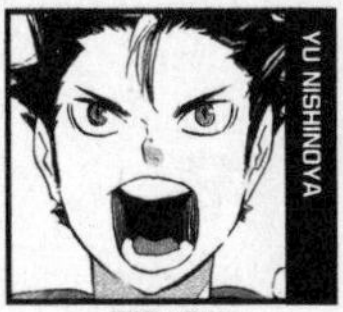
YU NISHINOYA
2ND YEAR
LIBERO

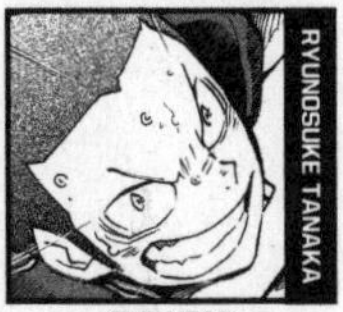
RYUNOSUKE TANAKA
2ND YEAR
WING SPIKER

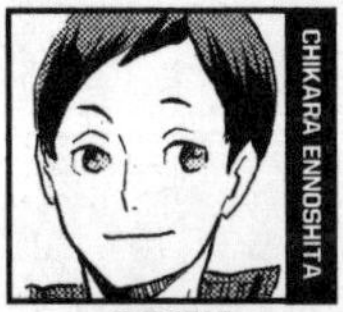
CHIKARA ENNOSHITA
2ND YEAR
WING SPIKER

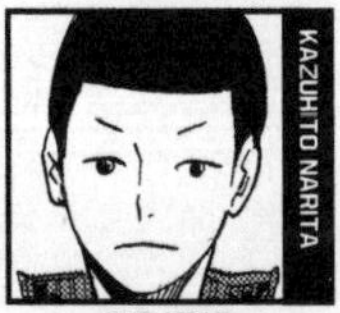
KAZUHITO NARITA
2ND YEAR
MIDDLE BLOCKER

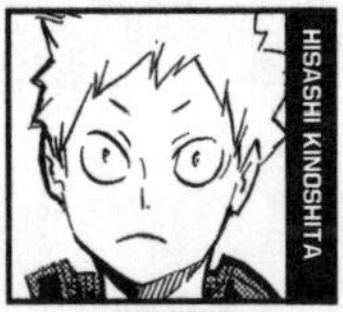
HISASHI KINOSHITA
2ND YEAR
WING SPIKER

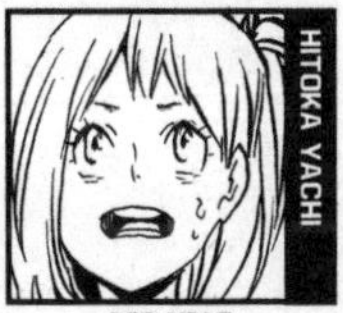
HITOKA YACHI
1ST YEAR
MANAGER

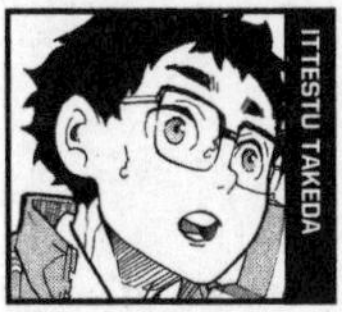
ITTETSU TAKEDA
ADVISER

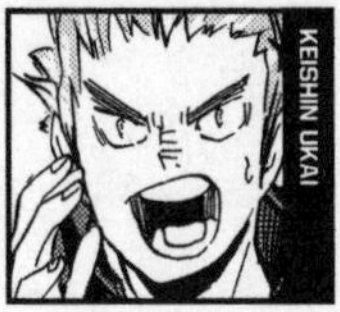
KEISHIN UKAI
COACH

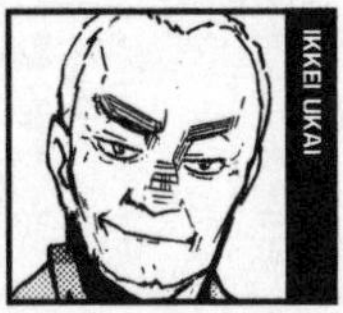
IKKEI UKAI
FORMER HEAD COACH

Ever since he saw the legendary player known as "the Little Giant" compete at the national volleyball finals, Shoyo Hinata has been aiming to be the best volleyball player ever! He decides to join the volleyball club at his middle school and gets to play in an official tournament during his third year. His team is crushed by a team led by volleyball prodigy Tobio Kageyama, also known as "the King of the Court." Swearing revenge on Kageyama, Hinata graduates middle school and enters Karasuno High School, the school where the Little Giant played. However, upon joining the club, he finds out that Kageyama is there too! The two of them bicker constantly, but they bring out the best in each other's talents and become a powerful combo. After a long and bitterly fought game, Karasuno finally defeats Shiratorizawa and wins the Miyagi Prefecture Qualifiers! Meanwhile, Fukurodani beats Nekoma in the Tokyo Area Qualifiers, earning their ticket to the finals and the Spring Tournament. Nekoma's last hope is to snag a spot as the venue sponsor representative by beating the devious Nohebi team. Their star libero, Yaku, is out with an injury, but then the real meaning of teamwork finally clicks with Lev! He and backup libero Shibayama manage to lead Nekoma to victory! Now, as preparations for the Spring Tourney are getting under way, Karasuno receives unexpected news...!!

HAIKYU!!

24 FIRST SNOW

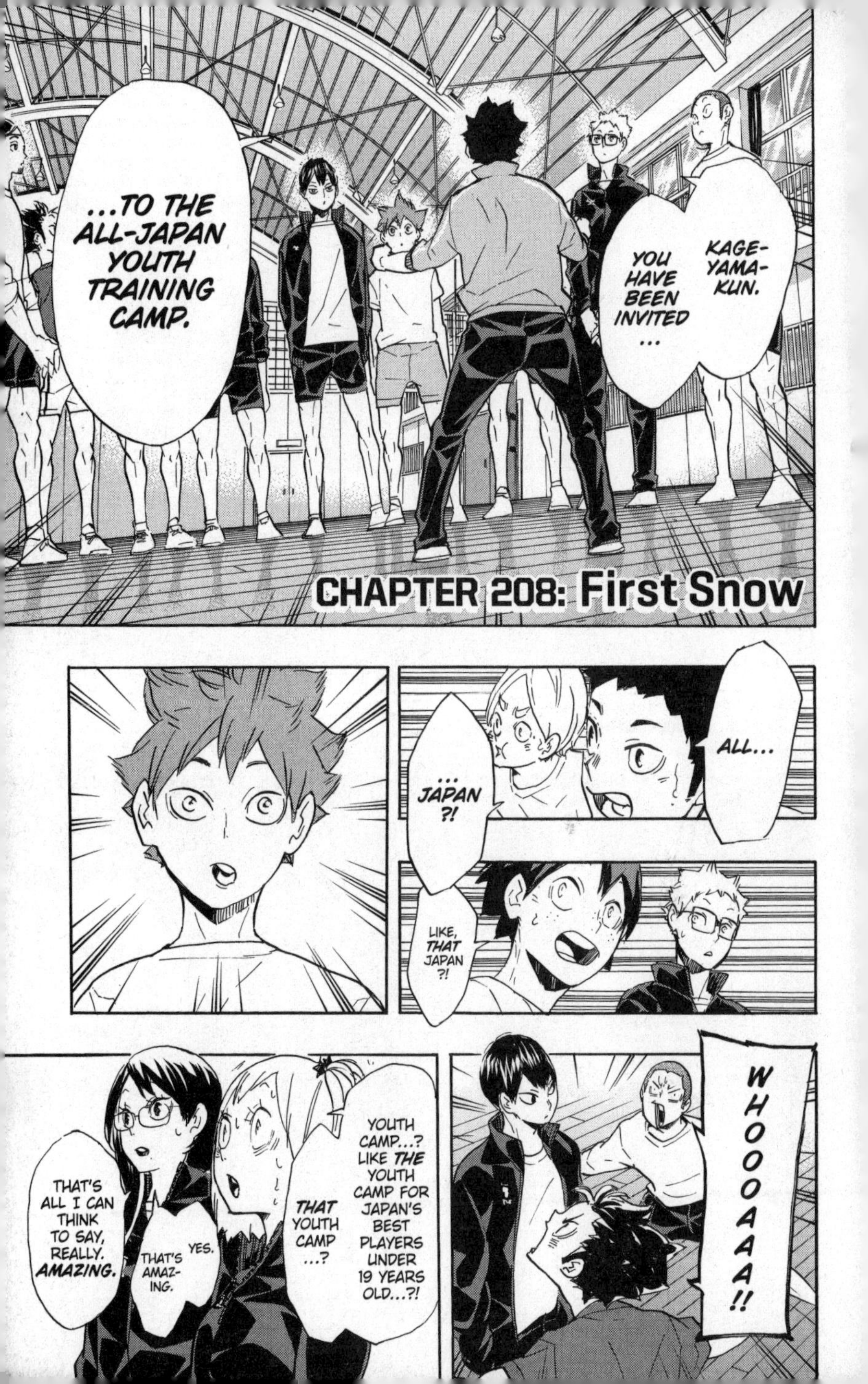
KAGE-YAMA-KUN.
YOU HAVE BEEN INVITED ...
...TO THE ALL-JAPAN YOUTH TRAINING CAMP.
CHAPTER 208: First Snow
ALL...
...JAPAN?!
LIKE, THAT JAPAN?!
WHOOOAAA!!
YOUTH CAMP...? LIKE THE YOUTH CAMP FOR JAPAN'S BEST PLAYERS UNDER 19 YEARS OLD...?!
THAT YOUTH CAMP...?
YES.
THAT'S AMAZING.
THAT'S ALL I CAN THINK TO SAY, REALLY. AMAZING.

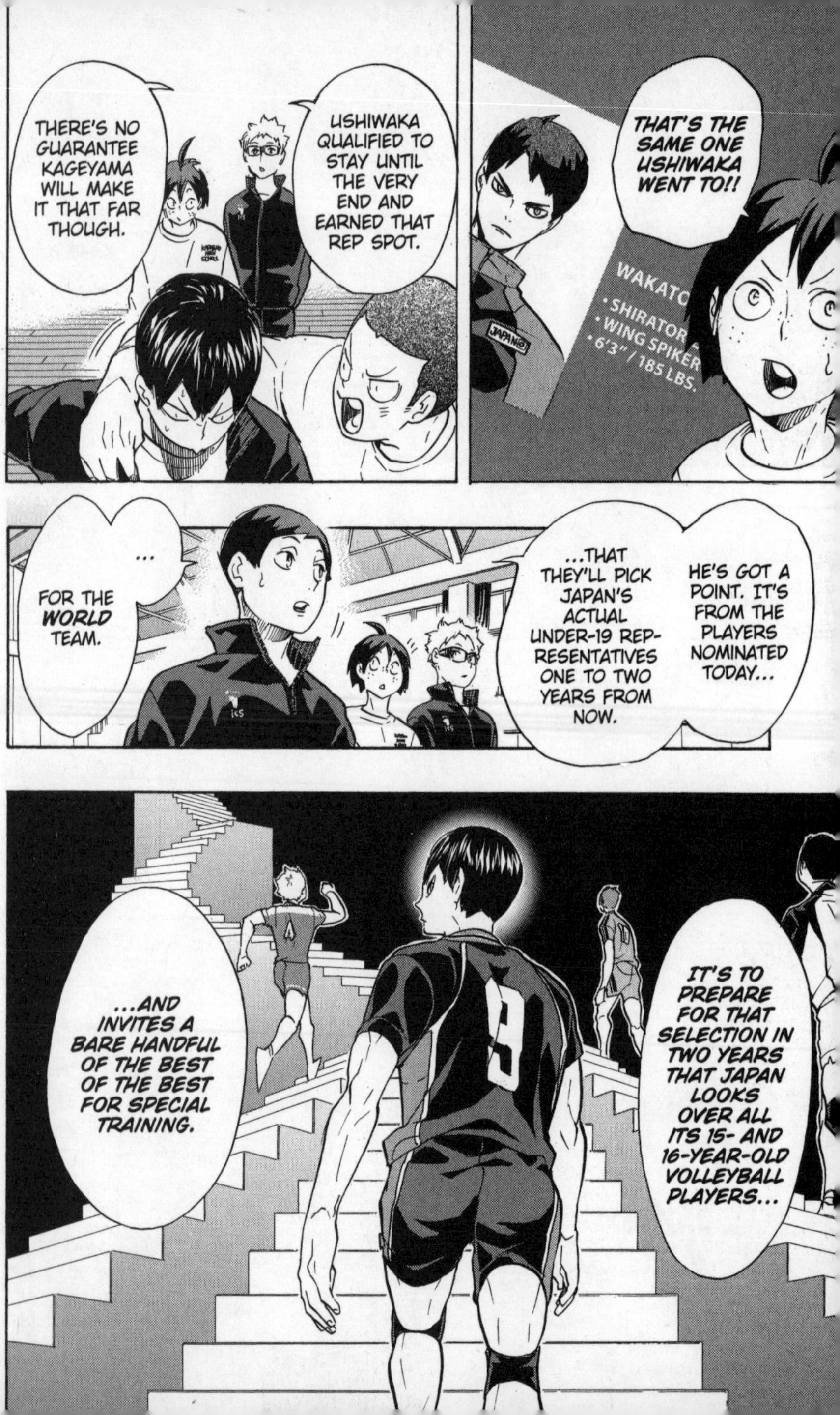
THAT'S THE SAME ONE USHIWAKA WENT TO!!
WAKATO
• SHIRATOR
• WING SPIKER
• 6'3" / 185 LBS.
USHIWAKA QUALIFIED TO STAY UNTIL THE VERY END AND EARNED THAT REP SPOT.
THERE'S NO GUARANTEE KAGEYAMA WILL MAKE IT THAT FAR THOUGH.
HE'S GOT A POINT. IT'S FROM THE PLAYERS NOMINATED TODAY...
...THAT THEY'LL PICK JAPAN'S ACTUAL UNDER-19 REPRESENTATIVES ONE TO TWO YEARS FROM NOW.
...
FOR THE WORLD TEAM.
IT'S TO PREPARE FOR THAT SELECTION IN TWO YEARS THAT JAPAN LOOKS OVER ALL ITS 15- AND 16-YEAR-OLD VOLLEYBALL PLAYERS...
...AND INVITES A BARE HANDFUL OF THE BEST OF THE BEST FOR SPECIAL TRAINING.

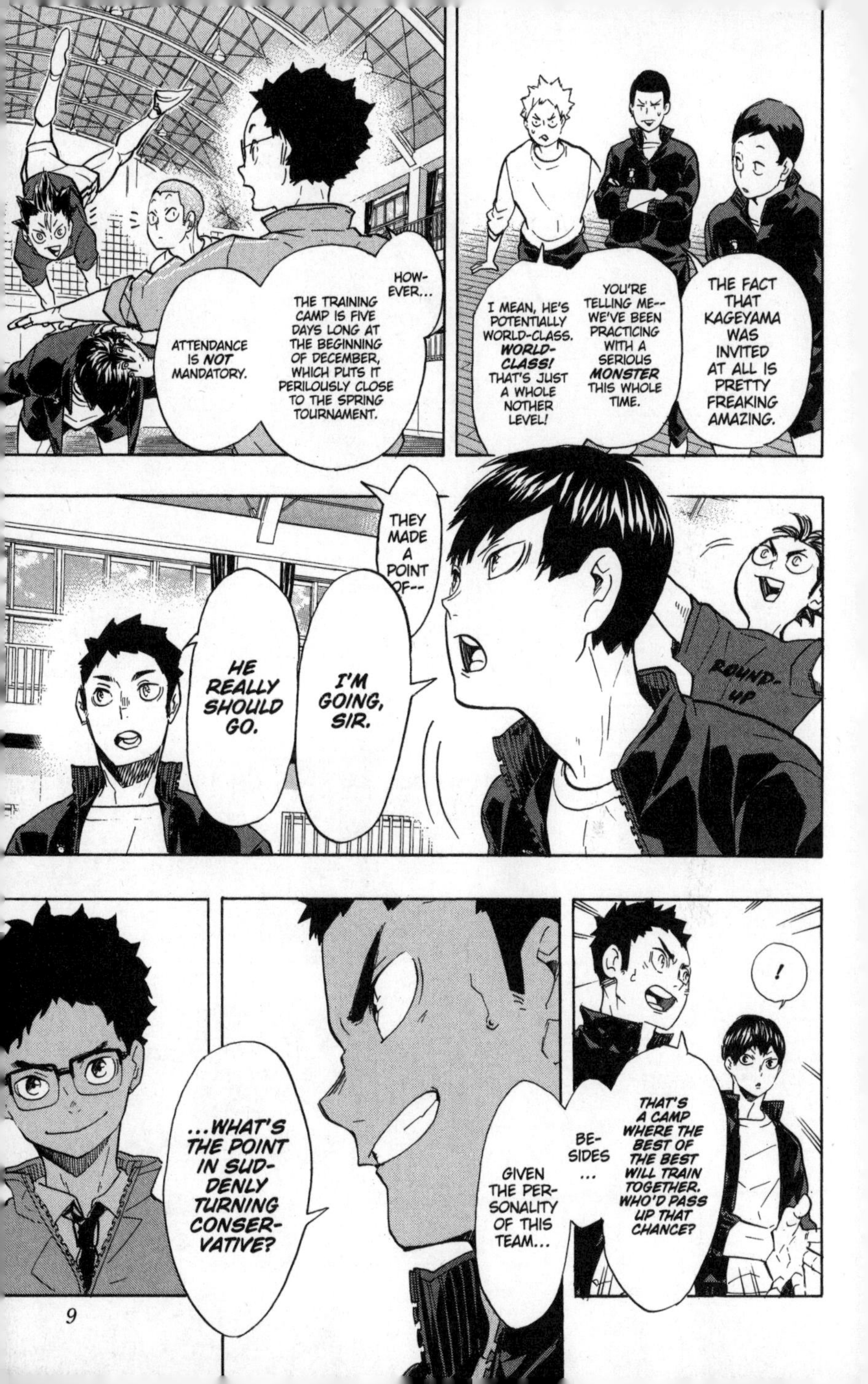
THE FACT THAT KAGEYAMA WAS INVITED AT ALL IS PRETTY FREAKING AMAZING.
YOU'RE TELLING ME-- WE'VE BEEN PRACTICING WITH A SERIOUS MONSTER THIS WHOLE TIME.
I MEAN, HE'S POTENTIALLY WORLD-CLASS. WORLD-CLASS! THAT'S JUST A WHOLE NOTHER LEVEL!
HOW-EVER...
THE TRAINING CAMP IS FIVE DAYS LONG AT THE BEGINNING OF DECEMBER, WHICH PUTS IT PERILOUSLY CLOSE TO THE SPRING TOURNAMENT.
ATTENDANCE IS NOT MANDATORY.
THEY MADE A POINT OF--
ROUND-UP
I'M GOING, SIR.
HE REALLY SHOULD GO.
!
THAT'S A CAMP WHERE THE BEST OF THE BEST WILL TRAIN TOGETHER. WHO'D PASS UP THAT CHANCE?
BE-SIDES...
GIVEN THE PER-SONALITY OF THIS TEAM...
...WHAT'S THE POINT IN SUD-DENLY TURNING CONSER-VATIVE?

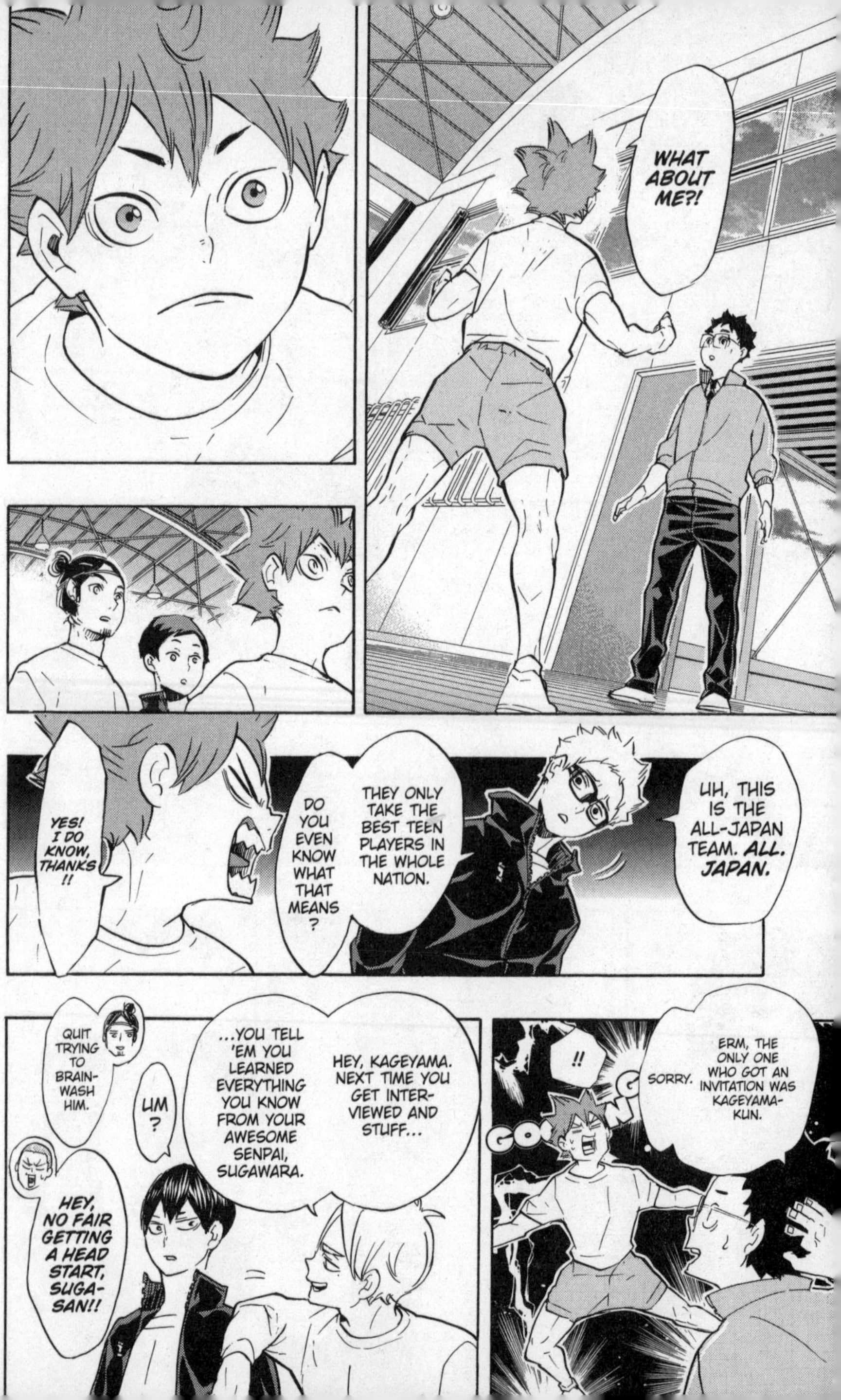
WHAT ABOUT ME?!
UH, THIS IS THE ALL-JAPAN TEAM. ALL. JAPAN.
THEY ONLY TAKE THE BEST TEEN PLAYERS IN THE WHOLE NATION.
DO YOU EVEN KNOW WHAT THAT MEANS?
YES! I DO KNOW, THANKS!!
ERM, THE ONLY ONE WHO GOT AN INVITATION WAS KAGEYAMA-KUN.
SORRY.
!!
HEY, KAGEYAMA. NEXT TIME YOU GET INTER-VIEWED AND STUFF...
...YOU TELL 'EM YOU LEARNED EVERYTHING YOU KNOW FROM YOUR AWESOME SENPAI, SUGAWARA.
UM?
QUIT TRYING TO BRAIN-WASH HIM.
HEY, NO FAIR GETTING A HEAD START, SUGA-SAN!!

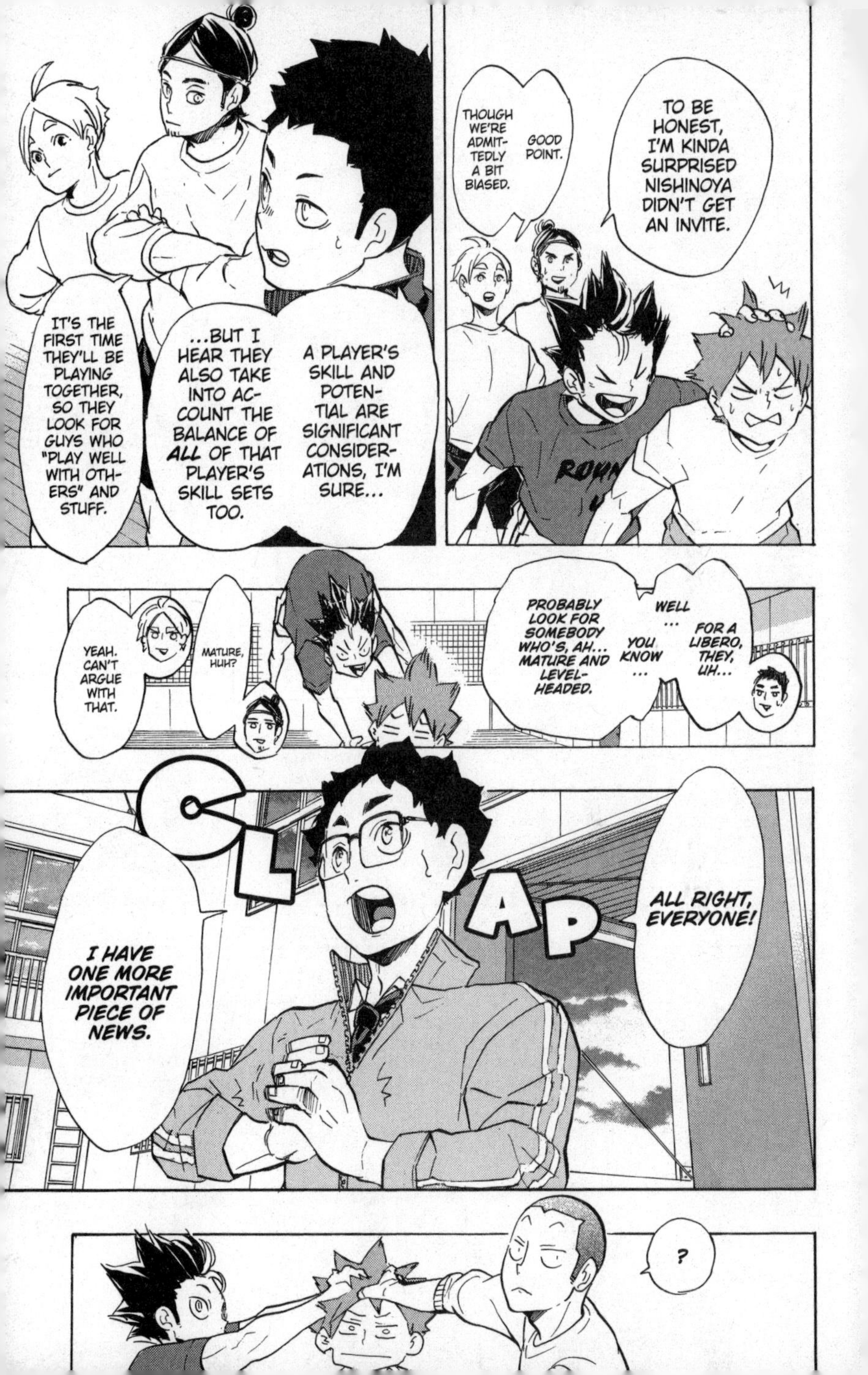
TO BE HONEST, I'M KINDA SURPRISED NISHINOYA DIDN'T GET AN INVITE.
GOOD POINT.
THOUGH WE'RE ADMITTEDLY A BIT BIASED.
A PLAYER'S SKILL AND POTENTIAL ARE SIGNIFICANT CONSIDERATIONS, I'M SURE...
...BUT I HEAR THEY ALSO TAKE INTO ACCOUNT THE BALANCE OF ALL OF THAT PLAYER'S SKILL SETS TOO.
IT'S THE FIRST TIME THEY'LL BE PLAYING TOGETHER, SO THEY LOOK FOR GUYS WHO "PLAY WELL WITH OTHERS" AND STUFF.
FOR A LIBERO, THEY, UH...
WELL... YOU KNOW...
PROBABLY LOOK FOR SOMEBODY WHO'S, AH... MATURE AND LEVEL-HEADED.
MATURE, HUH?
YEAH. CAN'T ARGUE WITH THAT.
CLAP
ALL RIGHT, EVERYONE!
I HAVE ONE MORE IMPORTANT PIECE OF NEWS.
?

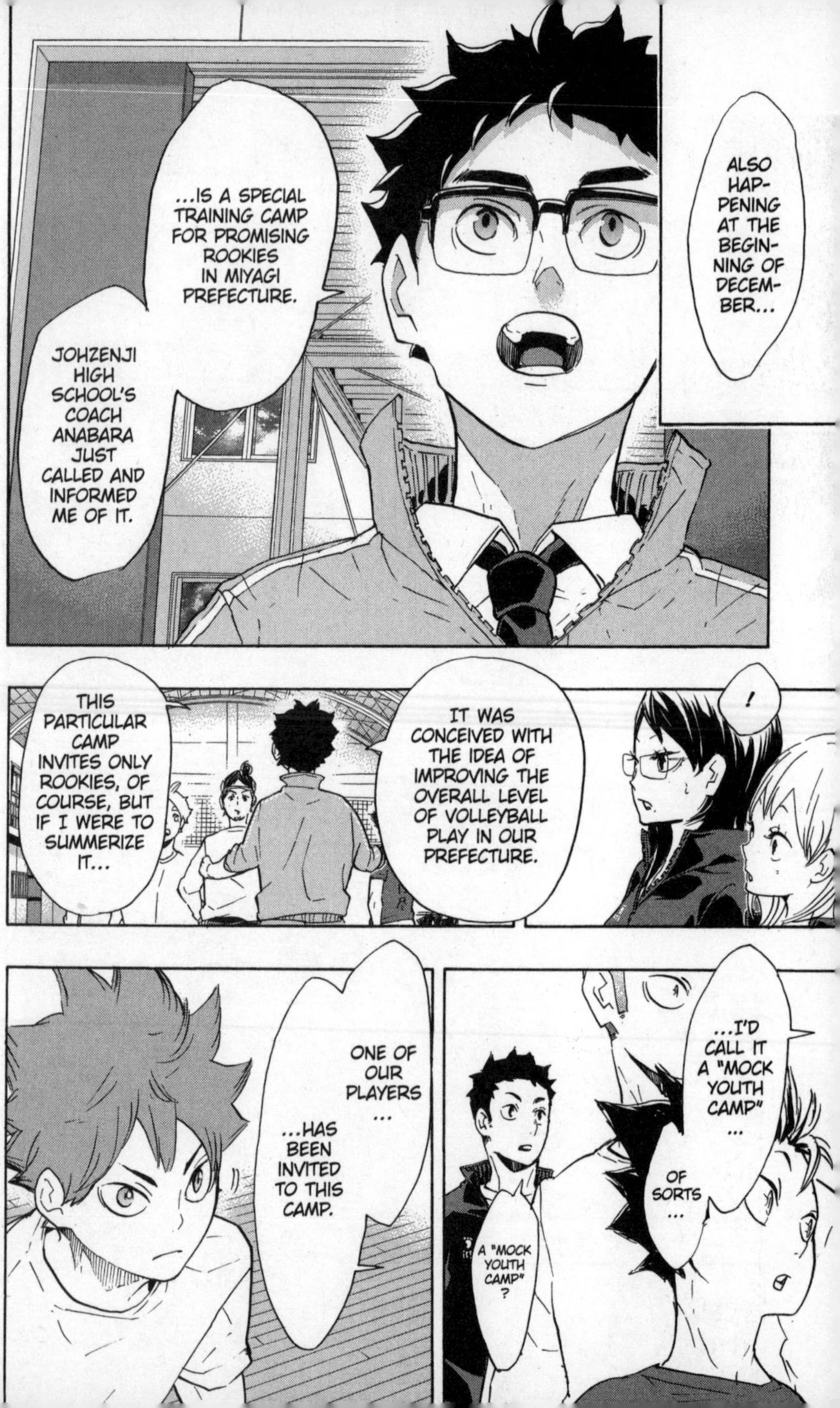
ALSO HAPPENING AT THE BEGINNING OF DECEMBER...
...IS A SPECIAL TRAINING CAMP FOR PROMISING ROOKIES IN MIYAGI PREFECTURE.
JOHZENJI HIGH SCHOOL'S COACH ANABARA JUST CALLED AND INFORMED ME OF IT.
!
IT WAS CONCEIVED WITH THE IDEA OF IMPROVING THE OVERALL LEVEL OF VOLLEYBALL PLAY IN OUR PREFECTURE.
THIS PARTICULAR CAMP INVITES ONLY ROOKIES, OF COURSE, BUT IF I WERE TO SUMMERIZE IT...
...I'D CALL IT A "MOCK YOUTH CAMP"...
OF SORTS...
A "MOCK YOUTH CAMP"?
ONE OF OUR PLAYERS...
...HAS BEEN INVITED TO THIS CAMP.

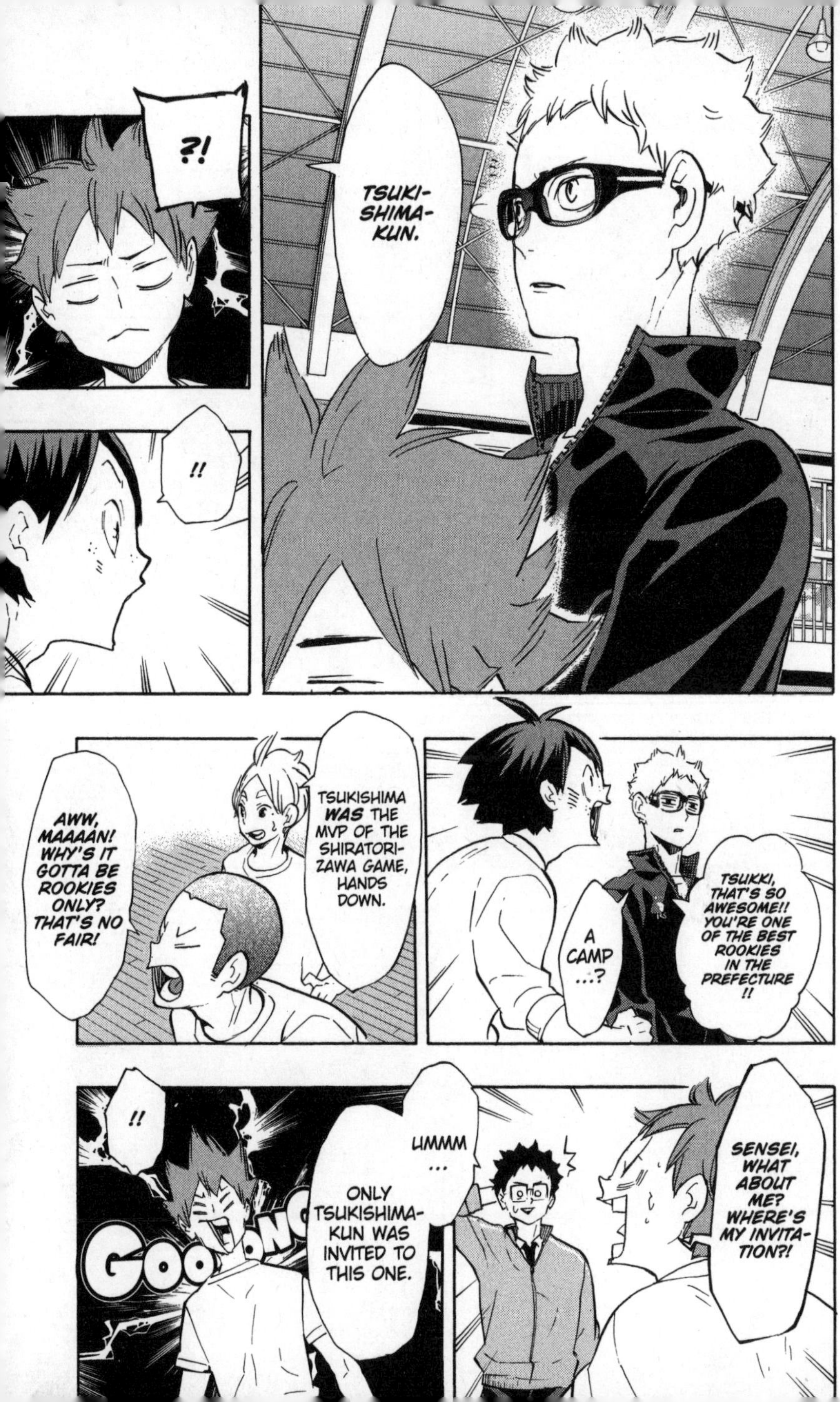
TSUKI-SHIMA-KUN.
?!
!!
TSUKKI, THAT'S SO AWESOME!! YOU'RE ONE OF THE BEST ROOKIES IN THE PREFECTURE !!
A CAMP ...?
TSUKISHIMA WAS THE MVP OF THE SHIRATORI-ZAWA GAME, HANDS DOWN.
AWW, MAAAAN! WHY'S IT GOTTA BE ROOKIES ONLY? THAT'S NO FAIR!
SENSEI, WHAT ABOUT ME? WHERE'S MY INVITATION?!
UMMM ...
ONLY TSUKISHIMA-KUN WAS INVITED TO THIS ONE.
!!
GOOONG

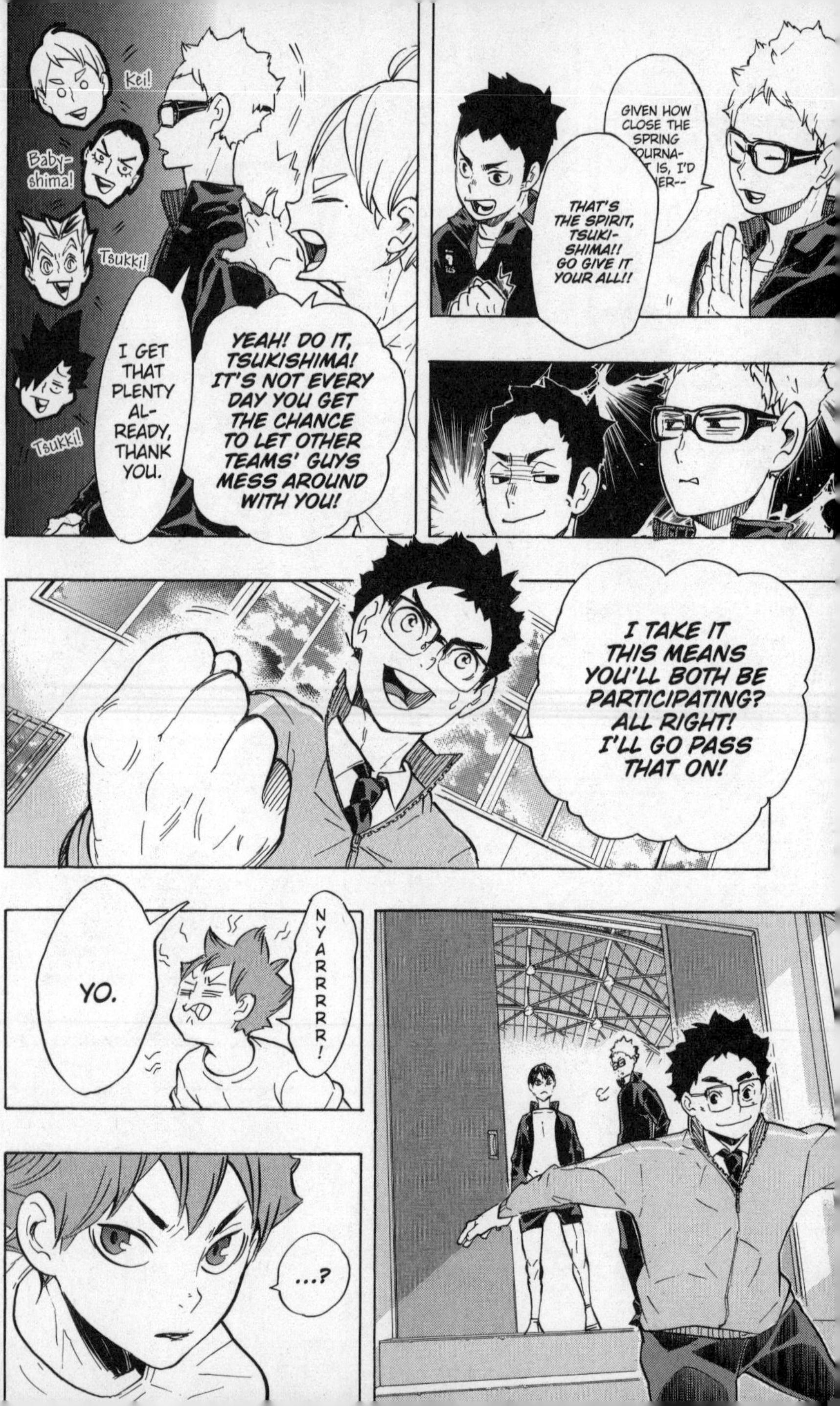
GIVEN HOW CLOSE THE SPRING TOURNA- ...T IS, I'D ...ER--
THAT'S THE SPIRIT, TSUKISHIMA!! GO GIVE IT YOUR ALL!!
Kei!
Baby-shima!
Tsukki!
Tsukki!
YEAH! DO IT, TSUKISHIMA! IT'S NOT EVERY DAY YOU GET THE CHANCE TO LET OTHER TEAMS' GUYS MESS AROUND WITH YOU!
I GET THAT PLENTY AL- READY, THANK YOU.
I TAKE IT THIS MEANS YOU'LL BOTH BE PARTICIPATING? ALL RIGHT! I'LL GO PASS THAT ON!
YO.
NYARRRRR!
...?

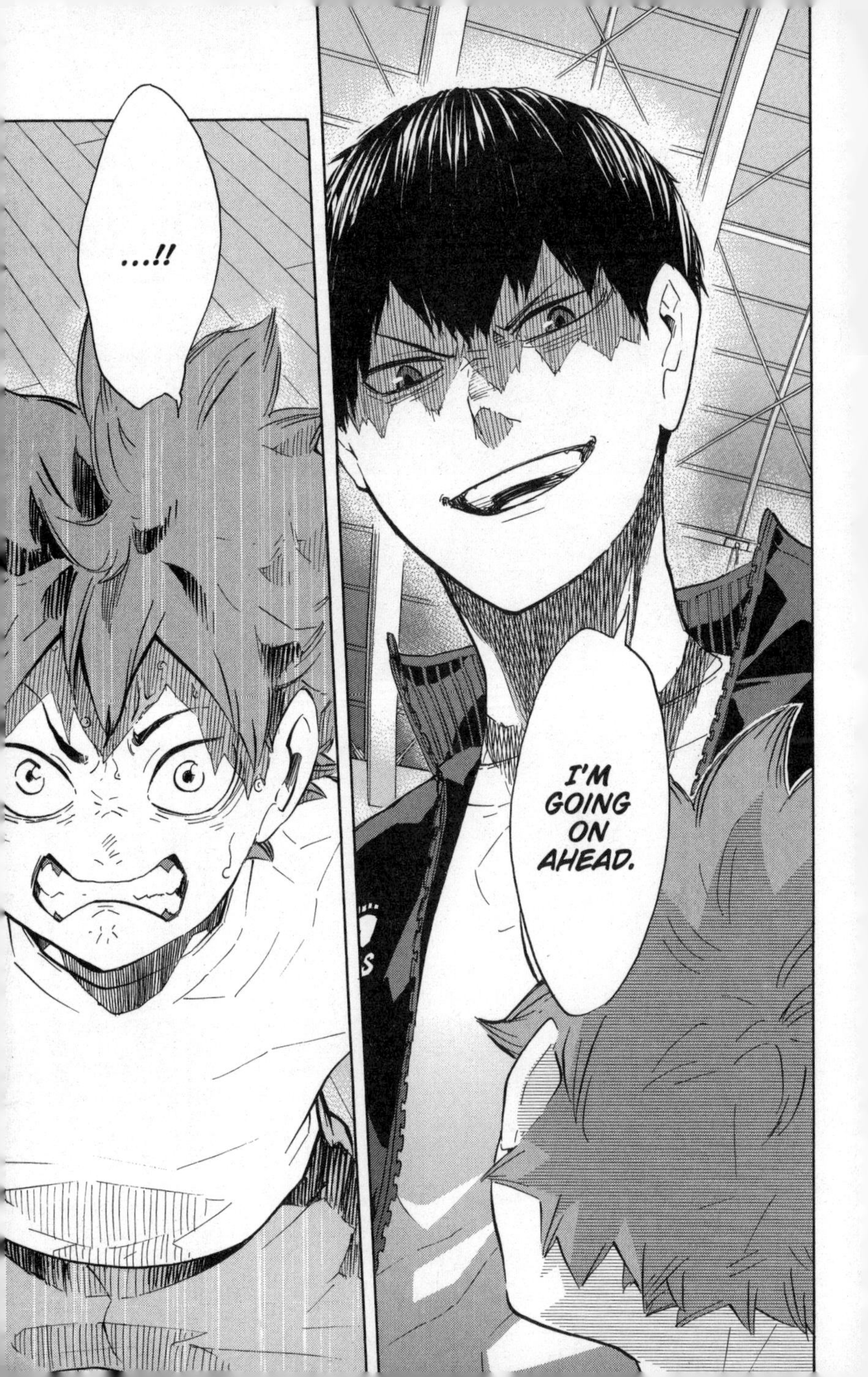
I'M GOING ON AHEAD.
...!!

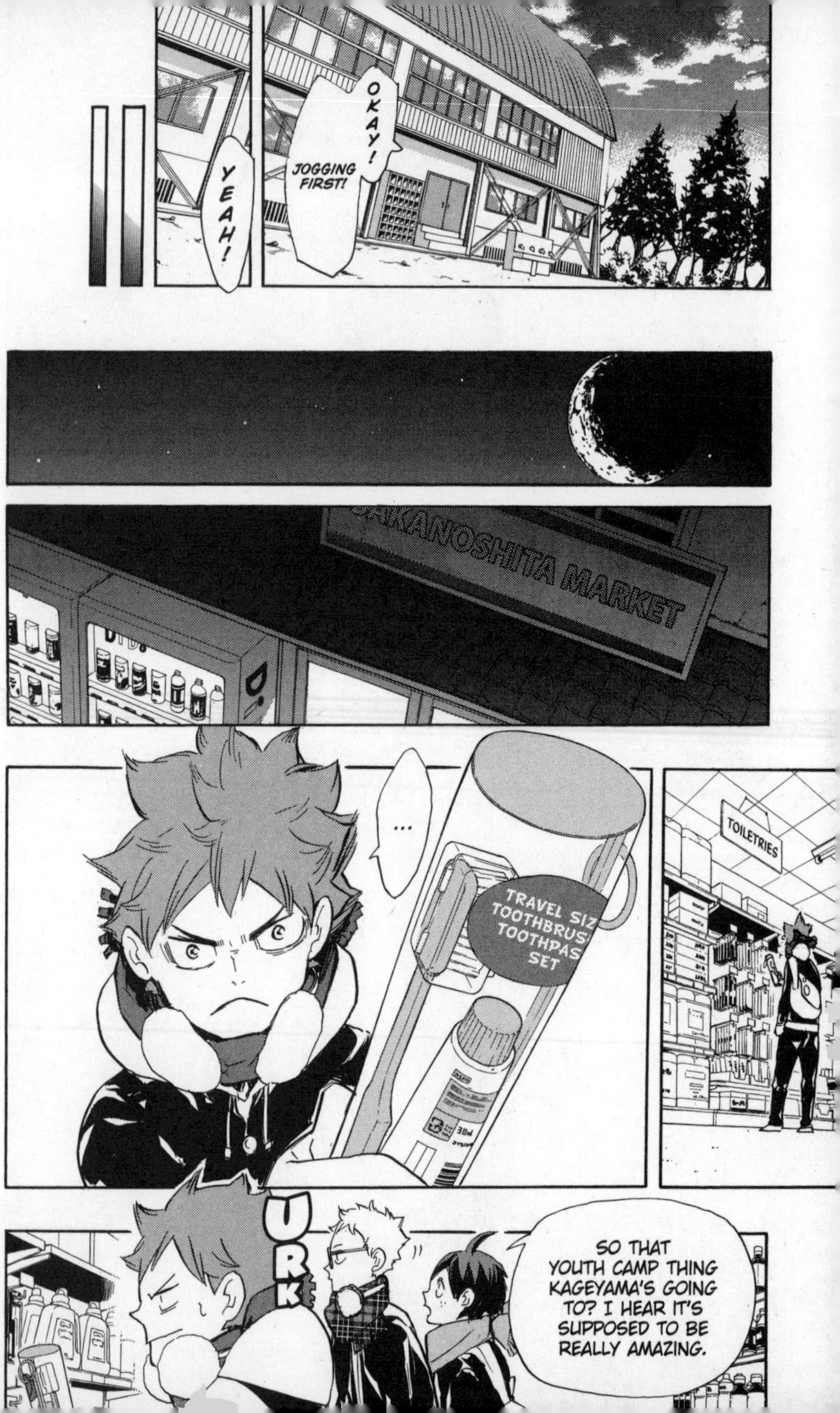
OKAY! JOGGING FIRST!
YEAH!
AKANOSHITA MARKET
TOILETRIES
...
TRAVEL SIZ
TOOTHBRUS
TOOTHPAS
SET
SO THAT YOUTH CAMP THING KAGEYAMA'S GOING TO? I HEAR IT'S SUPPOSED TO BE REALLY AMAZING.
URK

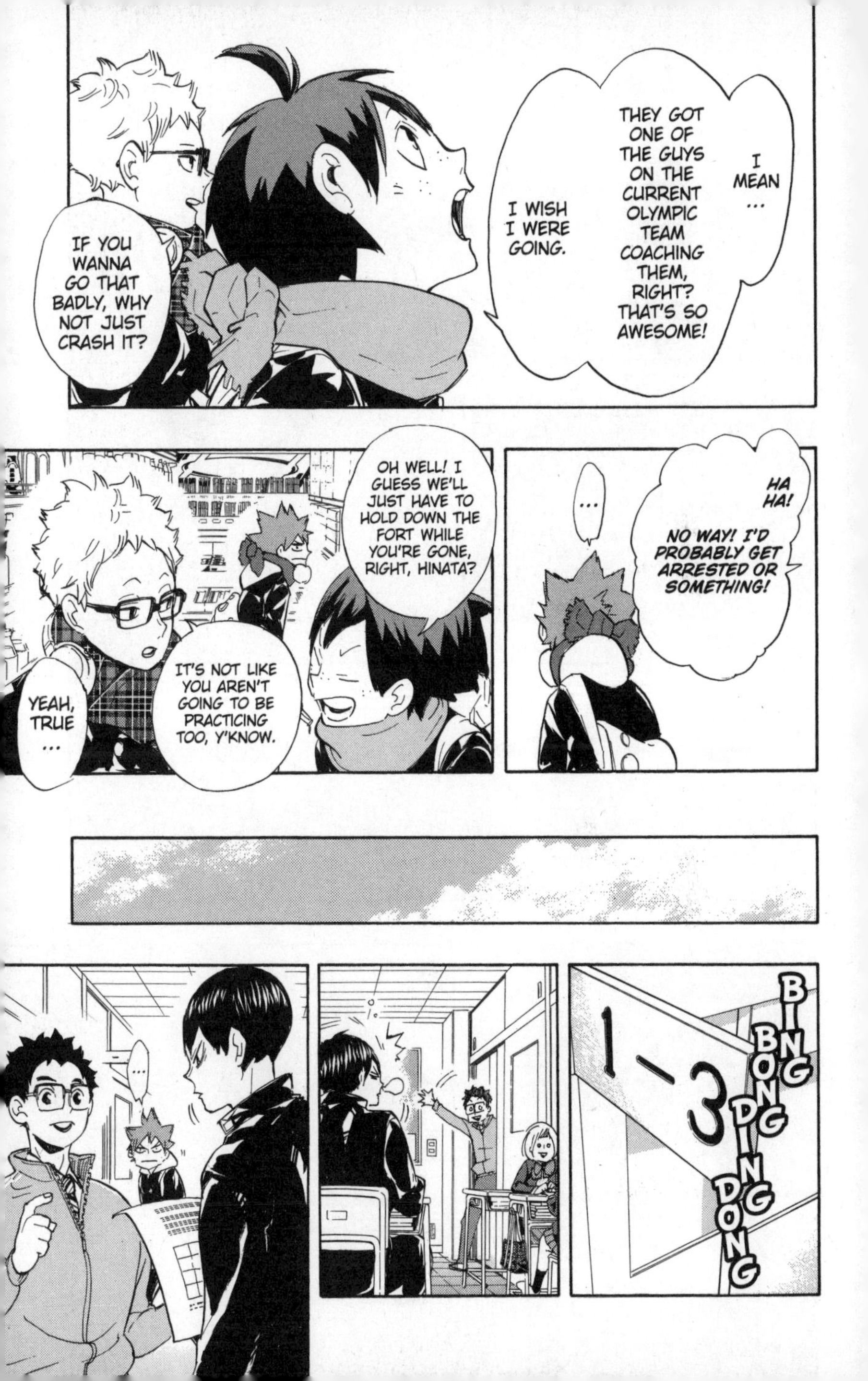
I MEAN ...
THEY GOT ONE OF THE GUYS ON THE CURRENT OLYMPIC TEAM COACHING THEM, RIGHT? THAT'S SO AWESOME!
I WISH I WERE GOING.
IF YOU WANNA GO THAT BADLY, WHY NOT JUST CRASH IT?
HA HA!
NO WAY! I'D PROBABLY GET ARRESTED OR SOMETHING!
...
OH WELL! I GUESS WE'LL JUST HAVE TO HOLD DOWN THE FORT WHILE YOU'RE GONE, RIGHT, HINATA?
IT'S NOT LIKE YOU AREN'T GOING TO BE PRACTICING TOO, Y'KNOW.
YEAH, TRUE ...
1-3
BING BONG DING DONG
...

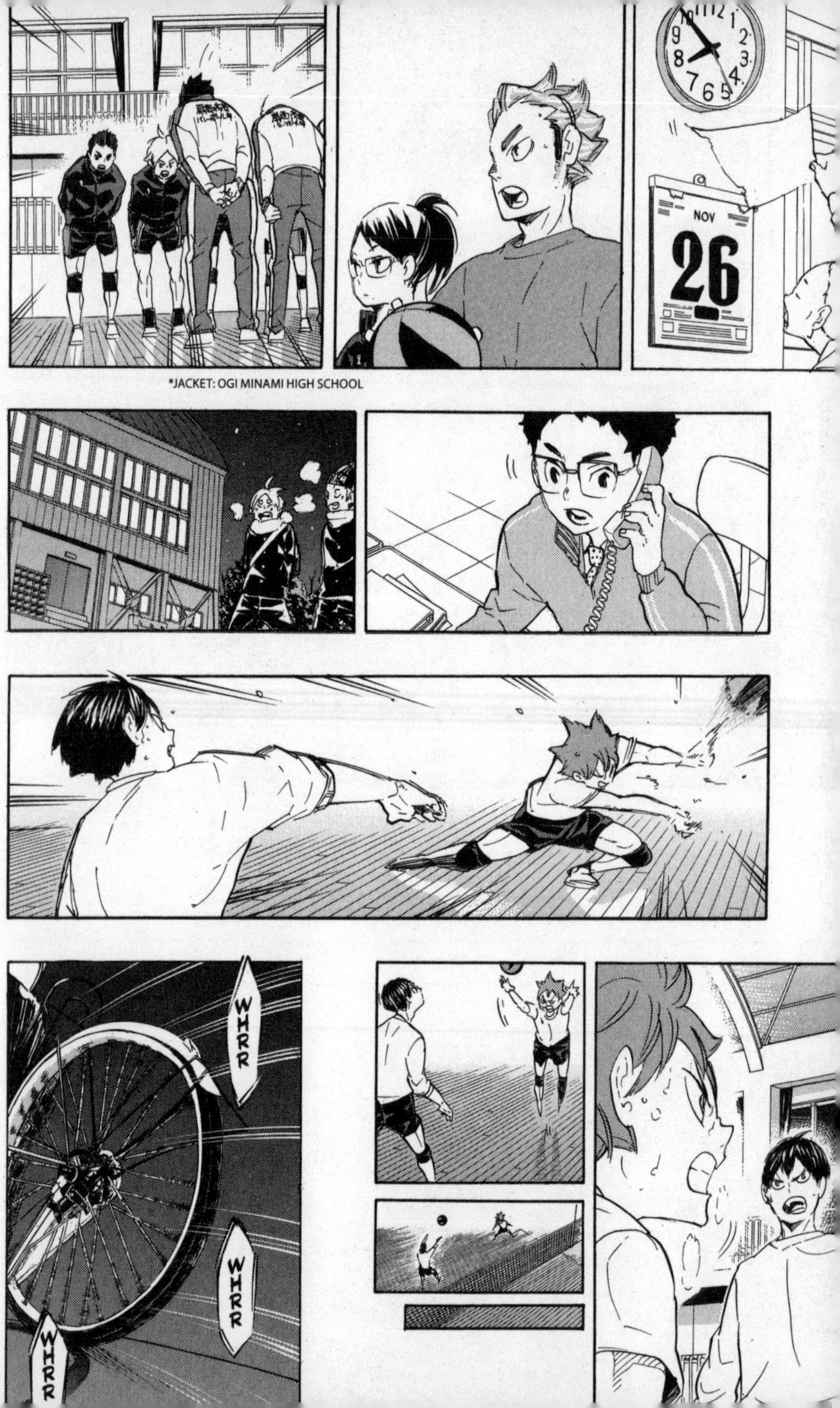
NOV
26
*JACKET: OGI MINAMI HIGH SCHOOL
WHRR
WHRR
WHRR

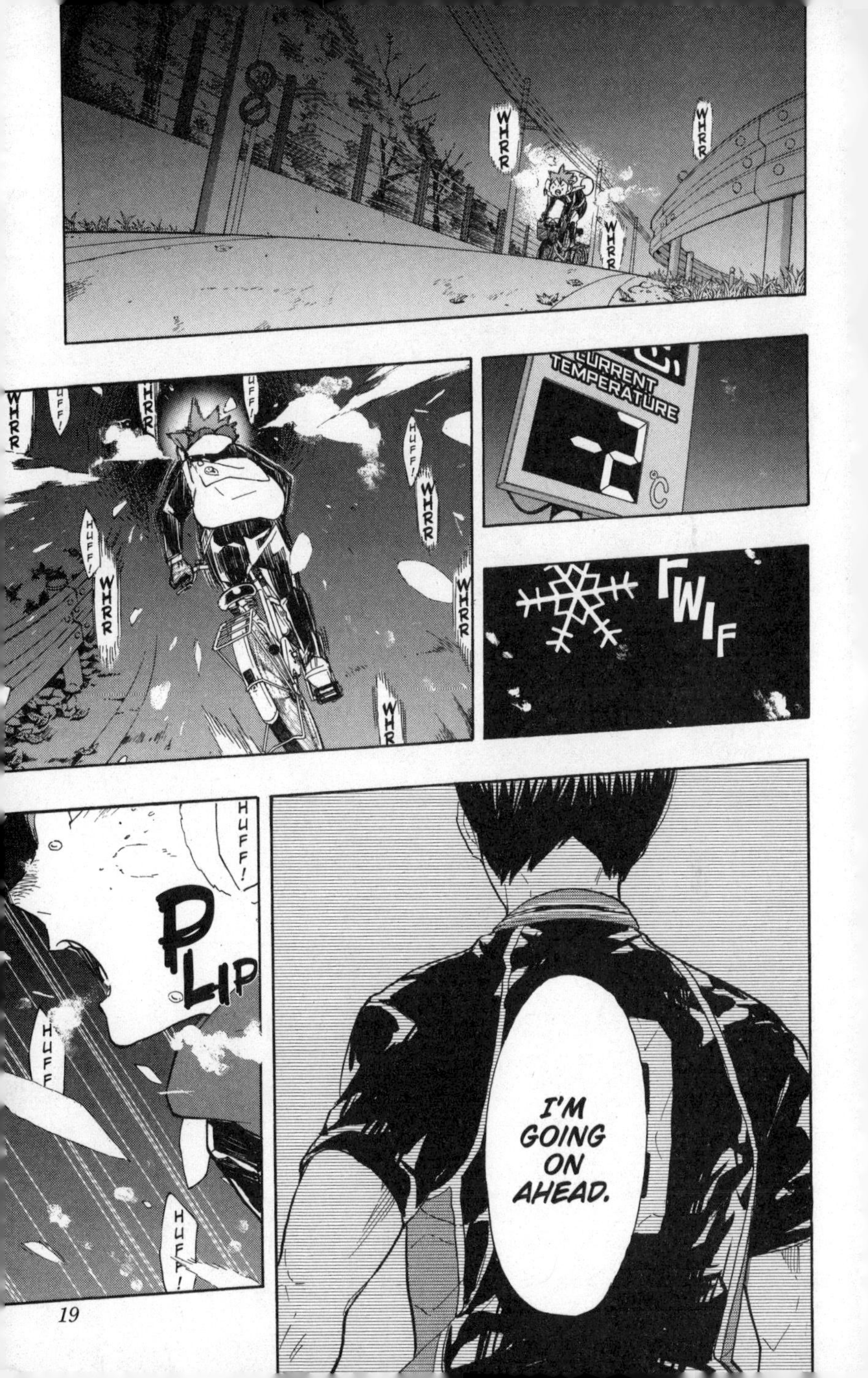
WHRR
WHRR
WHRR
CURRENT TEMPERATURE
-2 °C
FWIF
HUFF!
WHRR
HUFF!
WHRR
HUFF!
WHRR
WHRR
WHRR
WHR
I'M GOING ON AHEAD.
HUFF!
PLIP
HUFF
HUFF!

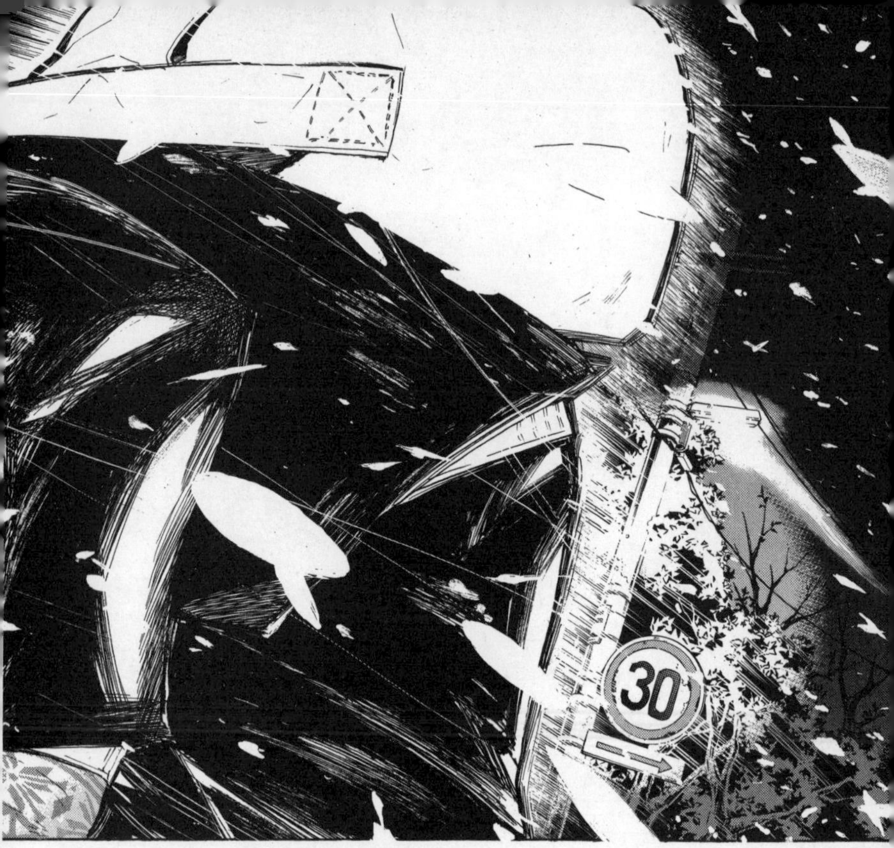
30

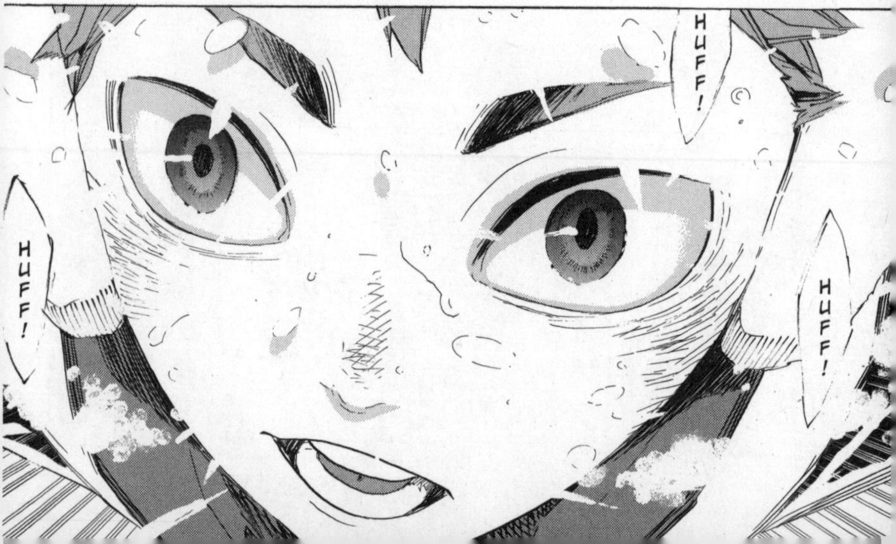
HUFF!
HUFF!
HUFF!

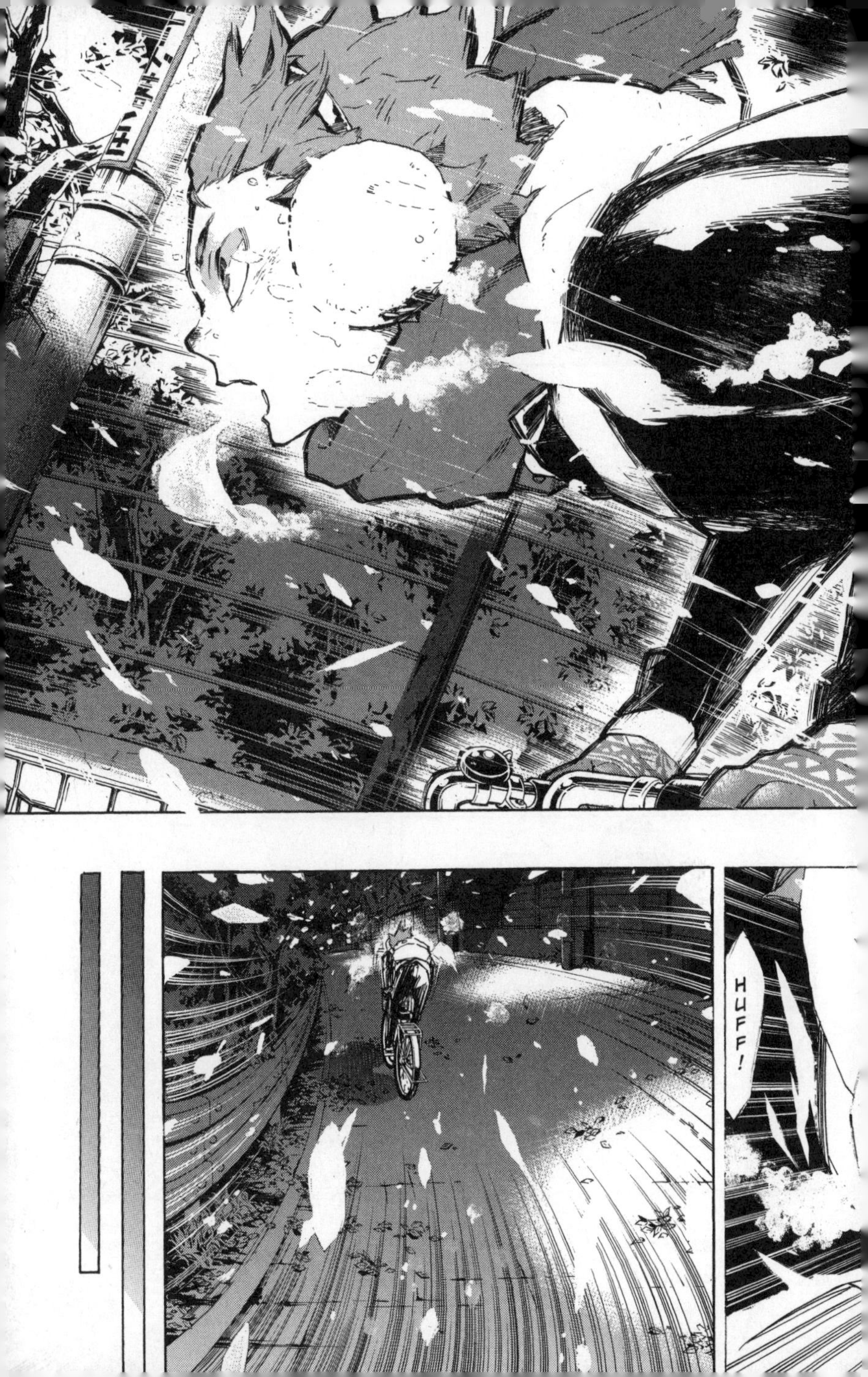
HUFF!

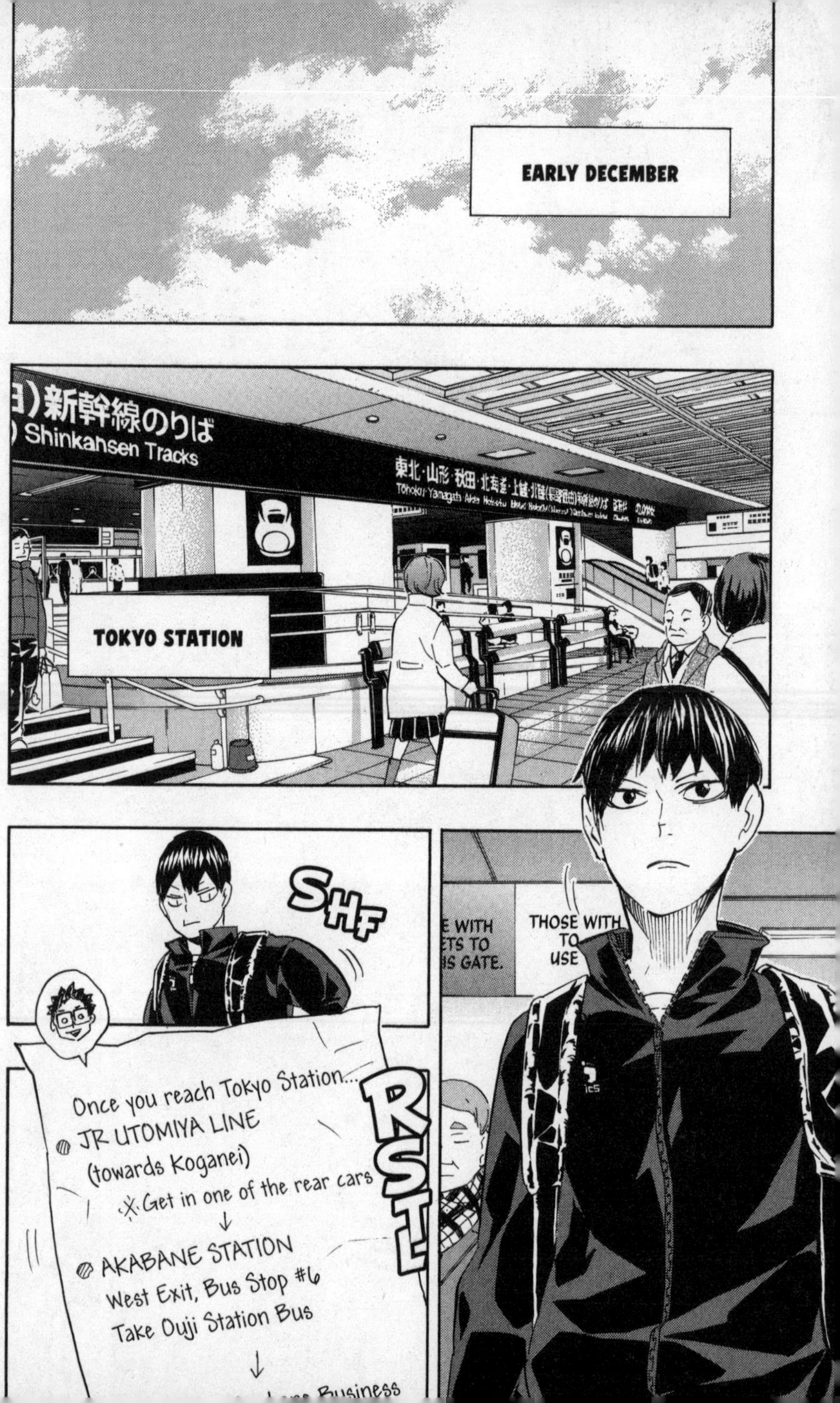
EARLY DECEMBER
新幹線のりば
Shinkansen Tracks
TOKYO STATION
THOSE WITH
TO
USE
E WITH
ETS TO
IS GATE.
SHF
Once you reach Tokyo Station...
JR UTOMIYA LINE
(towards Koganei)
※Get in one of the rear cars
↓
AKABANE STATION
West Exit, Bus Stop #6
Take Ouji Station Bus
↓
Business
RSTL

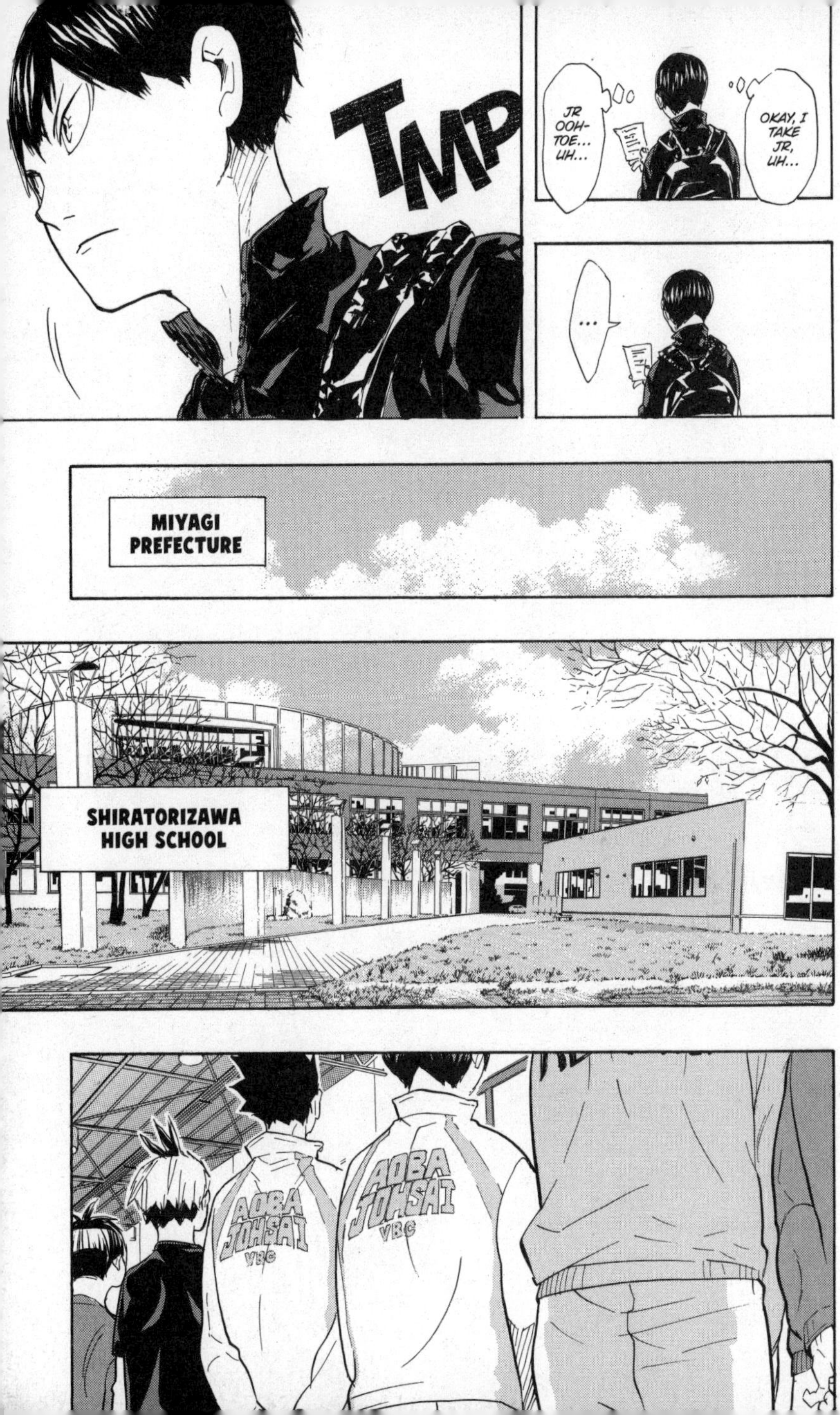
OKAY, I TAKE JR, UH...
JR OOH-TOE... UH...
...
TMP
MIYAGI PREFECTURE
SHIRATORIZAWA HIGH SCHOOL
AOBA JOHSAI VBC
AOBA JOHSAI VBC

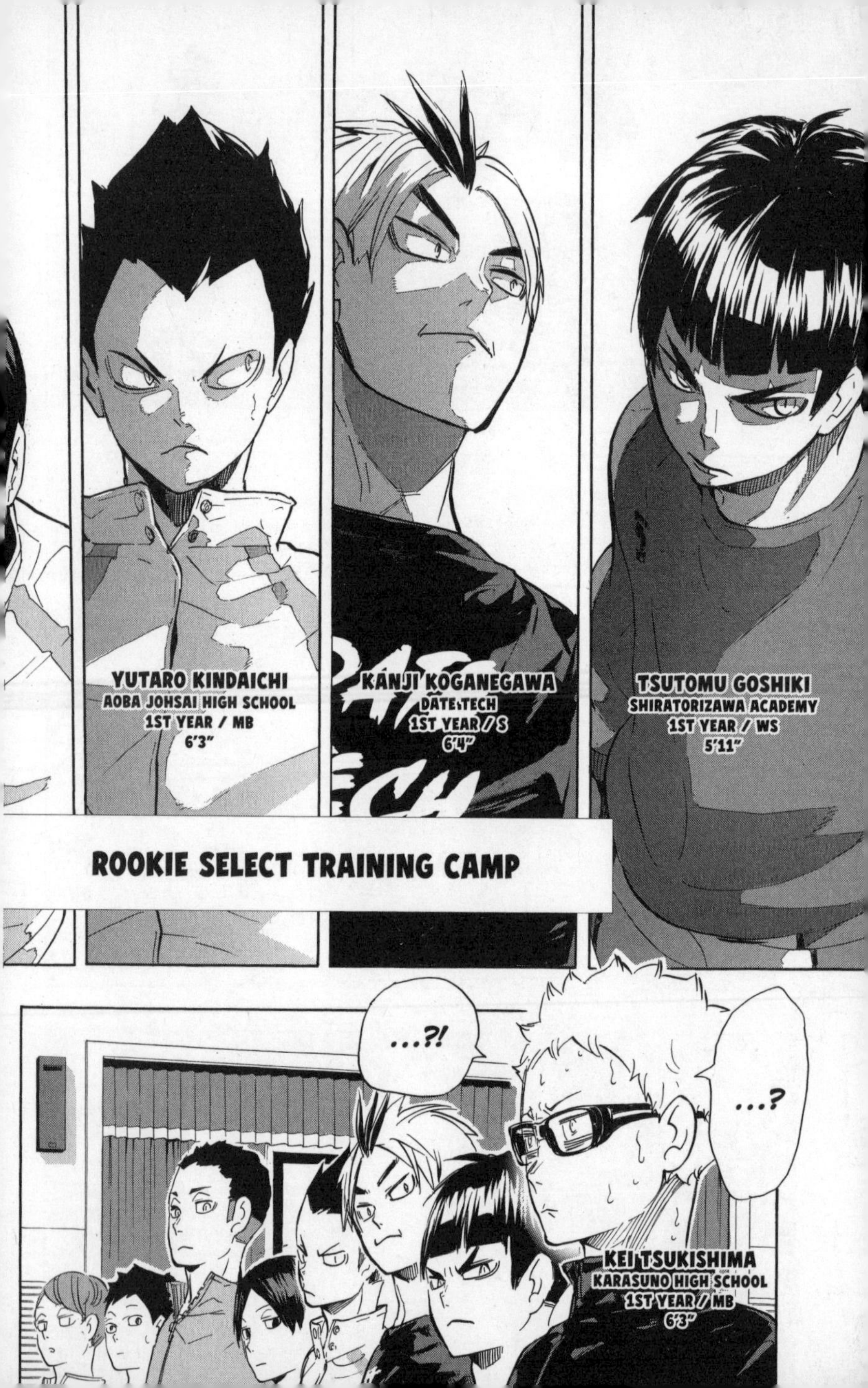
TSUTOMU GOSHIKI
SHIRATORIZAWA ACADEMY
1ST YEAR / WS
5'11"
KANJI KOGANEGAWA
DATE TECH
1ST YEAR / S
6'4"
YUTARO KINDAICHI
AOBA JOHSAI HIGH SCHOOL
1ST YEAR / MB
6'3"
ROOKIE SELECT TRAINING CAMP
...?
...?!
KEI TSUKISHIMA
KARASUNO HIGH SCHOOL
1ST YEAR / MB
6'3"

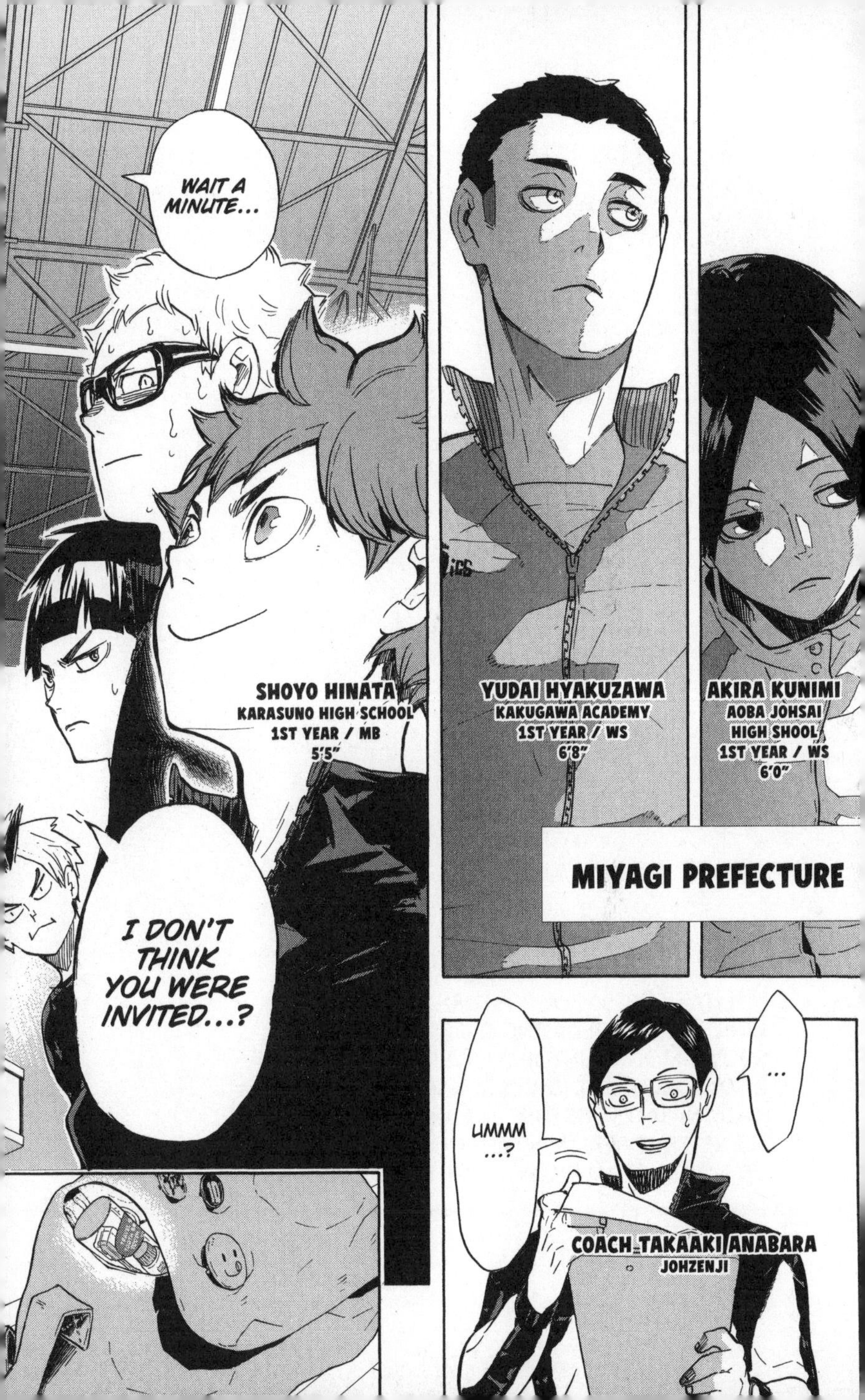
AKIRA KUNIMI
AOBA JOHSAI HIGH SHOOL
1ST YEAR / WS
6'0"
YUDAI HYAKUZAWA
KAKUGAWA ACADEMY
1ST YEAR / WS
6'8"
MIYAGI PREFECTURE
...
UMMM ...?
COACH TAKAAKI ANABARA
JOHZENJI
WAIT A MINUTE...
SHOYO HINATA
KARASUNO HIGH SCHOOL
1ST YEAR / MB
5'5"
I DON'T THINK YOU WERE INVITED...?

HINATA'S SUPERCOOL POSTURE
WHILE HE WAS PEDALING OVER THAT
SNOWY MOUNTAINTOP WAS INSPIRED
BY *MONDAY LATESHOW* REGULAR
KIRITANI-SAN'S POSTURE IN A SIMILAR
SCENE. THAT REALLY IS THE COOLEST
STANDING-PEDALING POSTURE EVER.

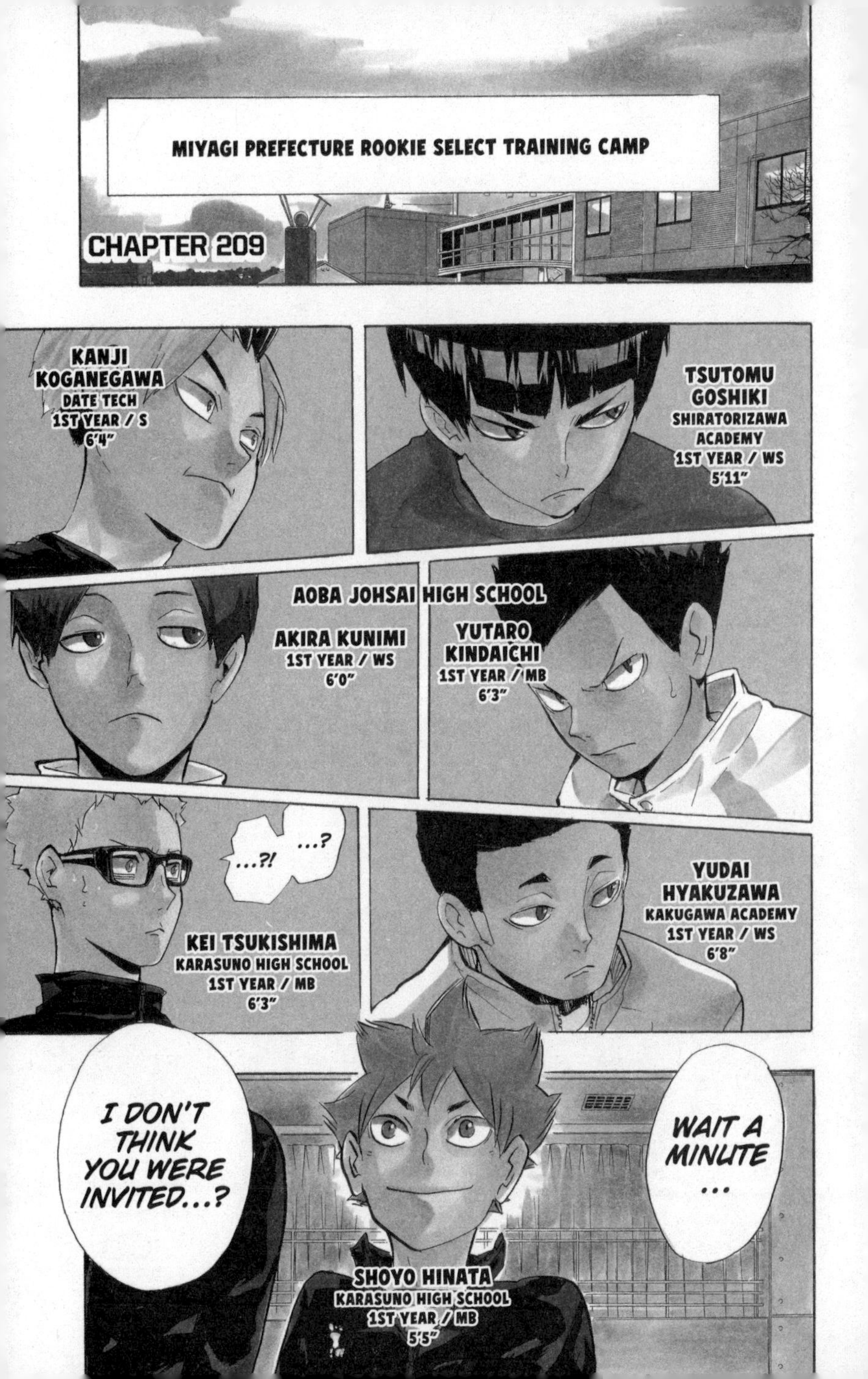
MIYAGI PREFECTURE ROOKIE SELECT TRAINING CAMP
CHAPTER 209
TSUTOMU GOSHIKI
SHIRATORIZAWA ACADEMY
1ST YEAR / WS
5'11"
KANJI KOGANEGAWA
DATE TECH
1ST YEAR / S
6'4"
AOBA JOHSAI HIGH SCHOOL
YUTARO KINDAICHI
1ST YEAR / MB
6'3"
AKIRA KUNIMI
1ST YEAR / WS
6'0"
YUDAI HYAKUZAWA
KAKUGAWA ACADEMY
1ST YEAR / WS
6'8"
...?
...?!
KEI TSUKISHIMA
KARASUNO HIGH SCHOOL
1ST YEAR / MB
6'3"
WAIT A MINUTE ...
I DON'T THINK YOU WERE INVITED...?
SHOYO HINATA
KARASUNO HIGH SCHOOL
1ST YEAR / MB
5'5"

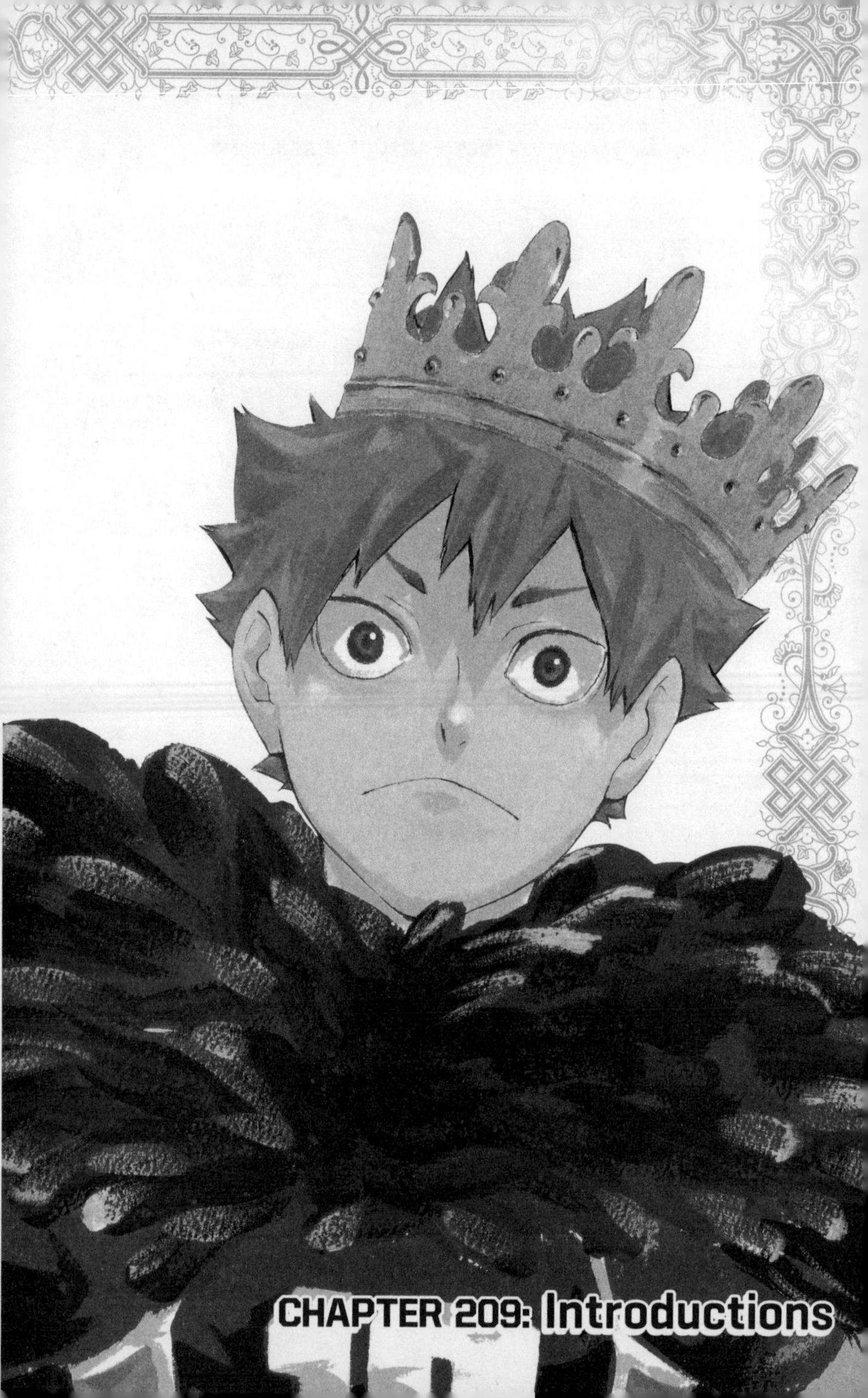

CHAPTER 209: Introductions

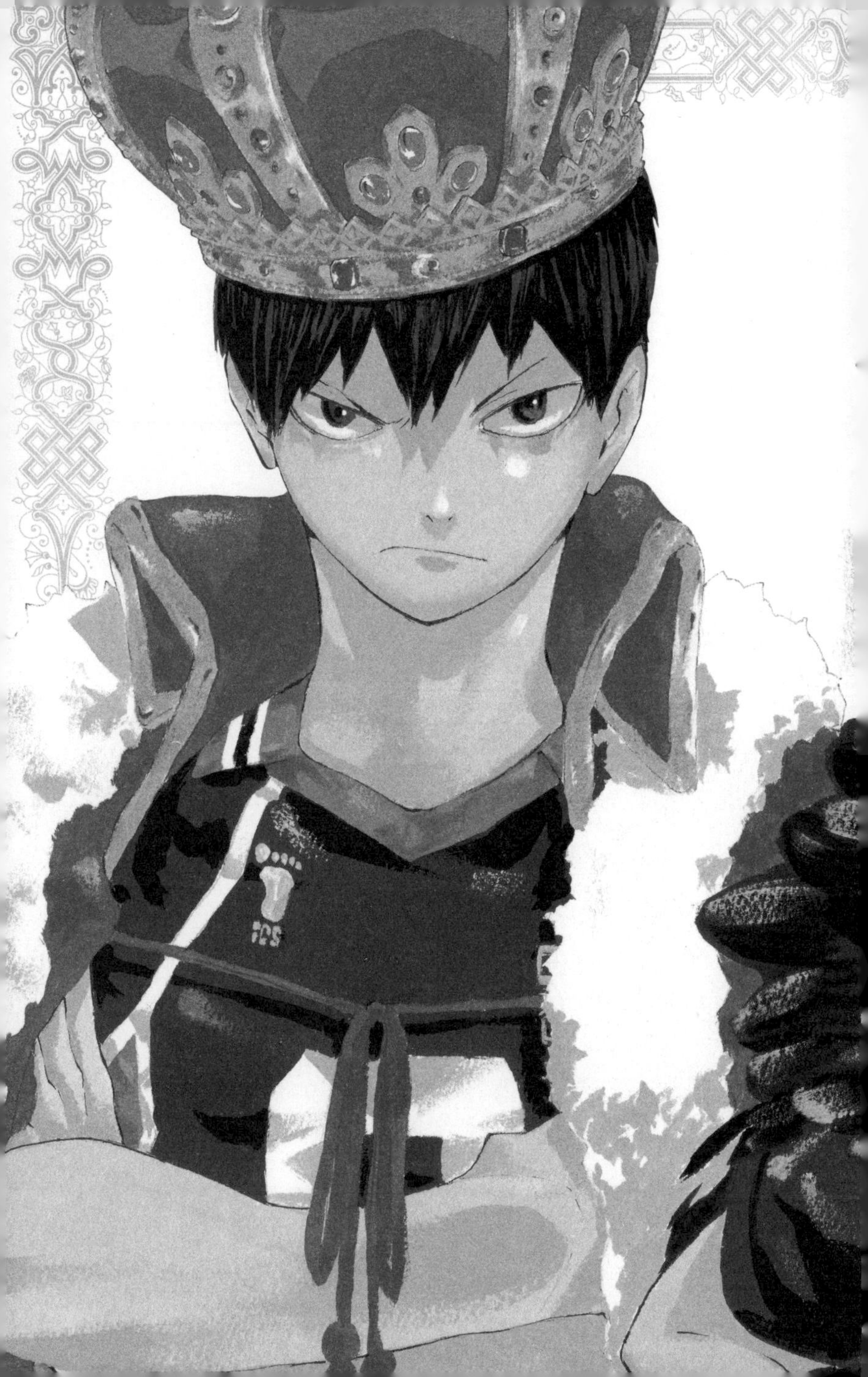

HAIKYU!!

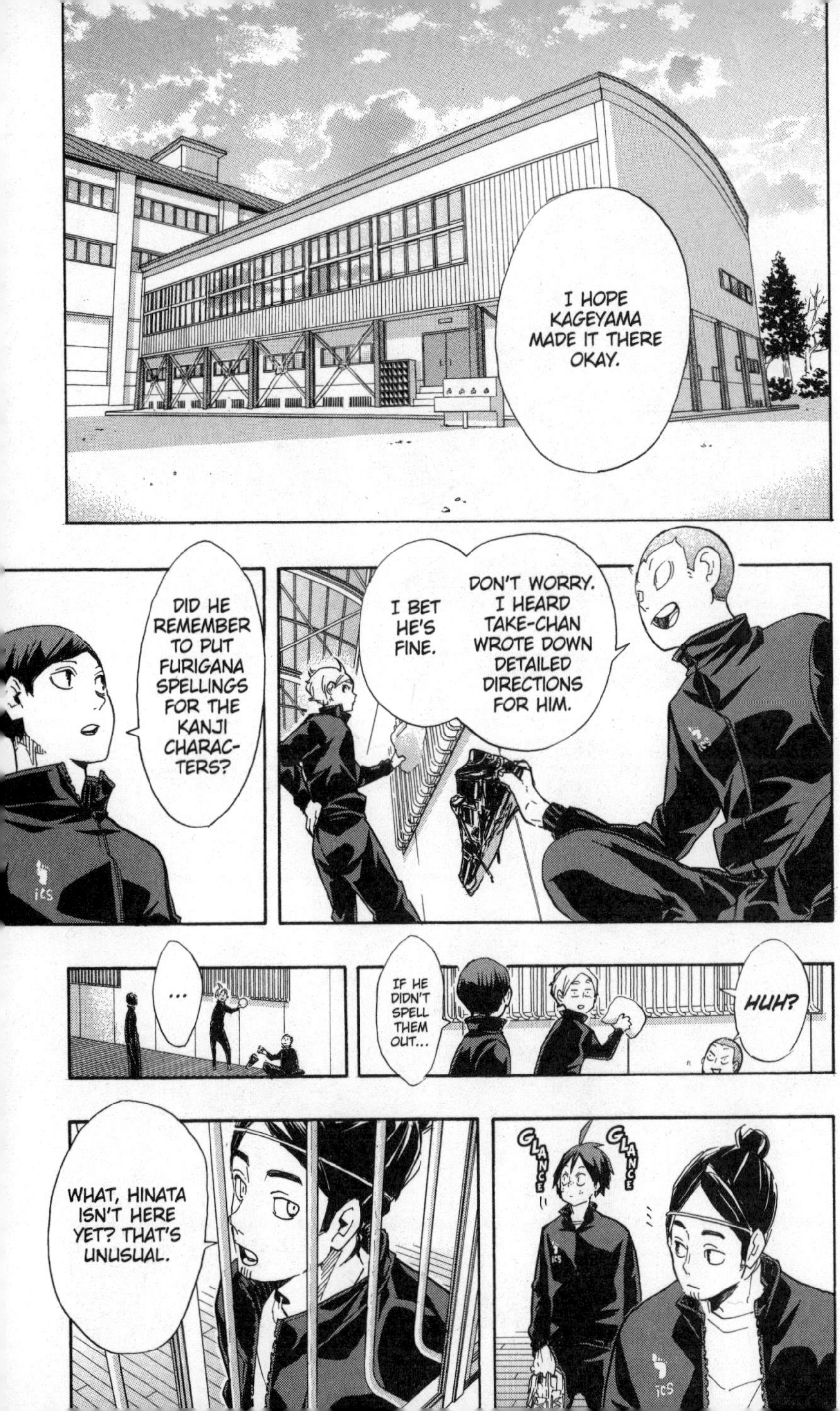
I HOPE KAGEYAMA MADE IT THERE OKAY.
DON'T WORRY. I HEARD TAKE-CHAN WROTE DOWN DETAILED DIRECTIONS FOR HIM.
I BET HE'S FINE.
DID HE REMEMBER TO PUT FURIGANA SPELLINGS FOR THE KANJI CHARAC-TERS?
HUH?
IF HE DIDN'T SPELL THEM OUT...
...
GLANCE
GLANCE
WHAT, HINATA ISN'T HERE YET? THAT'S UNUSUAL.

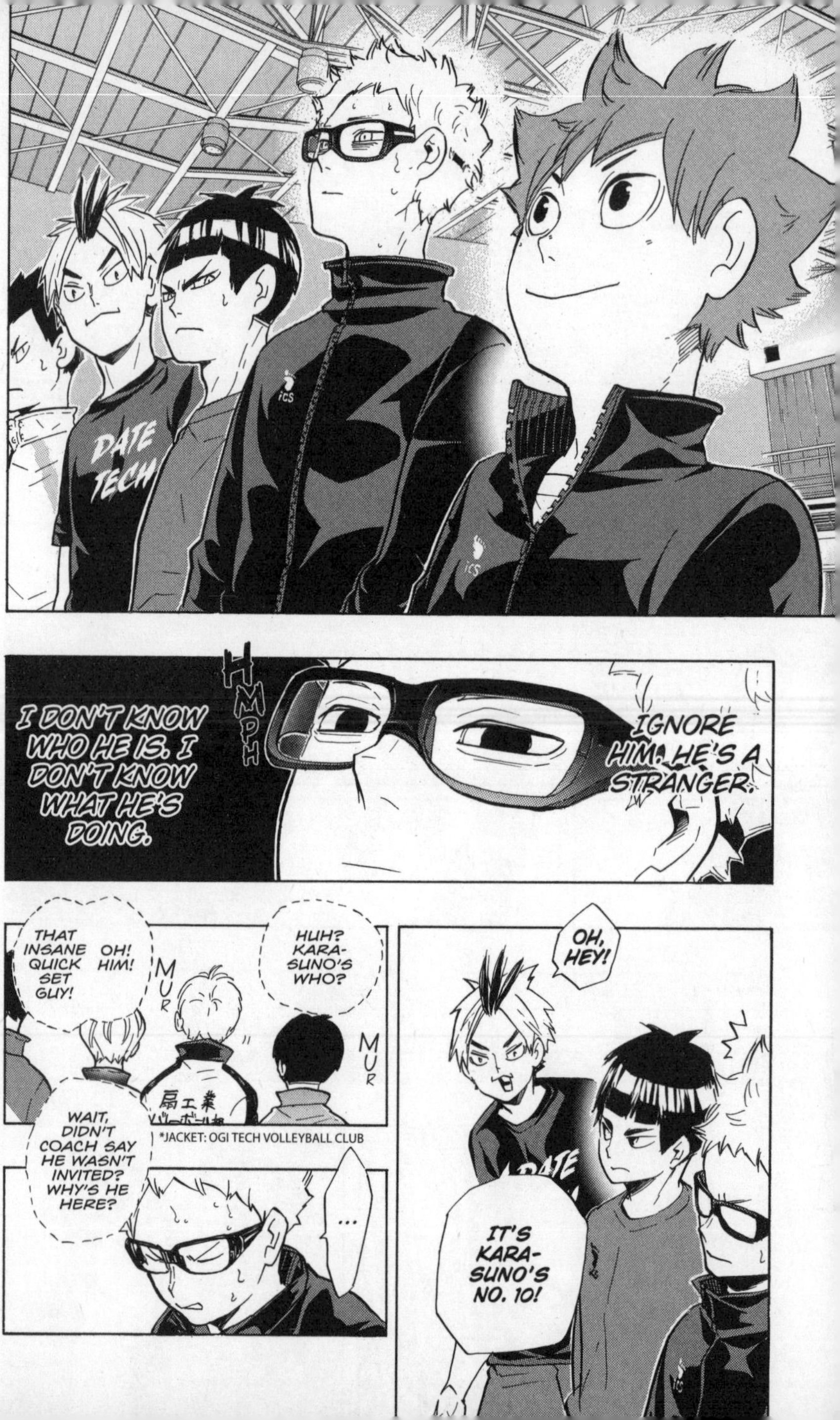
DATE TECH
IGNORE HIM. HE'S A STRANGER.
HMMPH
I DON'T KNOW WHO HE IS. I DON'T KNOW WHAT HE'S DOING.
OH, HEY!
IT'S KARA-SUNO'S NO. 10!
HUH? KARA-SUNO'S WHO?
OH! HIM!
THAT INSANE QUICK SET GUY!
MUR
MUR
扇工業
*JACKET: OGI TECH VOLLEYBALL CLUB
WAIT, DIDN'T COACH SAY HE WASN'T INVITED? WHY'S HE HERE?
...

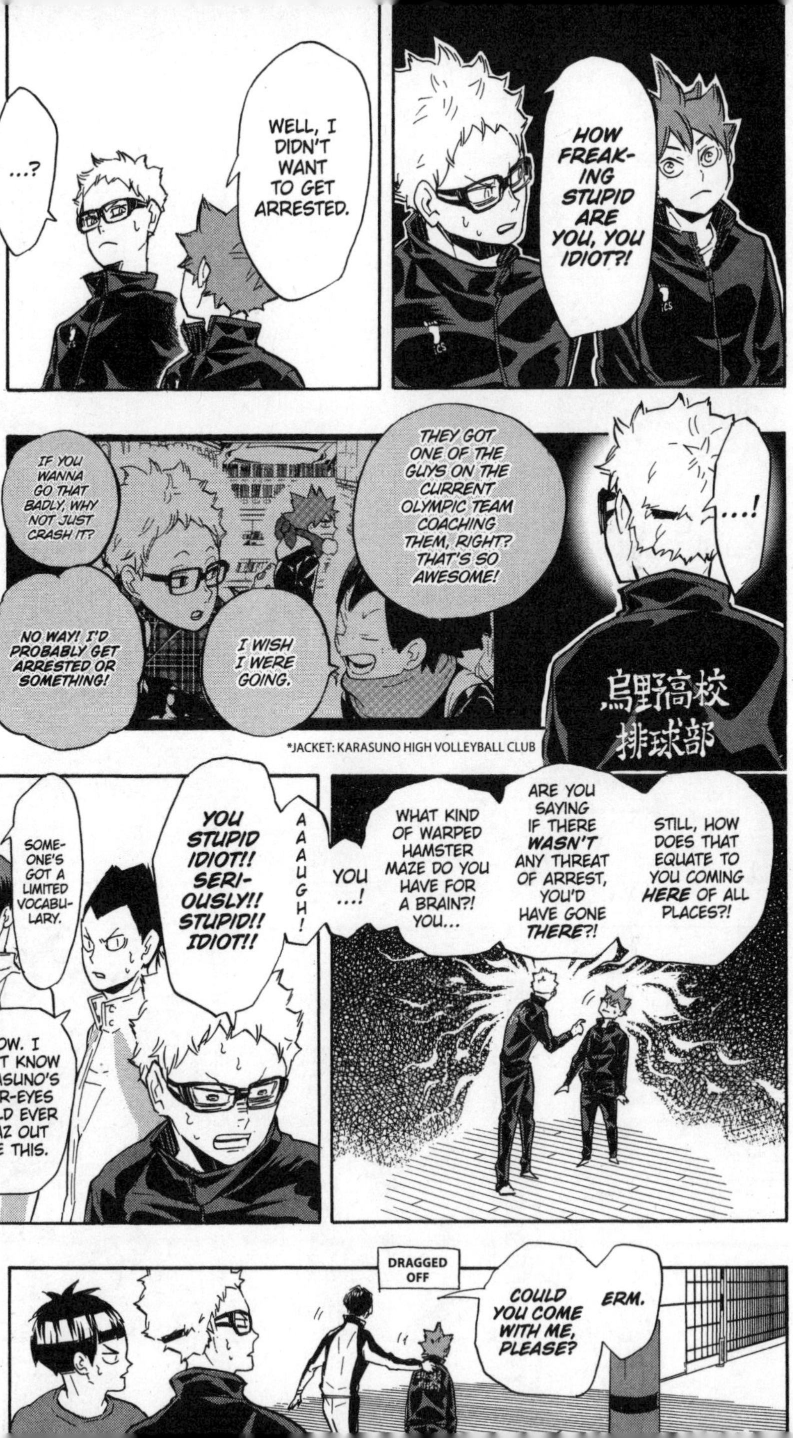
HOW FREAKING STUPID ARE YOU, YOU IDIOT?!
WELL, I DIDN'T WANT TO GET ARRESTED.
...?
...!
鳥野高校
排球部
*JACKET: KARASUNO HIGH VOLLEYBALL CLUB
THEY GOT ONE OF THE GUYS ON THE CURRENT OLYMPIC TEAM COACHING THEM, RIGHT? THAT'S SO AWESOME!
IF YOU WANNA GO THAT BADLY, WHY NOT JUST CRASH IT?
I WISH I WERE GOING.
NO WAY! I'D PROBABLY GET ARRESTED OR SOMETHING!
STILL, HOW DOES THAT EQUATE TO YOU COMING HERE OF ALL PLACES?!
ARE YOU SAYING IF THERE WASN'T ANY THREAT OF ARREST, YOU'D HAVE GONE THERE?!
WHAT KIND OF WARPED HAMSTER MAZE DO YOU HAVE FOR A BRAIN?! YOU...
YOU ...!
AAAAUGH!
YOU STUPID IDIOT!! SERIOUSLY!! STUPID!! IDIOT!!
SOMEONE'S GOT A LIMITED VOCABULARY.
WOW. I DIDN'T KNOW KARASUNO'S FOUR-EYES COULD EVER SPAZ OUT LIKE THIS.
ERM.
COULD YOU COME WITH ME, PLEASE?
DRAGGED OFF

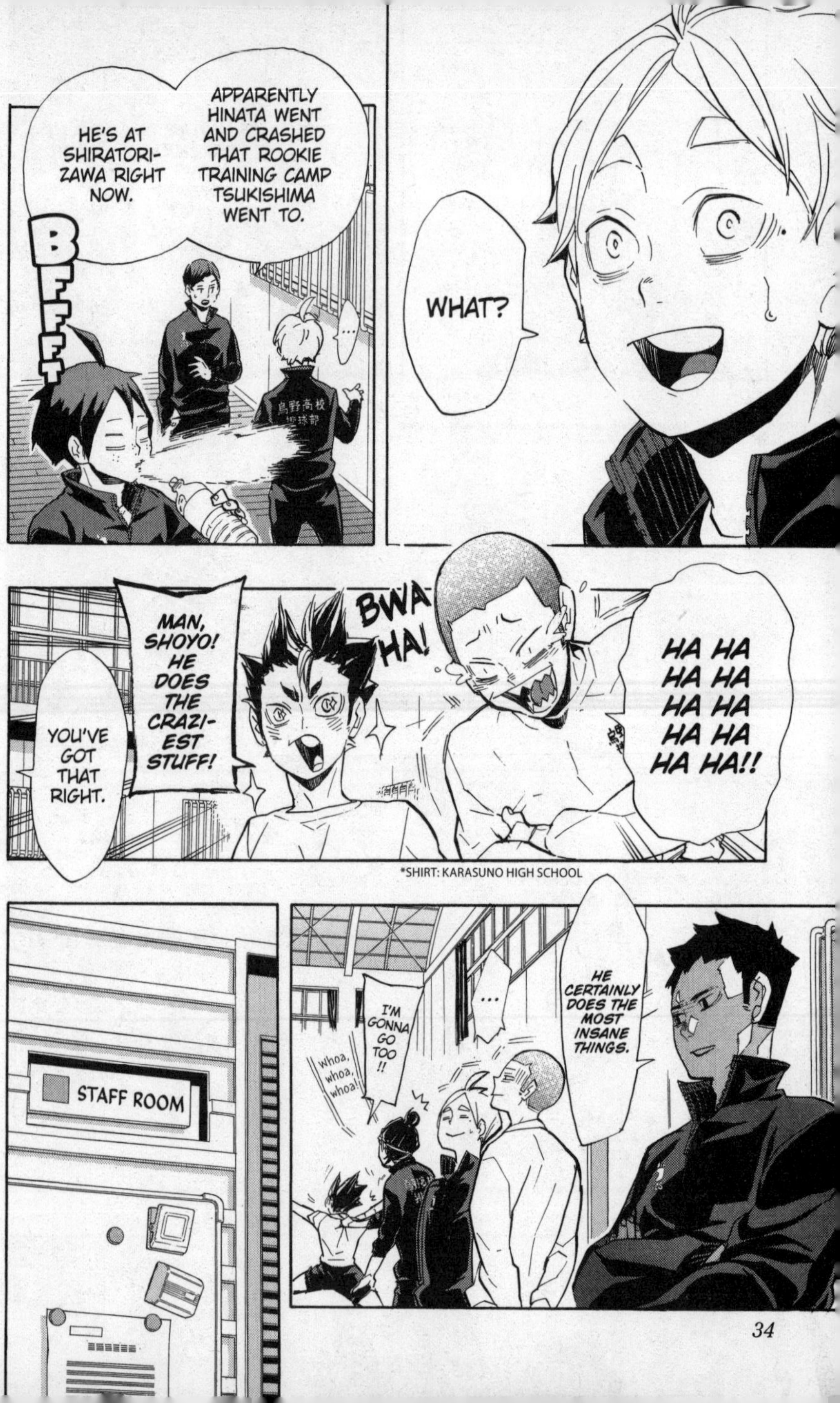
WHAT?
APPARENTLY HINATA WENT AND CRASHED THAT ROOKIE TRAINING CAMP TSUKISHIMA WENT TO.
HE'S AT SHIRATORI-ZAWA RIGHT NOW.
...
BFFFT
HA HA HA HA HA HA HA HA HA HA!!
BWA HA!
MAN, SHOYO! HE DOES THE CRAZI-EST STUFF!
YOU'VE GOT THAT RIGHT.
*SHIRT: KARASUNO HIGH SCHOOL
HE CERTAINLY DOES THE MOST INSANE THINGS.
...
I'M GONNA GO TOO!!
whoa, whoa, whoa!
STAFF ROOM

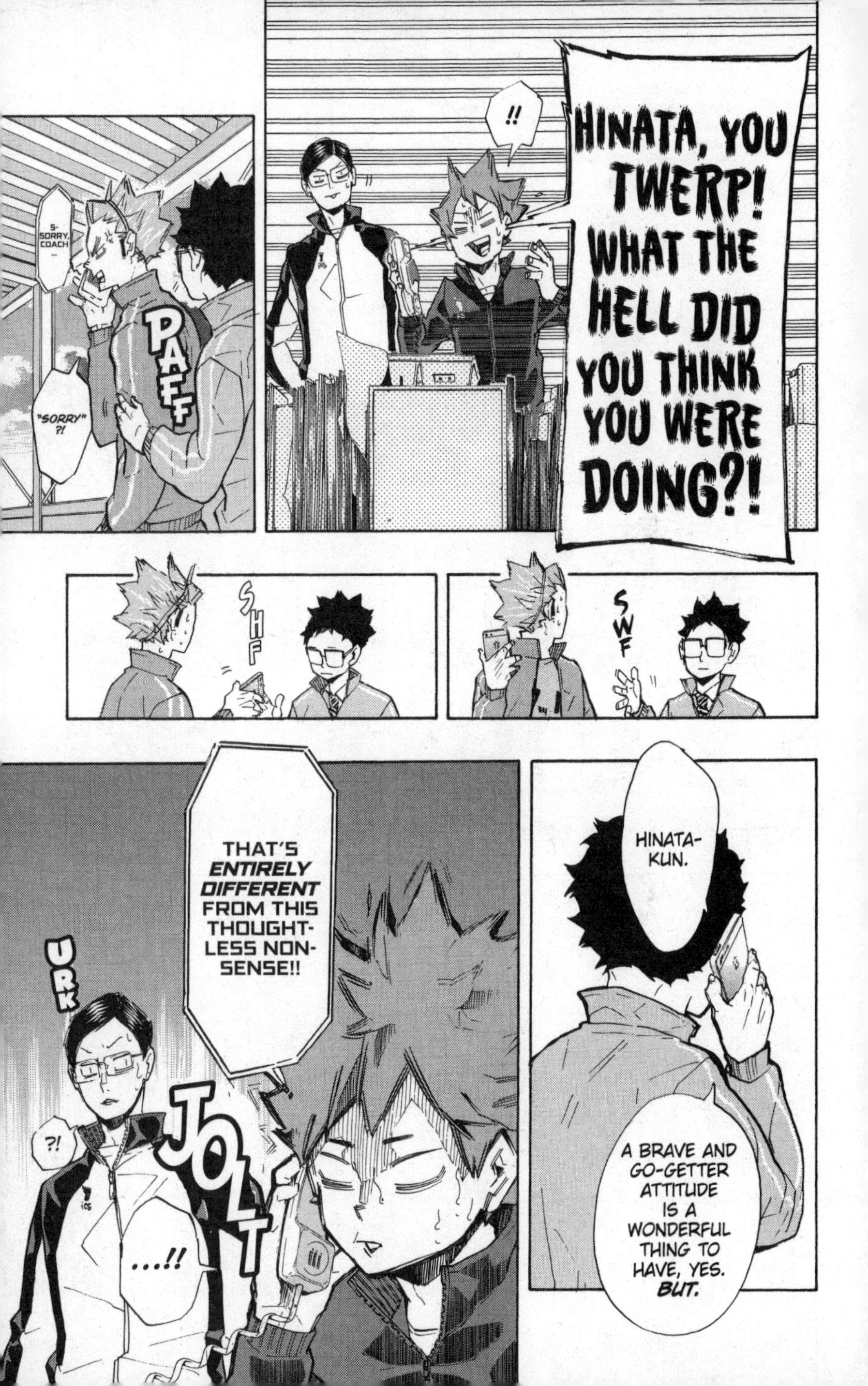
HINATA, YOU TWERP! WHAT THE HELL DID YOU THINK YOU WERE DOING?!
!!
S-SORRY, COACH ...
PAFF
"SORRY" ?!
SWF
SHF
HINATA-KUN.
A BRAVE AND GO-GETTER ATTITUDE IS A WONDERFUL THING TO HAVE, YES. *BUT.*
THAT'S *ENTIRELY DIFFERENT* FROM THIS THOUGHT-LESS NON-SENSE!!
URK
JOLT
?!
...!!

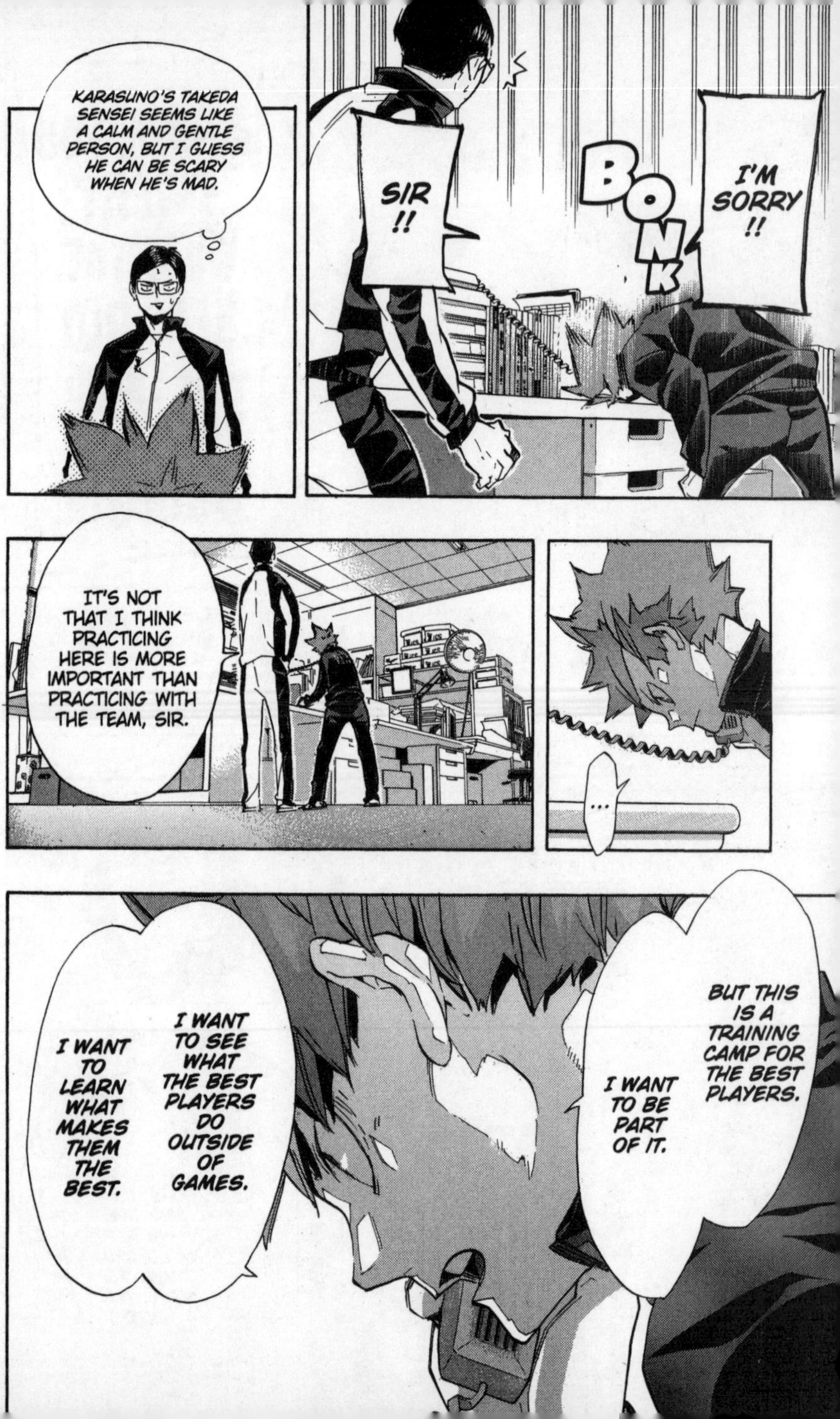
I'M SORRY!!
BONK
SIR!!
KARASUNO'S TAKEDA SENSEI SEEMS LIKE A CALM AND GENTLE PERSON, BUT I GUESS HE CAN BE SCARY WHEN HE'S MAD.
...
IT'S NOT THAT I THINK PRACTICING HERE IS MORE IMPORTANT THAN PRACTICING WITH THE TEAM, SIR.
BUT THIS IS A TRAINING CAMP FOR THE BEST PLAYERS.
I WANT TO BE PART OF IT.
I WANT TO SEE WHAT THE BEST PLAYERS DO OUTSIDE OF GAMES.
I WANT TO LEARN WHAT MAKES THEM THE BEST.

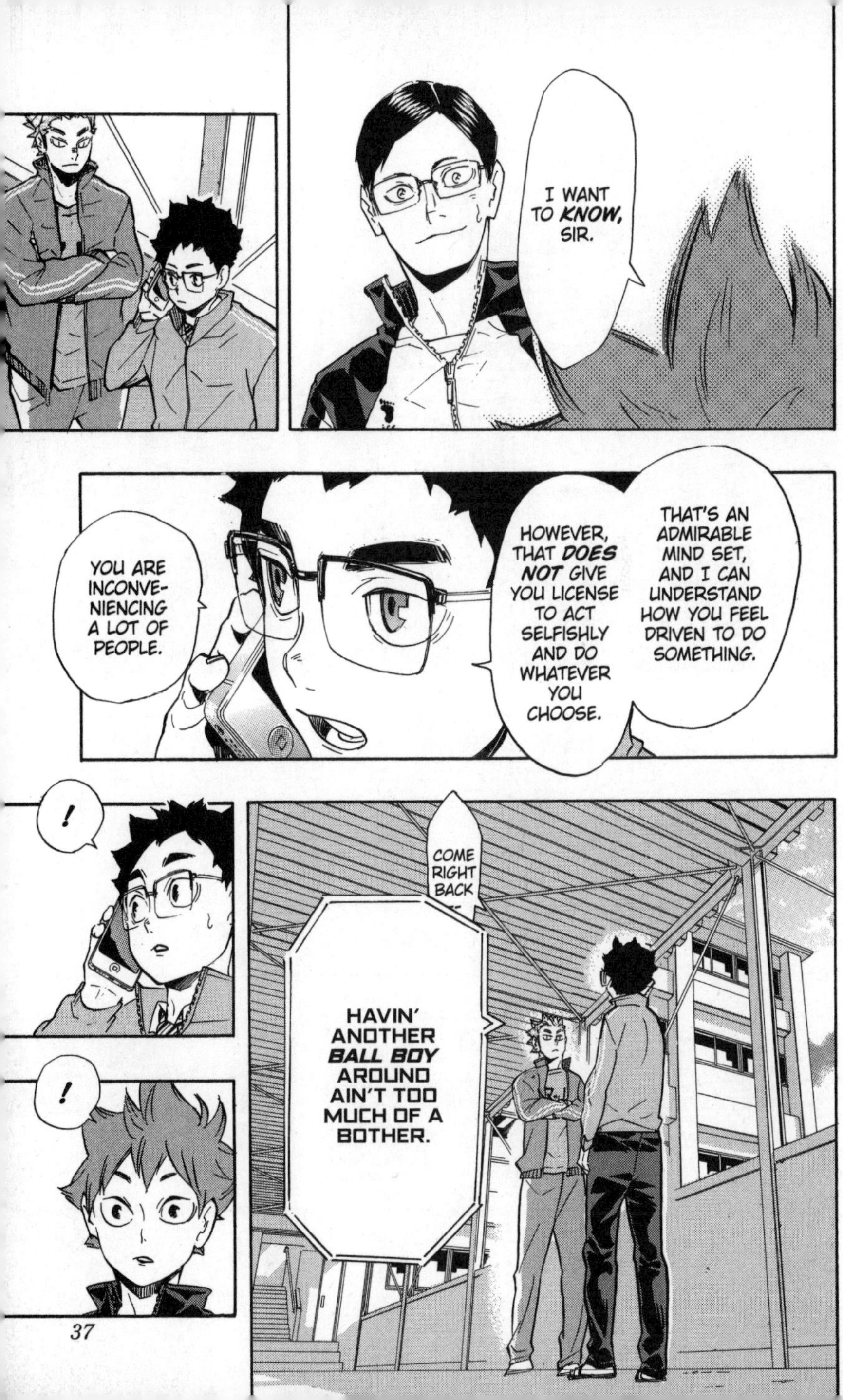
I WANT TO **KNOW,** SIR.
THAT'S AN ADMIRABLE MIND SET, AND I CAN UNDERSTAND HOW YOU FEEL DRIVEN TO DO SOMETHING.
HOWEVER, THAT **DOES NOT** GIVE YOU LICENSE TO ACT SELFISHLY AND DO WHATEVER YOU CHOOSE.
YOU ARE INCONVE-NIENCING A LOT OF PEOPLE.
COME RIGHT BACK
HAVIN' ANOTHER **BALL BOY** AROUND AIN'T TOO MUCH OF A BOTHER.
!
!

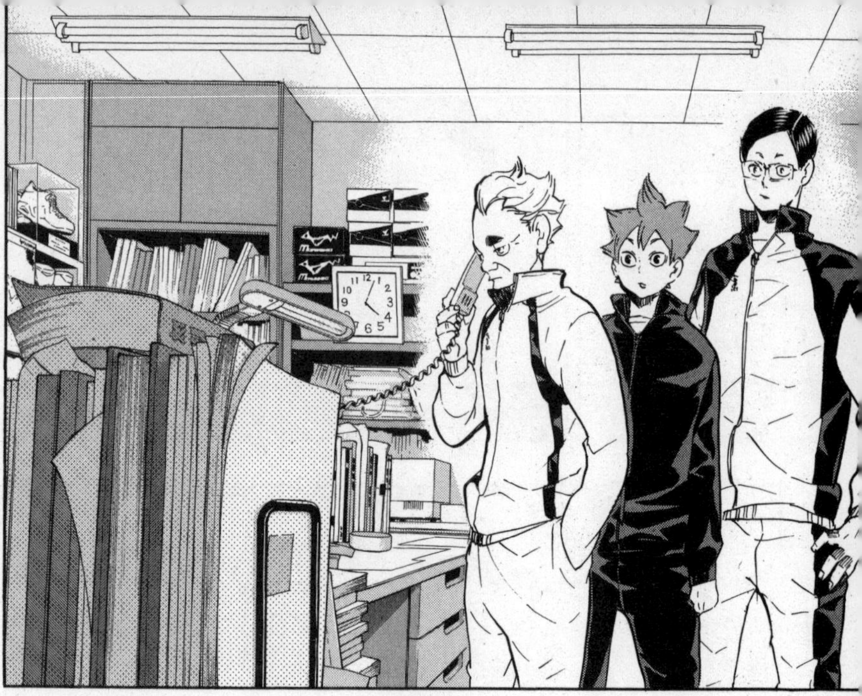

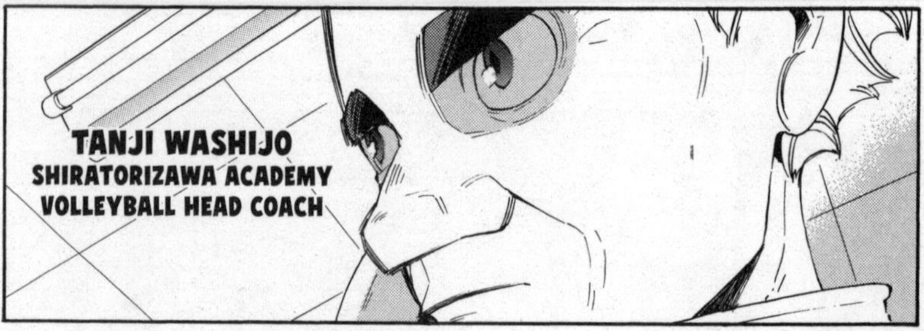
TANJI WASHIJO
SHIRATORIZAWA ACADEMY
VOLLEYBALL HEAD COACH

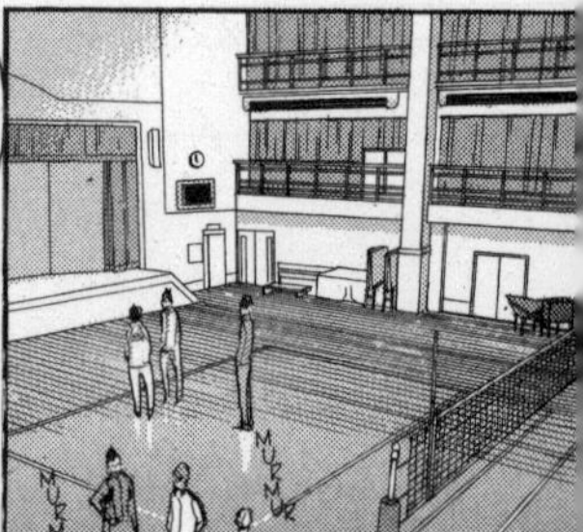

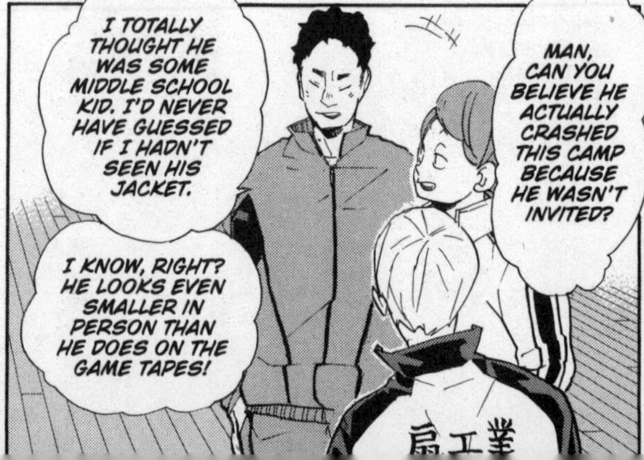
MAN, CAN YOU BELIEVE HE ACTUALLY CRASHED THIS CAMP BECAUSE HE WASN'T INVITED?
I TOTALLY THOUGHT HE WAS SOME MIDDLE SCHOOL KID. I'D NEVER HAVE GUESSED IF I HADN'T SEEN HIS JACKET.
I KNOW, RIGHT? HE LOOKS EVEN SMALLER IN PERSON THAN HE DOES ON THE GAME TAPES!

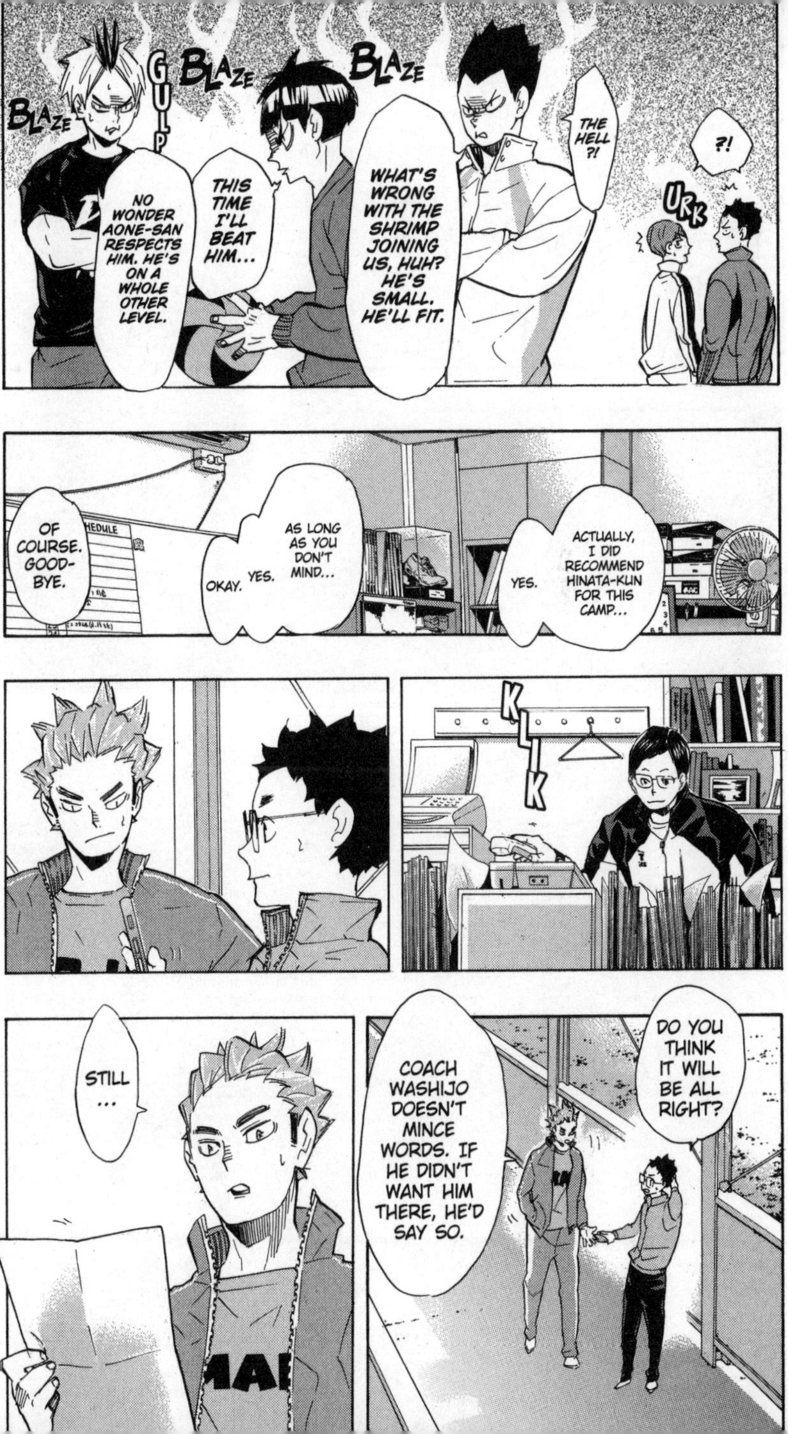
?!
URK
THE HELL?!
WHAT'S WRONG WITH THE SHRIMP JOINING US, HUH? HE'S SMALL. HE'LL FIT.
BLAZE
THIS TIME I'LL BEAT HIM...
BLAZE
GULP
NO WONDER AONE-SAN RESPECTS HIM. HE'S ON A WHOLE OTHER LEVEL.
BLAZE
ACTUALLY, I DID RECOMMEND HINATA-KUN FOR THIS CAMP...
YES.
AS LONG AS YOU DON'T MIND...
YES.
OKAY.
OF COURSE. GOOD-BYE.
KLIK
DO YOU THINK IT WILL BE ALL RIGHT?
COACH WASHIJO DOESN'T MINCE WORDS. IF HE DIDN'T WANT HIM THERE, HE'D SAY SO.
STILL...

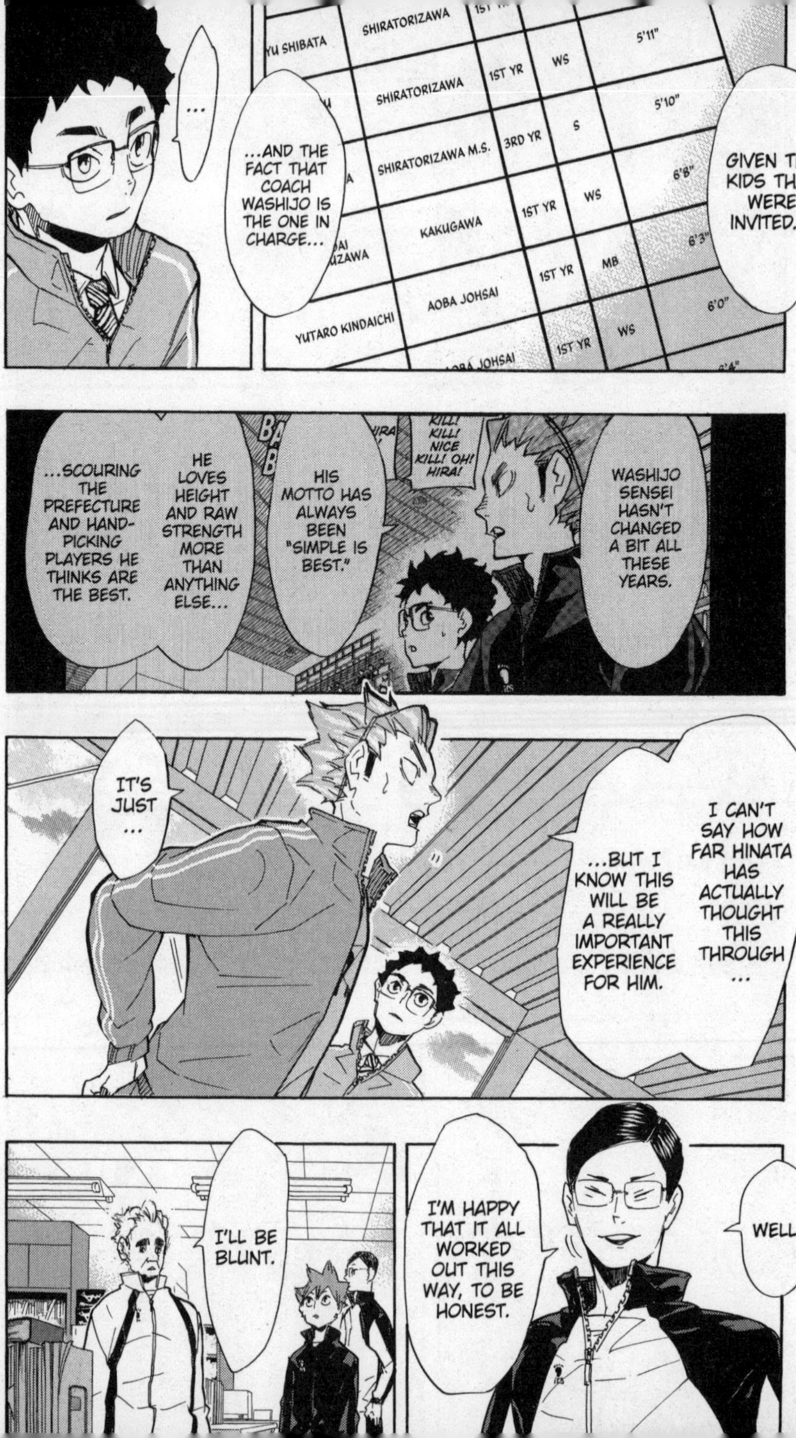
GIVEN THE KIDS THAT WERE INVITED...
...AND THE FACT THAT COACH WASHIJO IS THE ONE IN CHARGE...
YU SHIBATA
SHIRATORIZAWA
5'11"
1ST YR
WS
SHIRATORIZAWA
5'10"
S
3RD YR
SHIRATORIZAWA M.S.
6'8"
WS
1ST YR
KAKUGAWA
6'3"
MB
1ST YR
AOBA JOHSAI
6'0"
YUTARO KINDAICHI
WS
1ST YR
...
WASHIJO SENSEI HASN'T CHANGED A BIT ALL THESE YEARS.
KILL! KILL! NICE KILL! OH! HIRA!
HIS MOTTO HAS ALWAYS BEEN "SIMPLE IS BEST."
HE LOVES HEIGHT AND RAW STRENGTH MORE THAN ANYTHING ELSE...
...SCOURING THE PREFECTURE AND HAND-PICKING PLAYERS HE THINKS ARE THE BEST.
I CAN'T SAY HOW FAR HINATA HAS ACTUALLY THOUGHT THIS THROUGH...
...BUT I KNOW THIS WILL BE A REALLY IMPORTANT EXPERIENCE FOR HIM.
IT'S JUST...
WELL!
I'M HAPPY THAT IT ALL WORKED OUT THIS WAY, TO BE HONEST.
I'LL BE BLUNT.

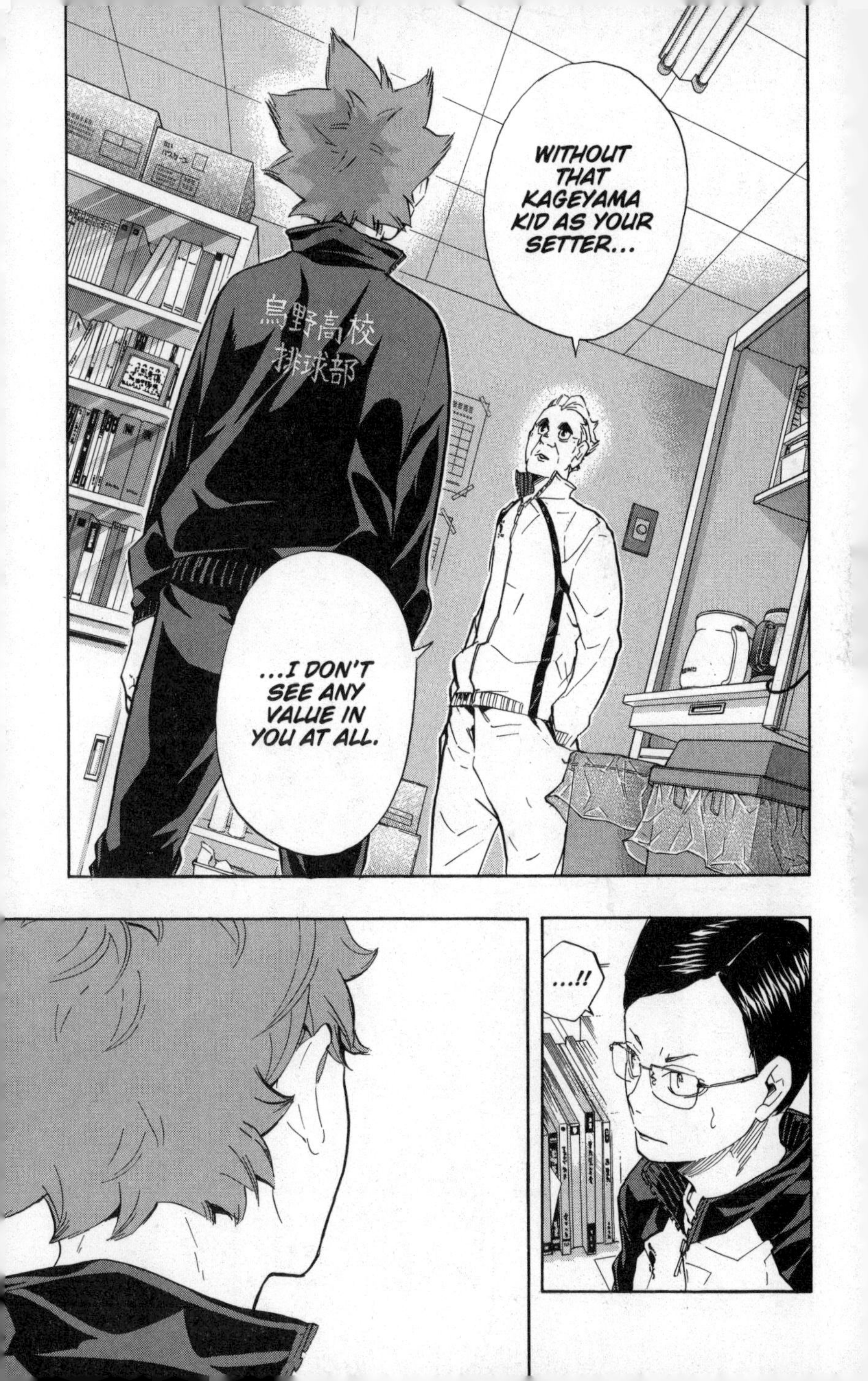
WITHOUT THAT KAGEYAMA KID AS YOUR SETTER...
烏野高校 排球部
...I DON'T SEE ANY VALUE IN YOU AT ALL.
...!!

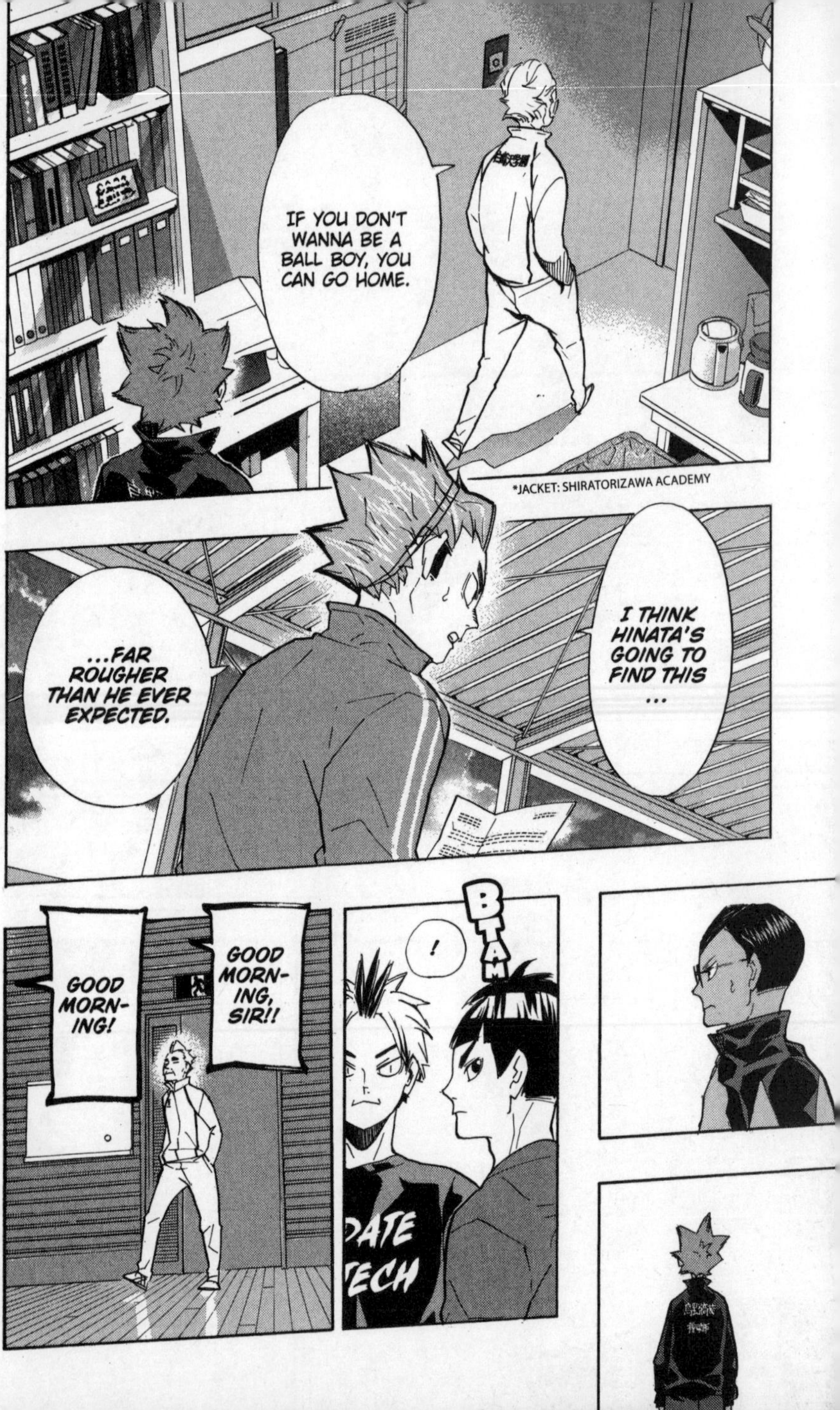
IF YOU DON'T WANNA BE A BALL BOY, YOU CAN GO HOME.
*JACKET: SHIRATORIZAWA ACADEMY
I THINK HINATA'S GOING TO FIND THIS ...
...FAR ROUGHER THAN HE EVER EXPECTED.
BTAM
!
DATE TECH
GOOD MORNING, SIR!!
GOOD MORNING!

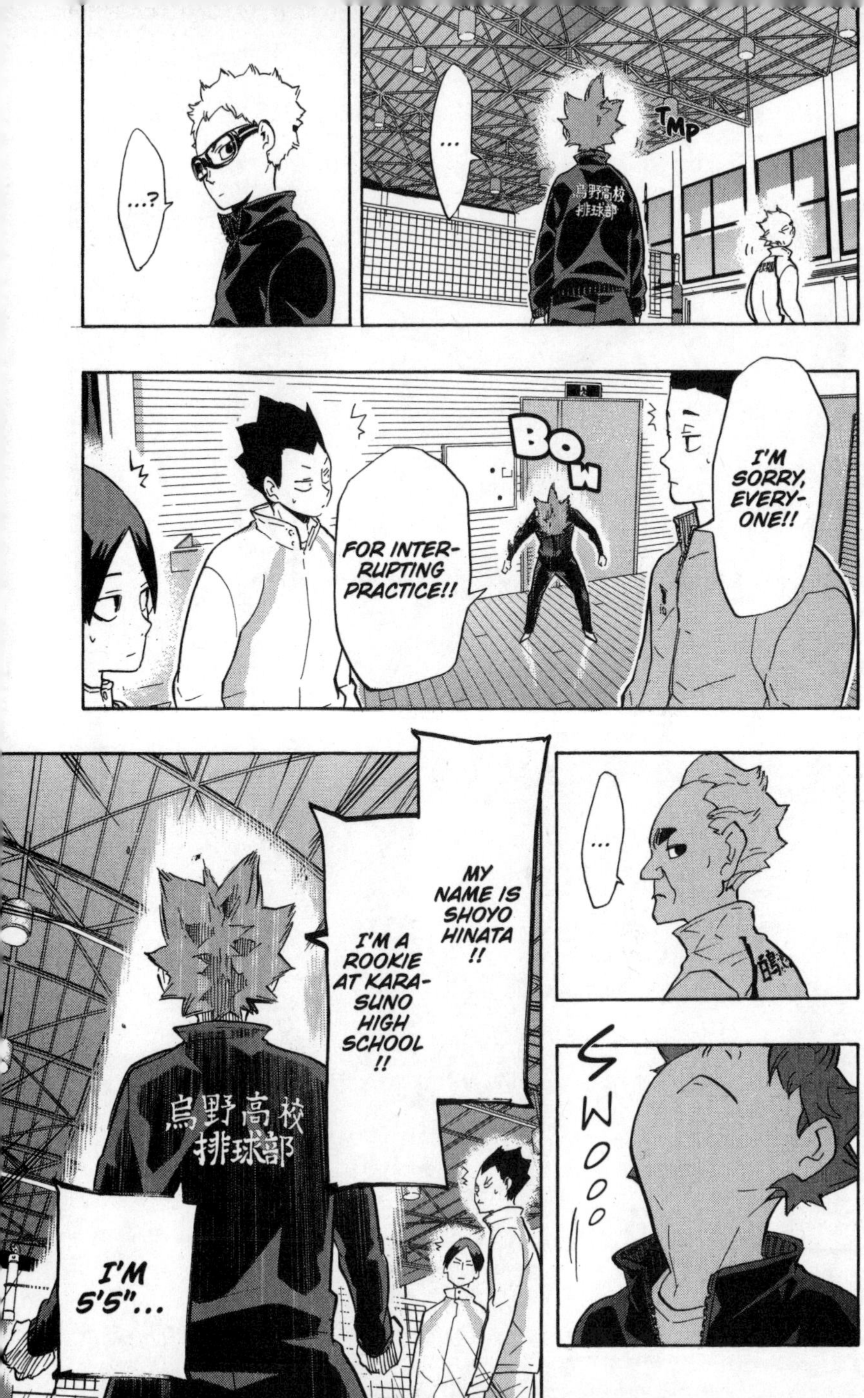
...
TMP
烏野高校 排球部
...?
I'M SORRY, EVERYONE!!
BOW
FOR INTER-RUPTING PRACTICE!!
...
SWOOO
MY NAME IS SHOYO HINATA!!
I'M A ROOKIE AT KARA-SUNO HIGH SCHOOL!!
烏野高校 排球部
I'M 5'5"...

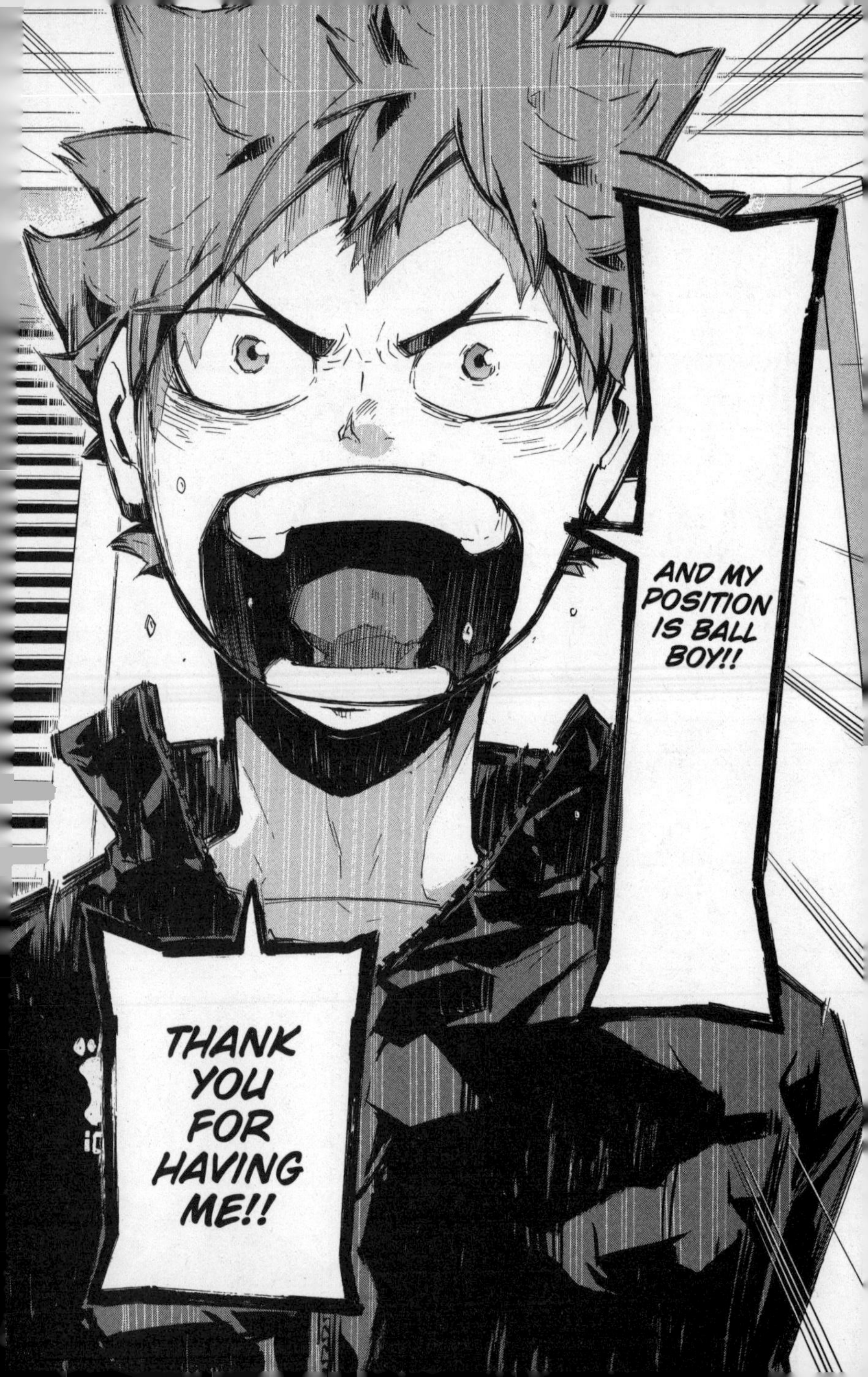
AND MY POSITION IS BALL BOY!!
THANK YOU FOR HAVING ME!!

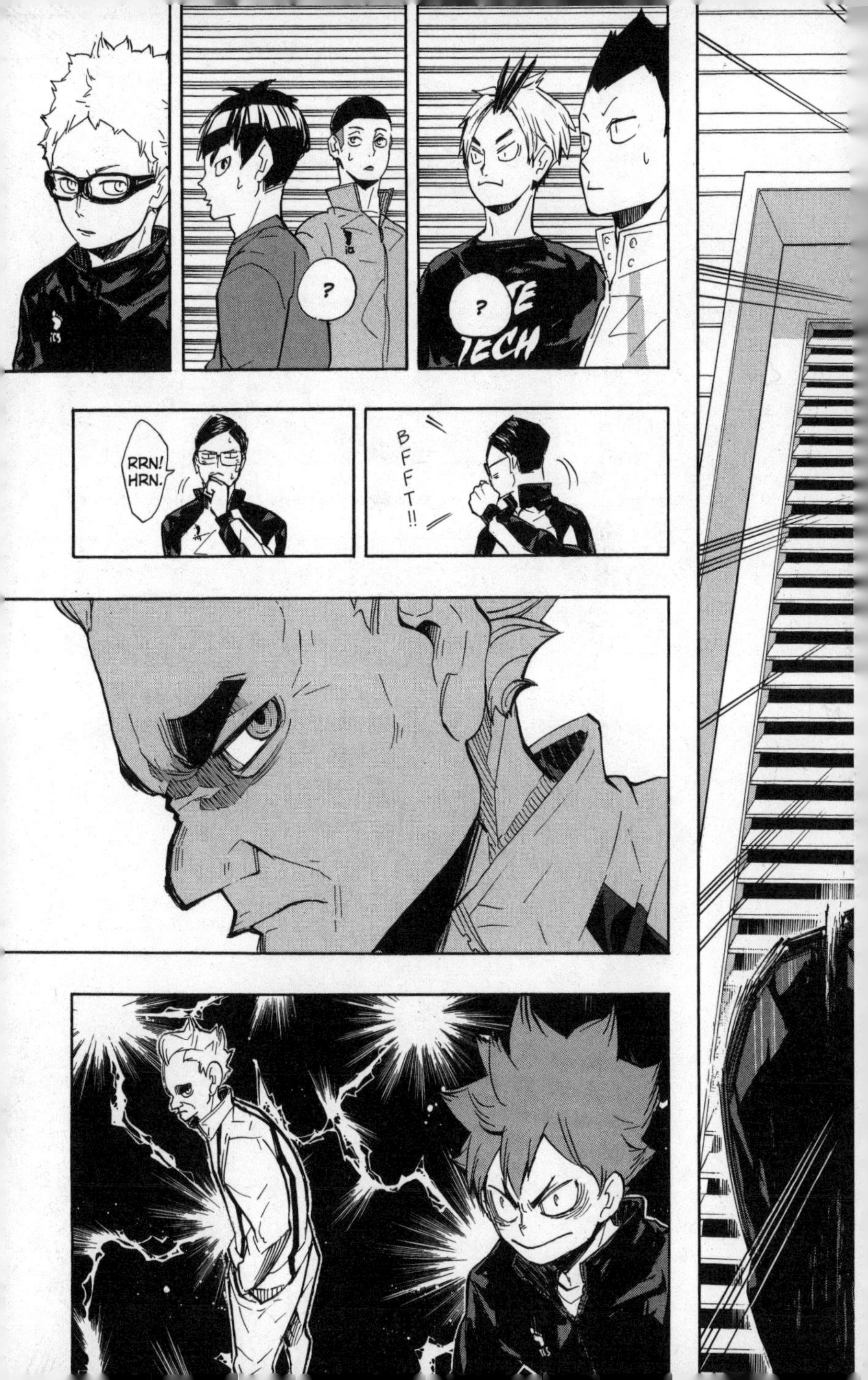
?
?
RRN! HRN.
BFFT!!

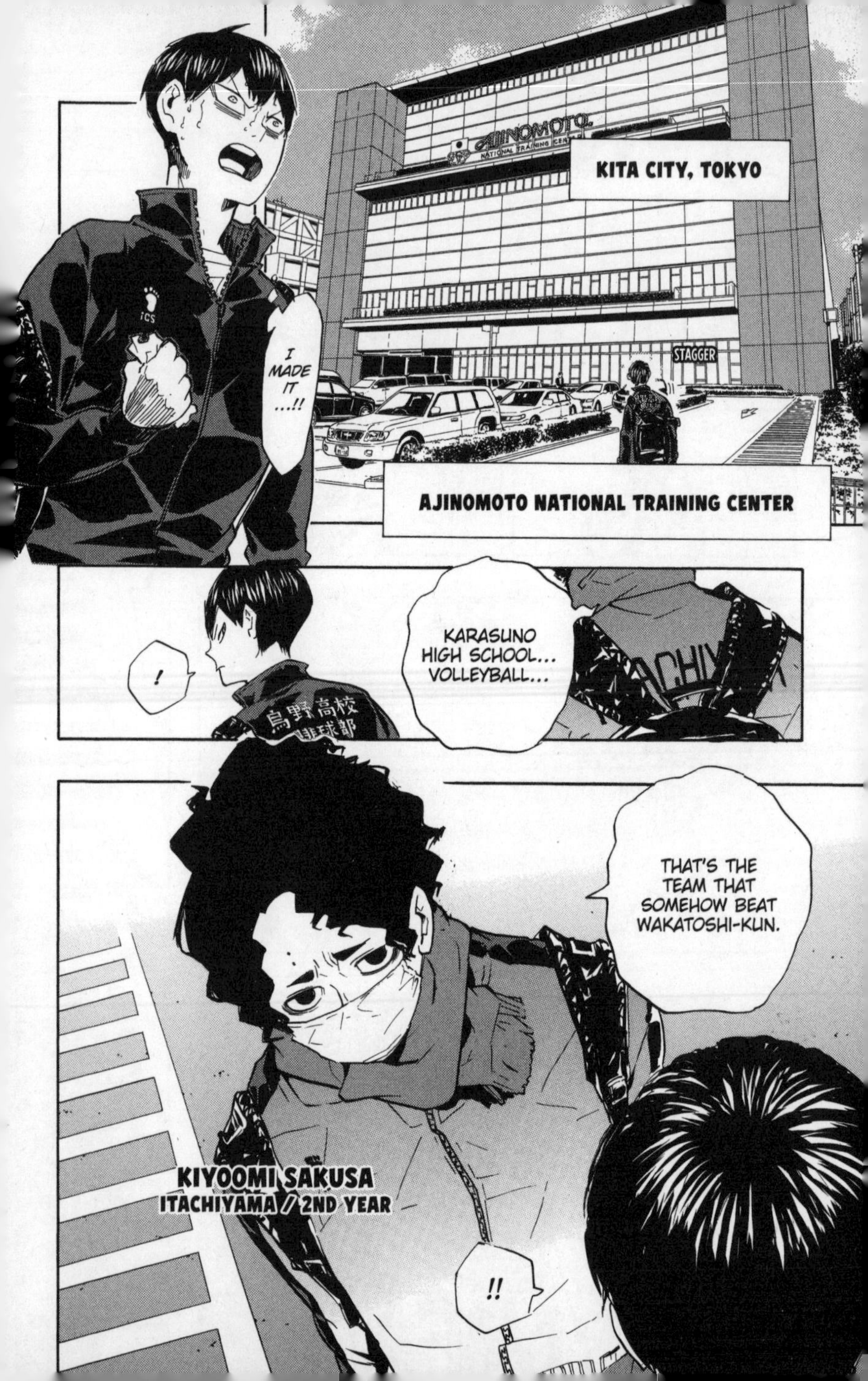
KITA CITY, TOKYO
AJINOMOTO
AJINOMOTO NATIONAL TRAINING CENTER
STAGGER
I MADE IT ...!!
KARASUNO HIGH SCHOOL... VOLLEYBALL...
!
THAT'S THE TEAM THAT SOMEHOW BEAT WAKATOSHI-KUN.
KIYOOMI SAKUSA
ITACHIYAMA / 2ND YEAR
!!

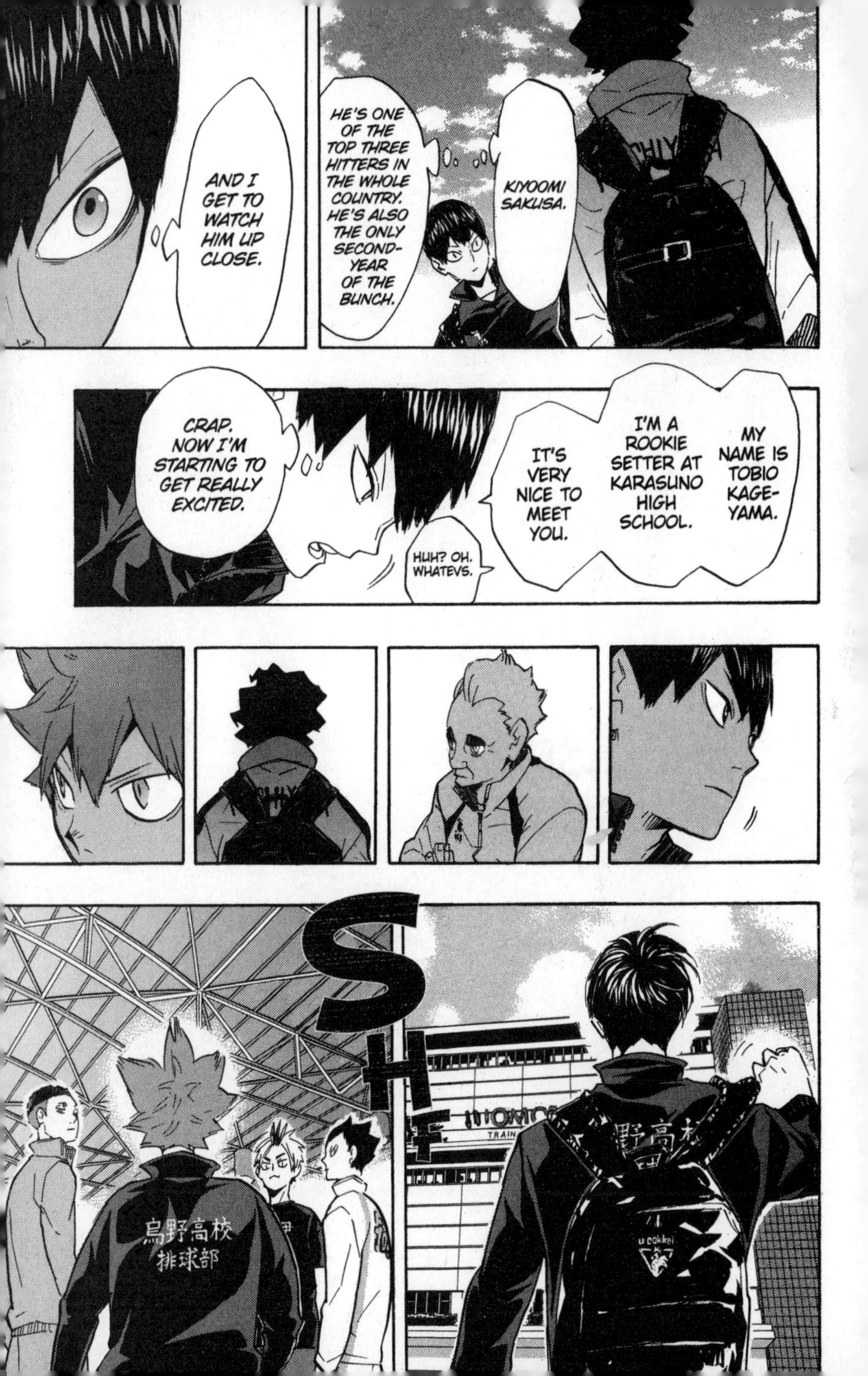
KIYOOMI SAKUSA.
HE'S ONE OF THE TOP THREE HITTERS IN THE WHOLE COUNTRY. HE'S ALSO THE ONLY SECOND-YEAR OF THE BUNCH.
AND I GET TO WATCH HIM UP CLOSE.
MY NAME IS TOBIO KAGE-YAMA.
I'M A ROOKIE SETTER AT KARASUNO HIGH SCHOOL.
IT'S VERY NICE TO MEET YOU.
HUH? OH. WHATEVS.
CRAP. NOW I'M STARTING TO GET REALLY EXCITED.
SHF
烏野高校
排球部

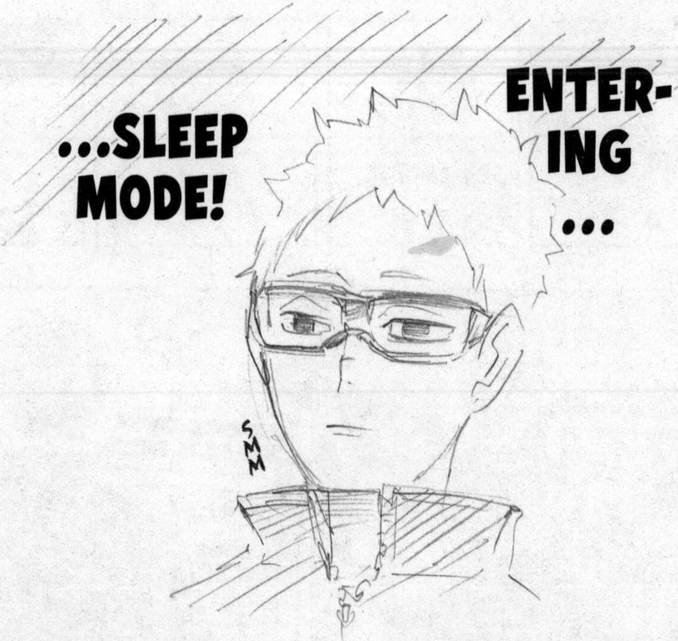
ENTER-ING...
...SLEEP MODE!
SMM

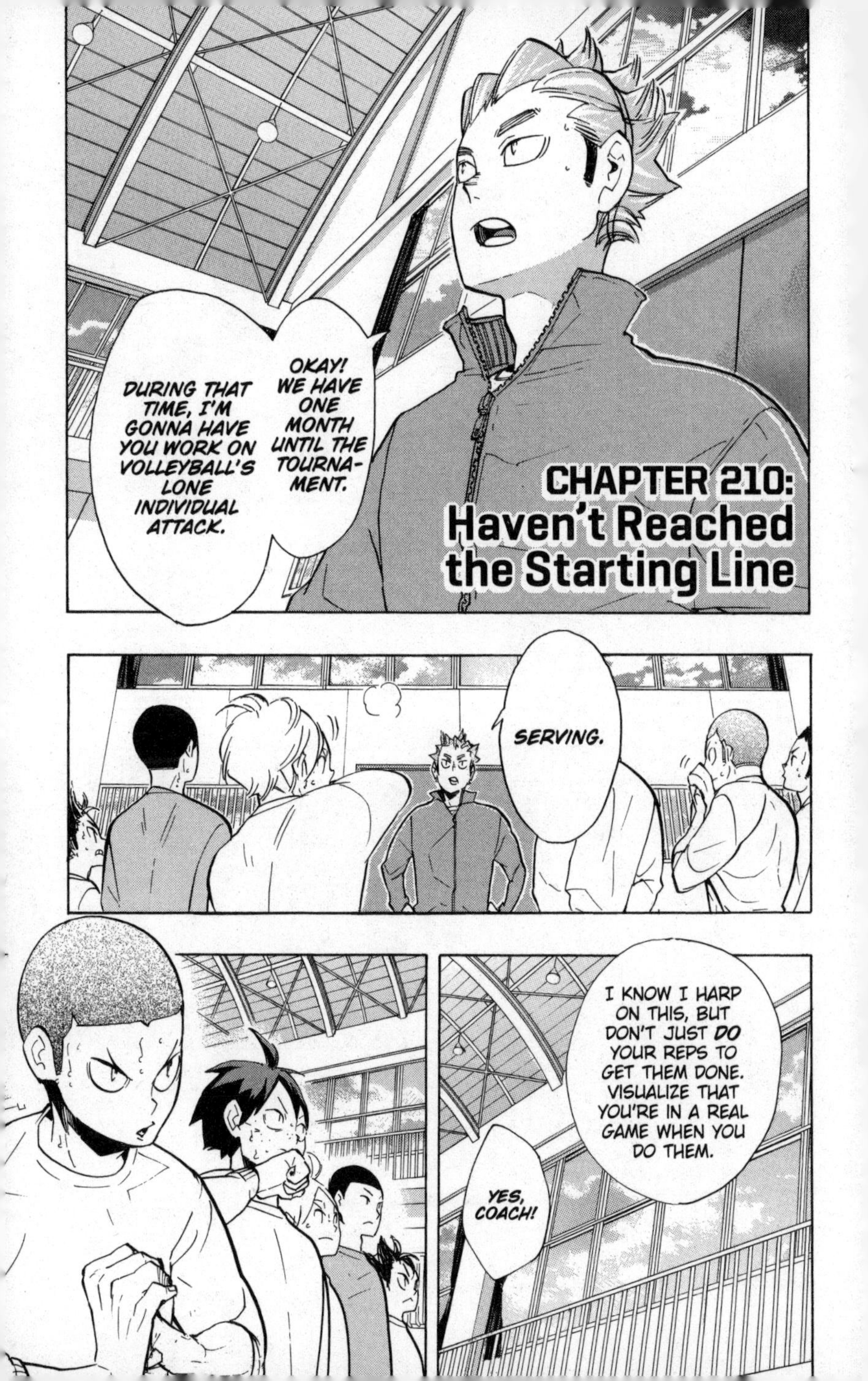
CHAPTER 210:
Haven't Reached the Starting Line
OKAY! WE HAVE ONE MONTH UNTIL THE TOURNAMENT.
DURING THAT TIME, I'M GONNA HAVE YOU WORK ON VOLLEYBALL'S LONE INDIVIDUAL ATTACK.
SERVING.
I KNOW I HARP ON THIS, BUT DON'T JUST *DO* YOUR REPS TO GET THEM DONE. VISUALIZE THAT YOU'RE IN A REAL GAME WHEN YOU DO THEM.
YES, COACH!

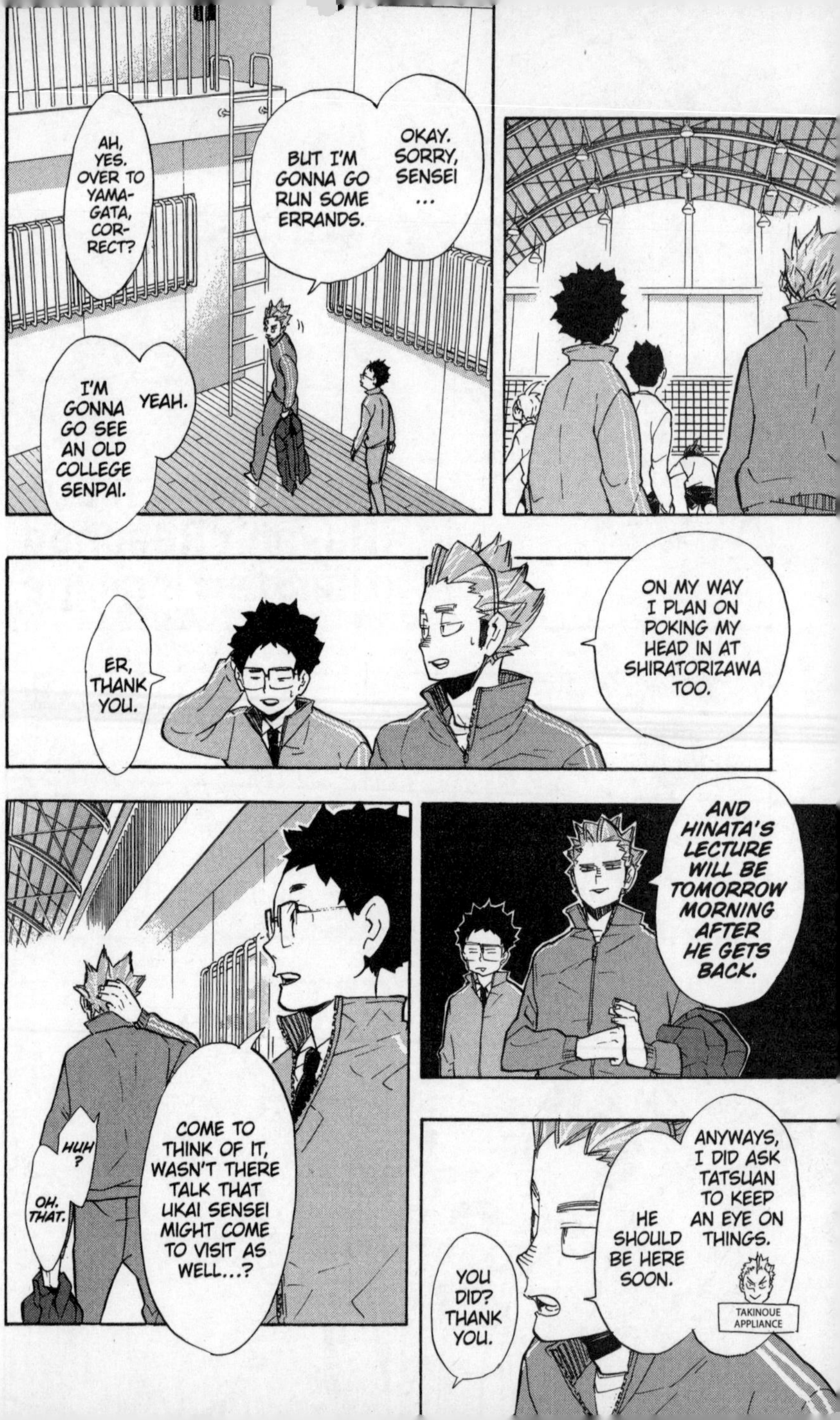
OKAY. SORRY, SENSEI...
BUT I'M GONNA GO RUN SOME ERRANDS.
AH, YES. OVER TO YAMAGATA, CORRECT?
YEAH.
I'M GONNA GO SEE AN OLD COLLEGE SENPAI.
ON MY WAY I PLAN ON POKING MY HEAD IN AT SHIRATORIZAWA TOO.
ER, THANK YOU.
AND HINATA'S LECTURE WILL BE TOMORROW MORNING AFTER HE GETS BACK.
ANYWAYS, I DID ASK TATSUAN TO KEEP AN EYE ON THINGS.
HE SHOULD BE HERE SOON.
TAKINOUE APPLIANCE
YOU DID? THANK YOU.
COME TO THINK OF IT, WASN'T THERE TALK THAT UKAI SENSEI MIGHT COME TO VISIT AS WELL...?
HUH?
OH. THAT.

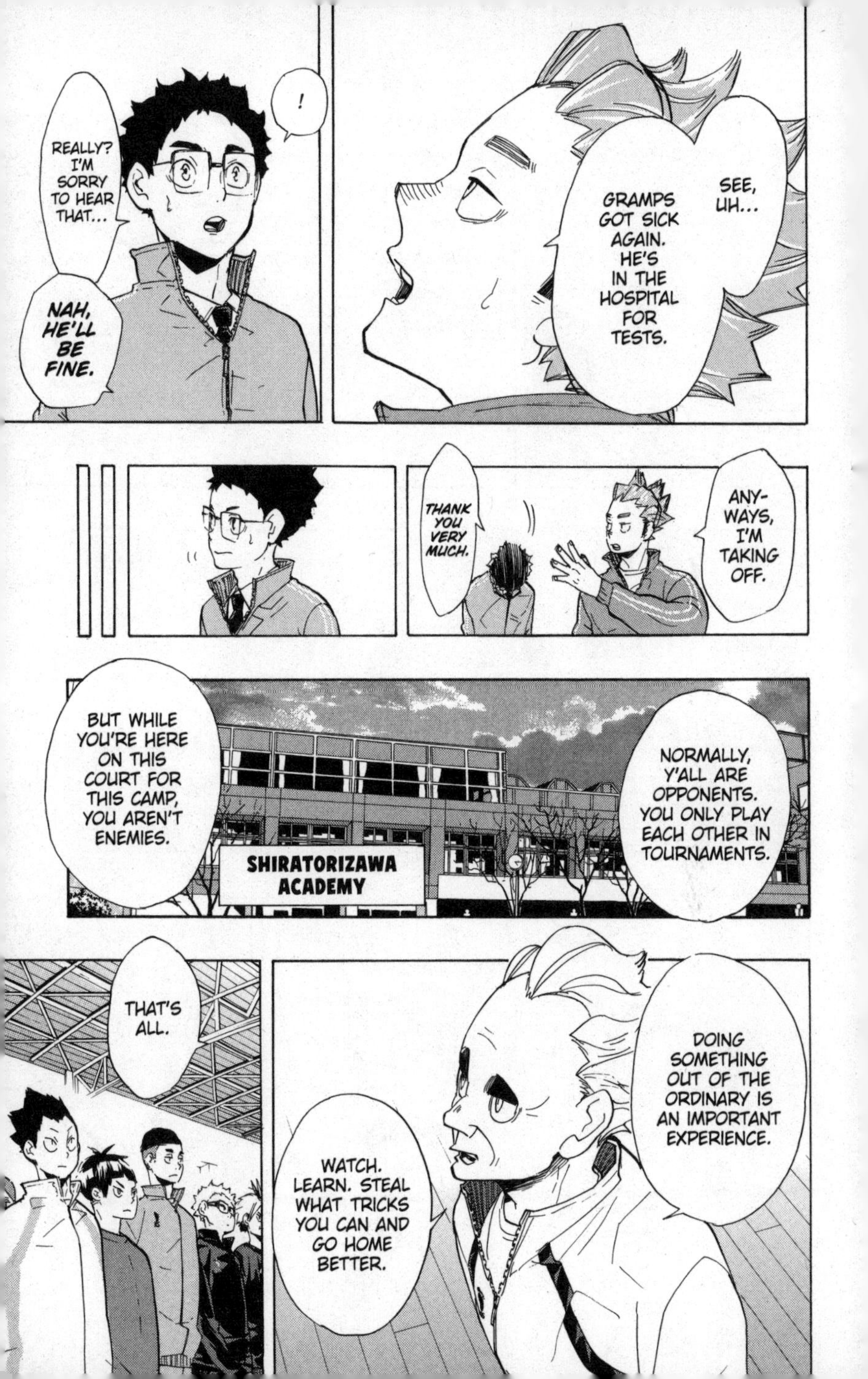
SEE, UH...
GRAMPS GOT SICK AGAIN. HE'S IN THE HOSPITAL FOR TESTS.
!
REALLY? I'M SORRY TO HEAR THAT...
NAH, HE'LL BE FINE.
ANY-WAYS, I'M TAKING OFF.
THANK YOU VERY MUCH.
NORMALLY, Y'ALL ARE OPPONENTS. YOU ONLY PLAY EACH OTHER IN TOURNAMENTS.
SHIRATORIZAWA ACADEMY
BUT WHILE YOU'RE HERE ON THIS COURT FOR THIS CAMP, YOU AREN'T ENEMIES.
DOING SOMETHING OUT OF THE ORDINARY IS AN IMPORTANT EXPERIENCE.
WATCH. LEARN. STEAL WHAT TRICKS YOU CAN AND GO HOME BETTER.
THAT'S ALL.

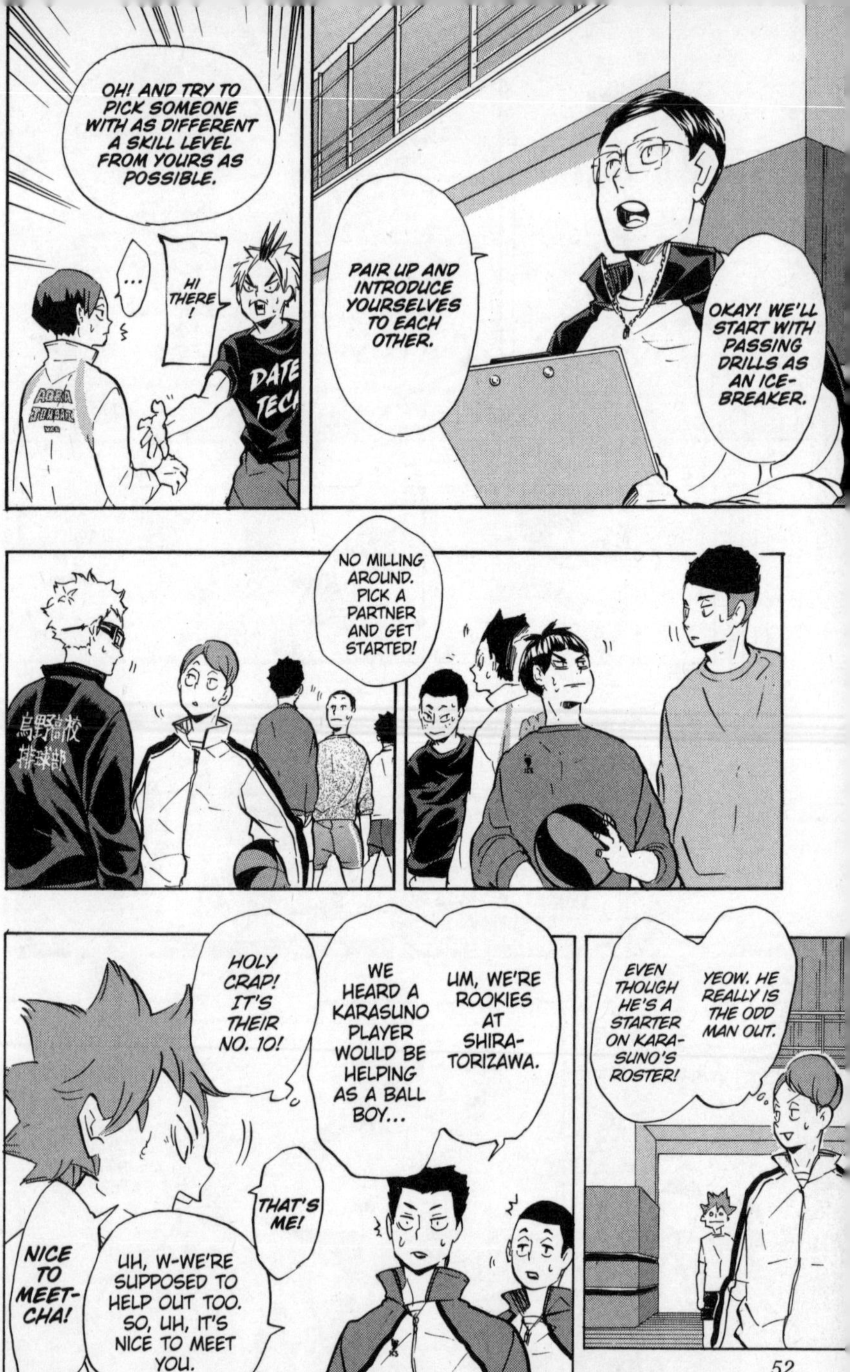
OKAY! WE'LL START WITH PASSING DRILLS AS AN ICE-BREAKER.
PAIR UP AND INTRODUCE YOURSELVES TO EACH OTHER.
OH! AND TRY TO PICK SOMEONE WITH AS DIFFERENT A SKILL LEVEL FROM YOURS AS POSSIBLE.
HI THERE!
...
DATE TECH
NO MILLING AROUND. PICK A PARTNER AND GET STARTED!
YEOW. HE REALLY IS THE ODD MAN OUT.
EVEN THOUGH HE'S A STARTER ON KARASUNO'S ROSTER!
UM, WE'RE ROOKIES AT SHIRATORIZAWA.
WE HEARD A KARASUNO PLAYER WOULD BE HELPING AS A BALL BOY...
HOLY CRAP! IT'S THEIR NO. 10!
THAT'S ME!
UH, W-WE'RE SUPPOSED TO HELP OUT TOO. SO, UH, IT'S NICE TO MEET YOU.
NICE TO MEET-CHA!

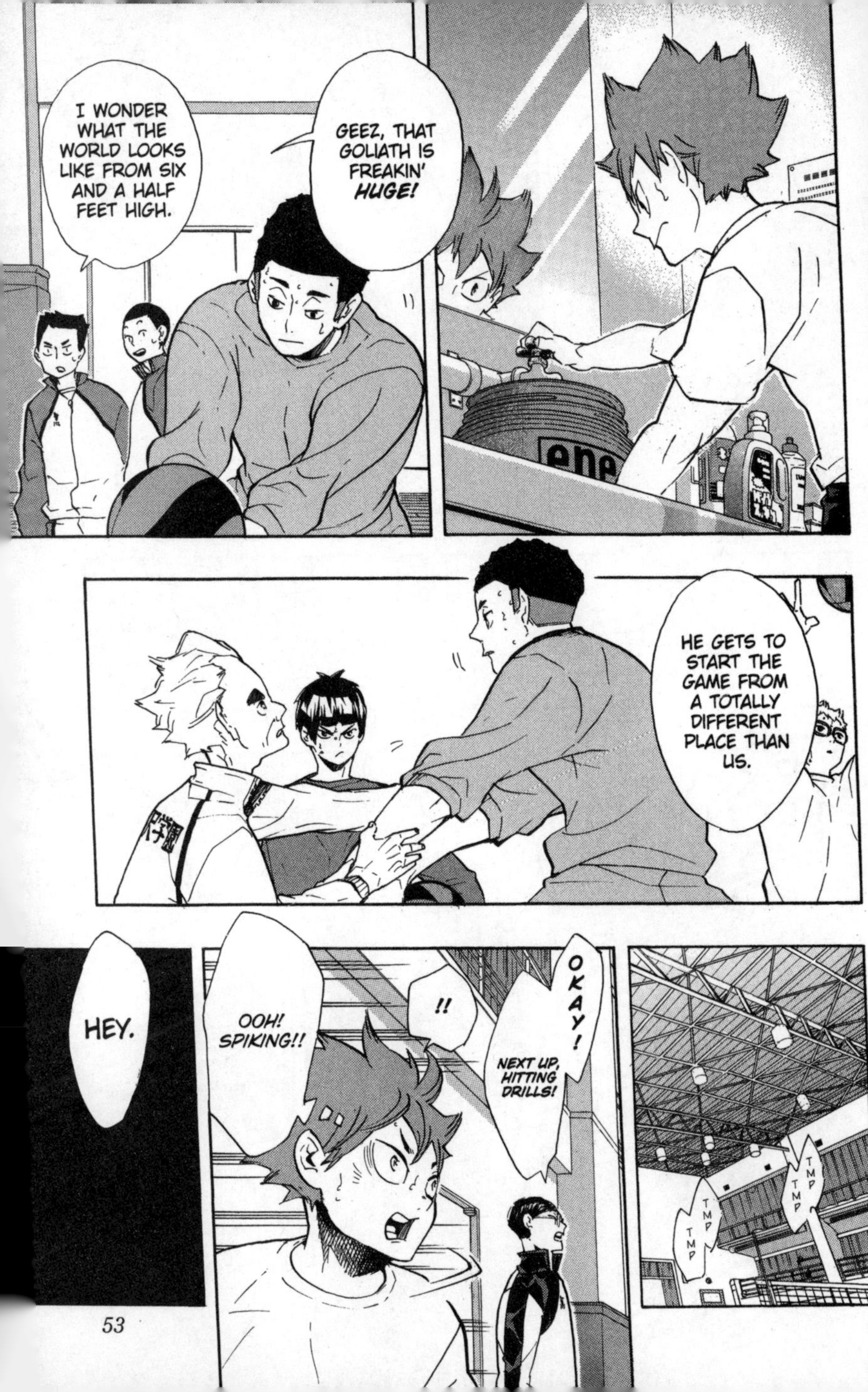
GEEZ, THAT GOLIATH IS FREAKIN' *HUGE!*
I WONDER WHAT THE WORLD LOOKS LIKE FROM SIX AND A HALF FEET HIGH.
HE GETS TO START THE GAME FROM A TOTALLY DIFFERENT PLACE THAN US.
TMP TMP
TMP TMP
OKAY!
NEXT UP, HITTING DRILLS!
!!
OOH! SPIKING!!
HEY.

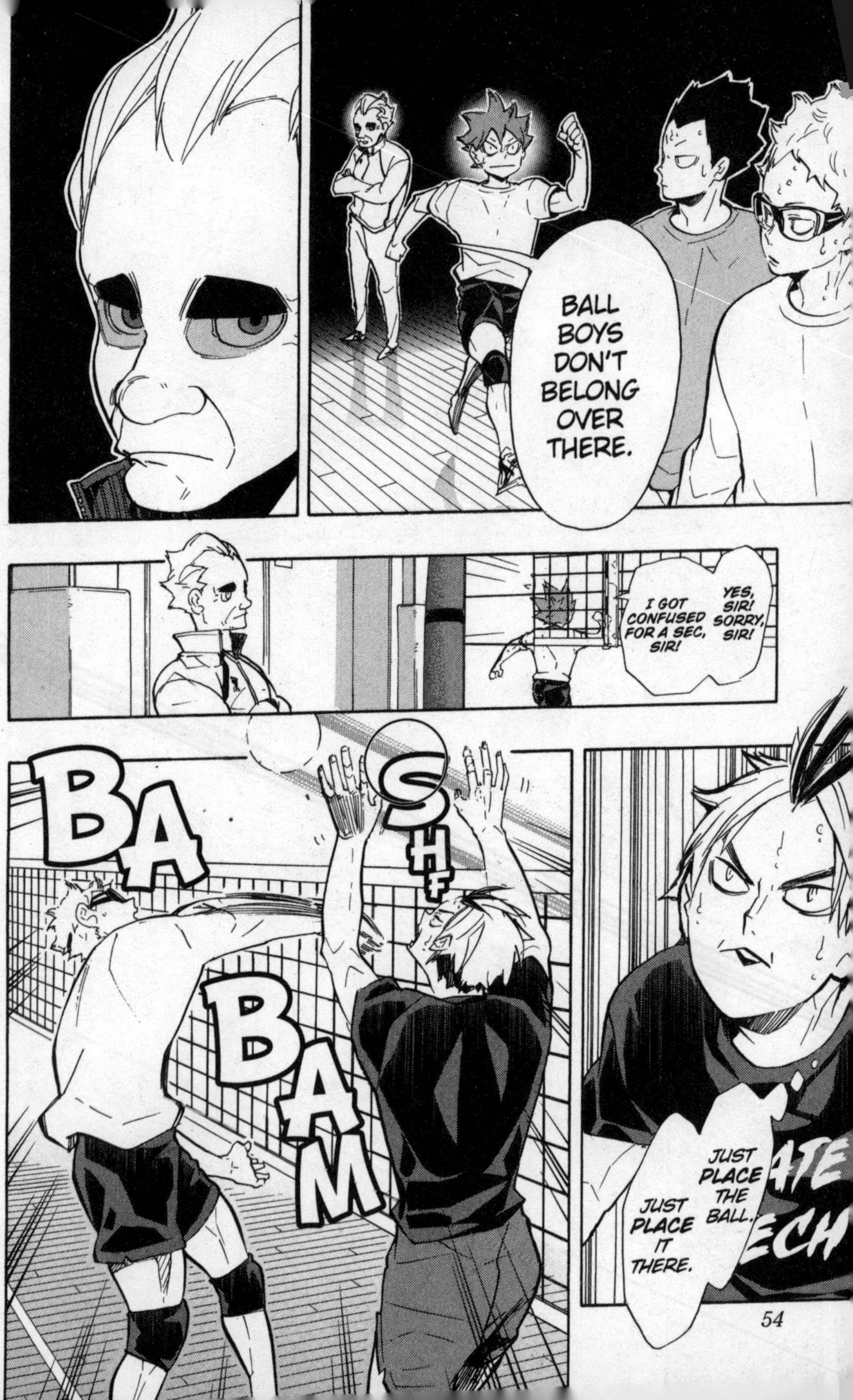
BALL BOYS DON'T BELONG OVER THERE.
YES, SIR! SORRY, SIR!
I GOT CONFUSED FOR A SEC, SIR!
JUST PLACE THE BALL.
JUST PLACE IT THERE.
BA
SHF
BBAM

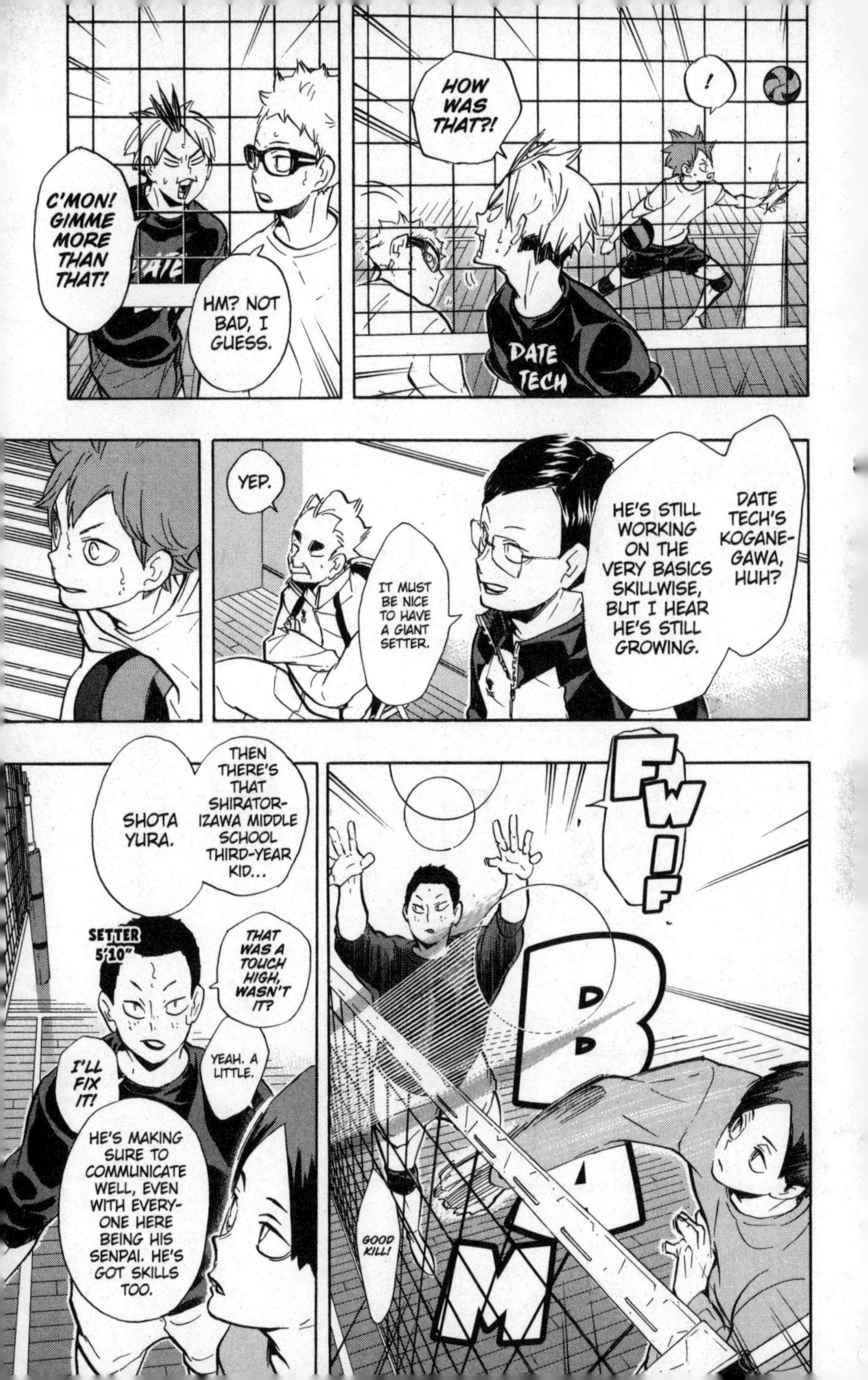
!
HOW WAS THAT?!
DATE TECH
HM? NOT BAD, I GUESS.
C'MON! GIMME MORE THAN THAT!
DATE TECH'S KOGANE-GAWA, HUH?
HE'S STILL WORKING ON THE VERY BASICS SKILLWISE, BUT I HEAR HE'S STILL GROWING.
IT MUST BE NICE TO HAVE A GIANT SETTER.
YEP.
FWIF
BAM
GOOD KILL!
THEN THERE'S THAT SHIRATOR-IZAWA MIDDLE SCHOOL THIRD-YEAR KID...
SHOTA YURA.
SETTER 5'10"
THAT WAS A TOUCH HIGH, WASN'T IT?
YEAH. A LITTLE.
I'LL FIX IT!
HE'S MAKING SURE TO COMMUNICATE WELL, EVEN WITH EVERY-ONE HERE BEING HIS SENPAI. HE'S GOT SKILLS TOO.

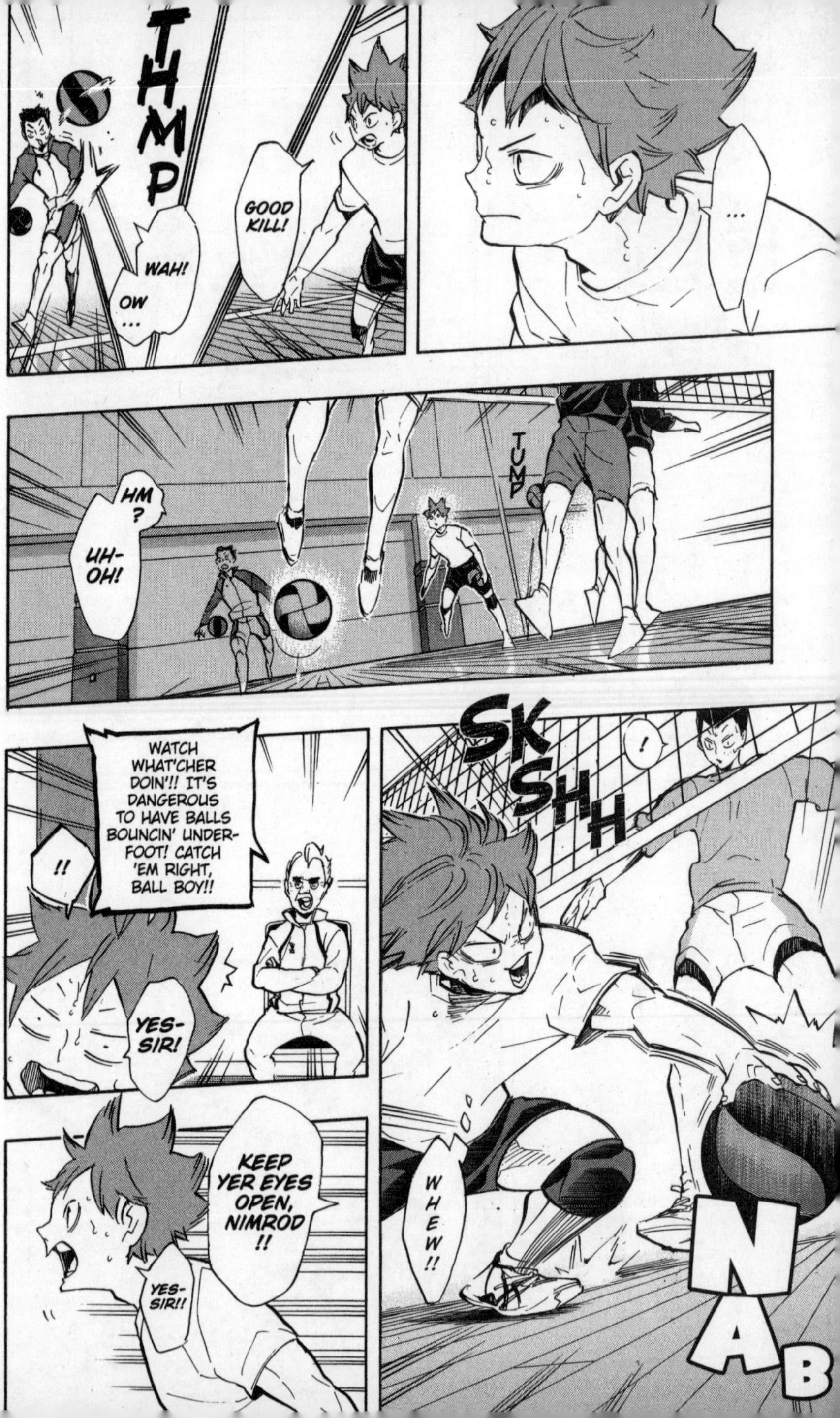
...
GOOD KILL!
THMP
WAH!
OW ...
TUMP
HM?
UH-OH!
SK SHH
!
NAB
WHEW!!
WATCH WHAT'CHER DOIN'!! IT'S DANGEROUS TO HAVE BALLS BOUNCIN' UNDER-FOOT! CATCH 'EM RIGHT, BALL BOY!!
!!
YES-SIR!
KEEP YER EYES OPEN, NIMROD!!
YES-SIR!!

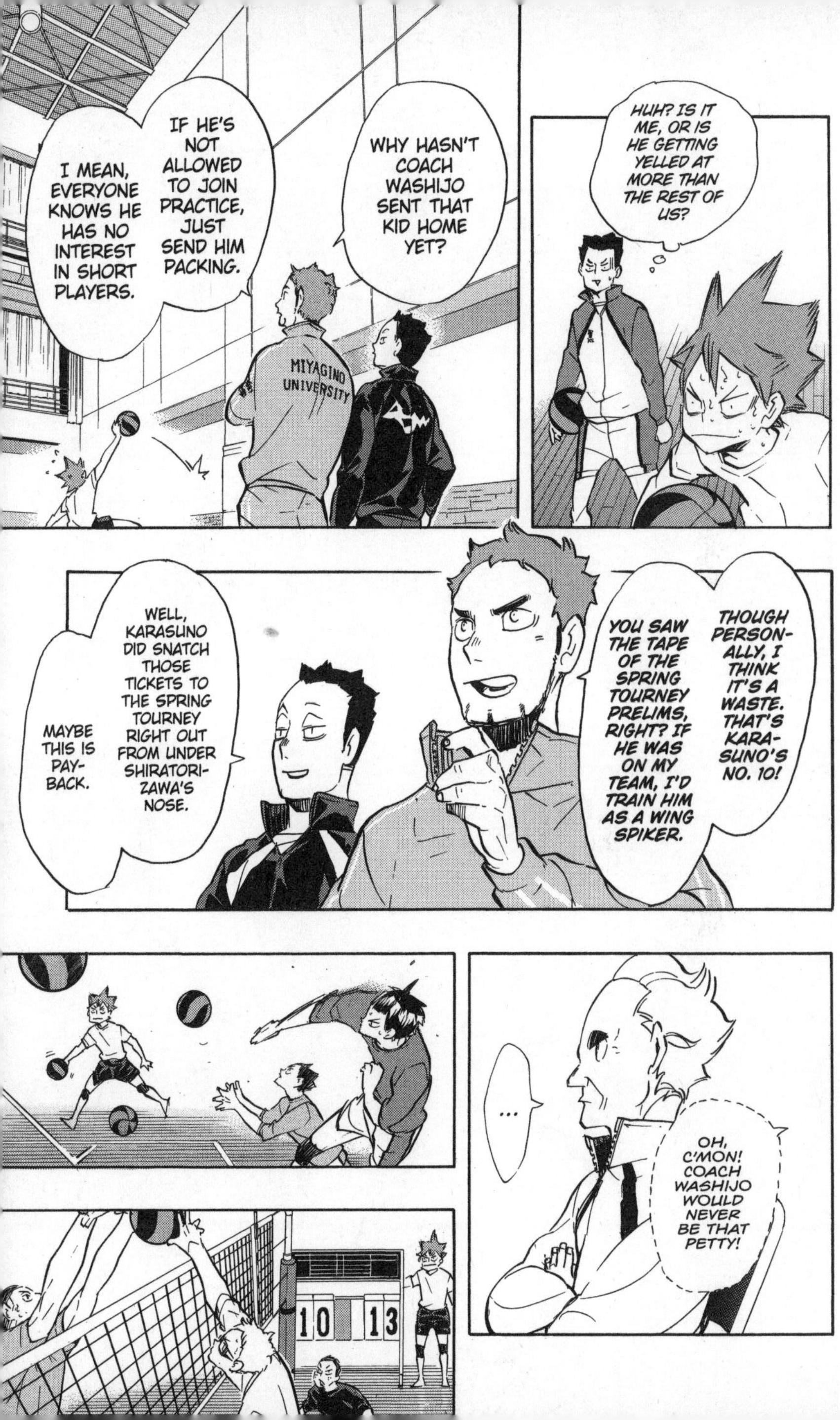
HUH? IS IT ME, OR IS HE GETTING YELLED AT MORE THAN THE REST OF US?
WHY HASN'T COACH WASHIJO SENT THAT KID HOME YET?
IF HE'S NOT ALLOWED TO JOIN PRACTICE, JUST SEND HIM PACKING.
I MEAN, EVERYONE KNOWS HE HAS NO INTEREST IN SHORT PLAYERS.
MIYAGINO UNIVERSITY
THOUGH PERSONALLY, I THINK IT'S A WASTE. THAT'S KARASUNO'S NO. 10!
YOU SAW THE TAPE OF THE SPRING TOURNEY PRELIMS, RIGHT? IF HE WAS ON MY TEAM, I'D TRAIN HIM AS A WING SPIKER.
WELL, KARASUNO DID SNATCH THOSE TICKETS TO THE SPRING TOURNEY RIGHT OUT FROM UNDER SHIRATORIZAWA'S NOSE.
MAYBE THIS IS PAYBACK.
...
OH, C'MON! COACH WASHIJO WOULD NEVER BE THAT PETTY!
10
13

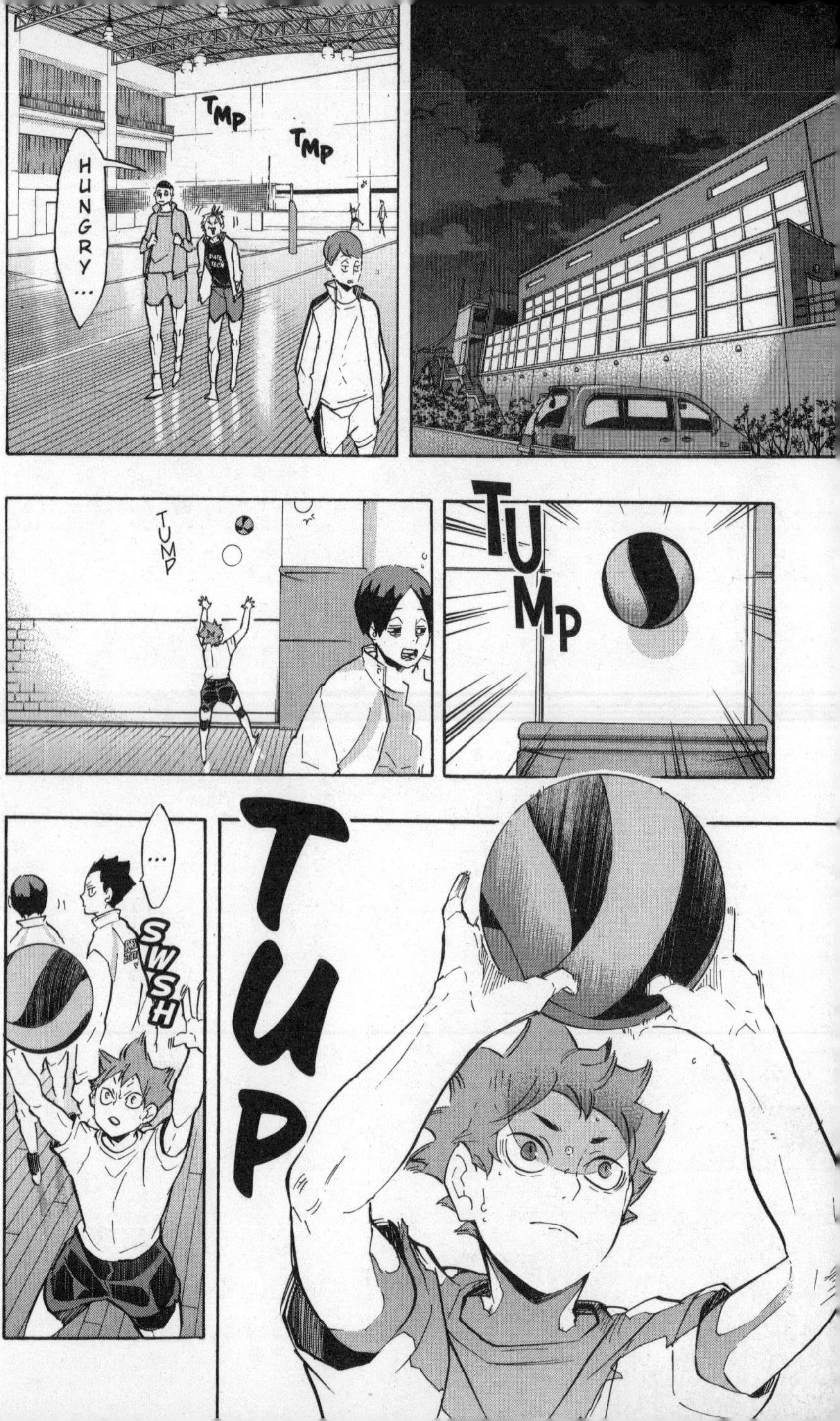
HUNGRY...
TMP
TMP
TUMP
TUMP
TUP
...
SWSH

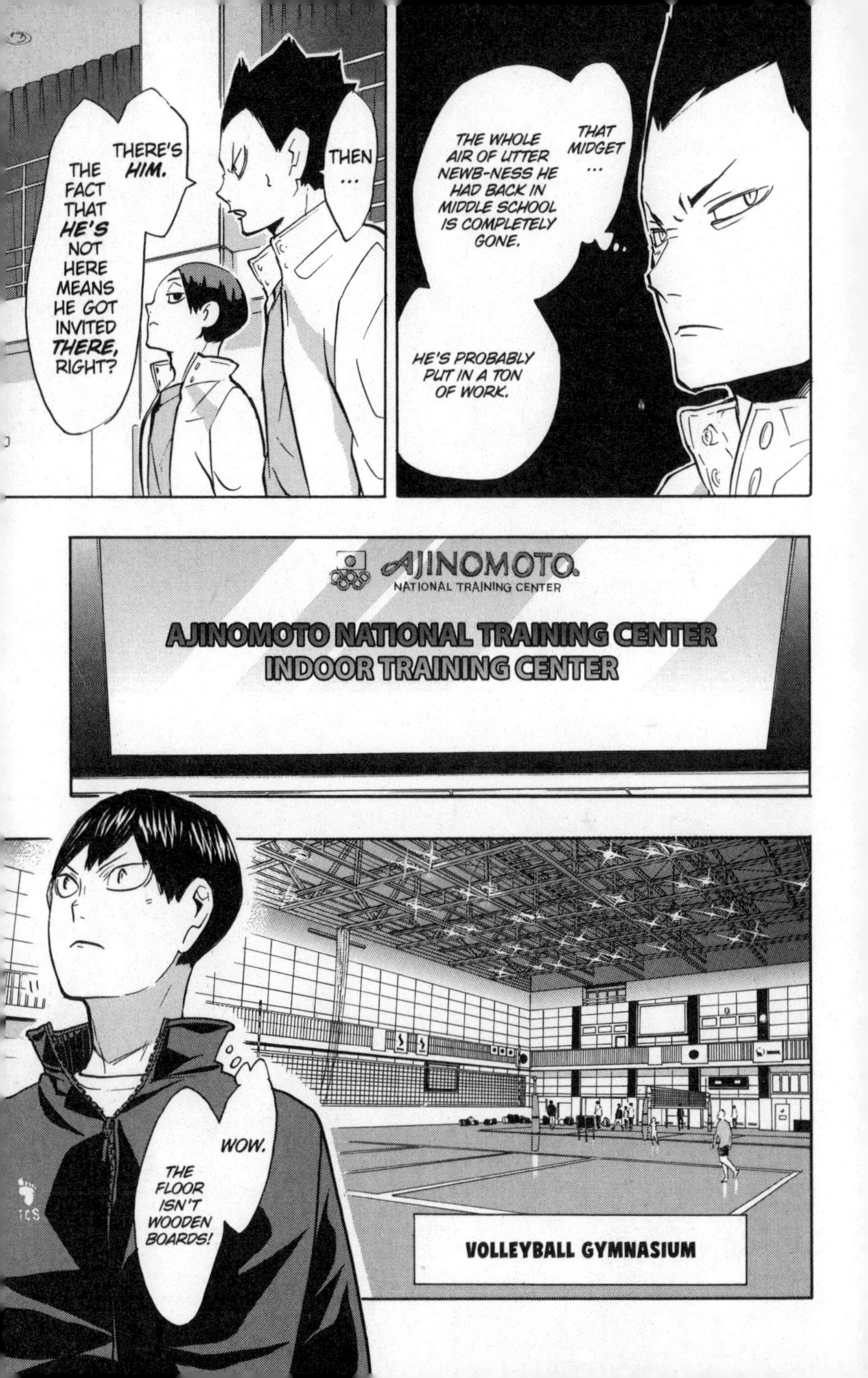
THAT MIDGET...
THE WHOLE AIR OF UTTER NEWB-NESS HE HAD BACK IN MIDDLE SCHOOL IS COMPLETELY GONE.
HE'S PROBABLY PUT IN A TON OF WORK.
THEN...
THERE'S HIM. THE FACT THAT HE'S NOT HERE MEANS HE GOT INVITED THERE, RIGHT?
AJINOMOTO NATIONAL TRAINING CENTER
AJINOMOTO NATIONAL TRAINING CENTER
INDOOR TRAINING CENTER
VOLLEYBALL GYMNASIUM
WOW.
THE FLOOR ISN'T WOODEN BOARDS!

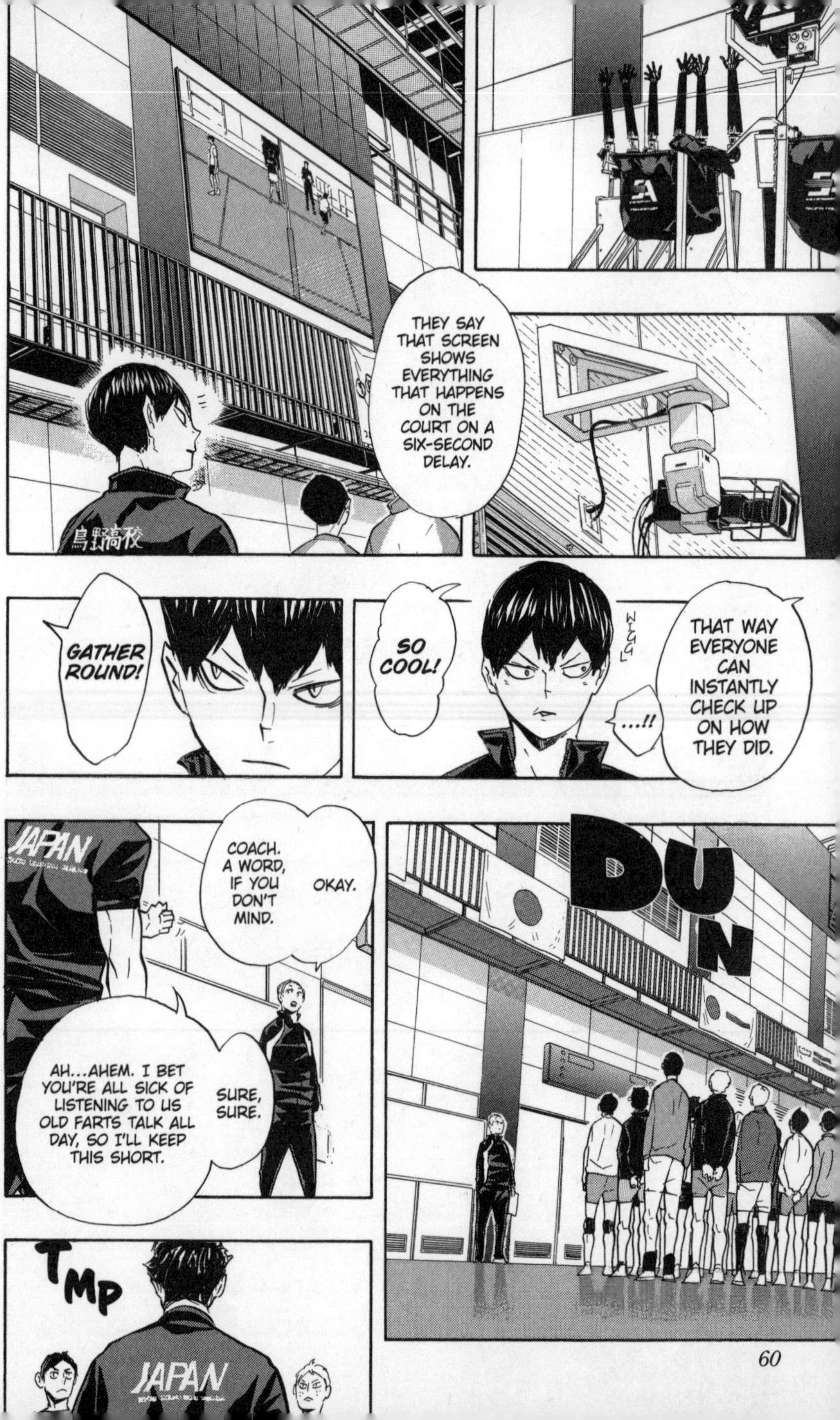
THEY SAY THAT SCREEN SHOWS EVERYTHING THAT HAPPENS ON THE COURT ON A SIX-SECOND DELAY.
THAT WAY EVERYONE CAN INSTANTLY CHECK UP ON HOW THEY DID.
...!!
WIGGL
SO COOL!
GATHER ROUND!
DUN
OKAY.
COACH. A WORD, IF YOU DON'T MIND.
SURE, SURE.
AH...AHEM. I BET YOU'RE ALL SICK OF LISTENING TO US OLD FARTS TALK ALL DAY, SO I'LL KEEP THIS SHORT.
TMP

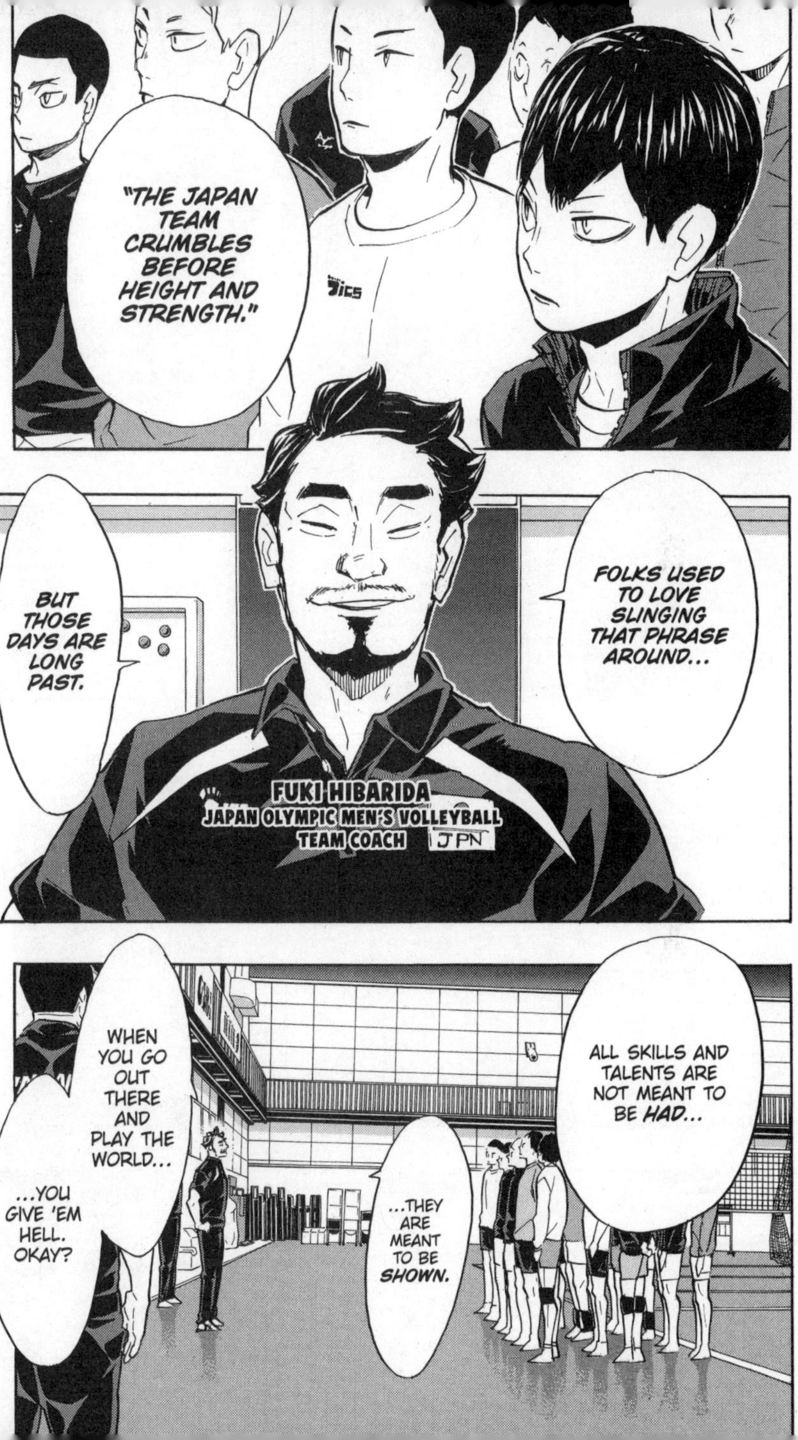
"THE JAPAN TEAM CRUMBLES BEFORE HEIGHT AND STRENGTH."
FOLKS USED TO LOVE SLINGING THAT PHRASE AROUND...
BUT THOSE DAYS ARE LONG PAST.
FUKI HIBARIDA
JAPAN OLYMPIC MEN'S VOLLEYBALL TEAM COACH
JPN
ALL SKILLS AND TALENTS ARE NOT MEANT TO BE *HAD*...
...THEY ARE MEANT TO BE *SHOWN*.
WHEN YOU GO OUT THERE AND PLAY THE WORLD...
...YOU GIVE 'EM HELL. OKAY?

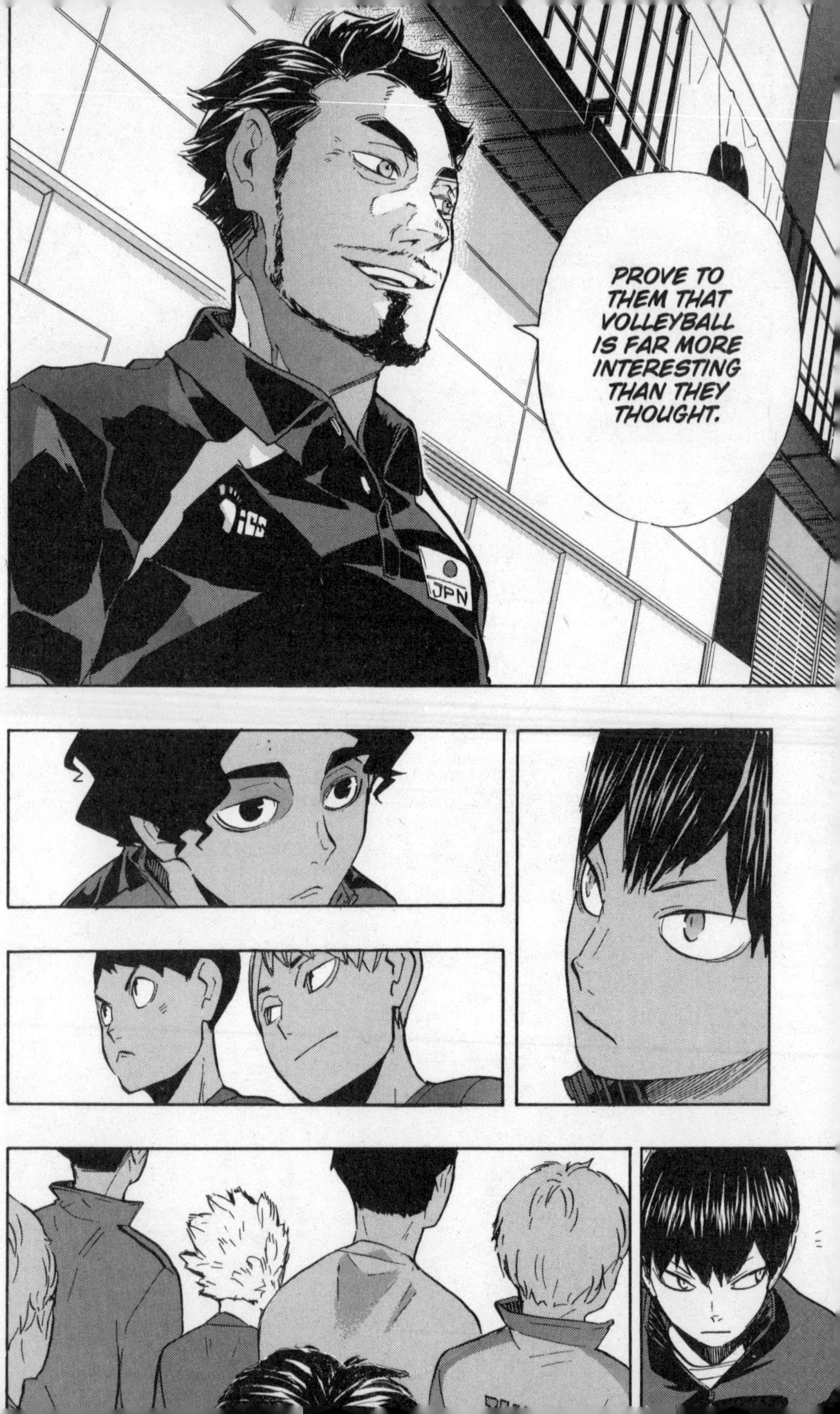
PROVE TO THEM THAT VOLLEYBALL IS FAR MORE INTERESTING THAN THEY THOUGHT.
JPN

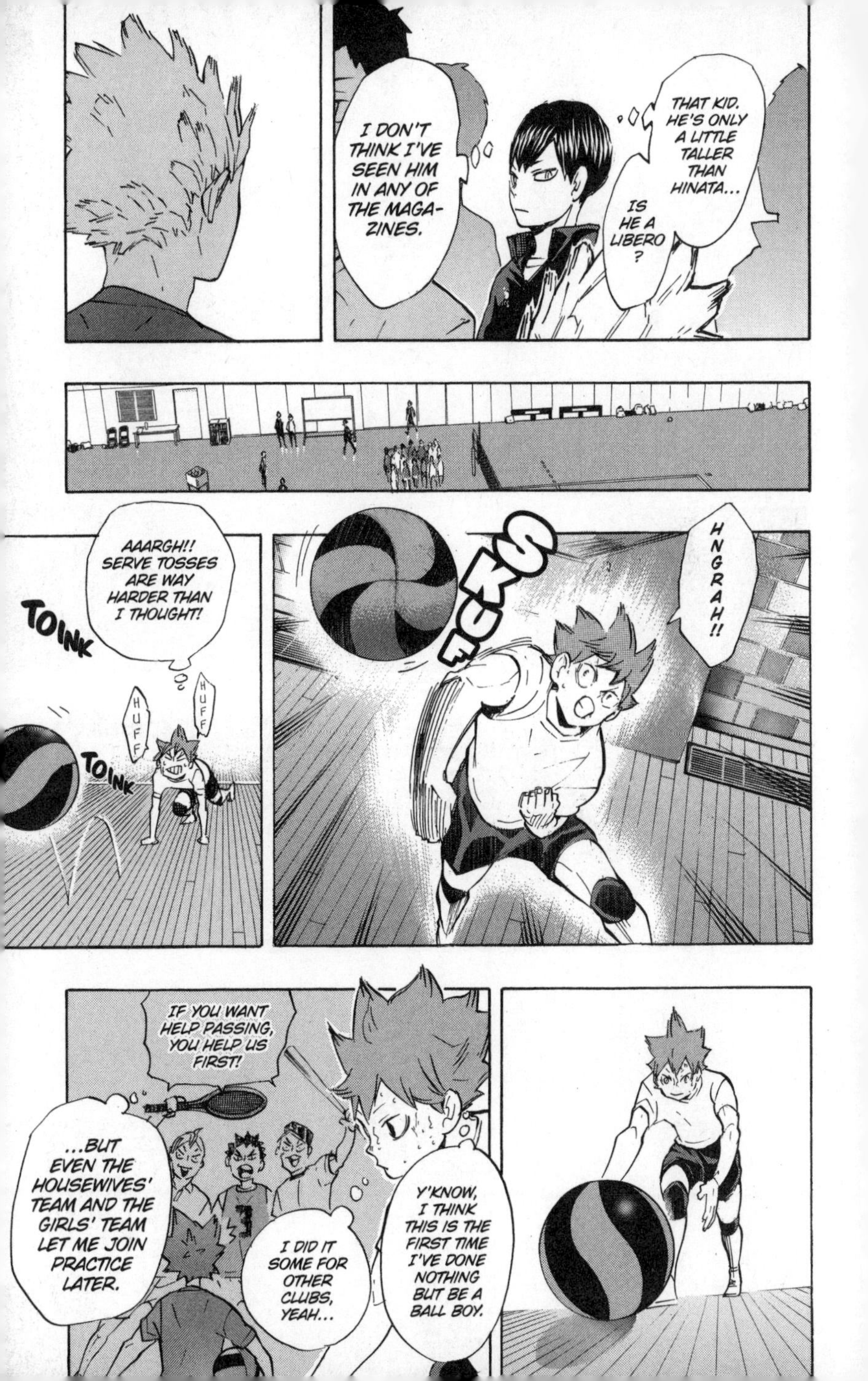
THAT KID. HE'S ONLY A LITTLE TALLER THAN HINATA...
IS HE A LIBERO?
I DON'T THINK I'VE SEEN HIM IN ANY OF THE MAGA-ZINES.
HNGRAH!!
SKUF
AAARGH!! SERVE TOSSES ARE WAY HARDER THAN I THOUGHT!
TOINK
HUFF
HUFF
TOINK
Y'KNOW, I THINK THIS IS THE FIRST TIME I'VE DONE NOTHING BUT BE A BALL BOY.
I DID IT SOME FOR OTHER CLUBS, YEAH...
IF YOU WANT HELP PASSING, YOU HELP US FIRST!
...BUT EVEN THE HOUSEWIVES' TEAM AND THE GIRLS' TEAM LET ME JOIN PRACTICE LATER.

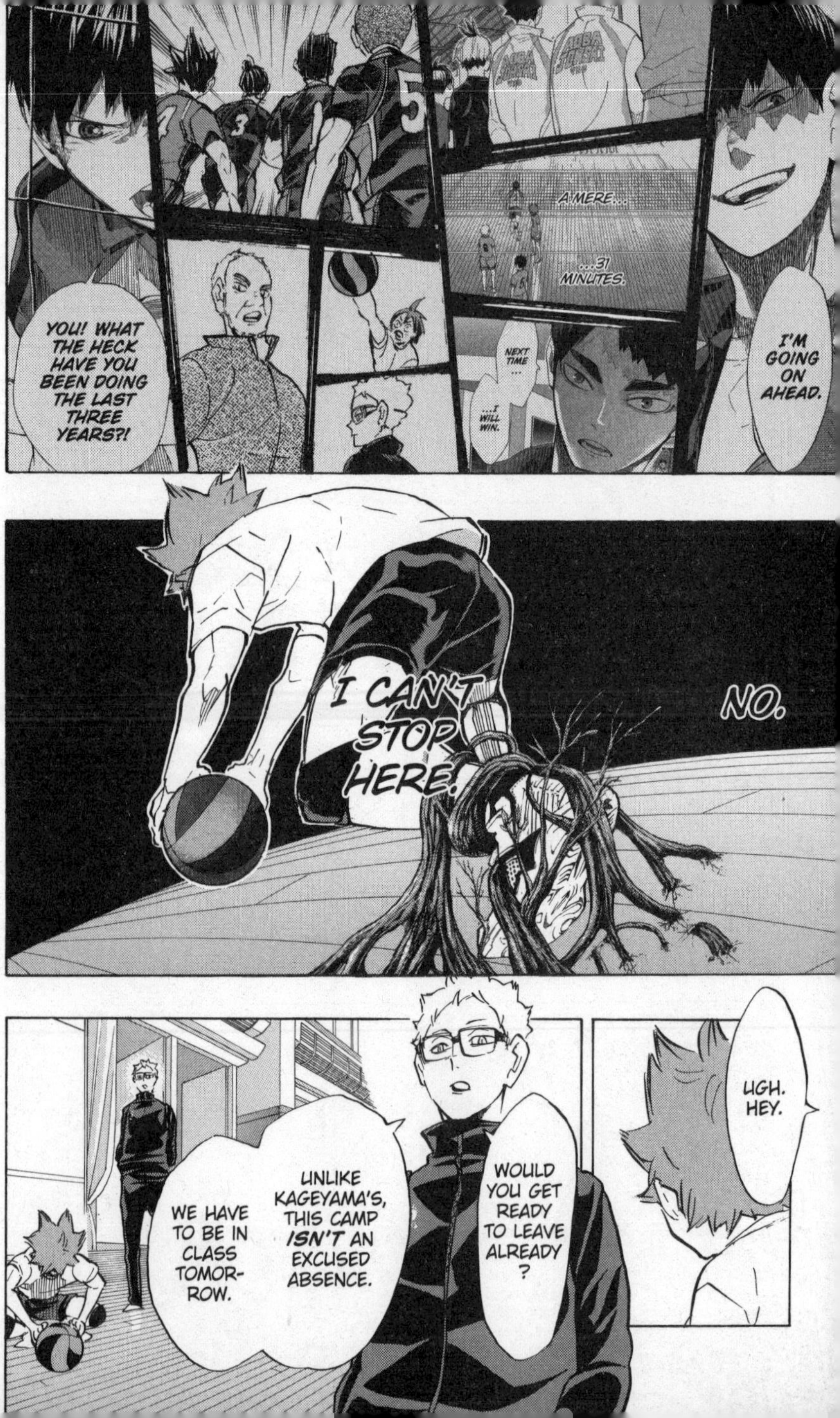
I'M GOING ON AHEAD.
A MERE...
...31 MINUTES.
NEXT TIME...
...I WILL WIN.
YOU! WHAT THE HECK HAVE YOU BEEN DOING THE LAST THREE YEARS?!
NO.
I CAN'T STOP HERE.
UGH. HEY.
WOULD YOU GET READY TO LEAVE ALREADY?
UNLIKE KAGEYAMA'S, THIS CAMP *ISN'T* AN EXCUSED ABSENCE.
WE HAVE TO BE IN CLASS TOMORROW.

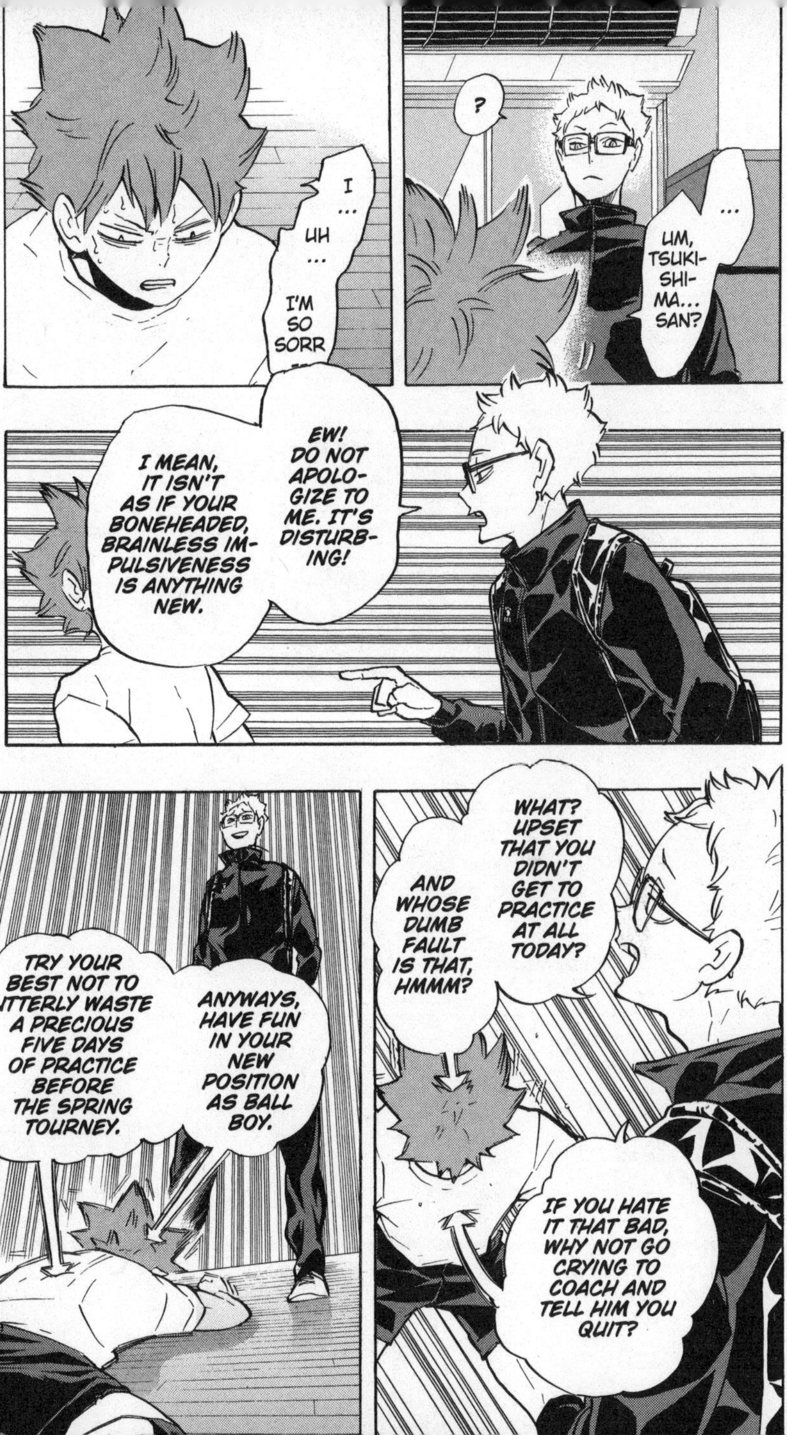
?
... UM, TSUKISHIMA... SAN?
I ... UH ... I'M SO SORR
EW! DO NOT APOLOGIZE TO ME. IT'S DISTURBING!
I MEAN, IT ISN'T AS IF YOUR BONEHEADED, BRAINLESS IMPULSIVENESS IS ANYTHING NEW.
WHAT? UPSET THAT YOU DIDN'T GET TO PRACTICE AT ALL TODAY?
AND WHOSE DUMB FAULT IS THAT, HMMM?
IF YOU HATE IT THAT BAD, WHY NOT GO CRYING TO COACH AND TELL HIM YOU QUIT?
ANYWAYS, HAVE FUN IN YOUR NEW POSITION AS BALL BOY.
TRY YOUR BEST NOT TO UTTERLY WASTE A PRECIOUS FIVE DAYS OF PRACTICE BEFORE THE SPRING TOURNEY.

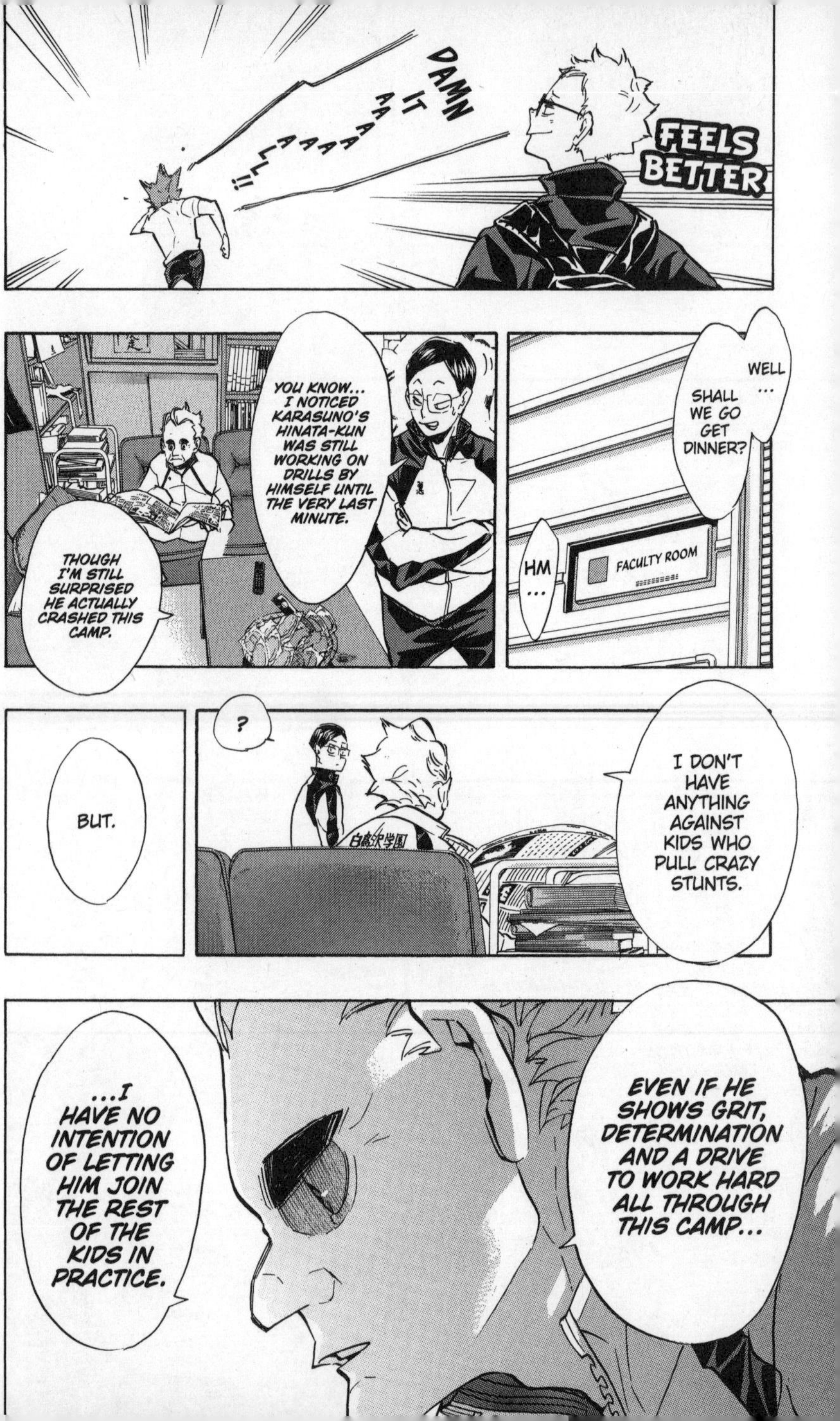
DAMN IT AAAAAALL!!
FEELS BETTER
WELL... SHALL WE GO GET DINNER?
FACULTY ROOM
HM...
YOU KNOW... I NOTICED KARASUNO'S HINATA-KUN WAS STILL WORKING ON DRILLS BY HIMSELF UNTIL THE VERY LAST MINUTE.
THOUGH I'M STILL SURPRISED HE ACTUALLY CRASHED THIS CAMP.
I DON'T HAVE ANYTHING AGAINST KIDS WHO PULL CRAZY STUNTS.
?
白鳥沢学園
BUT.
EVEN IF HE SHOWS GRIT, DETERMINATION AND A DRIVE TO WORK HARD ALL THROUGH THIS CAMP...
...I HAVE NO INTENTION OF LETTING HIM JOIN THE REST OF THE KIDS IN PRACTICE.

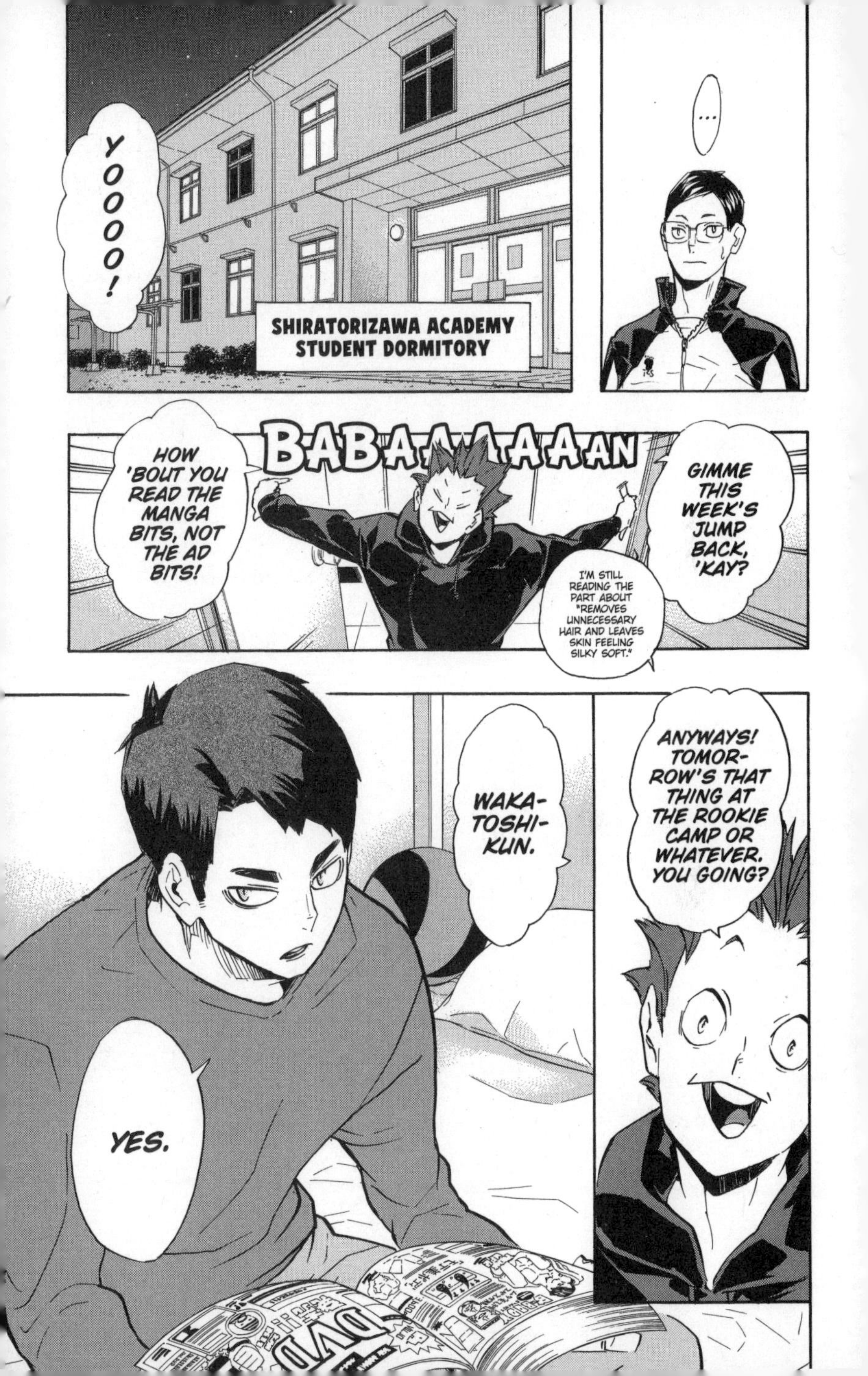
...
YOOOOO!
SHIRATORIZAWA ACADEMY STUDENT DORMITORY
BABAAAAAAAN
GIMME THIS WEEK'S JUMP BACK, 'KAY?
I'M STILL READING THE PART ABOUT "REMOVES UNNECESSARY HAIR AND LEAVES SKIN FEELING SILKY SOFT."
HOW 'BOUT YOU READ THE MANGA BITS, NOT THE AD BITS!
ANYWAYS! TOMOR-ROW'S THAT THING AT THE ROOKIE CAMP OR WHATEVER. YOU GOING?
WAKA-TOSHI-KUN.
YES.
DVD

Odd Man Out!

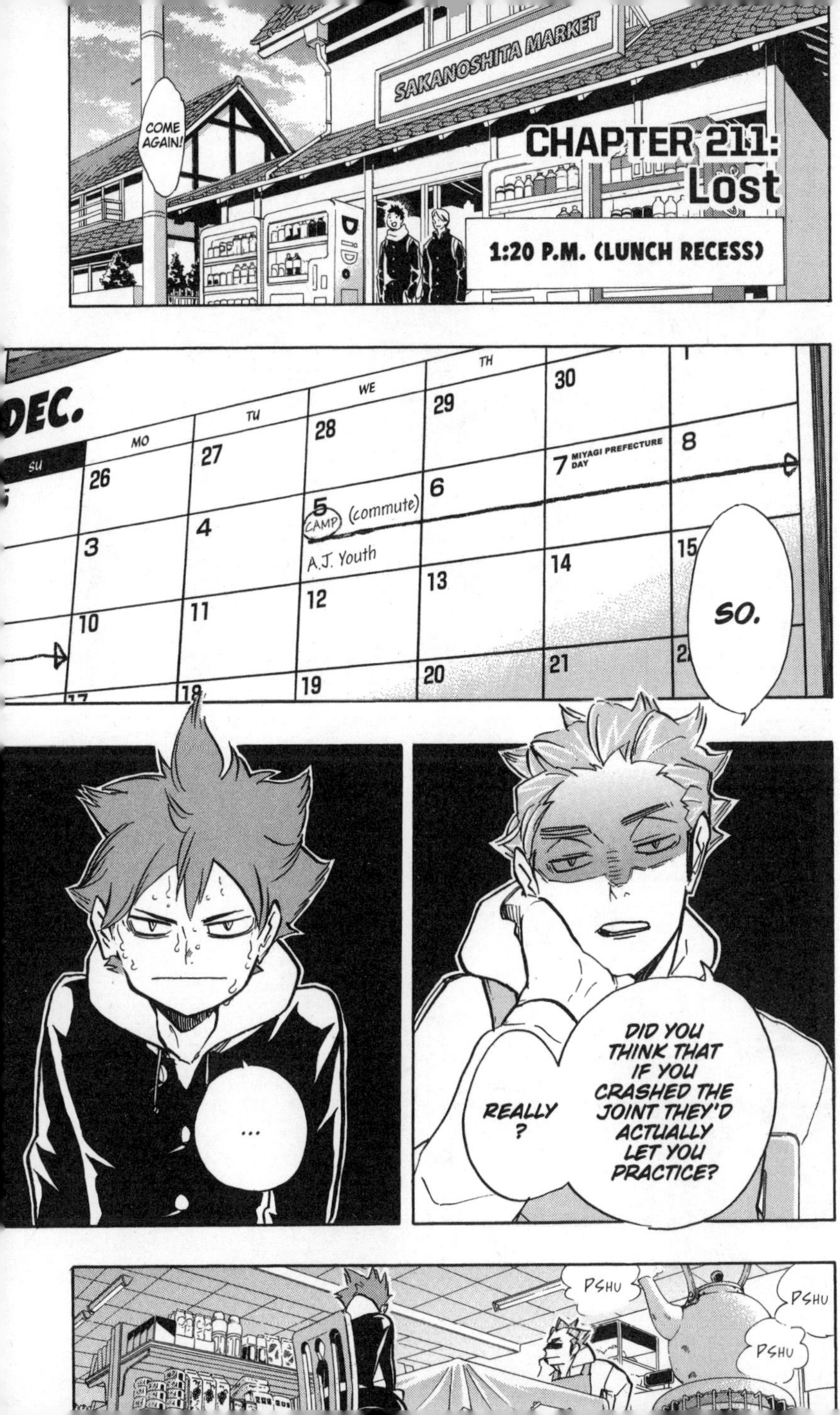
SAKANOSHITA MARKET
CHAPTER 211: Lost
1:20 P.M. (LUNCH RECESS)
COME AGAIN!
DEC.
SU
MO
TU
WE
TH
26
27
28
29
30
1
3
4
5
6
7 MIYAGI PREFECTURE DAY
8
CAMP (commute)
A.J. Youth
10
11
12
13
14
15
19
20
21
SO.
REALLY?
DID YOU THINK THAT IF YOU CRASHED THE JOINT THEY'D ACTUALLY LET YOU PRACTICE?
...
PSHU
PSHU
PSHU

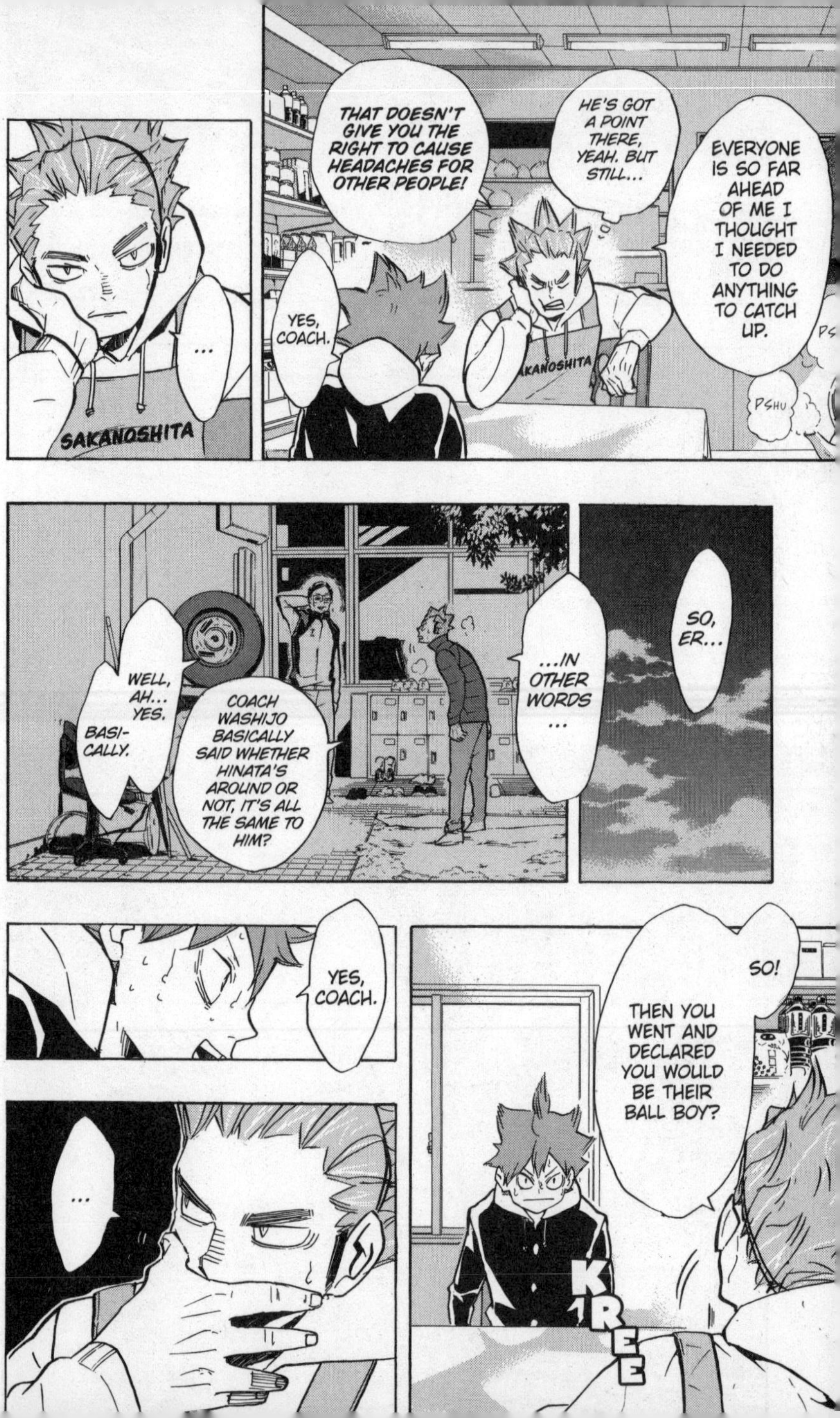
EVERYONE IS SO FAR AHEAD OF ME I THOUGHT I NEEDED TO DO ANYTHING TO CATCH UP.
PSHU
HE'S GOT A POINT THERE, YEAH. BUT STILL...
THAT DOESN'T GIVE YOU THE RIGHT TO CAUSE HEADACHES FOR OTHER PEOPLE!
YES, COACH.
SAKANOSHITA
...
SAKANOSHITA
SO, ER...
...IN OTHER WORDS...
COACH WASHIJO BASICALLY SAID WHETHER HINATA'S AROUND OR NOT, IT'S ALL THE SAME TO HIM?
WELL, AH... YES. BASI-CALLY.
SO!
THEN YOU WENT AND DECLARED YOU WOULD BE THEIR BALL BOY?
KREE
YES, COACH.
...

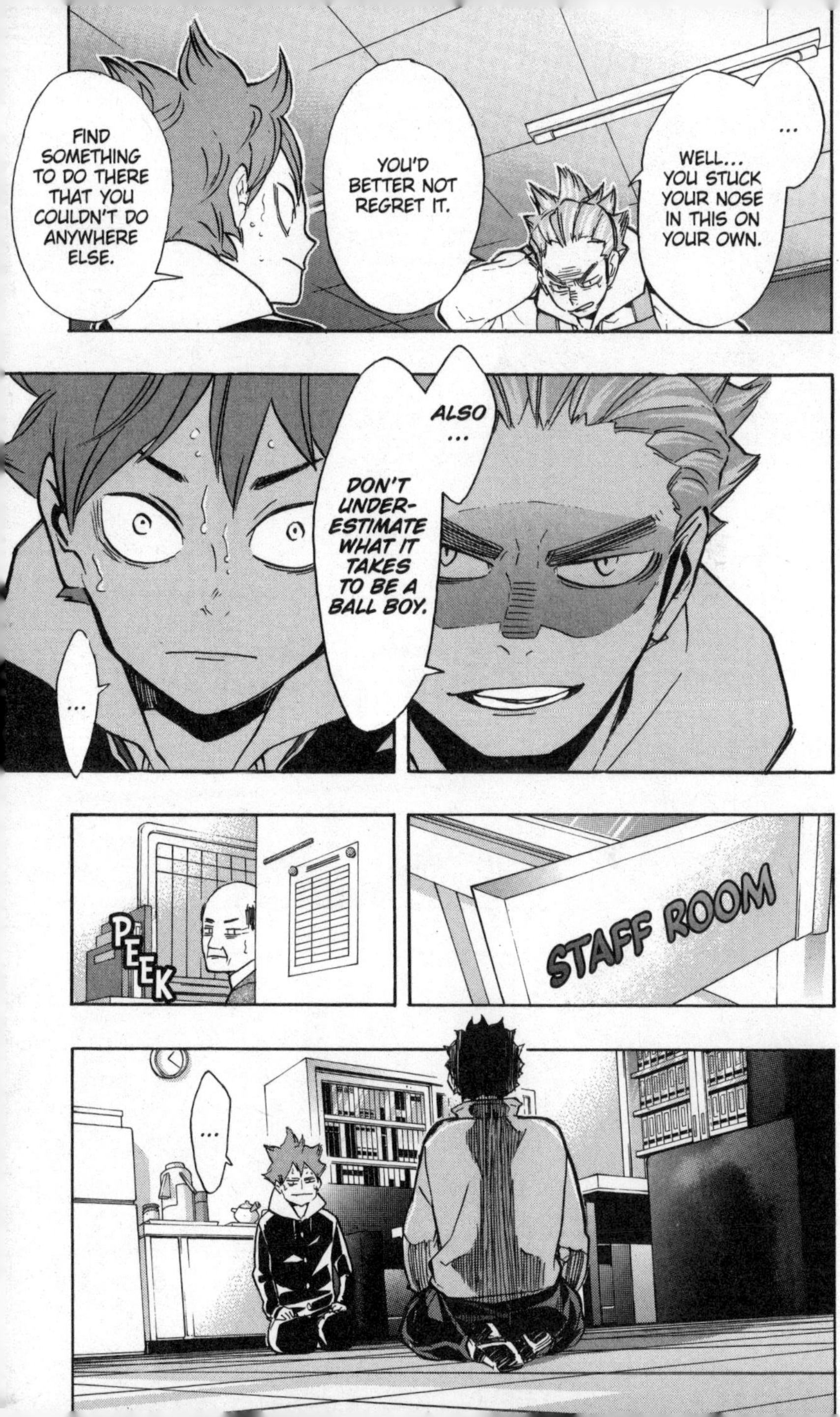
...
WELL... YOU STUCK YOUR NOSE IN THIS ON YOUR OWN.
YOU'D BETTER NOT REGRET IT.
FIND SOMETHING TO DO THERE THAT YOU COULDN'T DO ANYWHERE ELSE.
ALSO...
DON'T UNDER-ESTIMATE WHAT IT TAKES TO BE A BALL BOY.
...
STAFF ROOM
PEEK
...

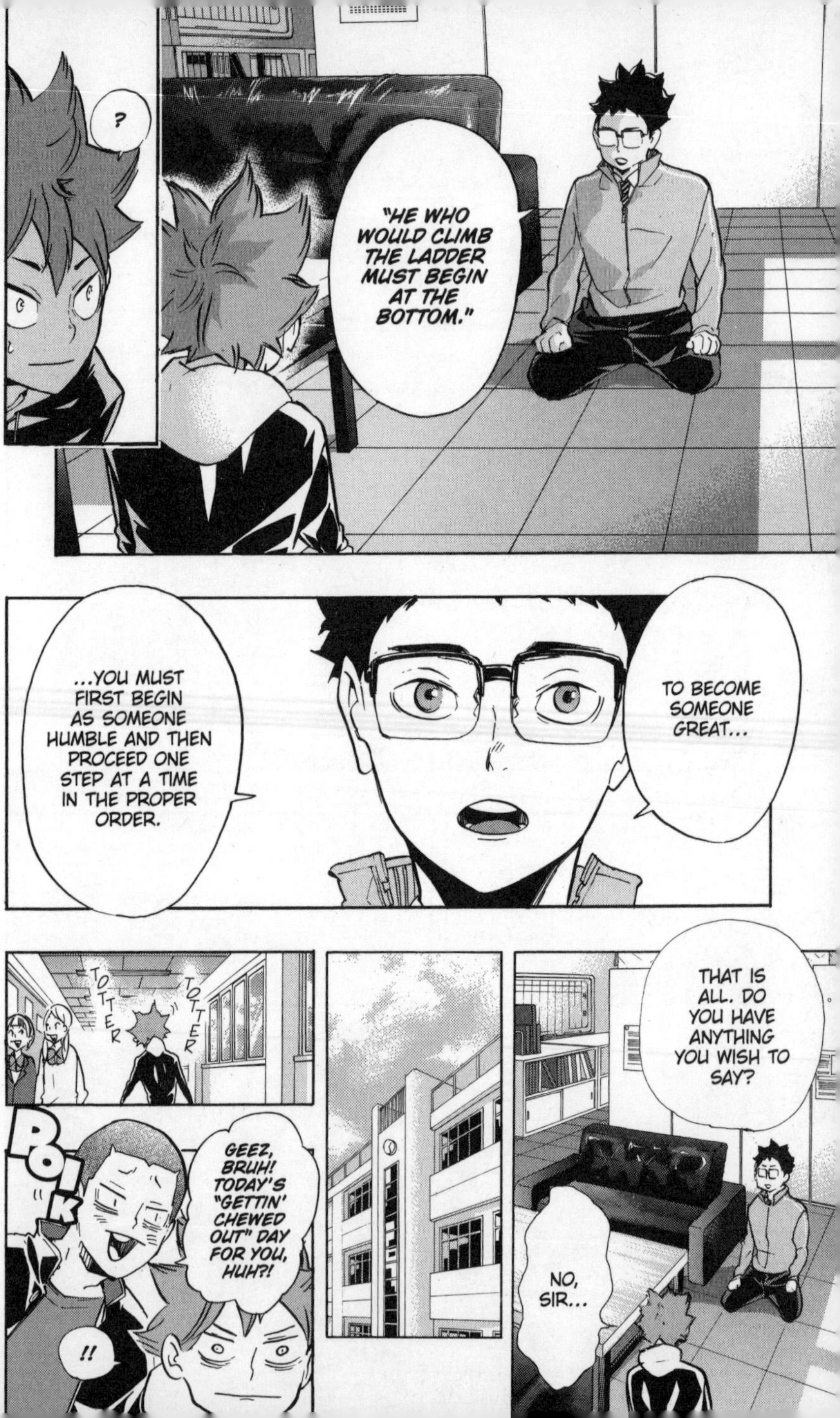
"HE WHO WOULD CLIMB THE LADDER MUST BEGIN AT THE BOTTOM."
?
TO BECOME SOMEONE GREAT...
...YOU MUST FIRST BEGIN AS SOMEONE HUMBLE AND THEN PROCEED ONE STEP AT A TIME IN THE PROPER ORDER.
THAT IS ALL. DO YOU HAVE ANYTHING YOU WISH TO SAY?
NO, SIR...
TOTTER
TOTTER
POIK
GEEZ, BRUH! TODAY'S "GETTIN' CHEWED OUT" DAY FOR YOU, HUH?!
!!

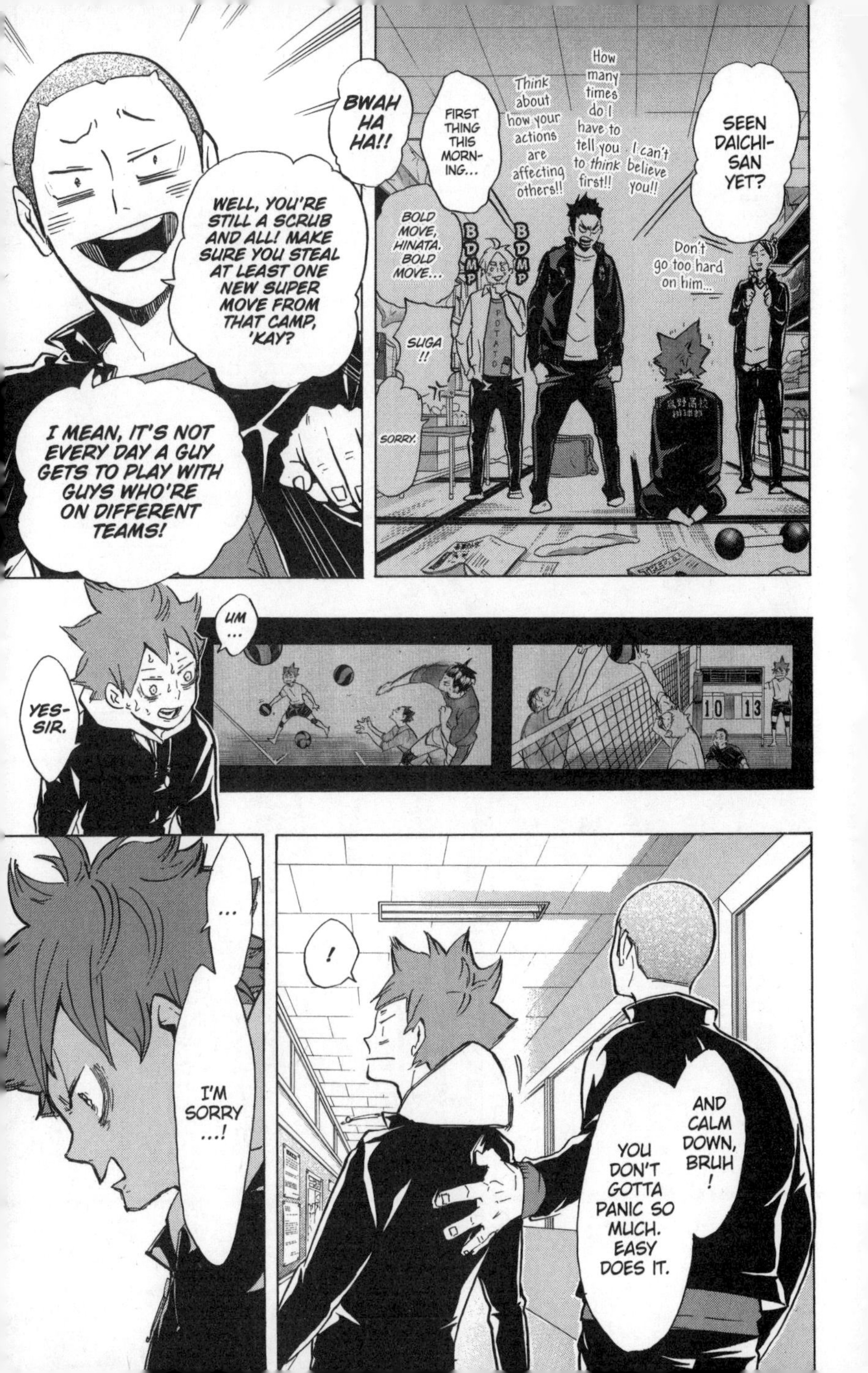
SEEN DAICHI-SAN YET?
Don't go too hard on him...
I can't believe you!!
How many times do I have to tell you to think first!!
Think about how your actions are affecting others!!
FIRST THING THIS MORNING...
BDMP
BDMP
BOLD MOVE, HINATA. BOLD MOVE...
SUGA!!
SORRY.
BWAH HA HA!!
WELL, YOU'RE STILL A SCRUB AND ALL! MAKE SURE YOU STEAL AT LEAST ONE NEW SUPER MOVE FROM THAT CAMP, 'KAY?
I MEAN, IT'S NOT EVERY DAY A GUY GETS TO PLAY WITH GUYS WHO'RE ON DIFFERENT TEAMS!
10 13
UM ...
YES-SIR.
AND CALM DOWN, BRUH!
YOU DON'T GOTTA PANIC SO MUCH. EASY DOES IT.
!
...
I'M SORRY ...!

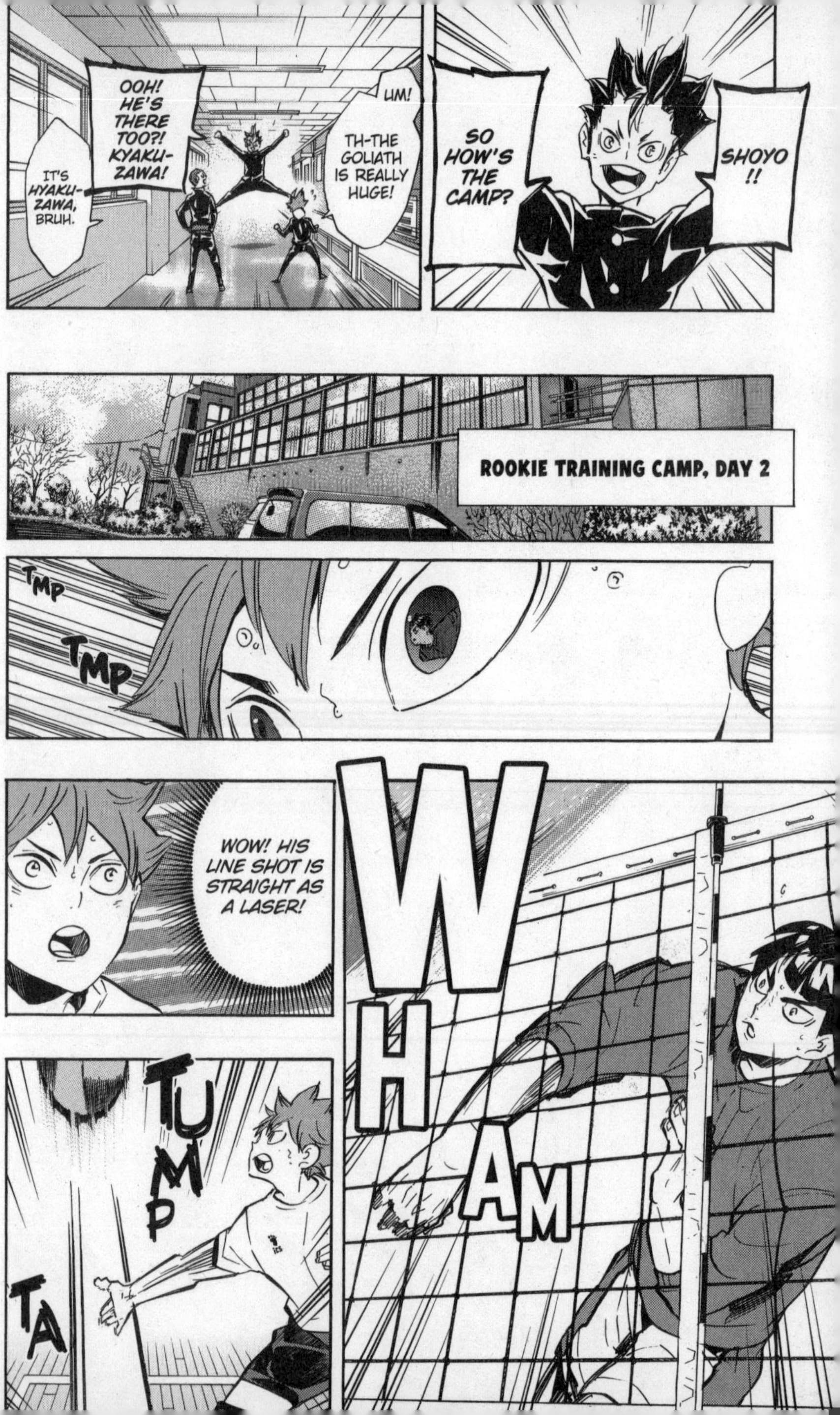
SHOYO !!
SO HOW'S THE CAMP?
UM!
TH-THE GOLIATH IS REALLY HUGE!
OOH! HE'S THERE TOO?! KYAKU-ZAWA!
IT'S HYAKU-ZAWA, BRUH.
ROOKIE TRAINING CAMP, DAY 2
TMP
TMP
WHAM
WOW! HIS LINE SHOT IS STRAIGHT AS A LASER!
TUMP
TA

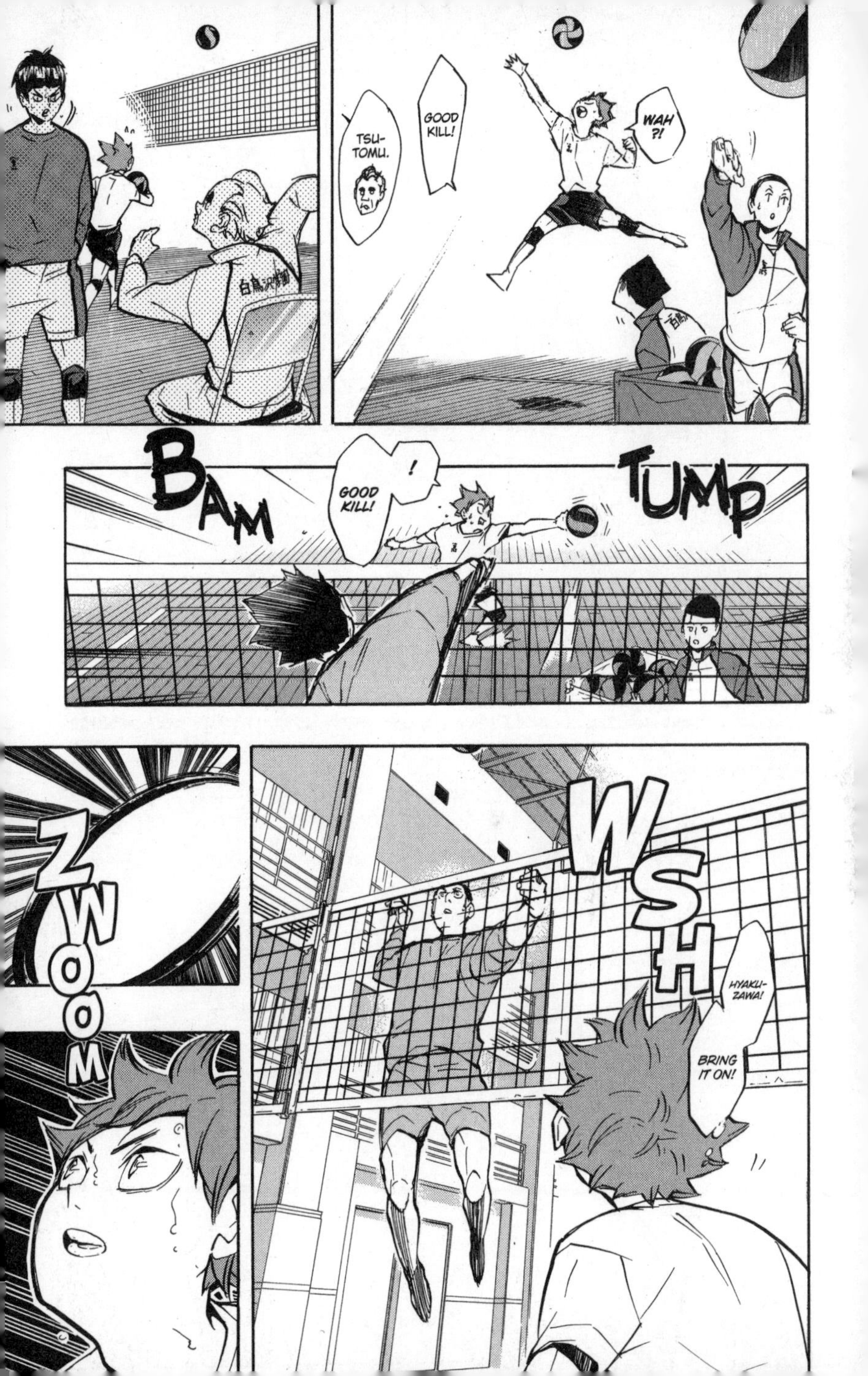
WAH ?!
GOOD KILL!
TSU-TOMU.
TUMP
!
GOOD KILL!
BAM
WSH
HYAKU-ZAWA!
BRING IT ON!
ZWOOOM

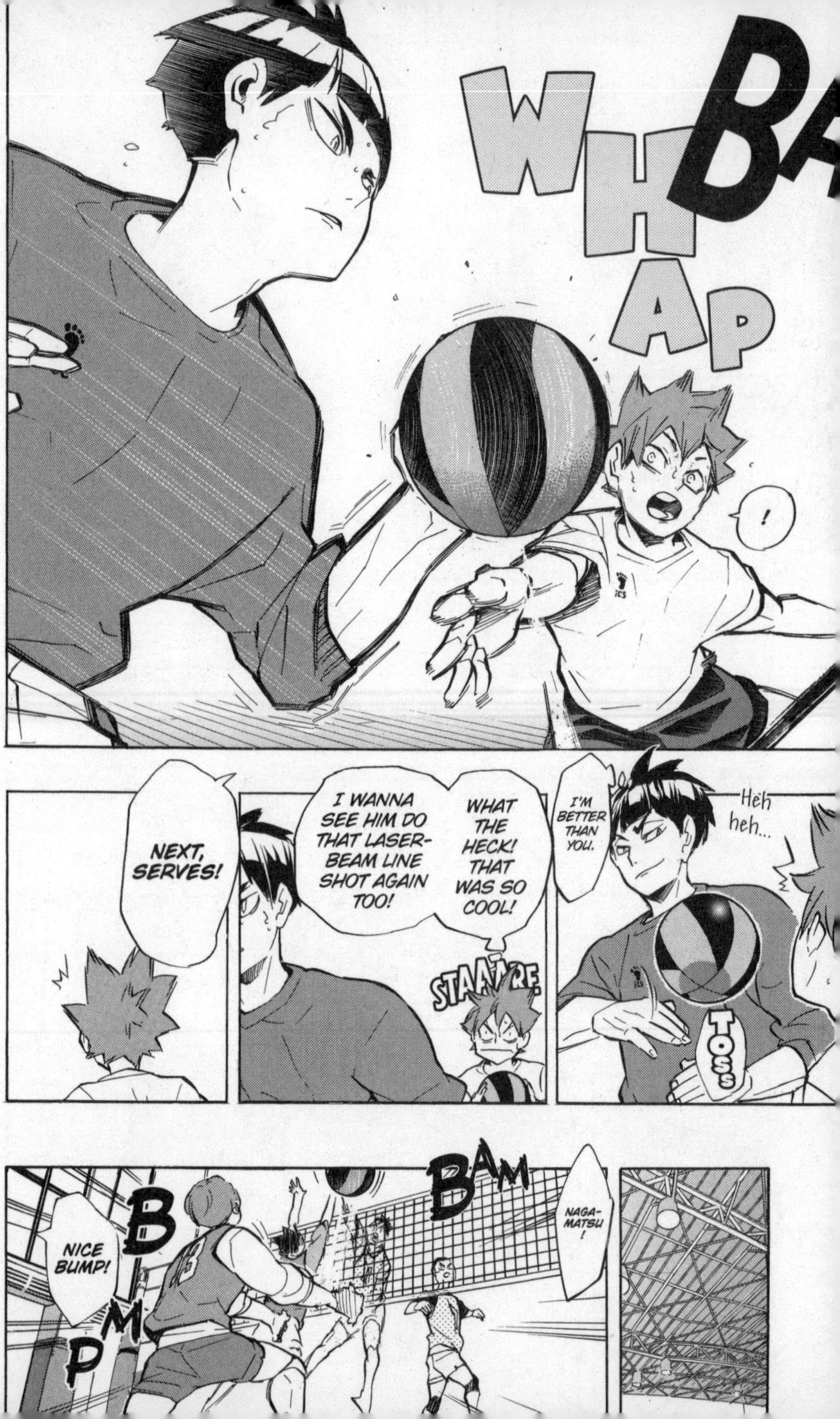

BA
WHAP
!
Heh heh...
I'M BETTER THAN YOU.
TOSS
WHAT THE HECK! THAT WAS SO COOL!
I WANNA SEE HIM DO THAT LASER-BEAM LINE SHOT AGAIN TOO!
STAAARE
NEXT, SERVES!
NAGAMATSU!
BAM
NICE BUMP!
BUMP

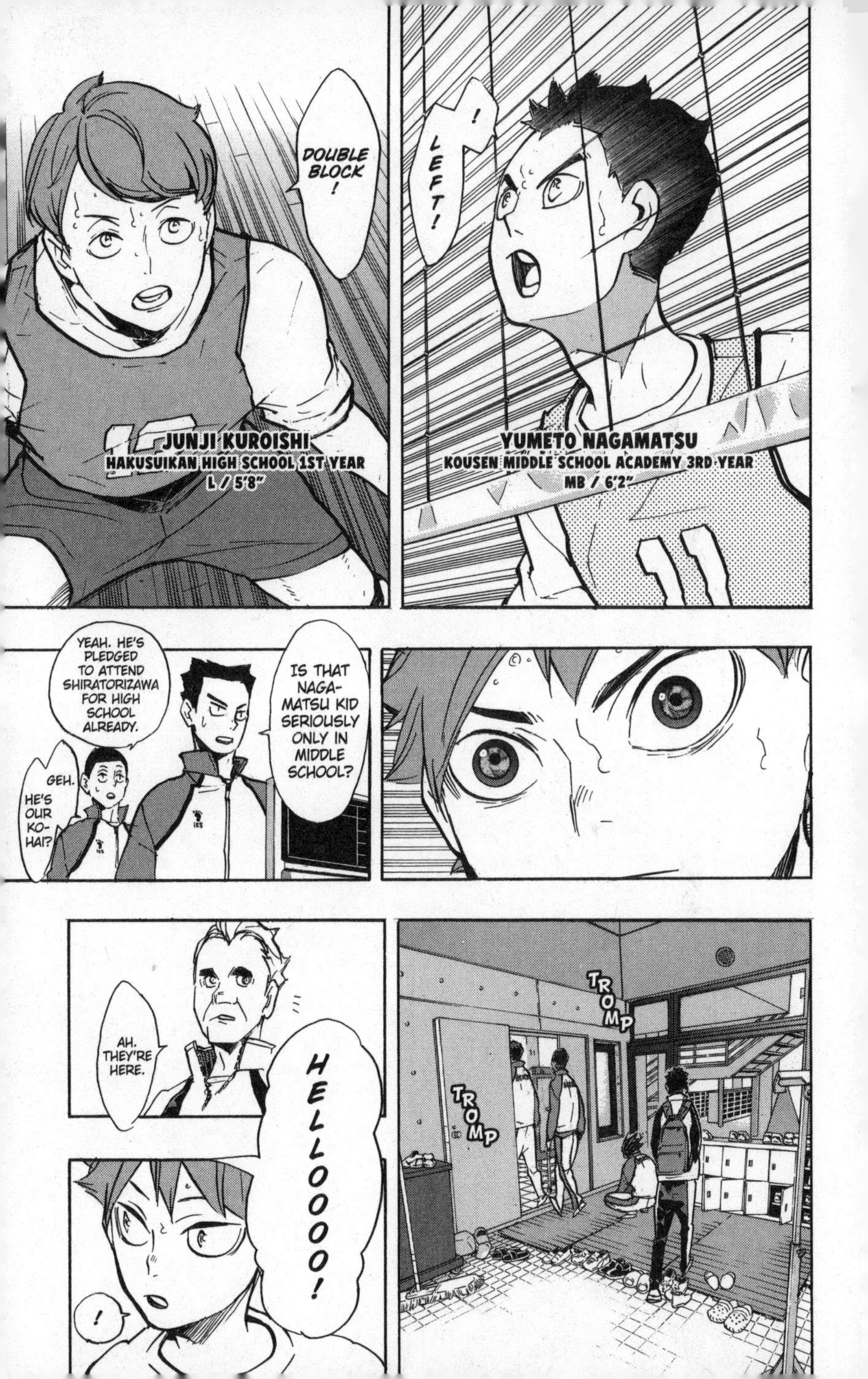
!
LEFT!
YUMETO NAGAMATSU
KOUSEN MIDDLE SCHOOL ACADEMY 3RD YEAR
MB / 6'2"
DOUBLE BLOCK!
JUNJI KUROISHI
HAKUSUIKAN HIGH SCHOOL 1ST YEAR
L / 5'8"
IS THAT NAGA-MATSU KID SERIOUSLY ONLY IN MIDDLE SCHOOL?
YEAH. HE'S PLEDGED TO ATTEND SHIRATORIZAWA FOR HIGH SCHOOL ALREADY.
GEH. HE'S OUR KO-HAI?
TROMP
TROMP
HELLOOOOO!
AH. THEY'RE HERE.
!

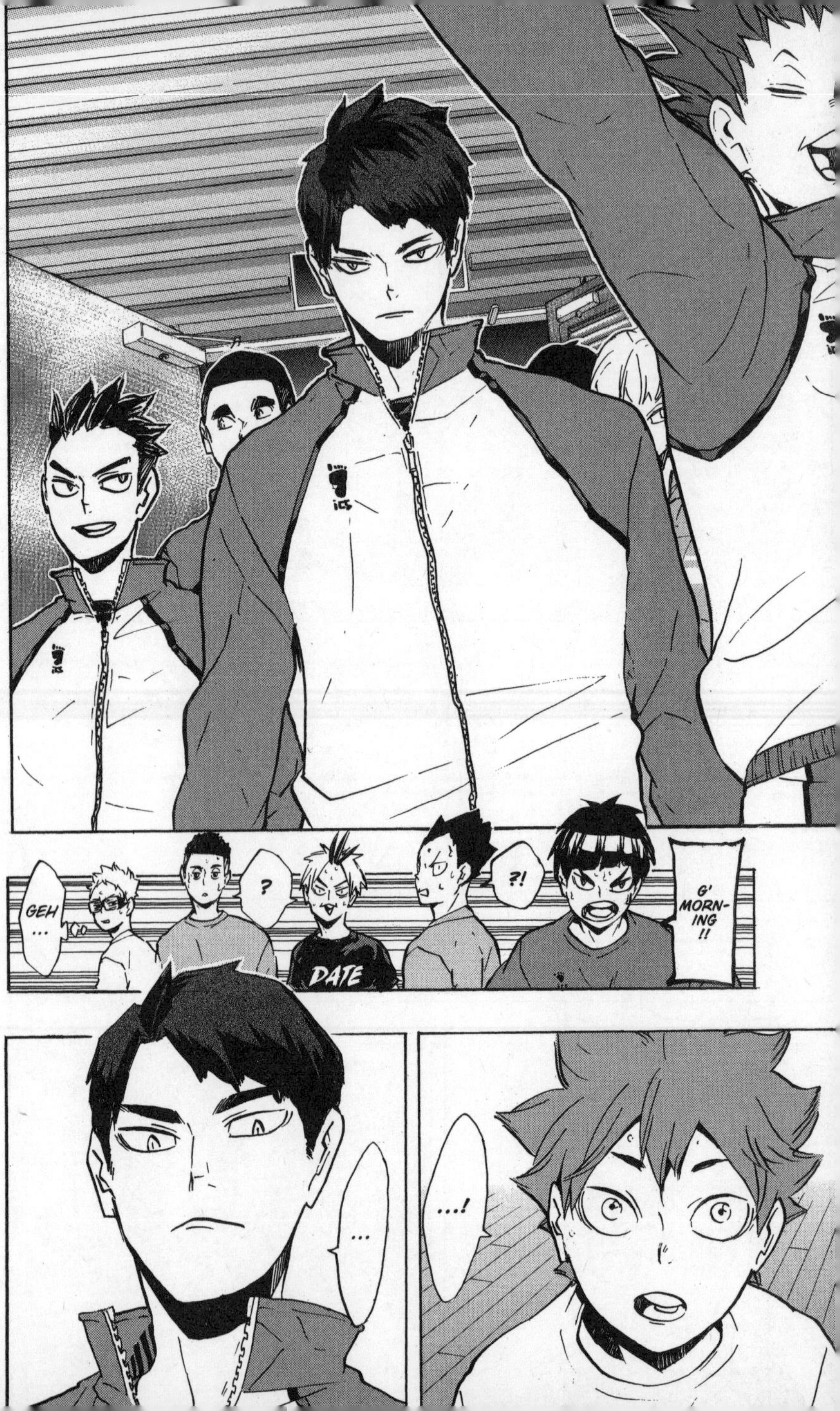
G' MORN-ING!!
?!
?
GEH ...
DATE
...!
...

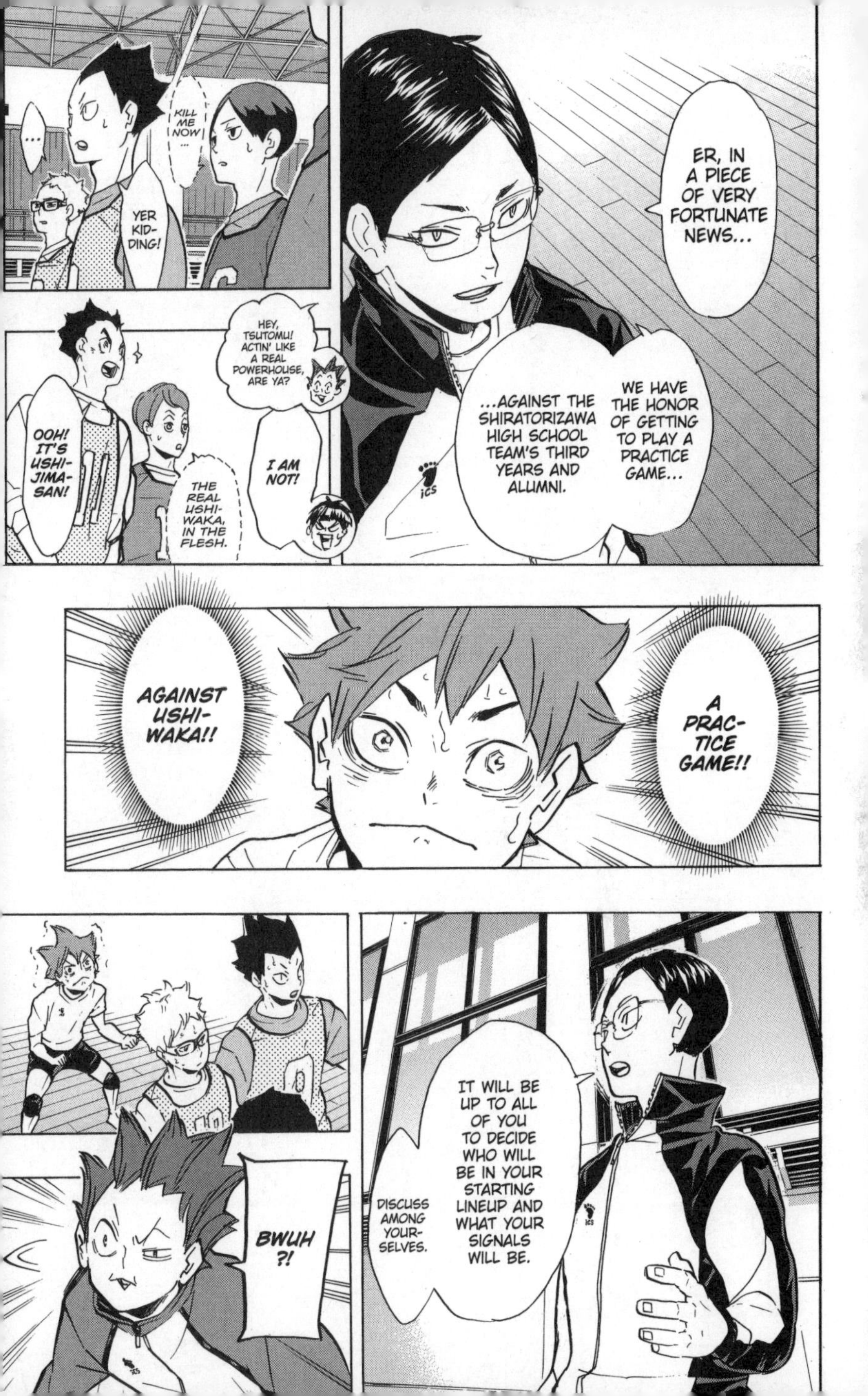
ER, IN A PIECE OF VERY FORTUNATE NEWS...
WE HAVE THE HONOR OF GETTING TO PLAY A PRACTICE GAME...
...AGAINST THE SHIRATORIZAWA HIGH SCHOOL TEAM'S THIRD YEARS AND ALUMNI.
KILL ME NOW...
...
YER KID-DING!
HEY, TSUTOMU! ACTIN' LIKE A REAL POWERHOUSE, ARE YA?
I AM NOT!
THE REAL USHI-WAKA, IN THE FLESH.
OOH! IT'S USHI-JIMA-SAN!
A PRAC-TICE GAME!!
AGAINST USHI-WAKA!!
IT WILL BE UP TO ALL OF YOU TO DECIDE WHO WILL BE IN YOUR STARTING LINEUP AND WHAT YOUR SIGNALS WILL BE.
DISCUSS AMONG YOUR-SELVES.
BWUH ?!

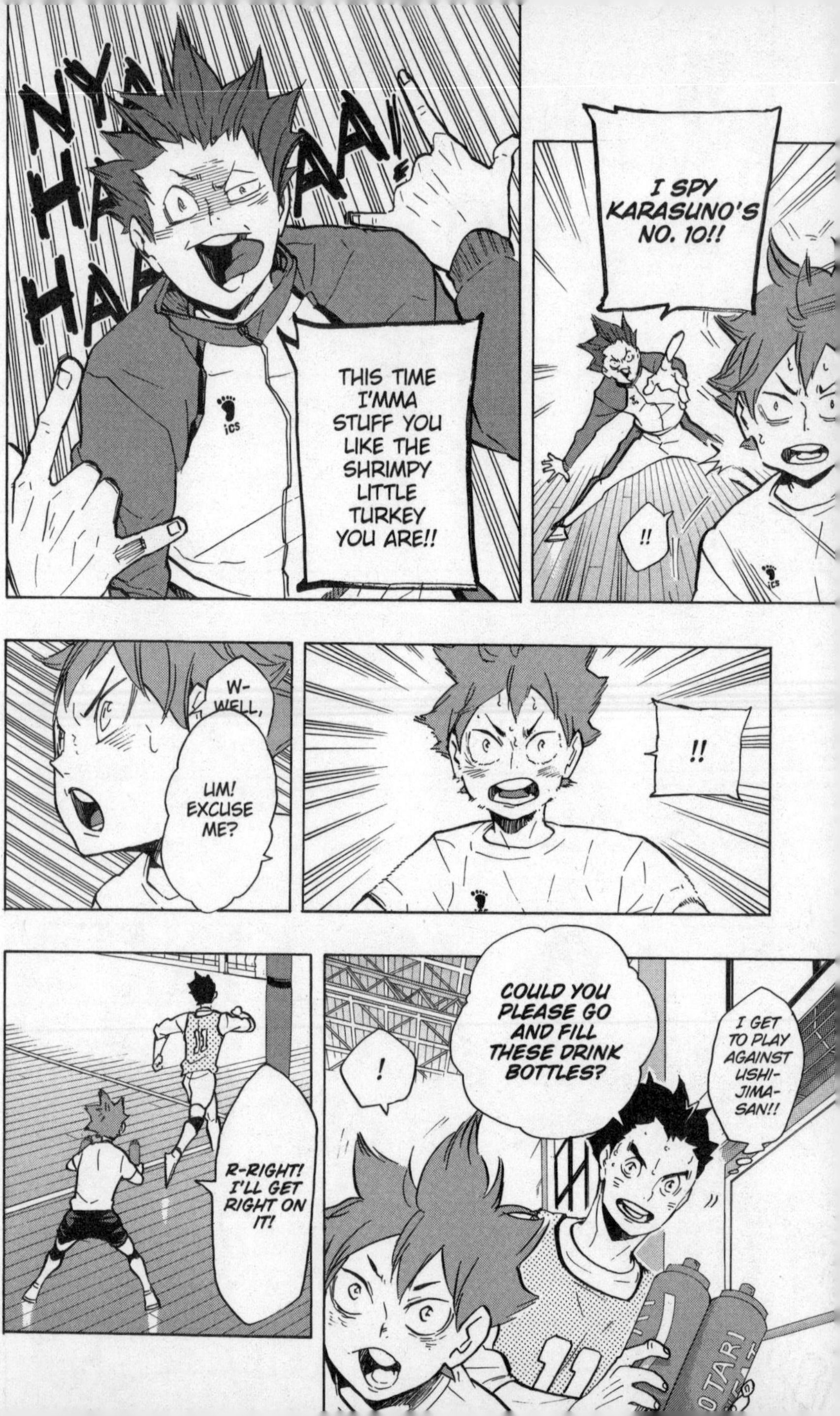
I SPY KARASUNO'S NO. 10!!
!!
NYA HA HAA AA!
THIS TIME I'MMA STUFF YOU LIKE THE SHRIMPY LITTLE TURKEY YOU ARE!!
!!
W-WELL,
UM! EXCUSE ME?
COULD YOU PLEASE GO AND FILL THESE DRINK BOTTLES?
!
I GET TO PLAY AGAINST USHIJIMA-SAN!!
R-RIGHT! I'LL GET RIGHT ON IT!

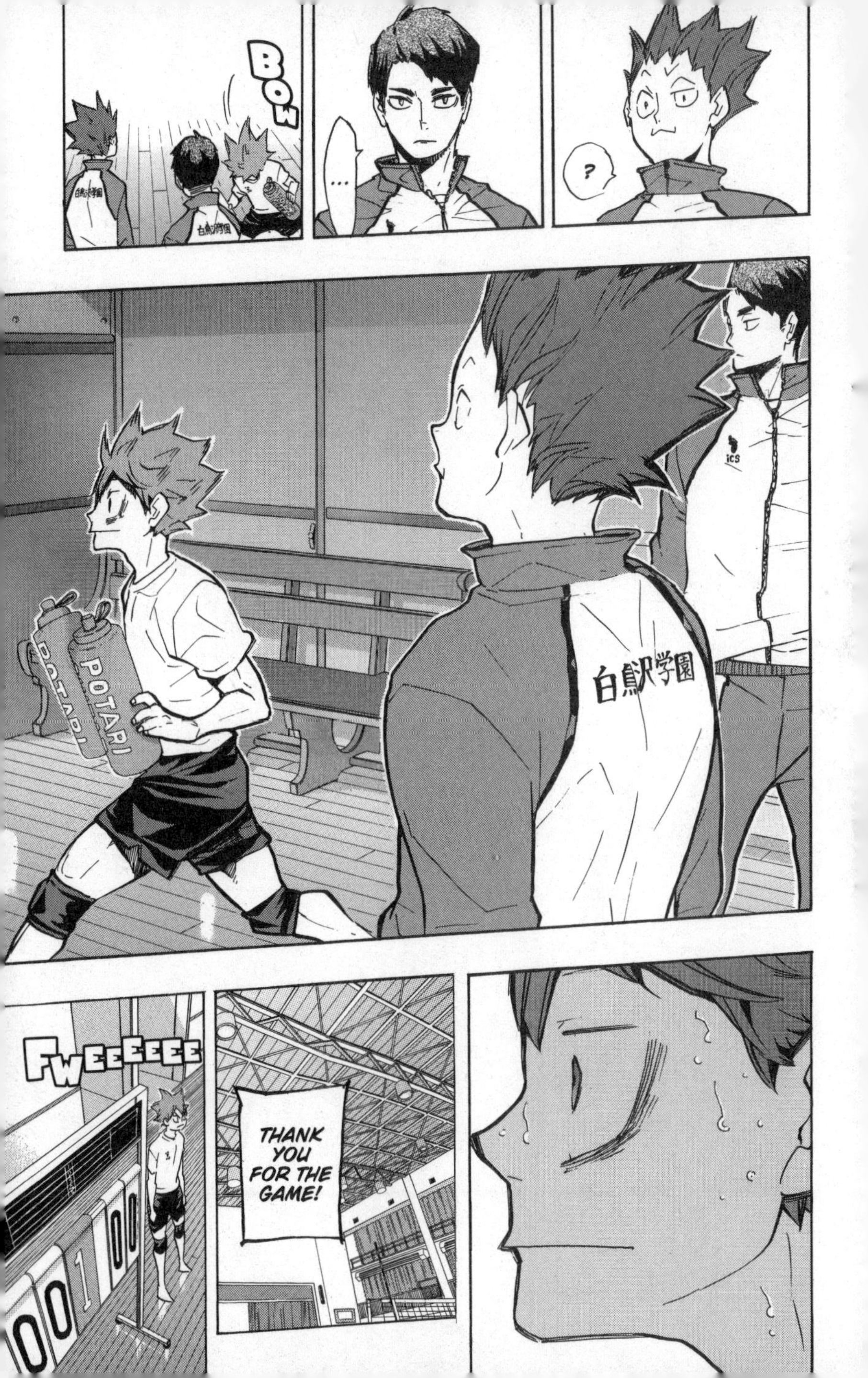
?
...
BOW
白鳥沢学園
白鳥沢学園
POTARI
POTARI
THANK YOU FOR THE GAME!
FWEEEEEE

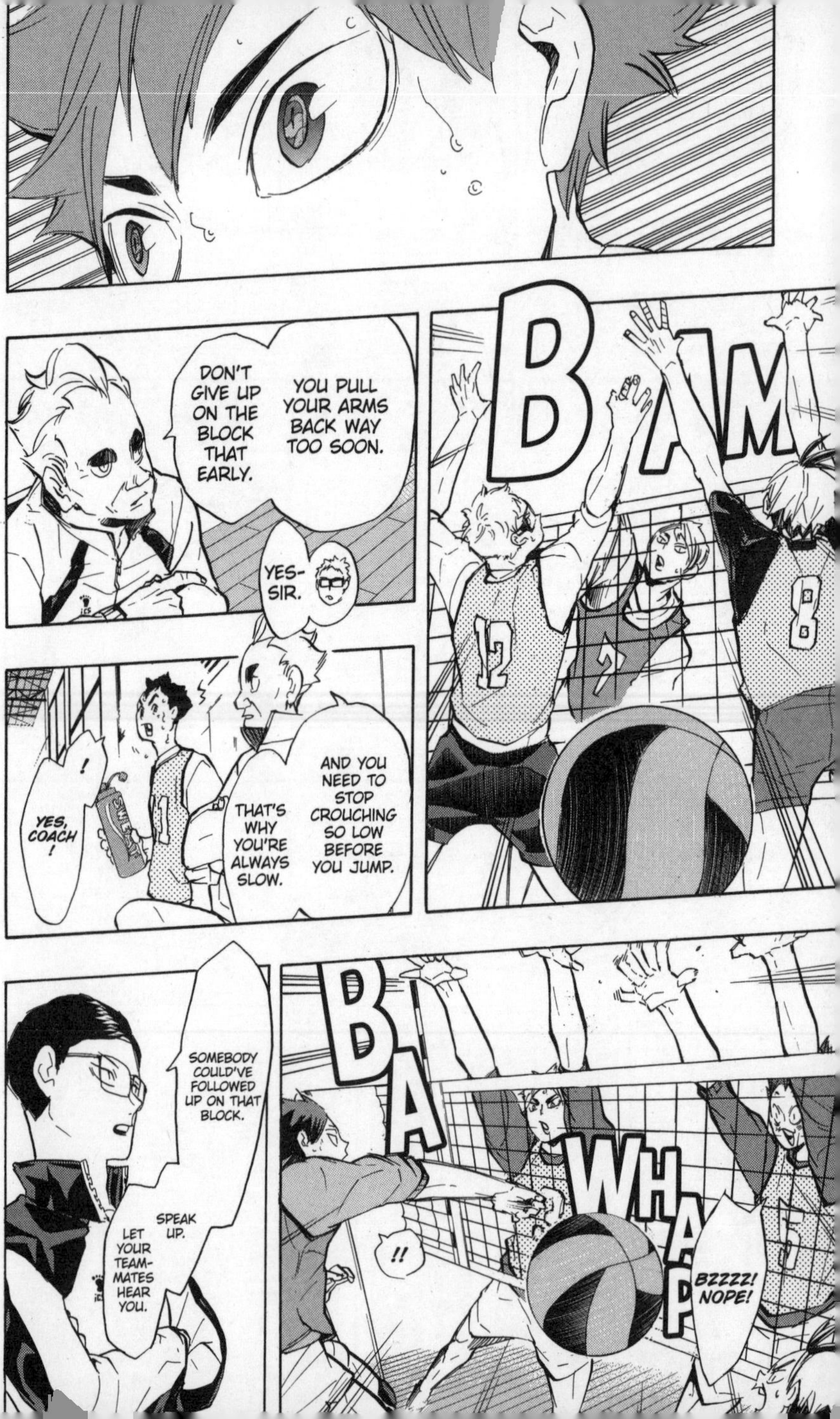
BAM
YOU PULL YOUR ARMS BACK WAY TOO SOON.
DON'T GIVE UP ON THE BLOCK THAT EARLY.
YES-SIR.
AND YOU NEED TO STOP CROUCHING SO LOW BEFORE YOU JUMP.
THAT'S WHY YOU'RE ALWAYS SLOW.
!
YES, COACH!
BA
WHAP
BZZZZ! NOPE!
!!
SOMEBODY COULD'VE FOLLOWED UP ON THAT BLOCK.
SPEAK UP.
LET YOUR TEAMMATES HEAR YOU.

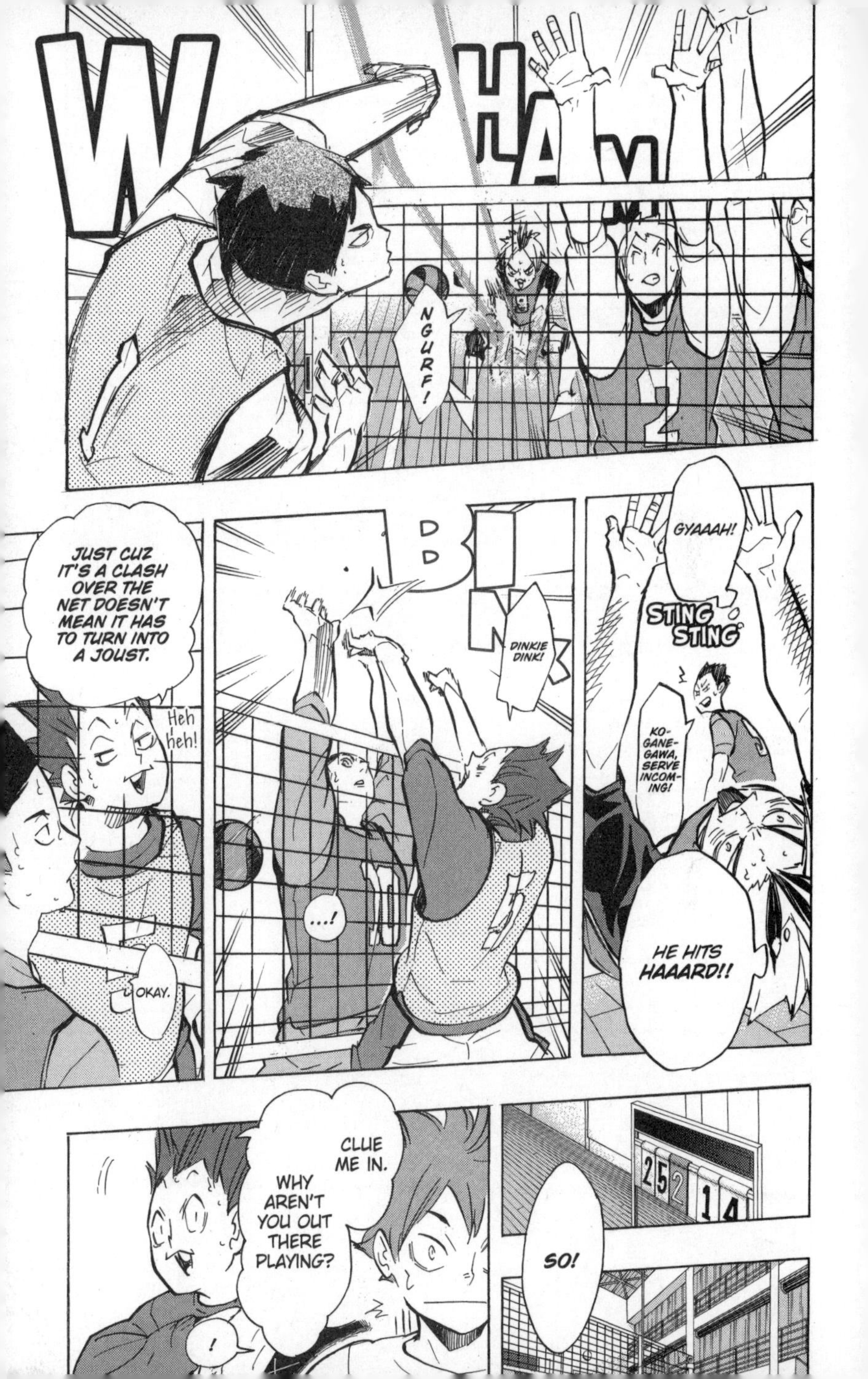
WHAM
NGURF!
GYAAAH!
STING STING
KOGANE-GAWA, SERVE INCOM-ING!
HE HITS HAAARD!!
DINKIE DINK!
...!
JUST CUZ IT'S A CLASH OVER THE NET DOESN'T MEAN IT HAS TO TURN INTO A JOUST.
Heh heh!
OKAY.
25 2 14
SO!
CLUE ME IN.
WHY AREN'T YOU OUT THERE PLAYING?
!

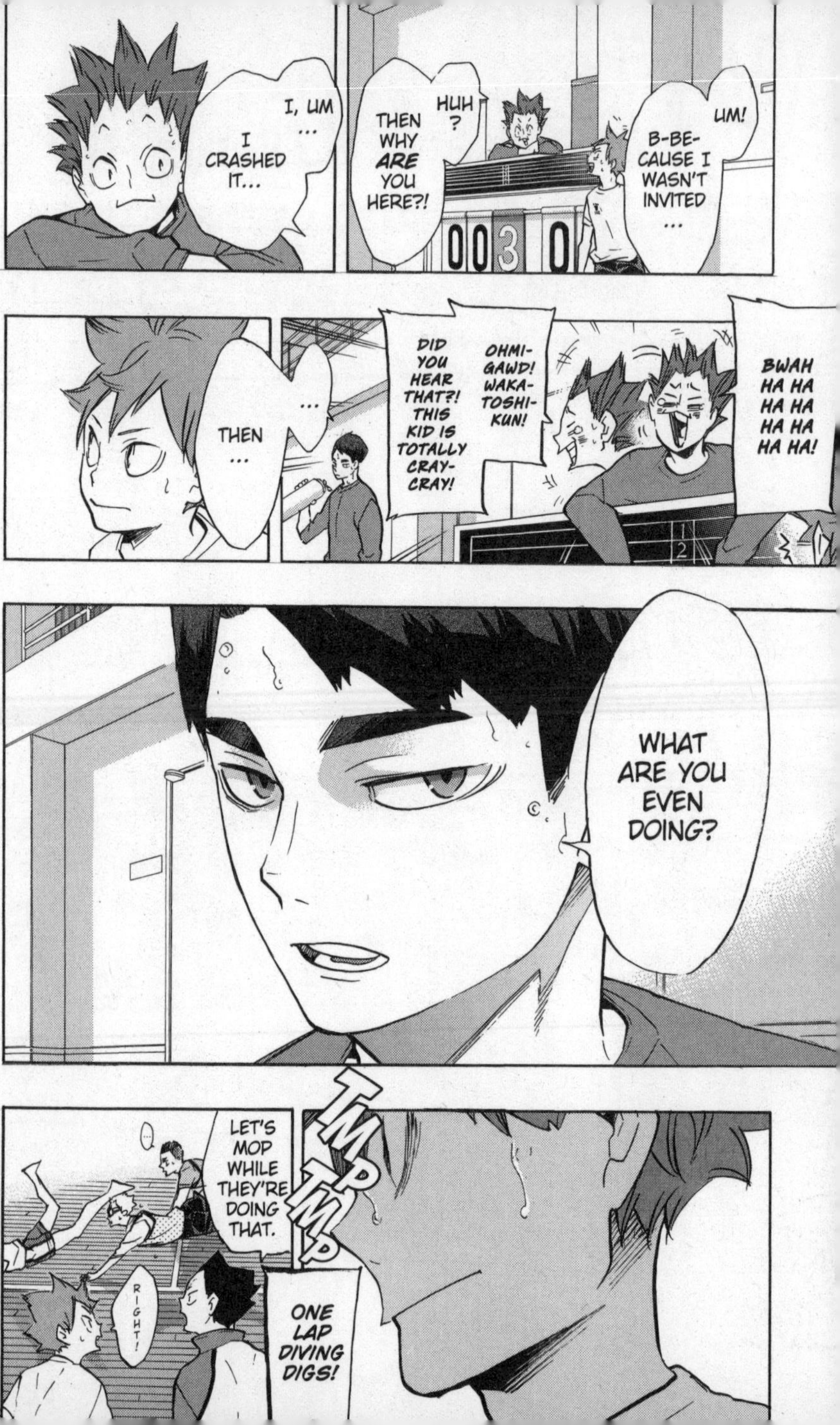
UM! B-BECAUSE I WASN'T INVITED ...
HUH? THEN WHY ARE YOU HERE?!
I, UM ... I CRASHED IT...
BWAH HA HA HA HA HA HA HA HA!
OHMI-GAWD! WAKA-TOSHI-KUN!
DID YOU HEAR THAT?! THIS KID IS TOTALLY CRAY-CRAY!
... THEN ...
WHAT ARE YOU EVEN DOING?
TMP TMP
ONE LAP DIVING DIGS!
...
LET'S MOP WHILE THEY'RE DOING THAT.
RIGHT!

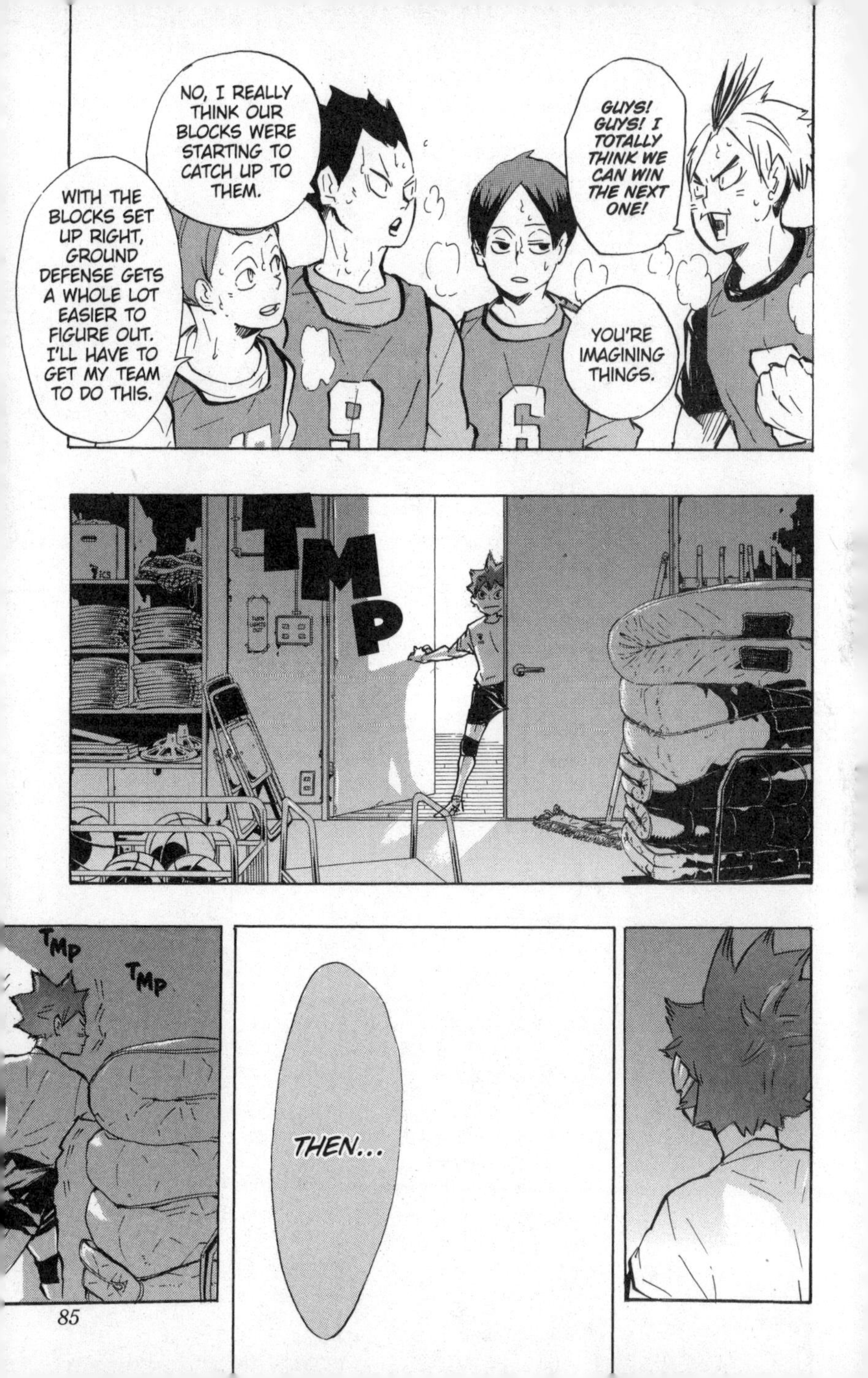
GUYS! GUYS! I TOTALLY THINK WE CAN WIN THE NEXT ONE!
YOU'RE IMAGINING THINGS.
NO, I REALLY THINK OUR BLOCKS WERE STARTING TO CATCH UP TO THEM.
WITH THE BLOCKS SET UP RIGHT, GROUND DEFENSE GETS A WHOLE LOT EASIER TO FIGURE OUT. I'LL HAVE TO GET MY TEAM TO DO THIS.
TMP
THEN...
TMP
TMP

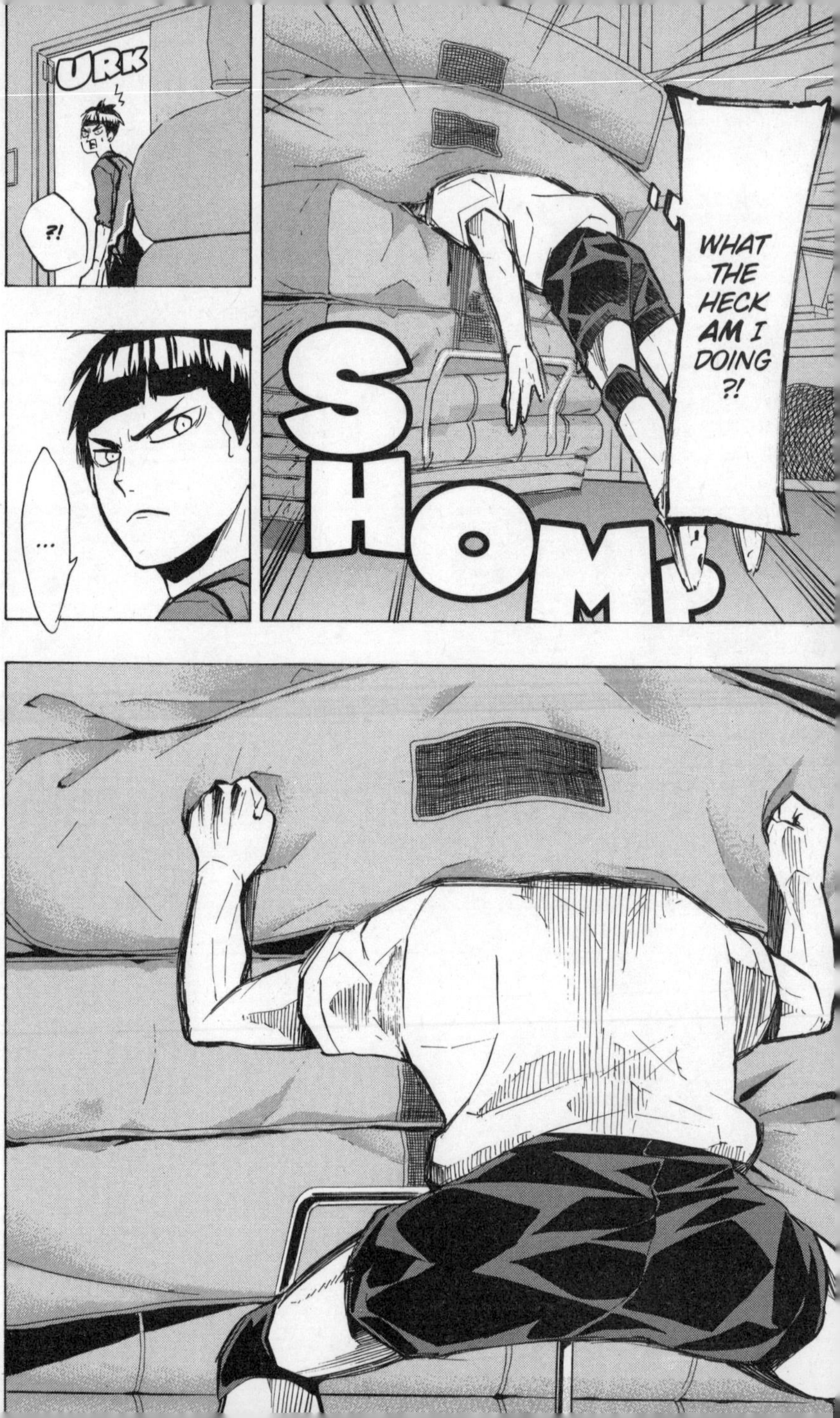
SHOMP
WHAT THE HECK AM I DOING ?!
URK
?!
...

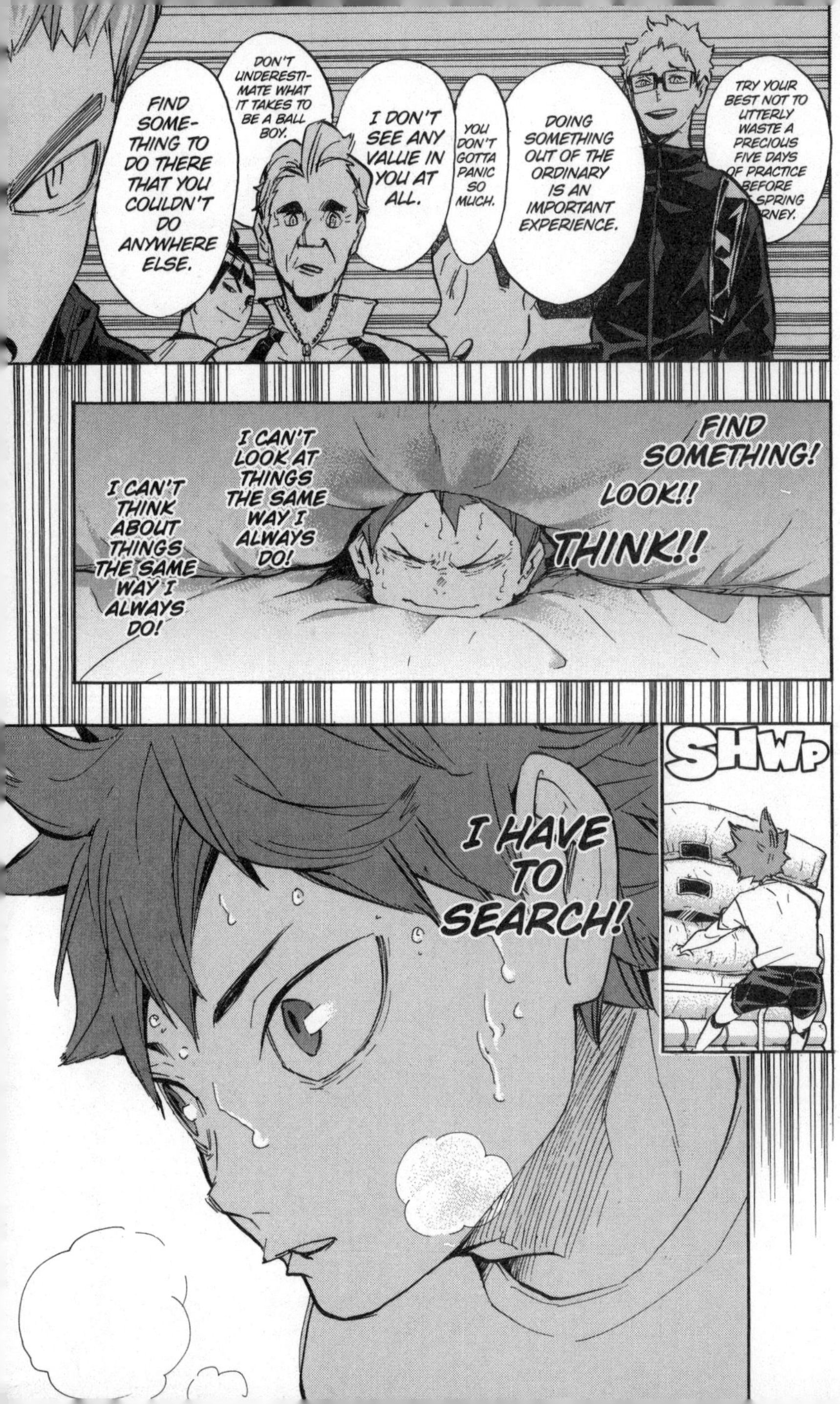
TRY YOUR BEST NOT TO UTTERLY WASTE A PRECIOUS FIVE DAYS OF PRACTICE BEFORE SPRING RNEY.
DOING SOMETHING OUT OF THE ORDINARY IS AN IMPORTANT EXPERIENCE.
YOU DON'T GOTTA PANIC SO MUCH.
I DON'T SEE ANY VALUE IN YOU AT ALL.
DON'T UNDERESTIMATE WHAT IT TAKES TO BE A BALL BOY.
FIND SOMETHING TO DO THERE THAT YOU COULDN'T DO ANYWHERE ELSE.
FIND SOMETHING!
LOOK!!
THINK!!
I CAN'T LOOK AT THINGS THE SAME WAY I ALWAYS DO!
I CAN'T THINK ABOUT THINGS THE SAME WAY I ALWAYS DO!
SHWP
I HAVE TO SEARCH!

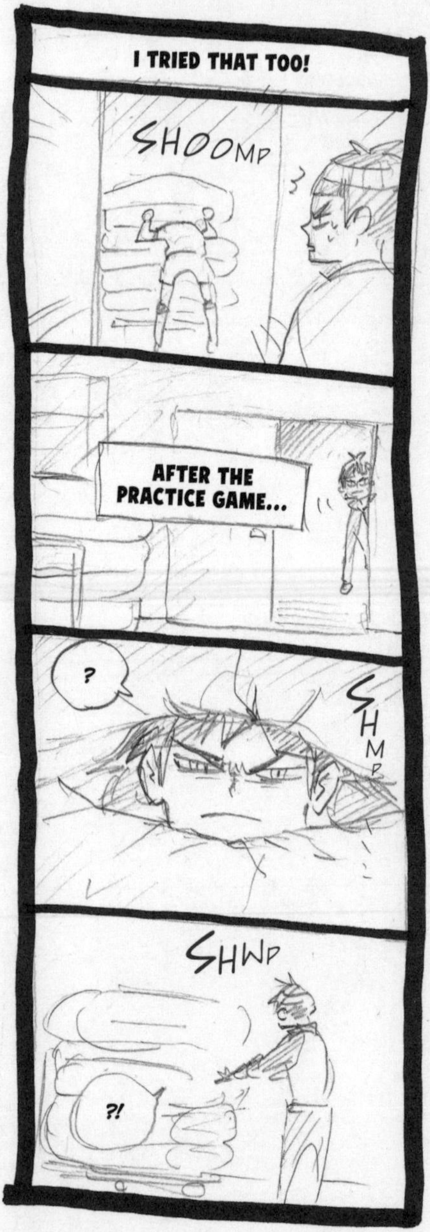
I TRIED THAT TOO!
SHOOMP
AFTER THE PRACTICE GAME...
?
SHMP
SHWP
?!

CHAPTER 212

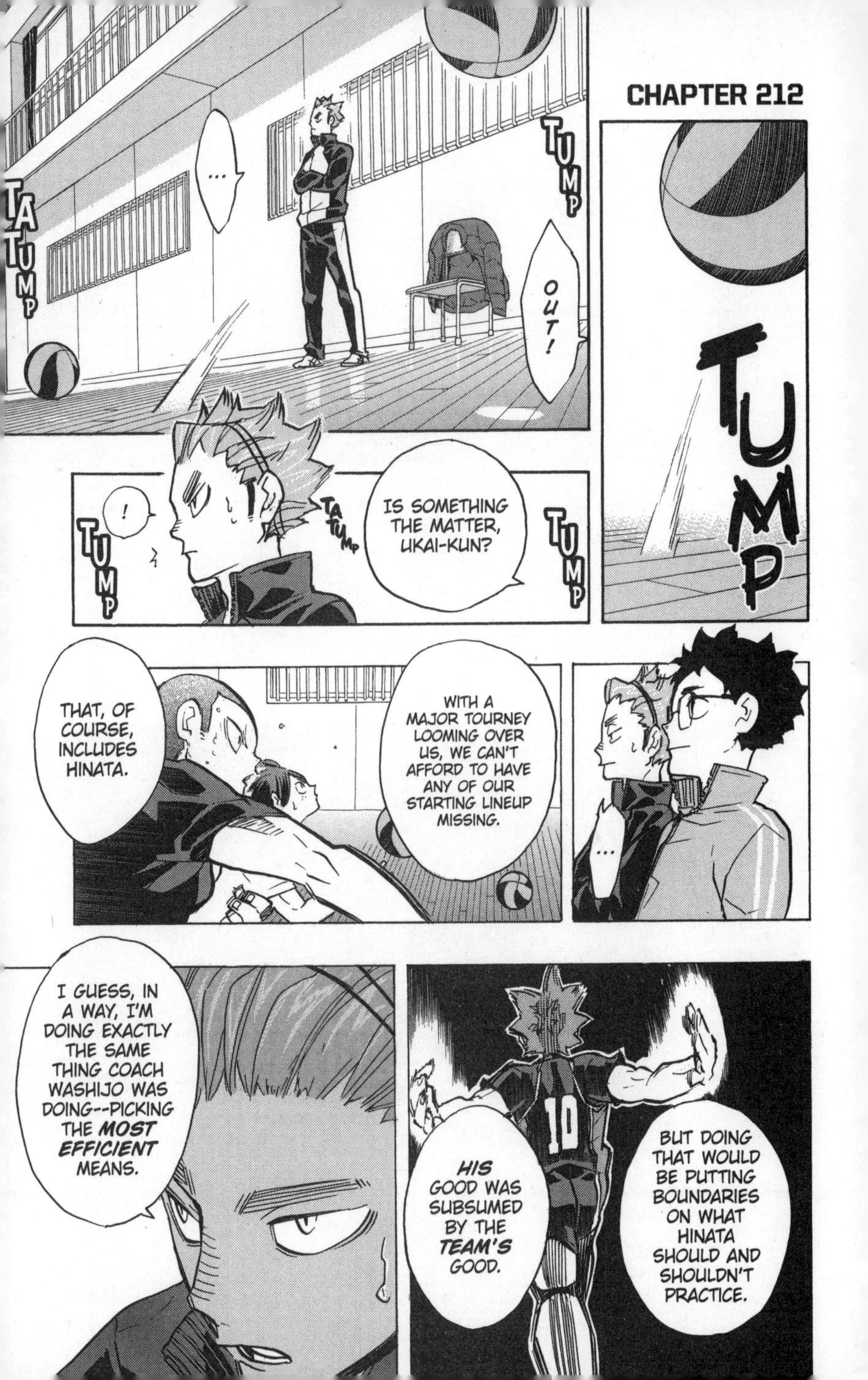
TUMP
...
OUT!
TUMP
TA TUMP
IS SOMETHING THE MATTER, UKAI-KUN?
TA TUMP
!
TUMP
TUMP
...
WITH A MAJOR TOURNEY LOOMING OVER US, WE CAN'T AFFORD TO HAVE ANY OF OUR STARTING LINEUP MISSING.
THAT, OF COURSE, INCLUDES HINATA.
I GUESS, IN A WAY, I'M DOING EXACTLY THE SAME THING COACH WASHIJO WAS DOING--PICKING THE MOST EFFICIENT MEANS.
HIS GOOD WAS SUBSUMED BY THE TEAM'S GOOD.
BUT DOING THAT WOULD BE PUTTING BOUNDARIES ON WHAT HINATA SHOULD AND SHOULDN'T PRACTICE.

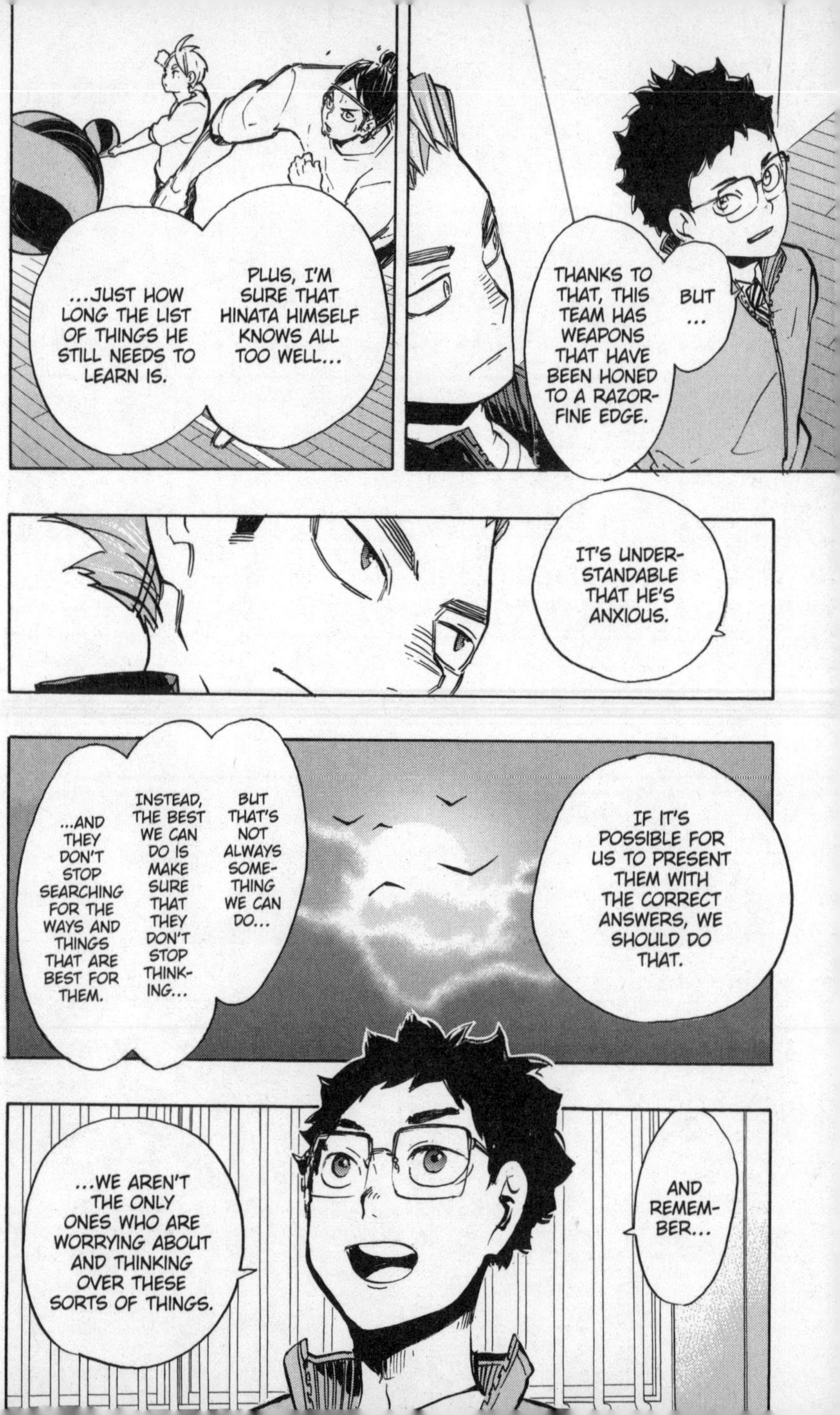
THANKS TO THAT, THIS TEAM HAS WEAPONS THAT HAVE BEEN HONED TO A RAZOR-FINE EDGE.
BUT ...
PLUS, I'M SURE THAT HINATA HIMSELF KNOWS ALL TOO WELL...
...JUST HOW LONG THE LIST OF THINGS HE STILL NEEDS TO LEARN IS.
IT'S UNDER-STANDABLE THAT HE'S ANXIOUS.
IF IT'S POSSIBLE FOR US TO PRESENT THEM WITH THE CORRECT ANSWERS, WE SHOULD DO THAT.
BUT THAT'S NOT ALWAYS SOME-THING WE CAN DO...
INSTEAD, THE BEST WE CAN DO IS MAKE SURE THAT THEY DON'T STOP THINK-ING...
...AND THEY DON'T STOP SEARCHING FOR THE WAYS AND THINGS THAT ARE BEST FOR THEM.
AND REMEM-BER...
...WE AREN'T THE ONLY ONES WHO ARE WORRYING ABOUT AND THINKING OVER THESE SORTS OF THINGS.

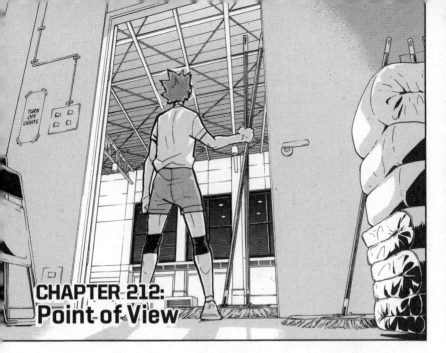

CHAPTER 212:
Point of View

DISTURBING, INNIT?

YES.

I HATE IT.

...

...

...

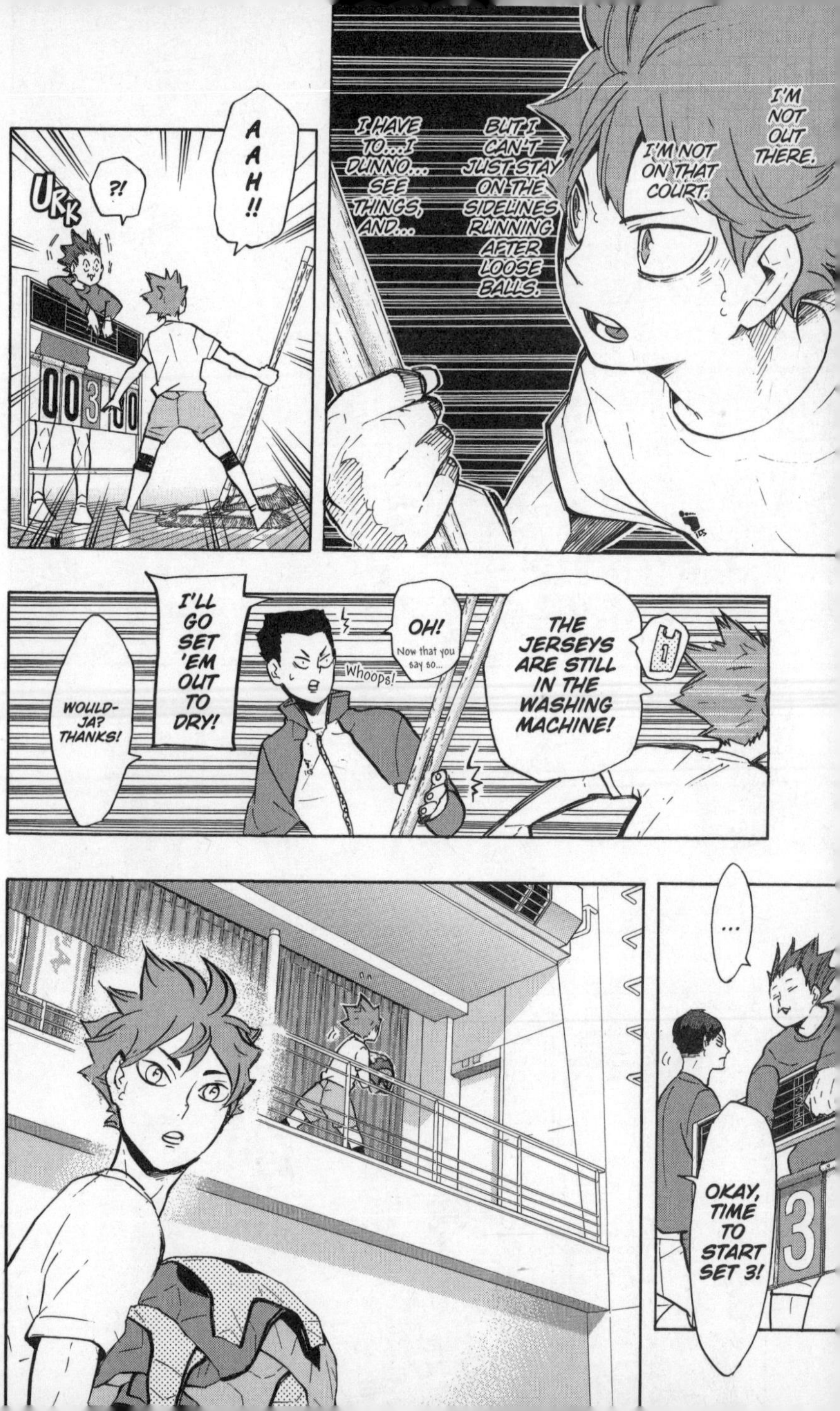
I'M NOT OUT THERE.
I'M NOT ON THAT COURT.
BUT I CAN'T JUST STAY ON THE SIDELINES RUNNING AFTER LOOSE BALLS.
I HAVE TO... I DUNNO... SEE THINGS, AND...
AAAH!!
?!
URK
THE JERSEYS ARE STILL IN THE WASHING MACHINE!
OH!
Now that you say so...
Whoops!
I'LL GO SET 'EM OUT TO DRY!
WOULD-JA? THANKS!
...
OKAY, TIME TO START SET 3!

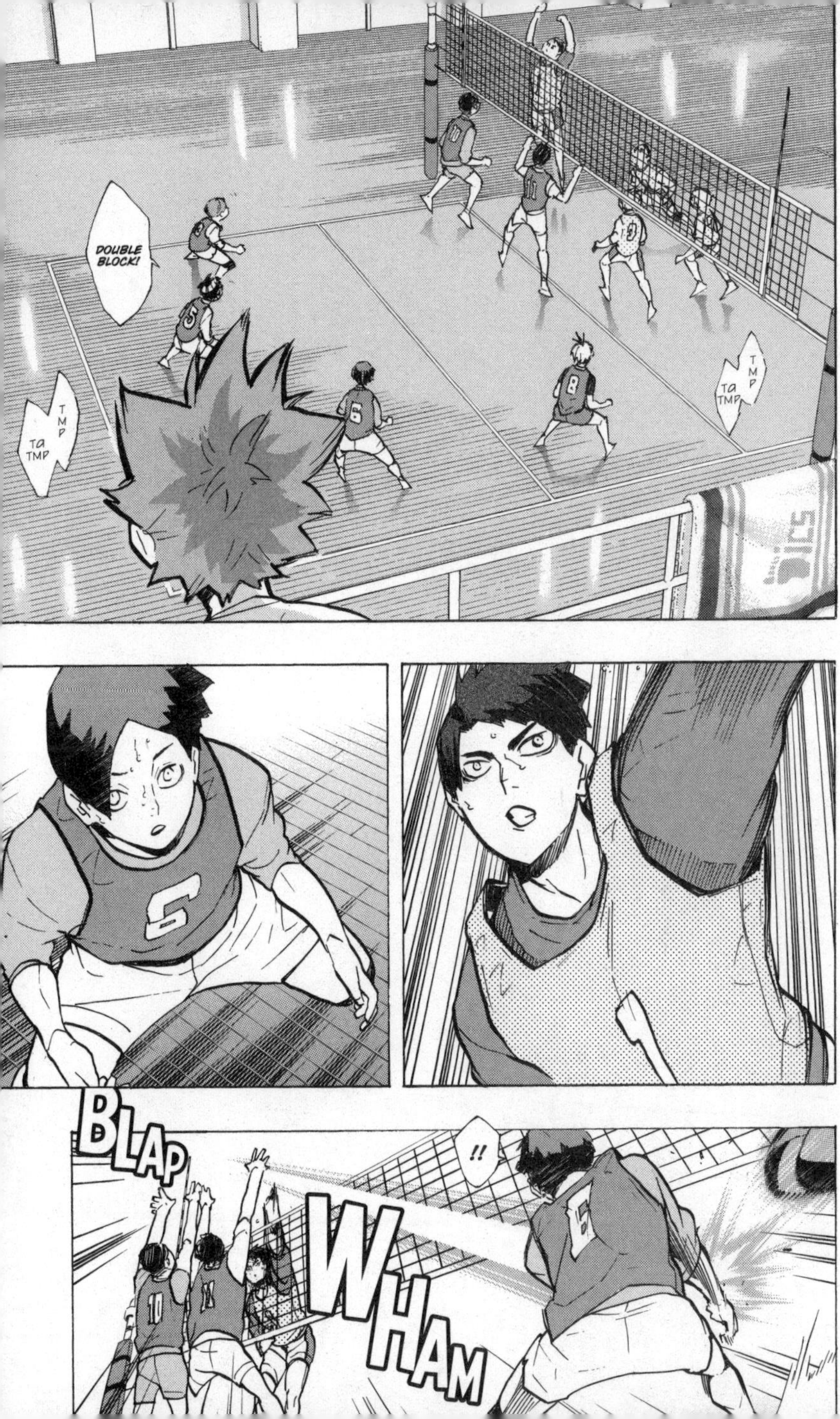
DOUBLE BLOCK!
TMP Ta TMP
TMP Ta TMP
!!
BLAP
WHAM

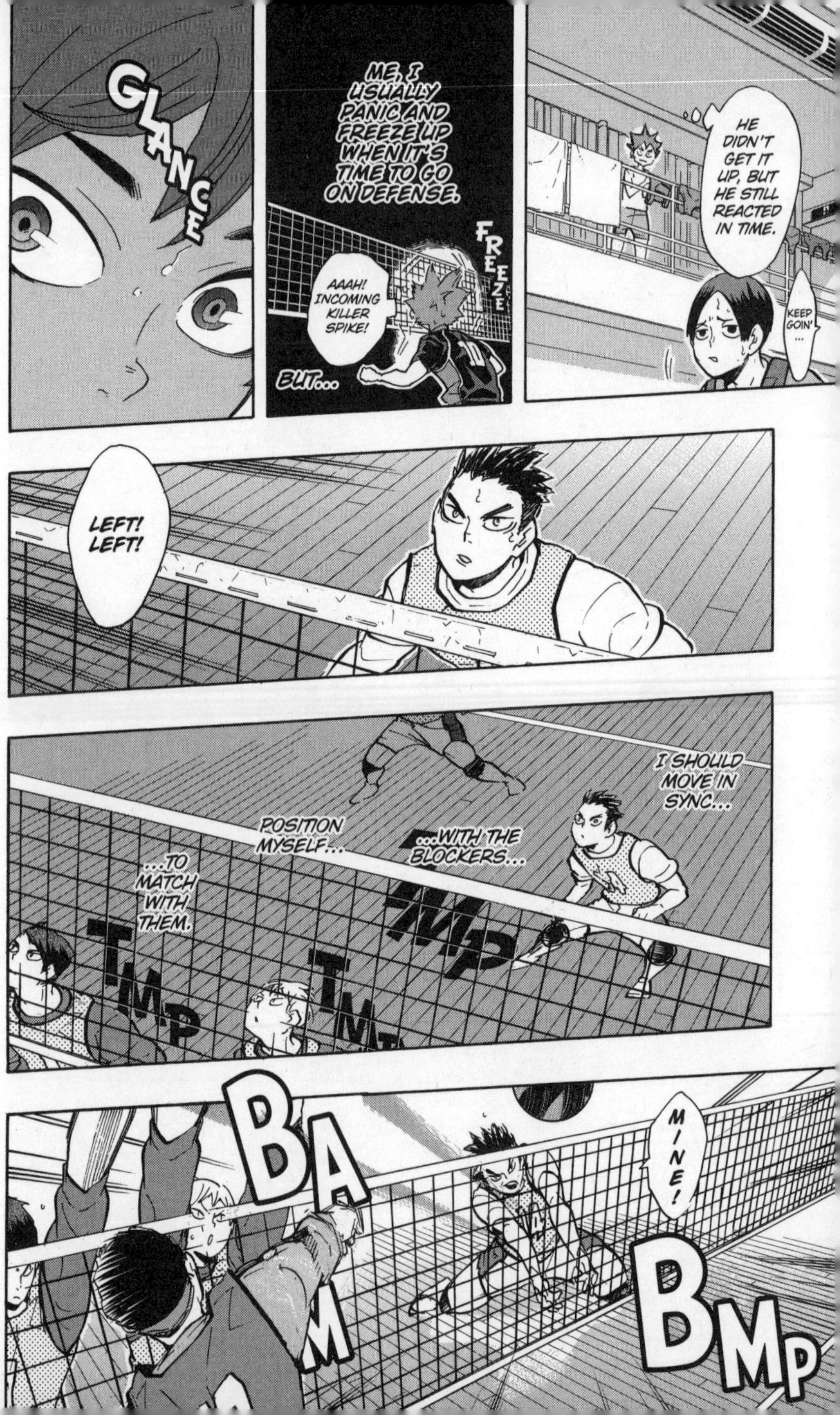

HE DIDN'T GET IT UP, BUT HE STILL REACTED IN TIME.
KEEP GOIN'...
ME, I USUALLY PANIC AND FREEZE UP WHEN IT'S TIME TO GO ON DEFENSE.
FREEZE
AAAH! INCOMING KILLER SPIKE!
BUT...
GLANCE
LEFT! LEFT!
I SHOULD MOVE IN SYNC...
...WITH THE BLOCKERS...
TMP
POSITION MYSELF...
...TO MATCH WITH THEM.
TMP
TMP
MINE!
BAM
BMP

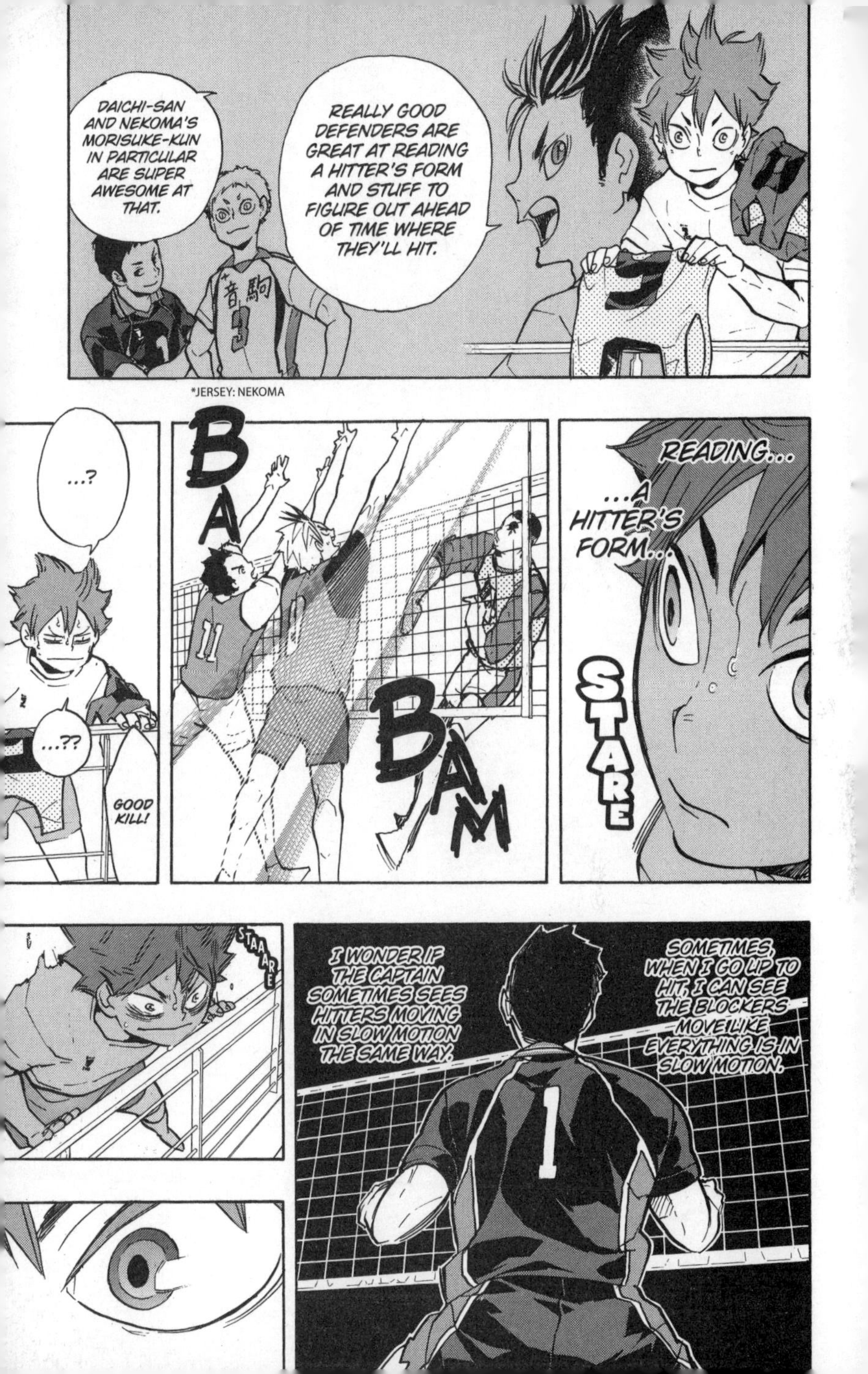
REALLY GOOD DEFENDERS ARE GREAT AT READING A HITTER'S FORM AND STUFF TO FIGURE OUT AHEAD OF TIME WHERE THEY'LL HIT.
DAICHI-SAN AND NEKOMA'S MORISUKE-KUN IN PARTICULAR ARE SUPER AWESOME AT THAT.
READING...
...A HITTER'S FORM...
STARE
BAM
BAM
...?
...??
GOOD KILL!
SOMETIMES, WHEN I GO UP TO HIT, I CAN SEE THE BLOCKERS MOVE LIKE EVERYTHING IS IN SLOW MOTION.
I WONDER IF THE CAPTAIN SOMETIMES SEES HITTERS MOVING IN SLOW MOTION THE SAME WAY.
STAAARE
*JERSEY: NEKOMA

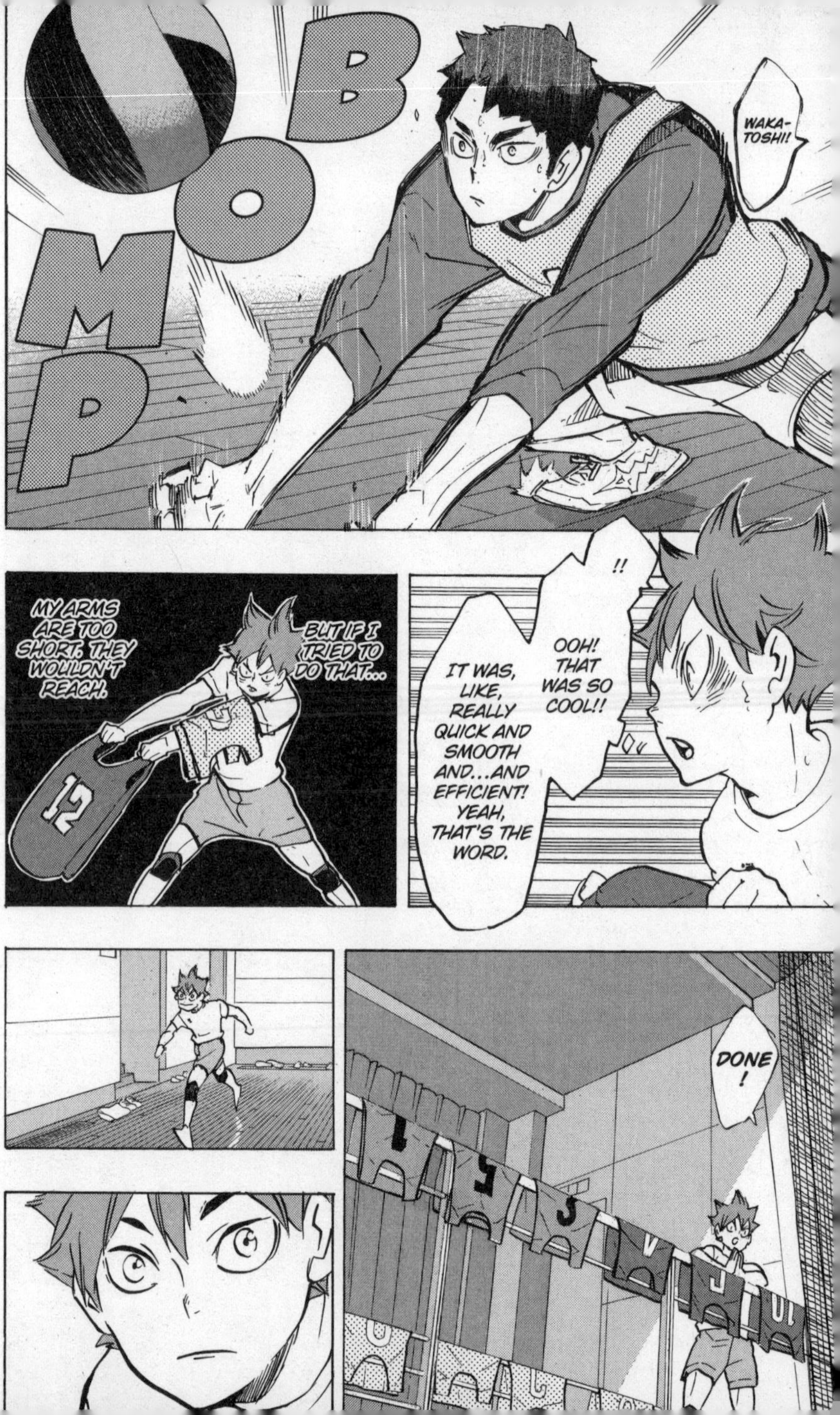
WAKA-TOSHI!
BOMP
!!
OOH! THAT WAS SO COOL!!
IT WAS, LIKE, REALLY QUICK AND SMOOTH AND...AND EFFICIENT! YEAH, THAT'S THE WORD.
BUT IF I TRIED TO DO THAT...
MY ARMS ARE TOO SHORT. THEY WOULDN'T REACH.
DONE!

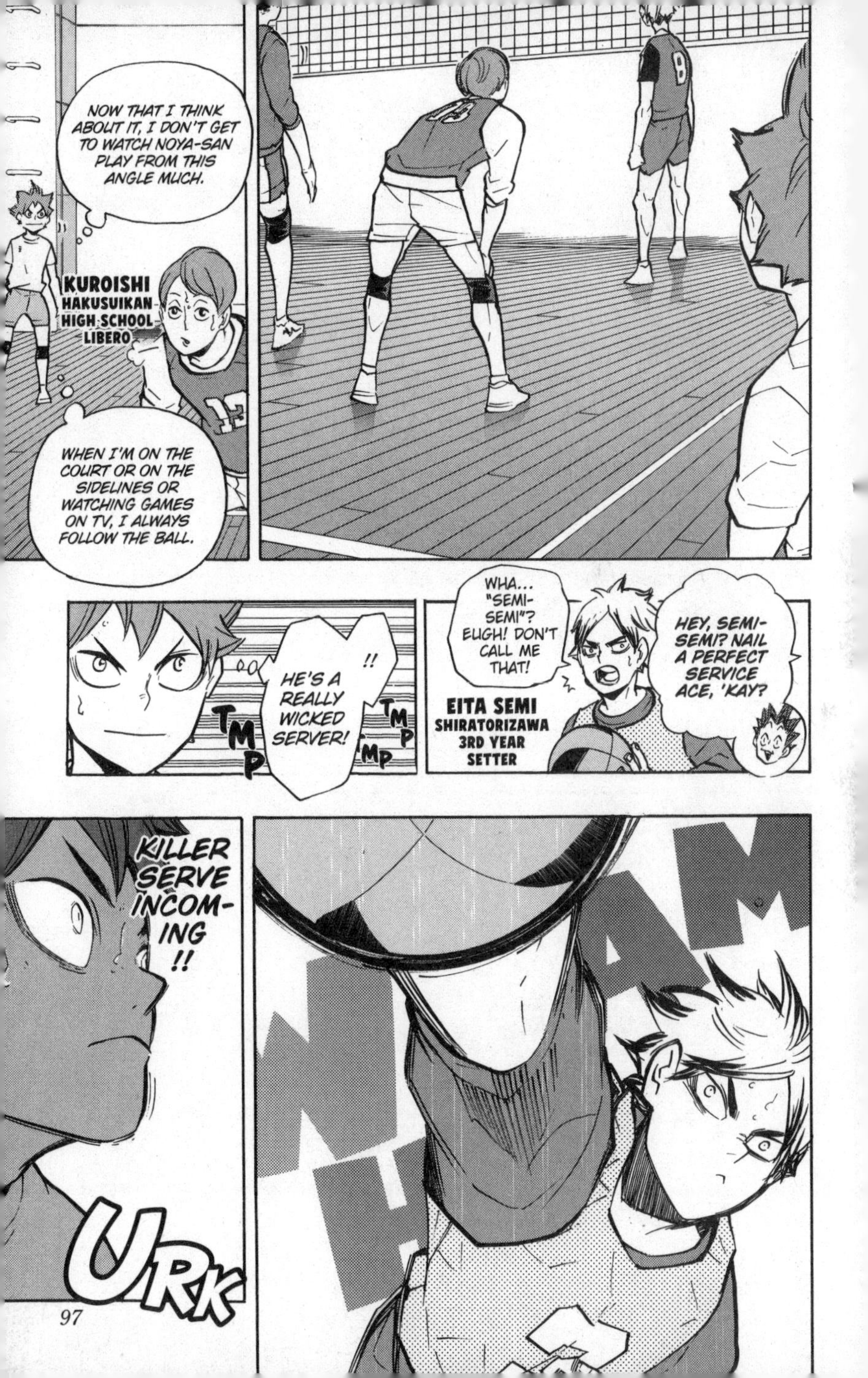
NOW THAT I THINK ABOUT IT, I DON'T GET TO WATCH NOYA-SAN PLAY FROM THIS ANGLE MUCH.
KUROISHI HAKUSUIKAN HIGH SCHOOL LIBERO
WHEN I'M ON THE COURT OR ON THE SIDELINES OR WATCHING GAMES ON TV, I ALWAYS FOLLOW THE BALL.
HEY, SEMI-SEMI? NAIL A PERFECT SERVICE ACE, 'KAY?
WHA... "SEMI-SEMI"? EUGH! DON'T CALL ME THAT!
EITA SEMI SHIRATORIZAWA 3RD YEAR SETTER
!!
HE'S A REALLY WICKED SERVER!
TMP TMP TMP
WHAM
KILLER SERVE INCOMING!!
URK

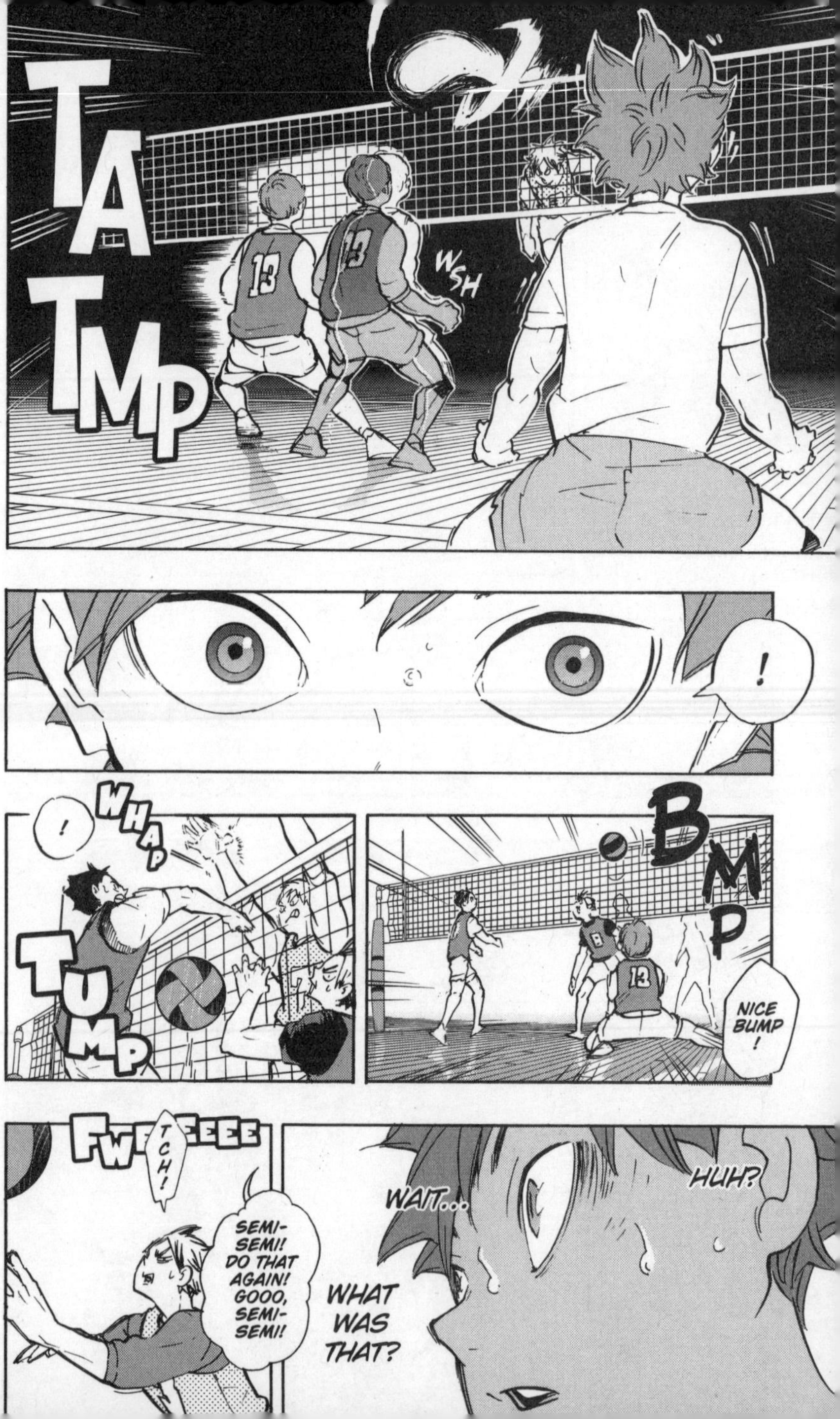
TATMP
WSH
!
BMP
NICE BUMP!
!
WHAP
TUMP
HUH?
WAIT...
WHAT WAS THAT?
FWEEEE
TCH!
SEMI-SEMI! DO THAT AGAIN! GOOO, SEMI-SEMI!

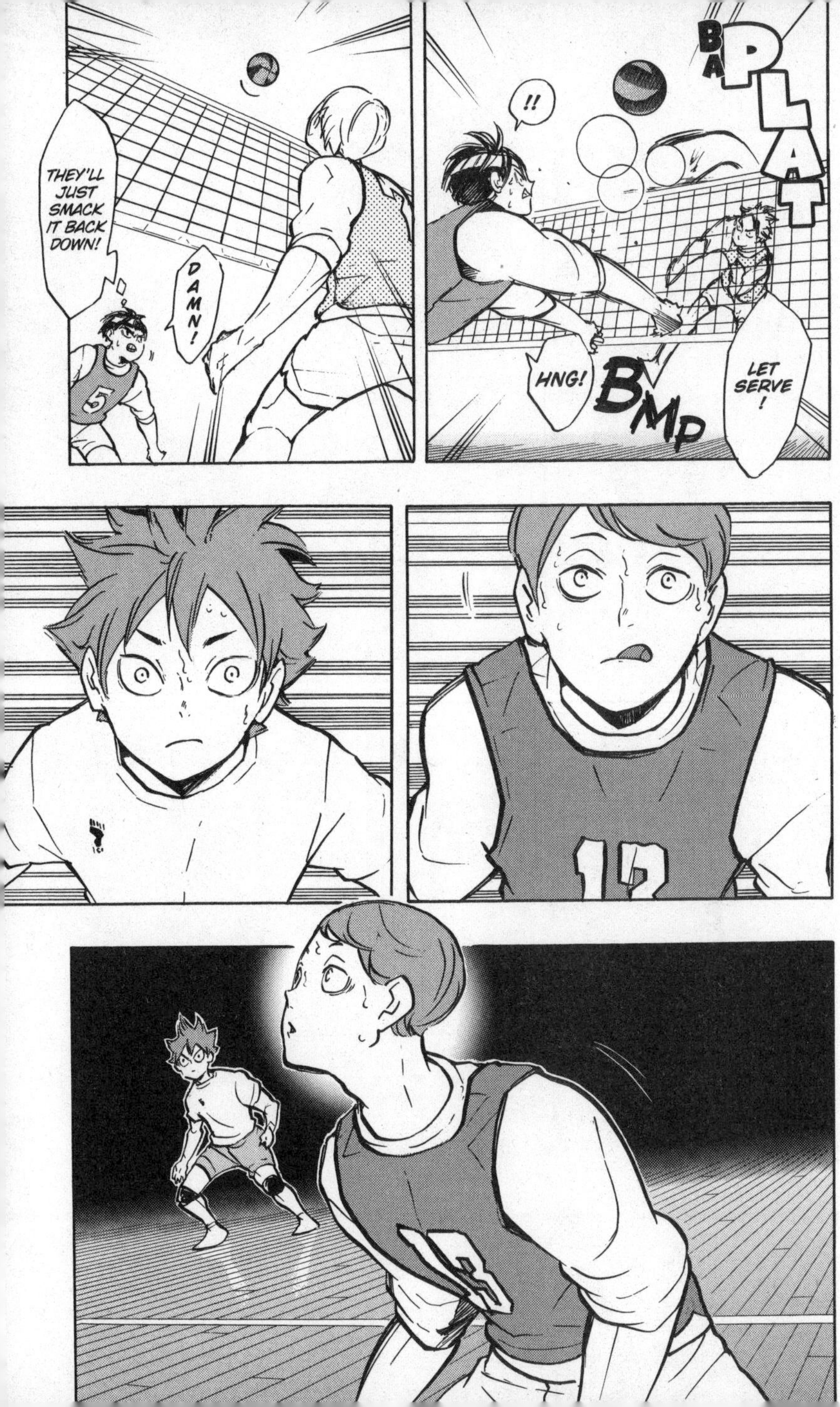
BA PLAT
!!
LET SERVE!
BMP
HNG!
DAMN!
THEY'LL JUST SMACK IT BACK DOWN!

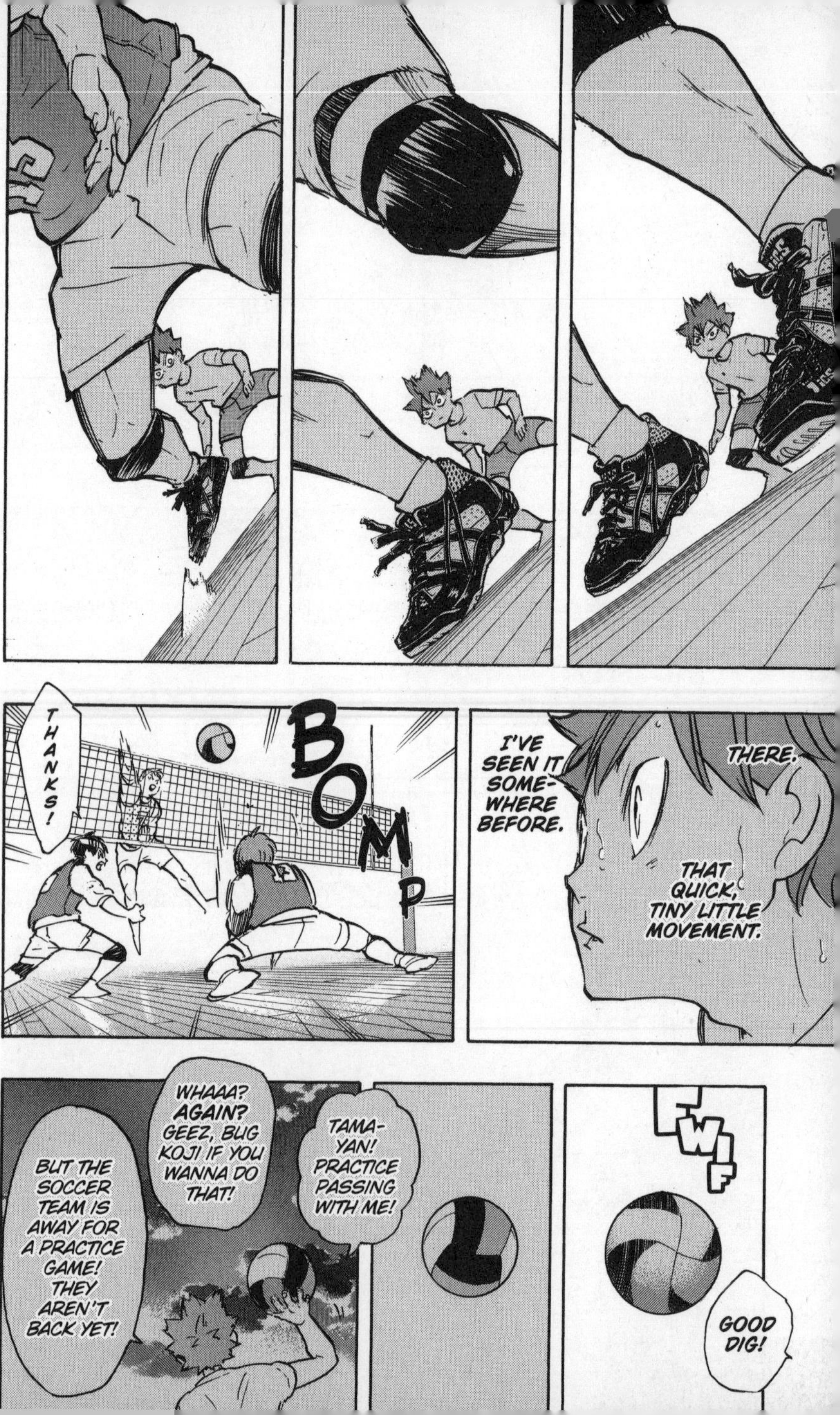
THERE.
I'VE SEEN IT SOMEWHERE BEFORE.
THAT QUICK, TINY LITTLE MOVEMENT.
BOMP
THANKS!
FWIF
GOOD DIG!
TAMA-YAN! PRACTICE PASSING WITH ME!
WHAAA? AGAIN? GEEZ, BUG KOJI IF YOU WANNA DO THAT!
BUT THE SOCCER TEAM IS AWAY FOR A PRACTICE GAME! THEY AREN'T BACK YET!

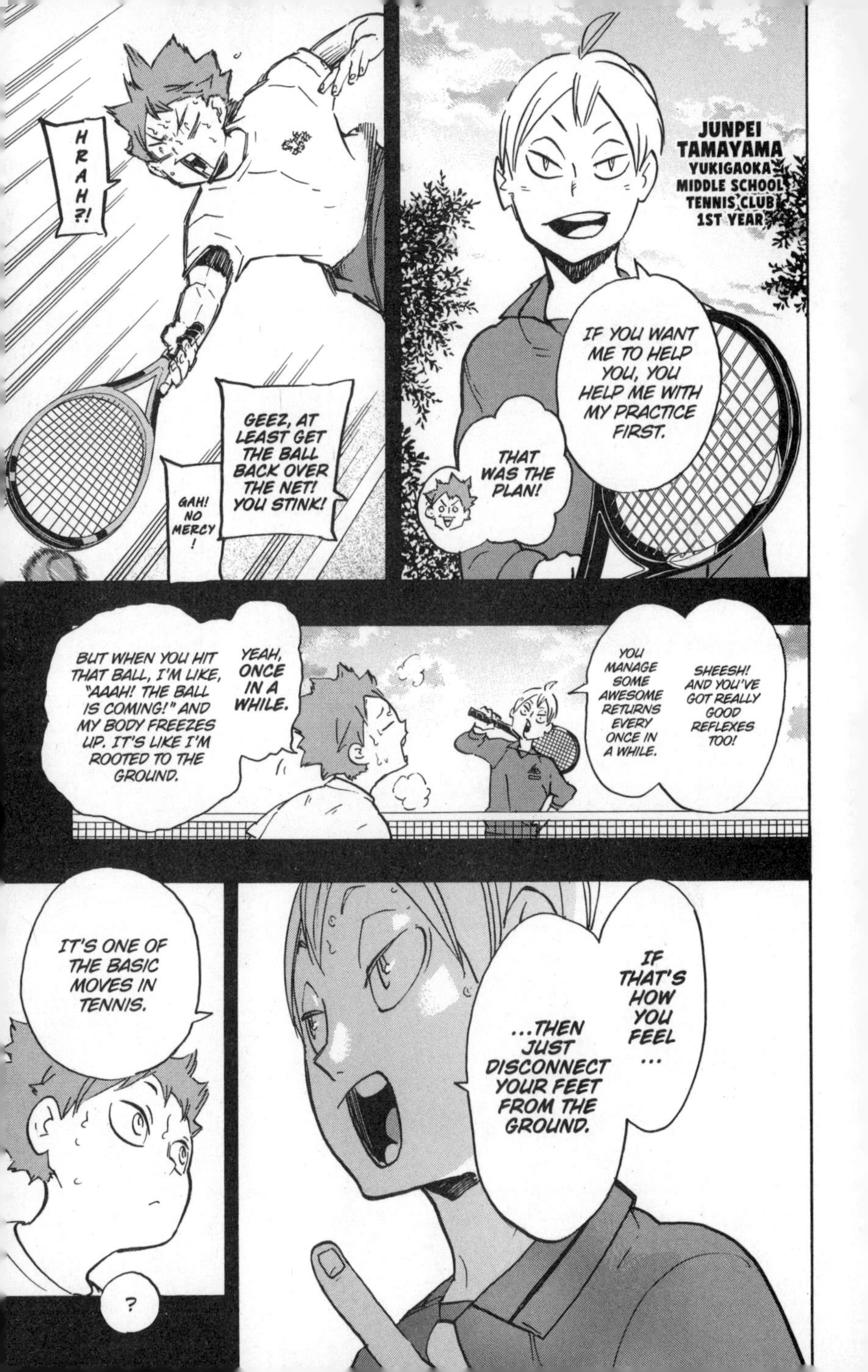
JUNPEI TAMAYAMA
YUKIGAOKA MIDDLE SCHOOL TENNIS CLUB 1ST YEAR
IF YOU WANT ME TO HELP YOU, YOU HELP ME WITH MY PRACTICE FIRST.
THAT WAS THE PLAN!
HRAH?!
GEEZ, AT LEAST GET THE BALL BACK OVER THE NET! YOU STINK!
GAH! NO MERCY!
SHEESH! AND YOU'VE GOT REALLY GOOD REFLEXES TOO!
YOU MANAGE SOME AWESOME RETURNS EVERY ONCE IN A WHILE.
YEAH, ONCE IN A WHILE.
BUT WHEN YOU HIT THAT BALL, I'M LIKE, "AAAH! THE BALL IS COMING!" AND MY BODY FREEZES UP. IT'S LIKE I'M ROOTED TO THE GROUND.
IF THAT'S HOW YOU FEEL...
...THEN JUST DISCONNECT YOUR FEET FROM THE GROUND.
IT'S ONE OF THE BASIC MOVES IN TENNIS.
?

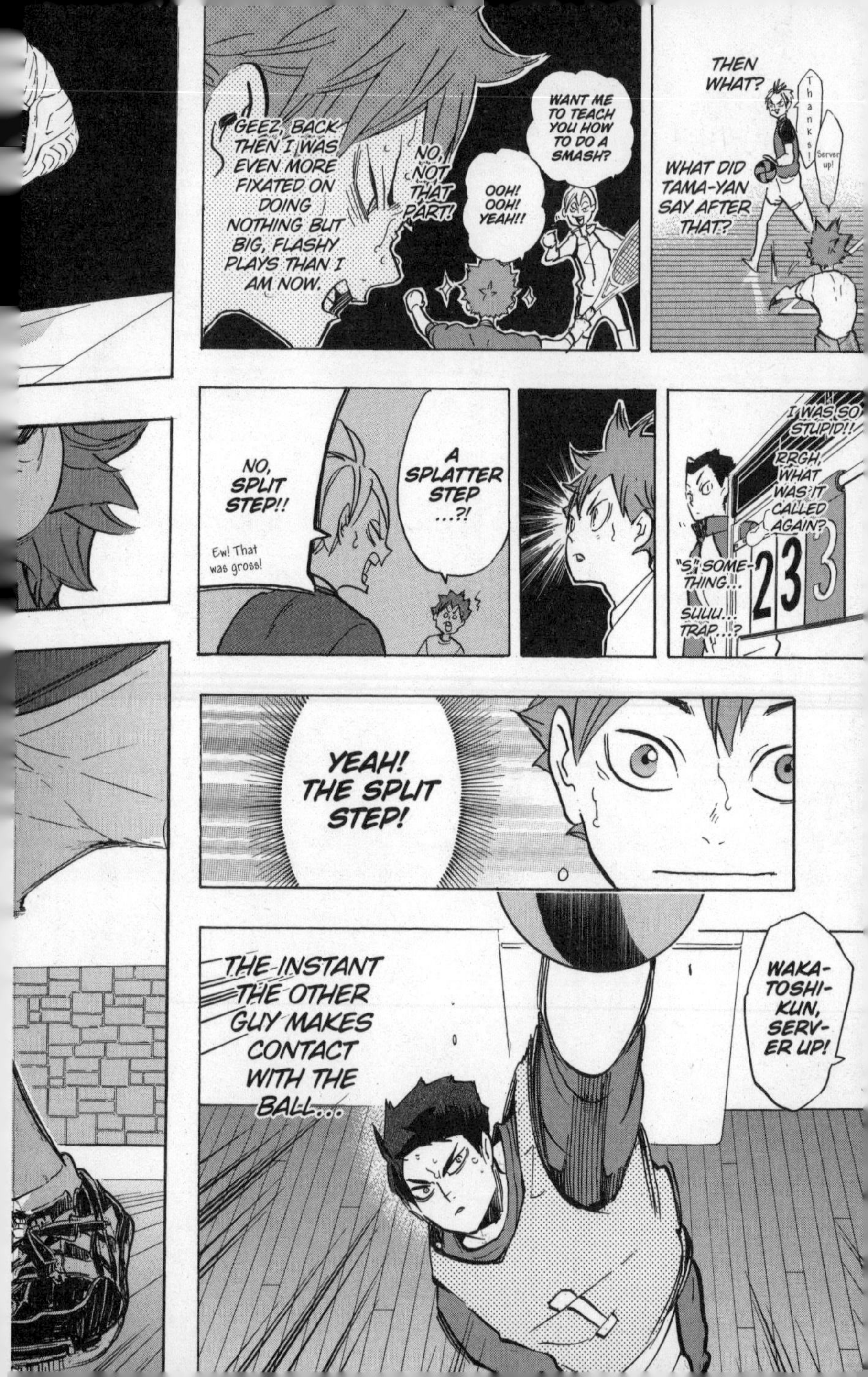
THEN WHAT?
Thanks!
Server up!
WHAT DID TAMA-YAN SAY AFTER THAT?
WANT ME TO TEACH YOU HOW TO DO A SMASH?
OOH! OOH! YEAH!!
NO, NOT THAT PART!
GEEZ, BACK THEN I WAS EVEN MORE FIXATED ON DOING NOTHING BUT BIG, FLASHY PLAYS THAN I AM NOW.
I WAS SO STUPID!!
RRGH, WHAT WAS IT CALLED AGAIN?
"S" SOMETHING...
SUUU... TRAP...?
A SPLATTER STEP ...?!
NO, SPLIT STEP!!
Ew! That was gross!
YEAH! THE SPLIT STEP!
WAKA-TOSHI-KUN, SERV-ER UP!
THE INSTANT THE OTHER GUY MAKES CONTACT WITH THE BALL...

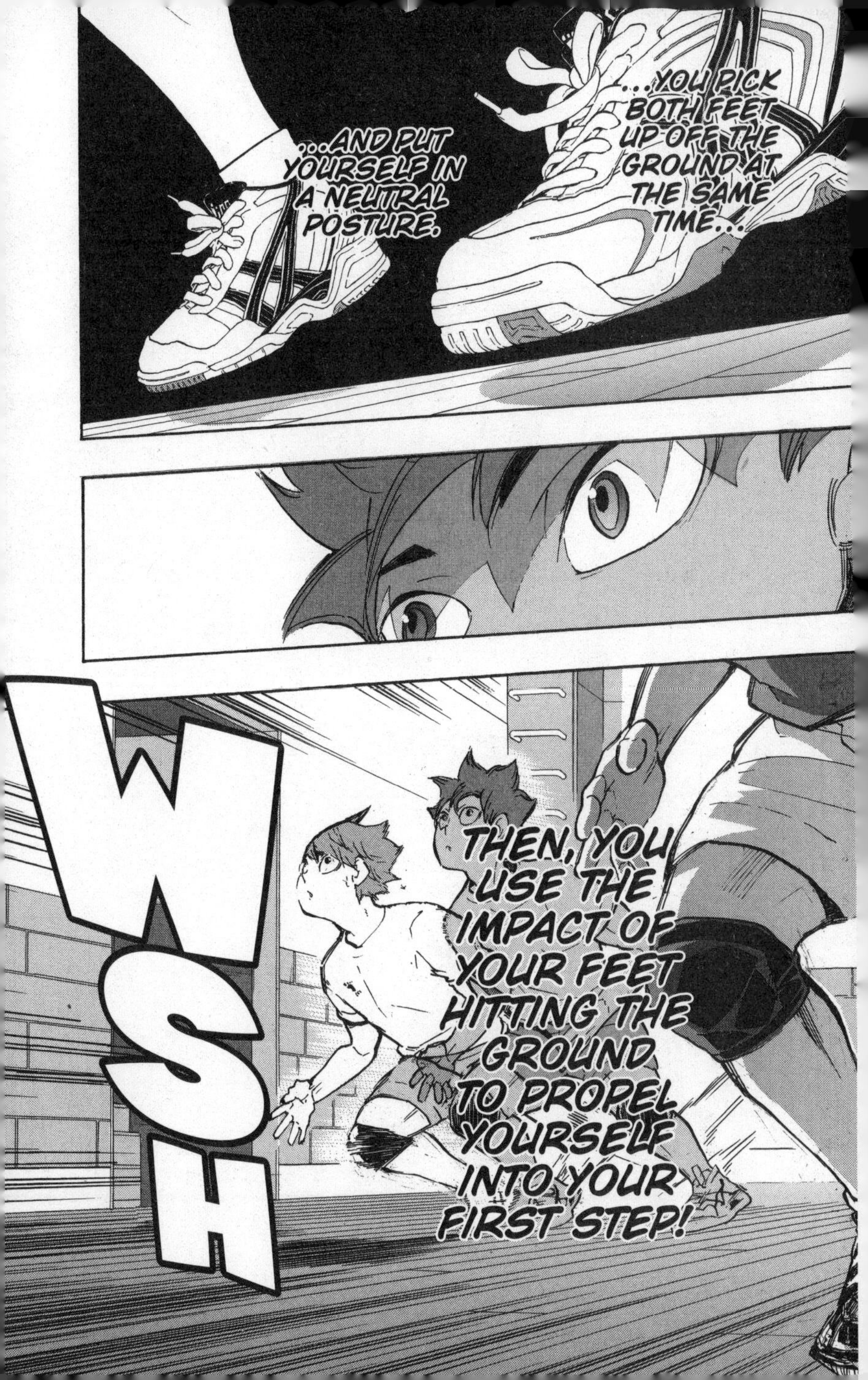
...YOU PICK BOTH FEET UP OFF THE GROUND AT THE SAME TIME...
...AND PUT YOURSELF IN A NEUTRAL POSTURE.
WSH
THEN, YOU USE THE IMPACT OF YOUR FEET HITTING THE GROUND TO PROPEL YOURSELF INTO YOUR FIRST STEP!

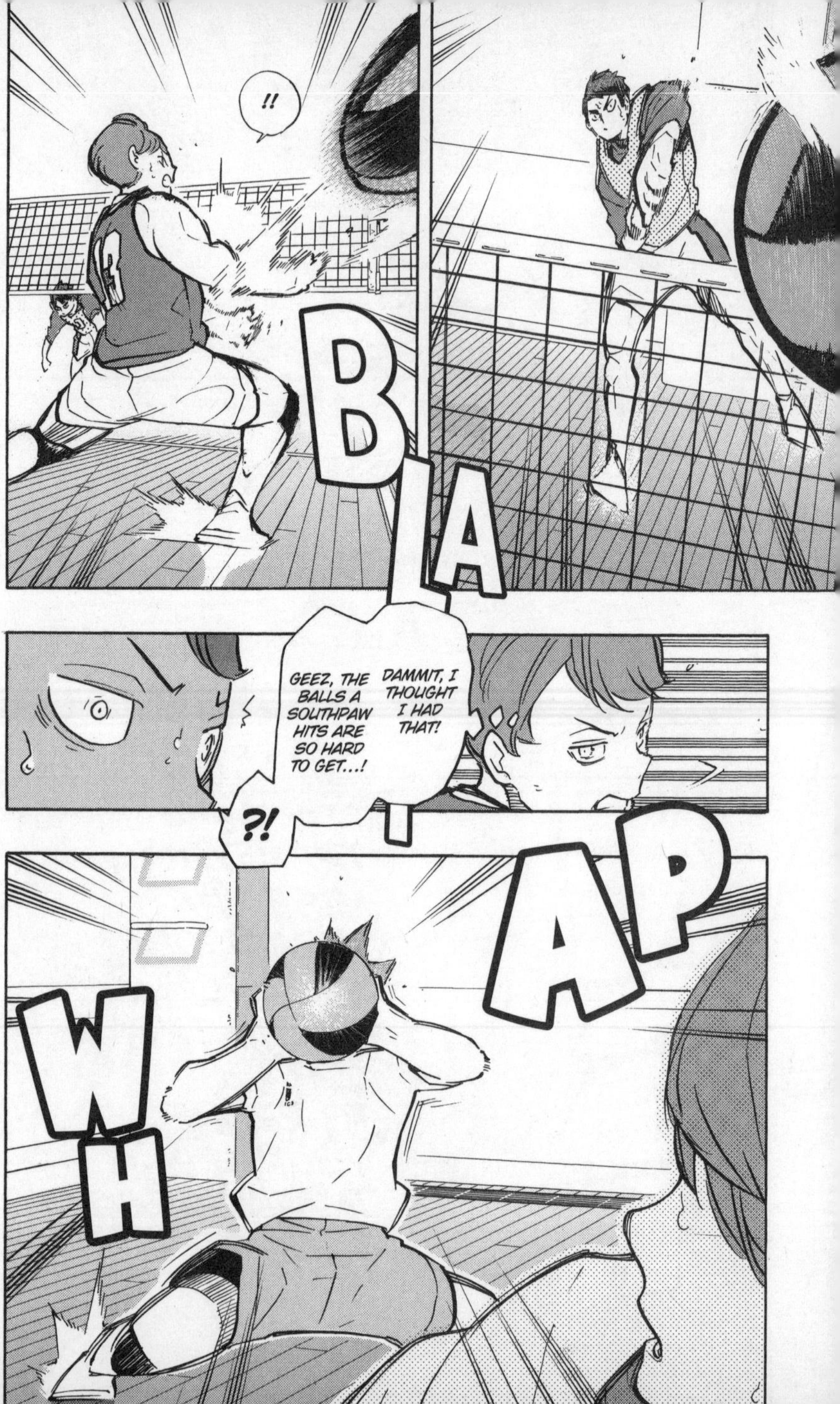

BLA
!!
DAMMIT, I THOUGHT I HAD THAT!
GEEZ, THE BALLS A SOUTHPAW HITS ARE SO HARD TO GET...!
?!
WHAP

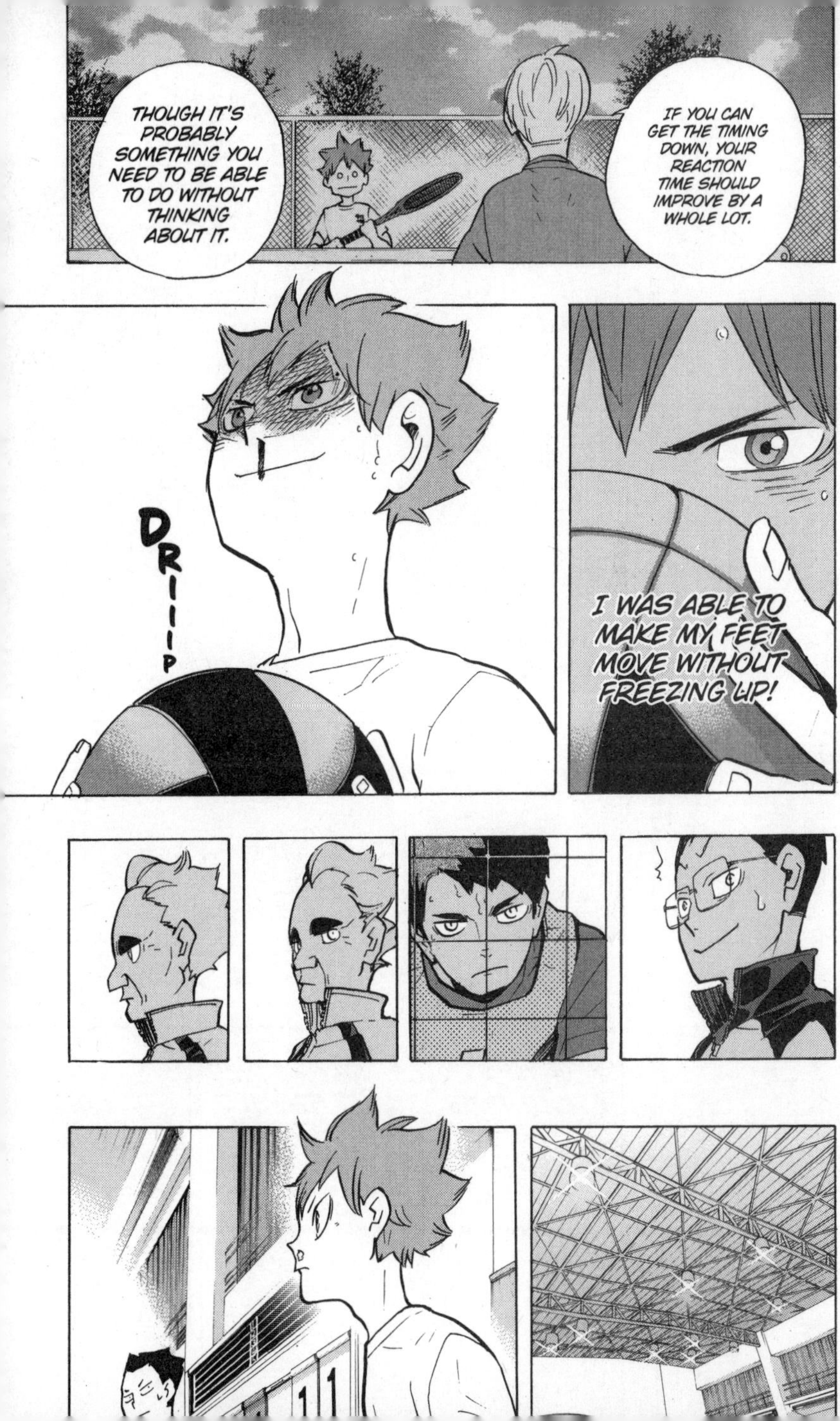
IF YOU CAN GET THE TIMING DOWN, YOUR REACTION TIME SHOULD IMPROVE BY A WHOLE LOT.
THOUGH IT'S PROBABLY SOMETHING YOU NEED TO BE ABLE TO DO WITHOUT THINKING ABOUT IT.
I WAS ABLE TO MAKE MY FEET MOVE WITHOUT FREEZING UP!
DRIIIP

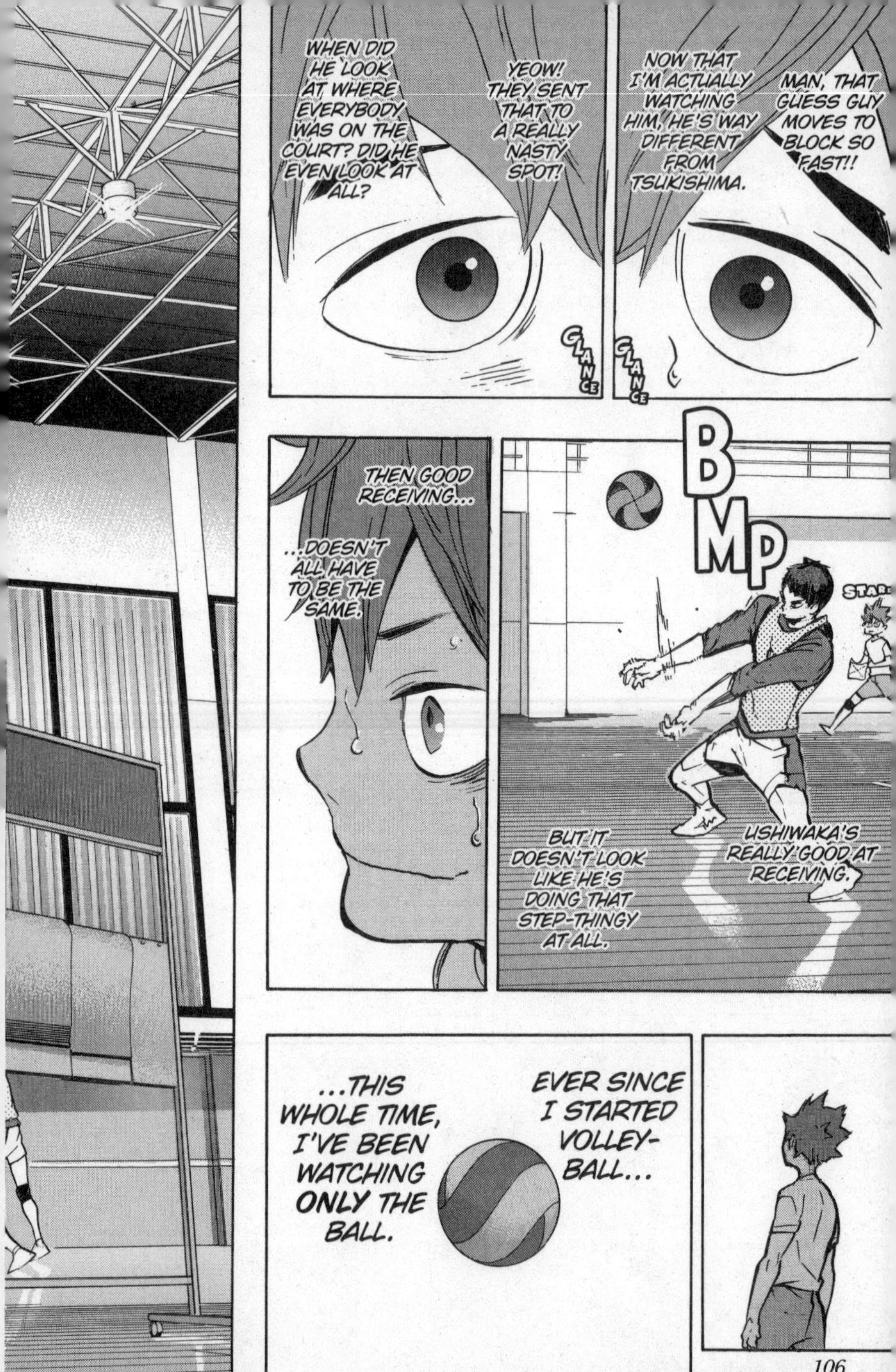
MAN, THAT GUESS GUY MOVES TO BLOCK SO FAST!!
NOW THAT I'M ACTUALLY WATCHING HIM, HE'S WAY DIFFERENT FROM TSUKISHIMA.
GLANCE
YEOW! THEY SENT THAT TO A REALLY NASTY SPOT!
WHEN DID HE LOOK AT WHERE EVERYBODY WAS ON THE COURT? DID HE EVEN LOOK AT ALL?
GLANCE
BMP
USHIWAKA'S REALLY GOOD AT RECEIVING.
BUT IT DOESN'T LOOK LIKE HE'S DOING THAT STEP-THINGY AT ALL.
THEN GOOD RECEIVING...
...DOESN'T ALL HAVE TO BE THE SAME.
EVER SINCE I STARTED VOLLEY-BALL...
...THIS WHOLE TIME, I'VE BEEN WATCHING ONLY THE BALL.

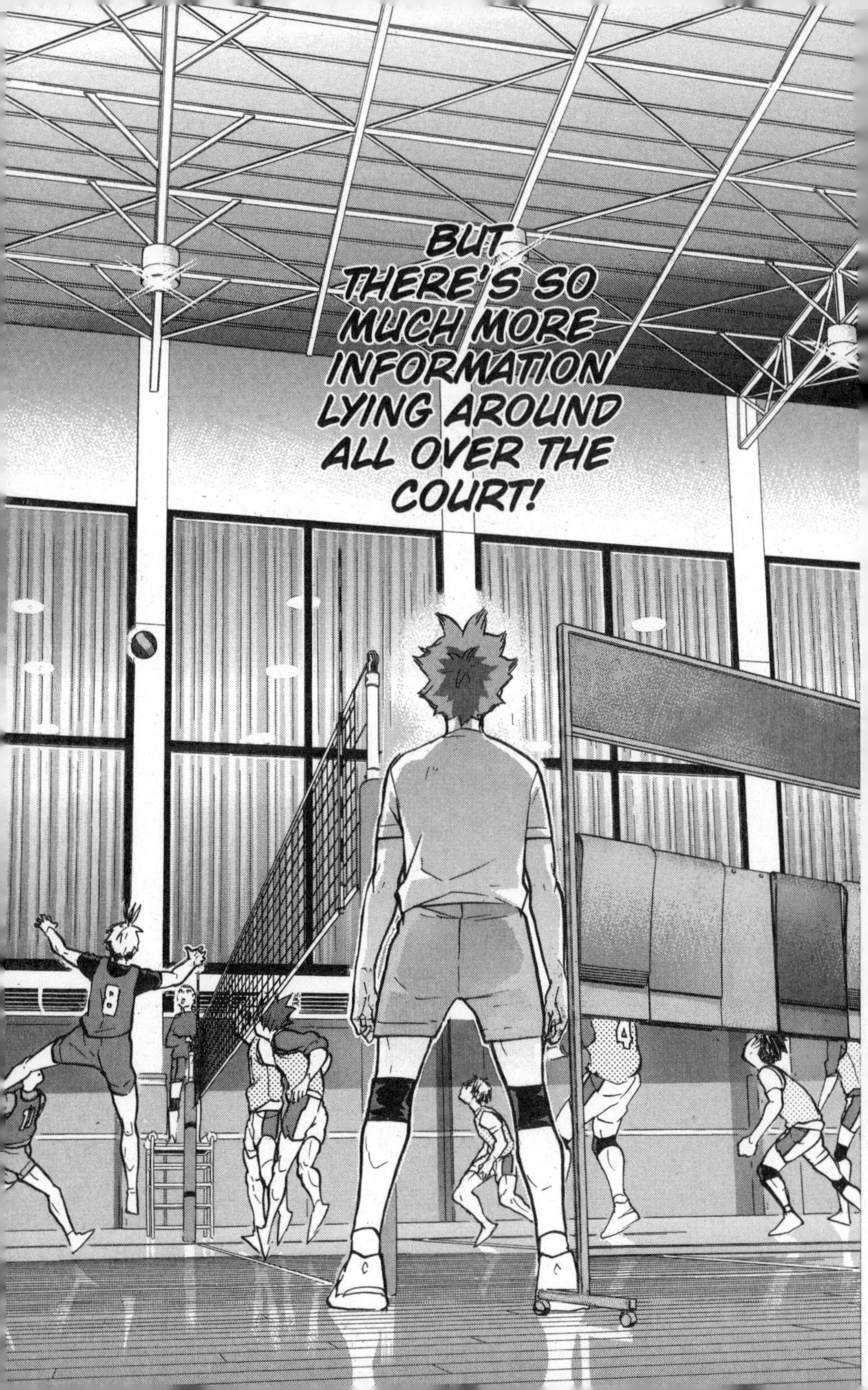
BUT THERE'S SO MUCH MORE INFORMATION LYING AROUND ALL OVER THE COURT!

Splatter Step

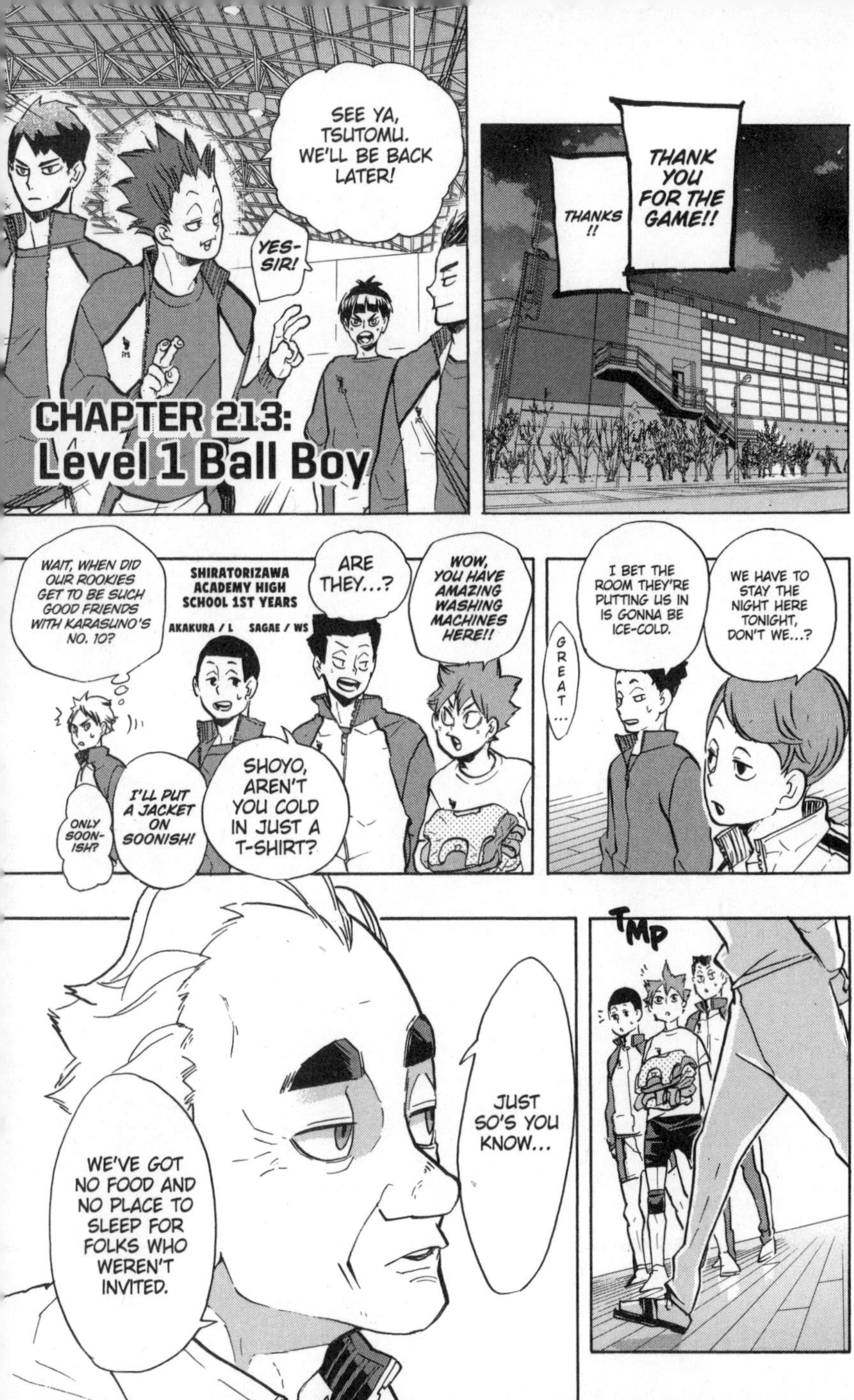
THANK YOU FOR THE GAME!!
THANKS!!
SEE YA, TSUTOMU. WE'LL BE BACK LATER!
YES-SIR!
CHAPTER 213:
Level 1 Ball Boy
WE HAVE TO STAY THE NIGHT HERE TONIGHT, DON'T WE...?
I BET THE ROOM THEY'RE PUTTING US IN IS GONNA BE ICE-COLD.
GREAT...
WOW, YOU HAVE AMAZING WASHING MACHINES HERE!!
ARE THEY...?
SHIRATORIZAWA ACADEMY HIGH SCHOOL 1ST YEARS
AKAKURA / L
SAGAE / WS
WAIT, WHEN DID OUR ROOKIES GET TO BE SUCH GOOD FRIENDS WITH KARASUNO'S NO. 10?
SHOYO, AREN'T YOU COLD IN JUST A T-SHIRT?
I'LL PUT A JACKET ON SOONISH!
ONLY SOONISH?
TMP
JUST SO'S YOU KNOW...
WE'VE GOT NO FOOD AND NO PLACE TO SLEEP FOR FOLKS WHO WEREN'T INVITED.

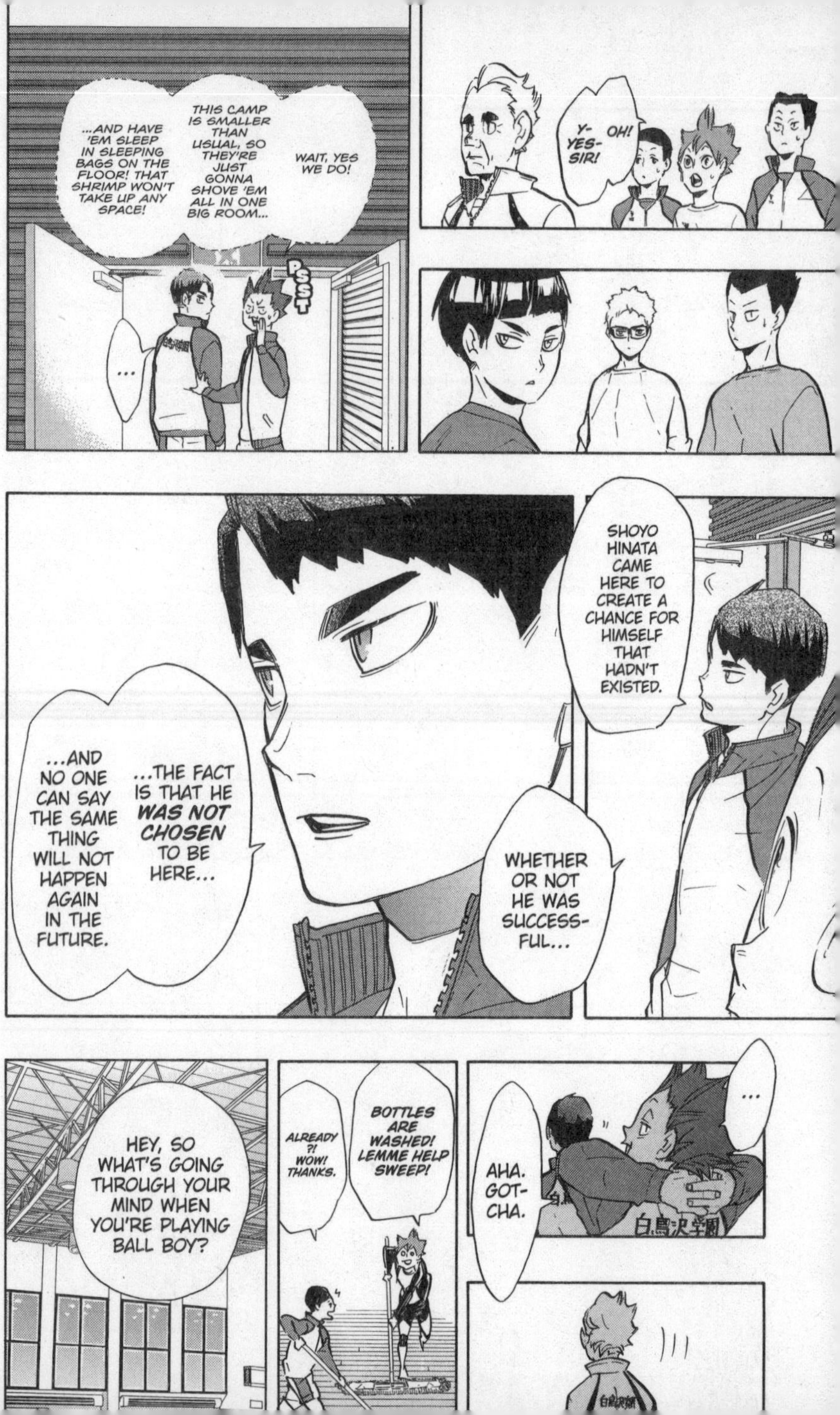
OH!
Y- YES-SIR!
WAIT, YES WE DO!
THIS CAMP IS SMALLER THAN USUAL, SO THEY'RE JUST GONNA SHOVE 'EM ALL IN ONE BIG ROOM...
...AND HAVE 'EM SLEEP IN SLEEPING BAGS ON THE FLOOR! THAT SHRIMP WON'T TAKE UP ANY SPACE!
PSST
...
SHOYO HINATA CAME HERE TO CREATE A CHANCE FOR HIMSELF THAT HADN'T EXISTED.
WHETHER OR NOT HE WAS SUCCESS-FUL...
...THE FACT IS THAT HE **WAS NOT CHOSEN** TO BE HERE...
...AND NO ONE CAN SAY THE SAME THING WILL NOT HAPPEN AGAIN IN THE FUTURE.
...
AHA. GOT-CHA.
BOTTLES ARE WASHED! LEMME HELP SWEEP!
ALREADY?! WOW! THANKS.
HEY, SO WHAT'S GOING THROUGH YOUR MIND WHEN YOU'RE PLAYING BALL BOY?

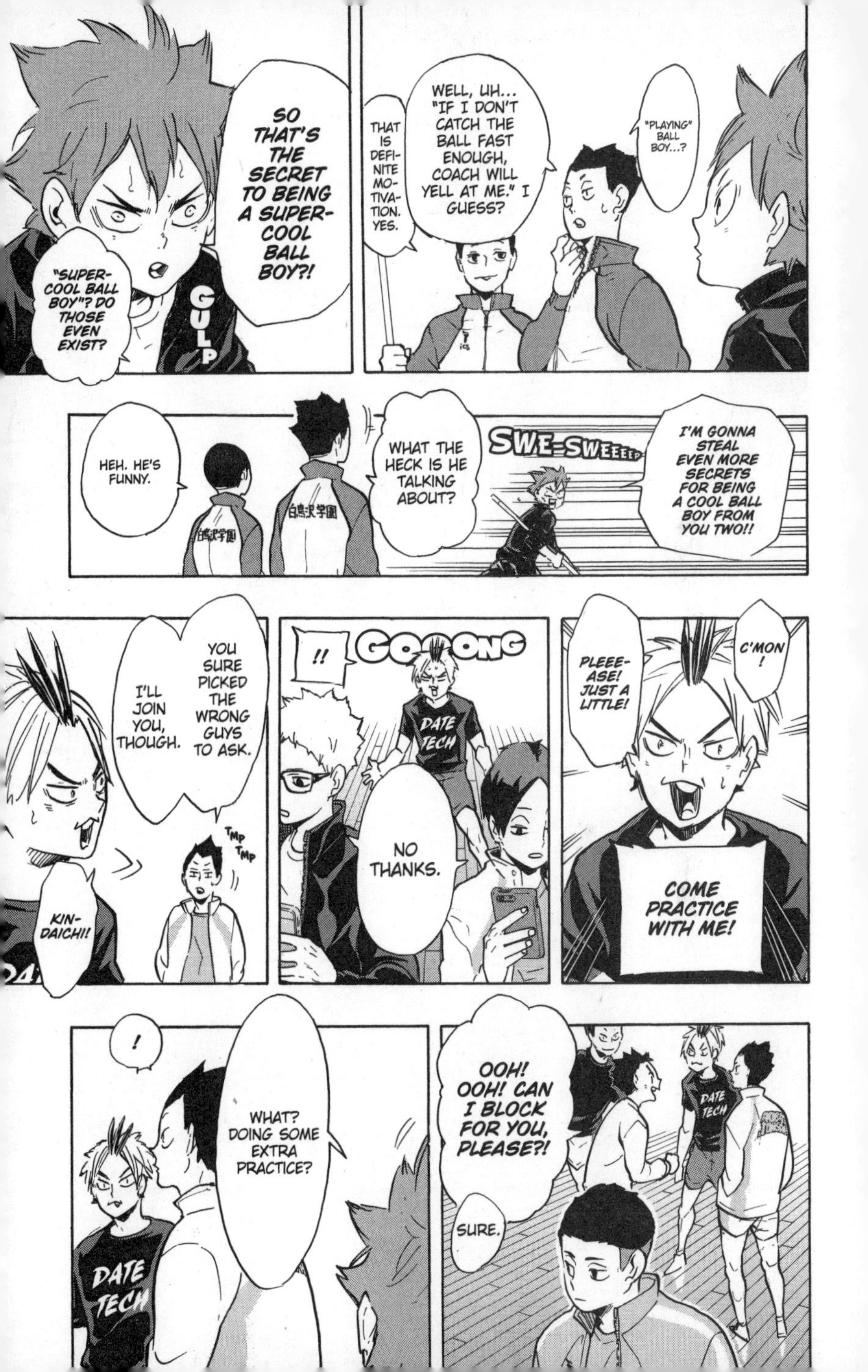
"PLAYING" BALL BOY...?
WELL, UH... "IF I DON'T CATCH THE BALL FAST ENOUGH, COACH WILL YELL AT ME." I GUESS?
THAT IS DEFINITE MOTIVATION. YES.
SO THAT'S THE SECRET TO BEING A SUPER-COOL BALL BOY?!
GULP
"SUPER-COOL BALL BOY"? DO THOSE EVEN EXIST?
I'M GONNA STEAL EVEN MORE SECRETS FOR BEING A COOL BALL BOY FROM YOU TWO!!
SWE-SWEEEEE
WHAT THE HECK IS HE TALKING ABOUT?
HEH. HE'S FUNNY.
C'MON!
PLEEE-ASE! JUST A LITTLE!
COME PRACTICE WITH ME!
!!
DATE TECH
NO THANKS.
YOU SURE PICKED THE WRONG GUYS TO ASK.
I'LL JOIN YOU, THOUGH.
TMP TMP
KIN-DAICHI!
OOH! OOH! CAN I BLOCK FOR YOU, PLEASE?!
SURE.
DATE TECH
!
WHAT? DOING SOME EXTRA PRACTICE?
DATE TECH

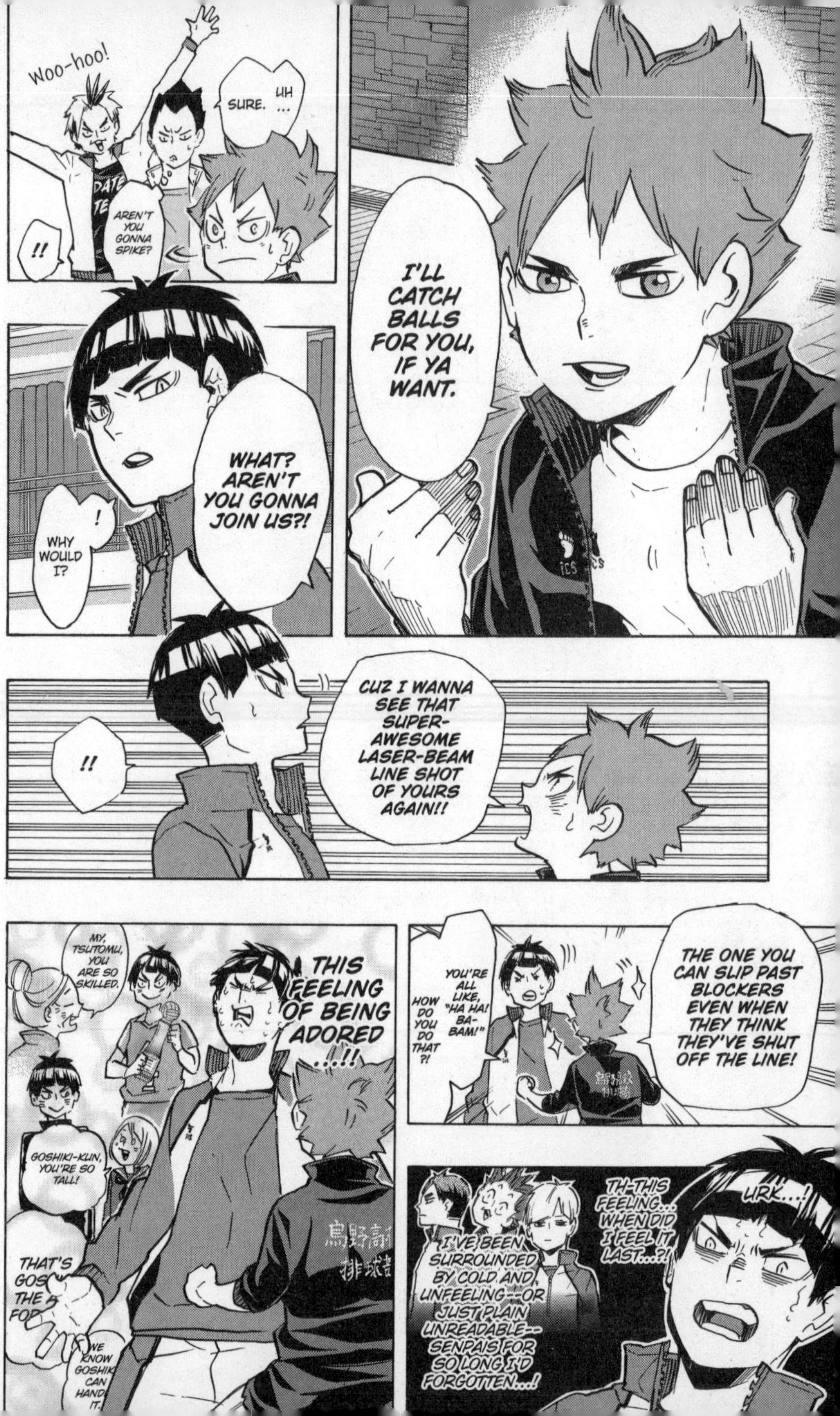

Woo-hoo!
UH ... SURE.
AREN'T YOU GONNA SPIKE?
!!
I'LL CATCH BALLS FOR YOU, IF YA WANT.
WHAT? AREN'T YOU GONNA JOIN US?!
!
WHY WOULD I?
CUZ I WANNA SEE THAT SUPER-AWESOME LASER-BEAM LINE SHOT OF YOURS AGAIN!!
!!
THE ONE YOU CAN SLIP PAST BLOCKERS EVEN WHEN THEY THINK THEY'VE SHUT OFF THE LINE!
YOU'RE ALL LIKE, "HA HA! BA-BAM!"
HOW DO YOU DO THAT?!
URK...!
TH-THIS FEELING... WHEN DID I FEEL IT LAST...?!
I'VE BEEN SURROUNDED BY COLD AND UNFEELING--OR JUST PLAIN UNREADABLE--SENPAIS FOR SO LONG I'D FORGOTTEN...!
THIS FEELING OF BEING ADORED...!!
MY, TSUTOMU, YOU ARE SO SKILLED.
GOSHIKI-KUN, YOU'RE SO TALL!

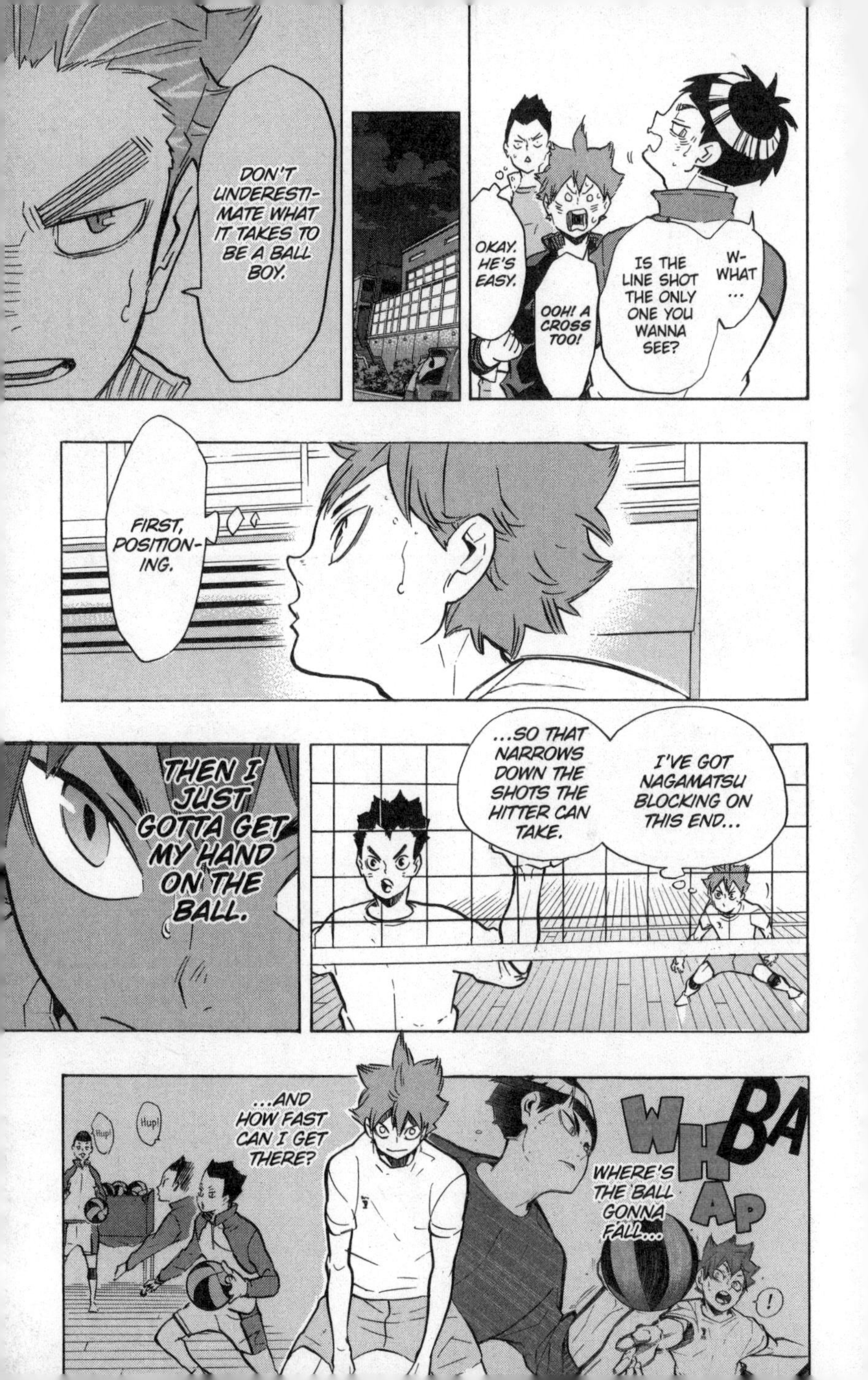
W-WHAT...
IS THE LINE SHOT THE ONLY ONE YOU WANNA SEE?
OOH! A CROSS TOO!
OKAY. HE'S EASY.
DON'T UNDERESTIMATE WHAT IT TAKES TO BE A BALL BOY.
FIRST, POSITIONING.
I'VE GOT NAGAMATSU BLOCKING ON THIS END...
...SO THAT NARROWS DOWN THE SHOTS THE HITTER CAN TAKE.
THEN I JUST GOTTA GET MY HAND ON THE BALL.
WHABAP
WHERE'S THE BALL GONNA FALL...
...AND HOW FAST CAN I GET THERE?
Hup!
Hup!
!

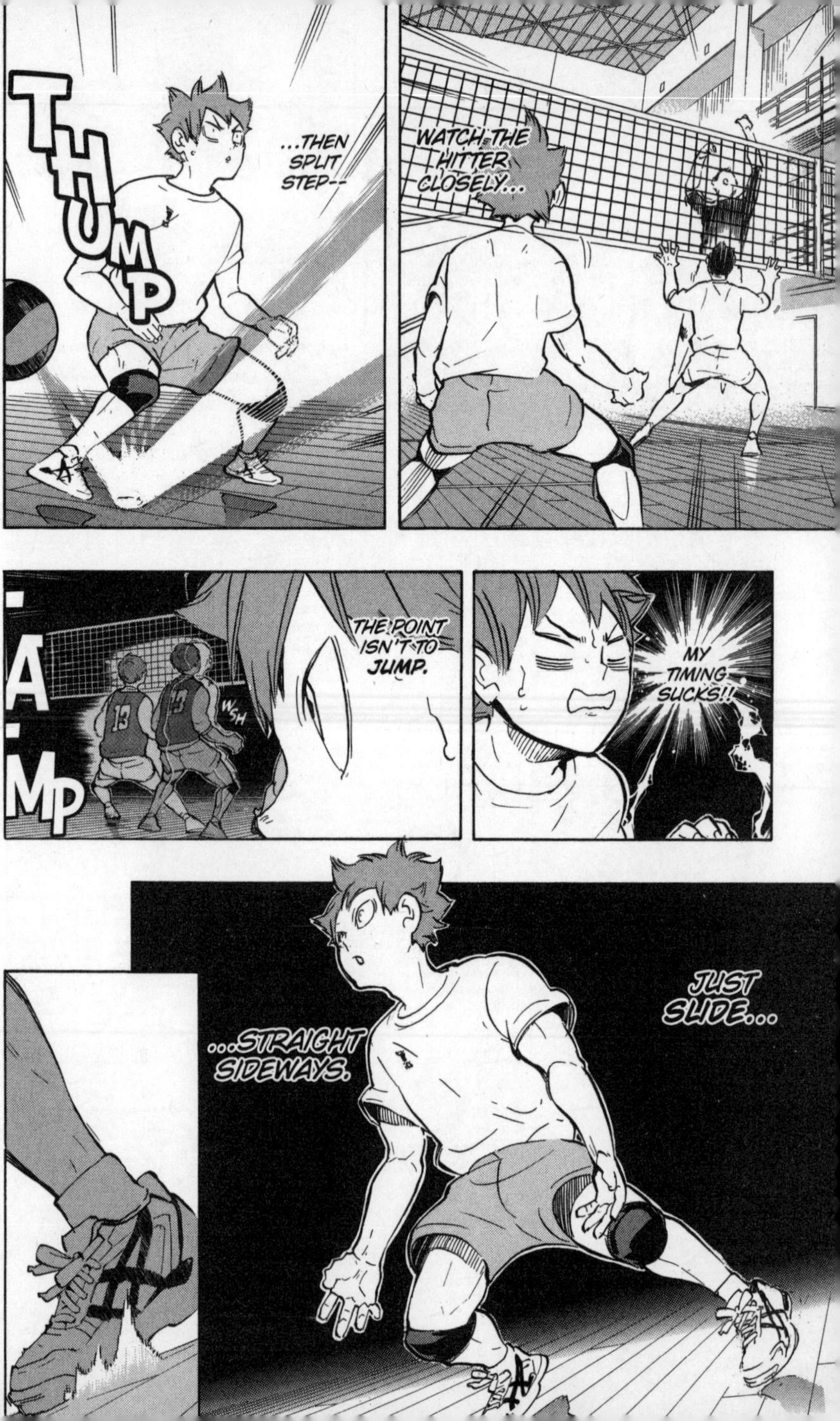
WATCH THE HITTER CLOSELY...
...THEN SPLIT STEP--
THUMP
MY TIMING SUCKS!!
THE POINT ISN'T TO JUMP.
WSH
JUST SLIDE...
...STRAIGHT SIDEWAYS.

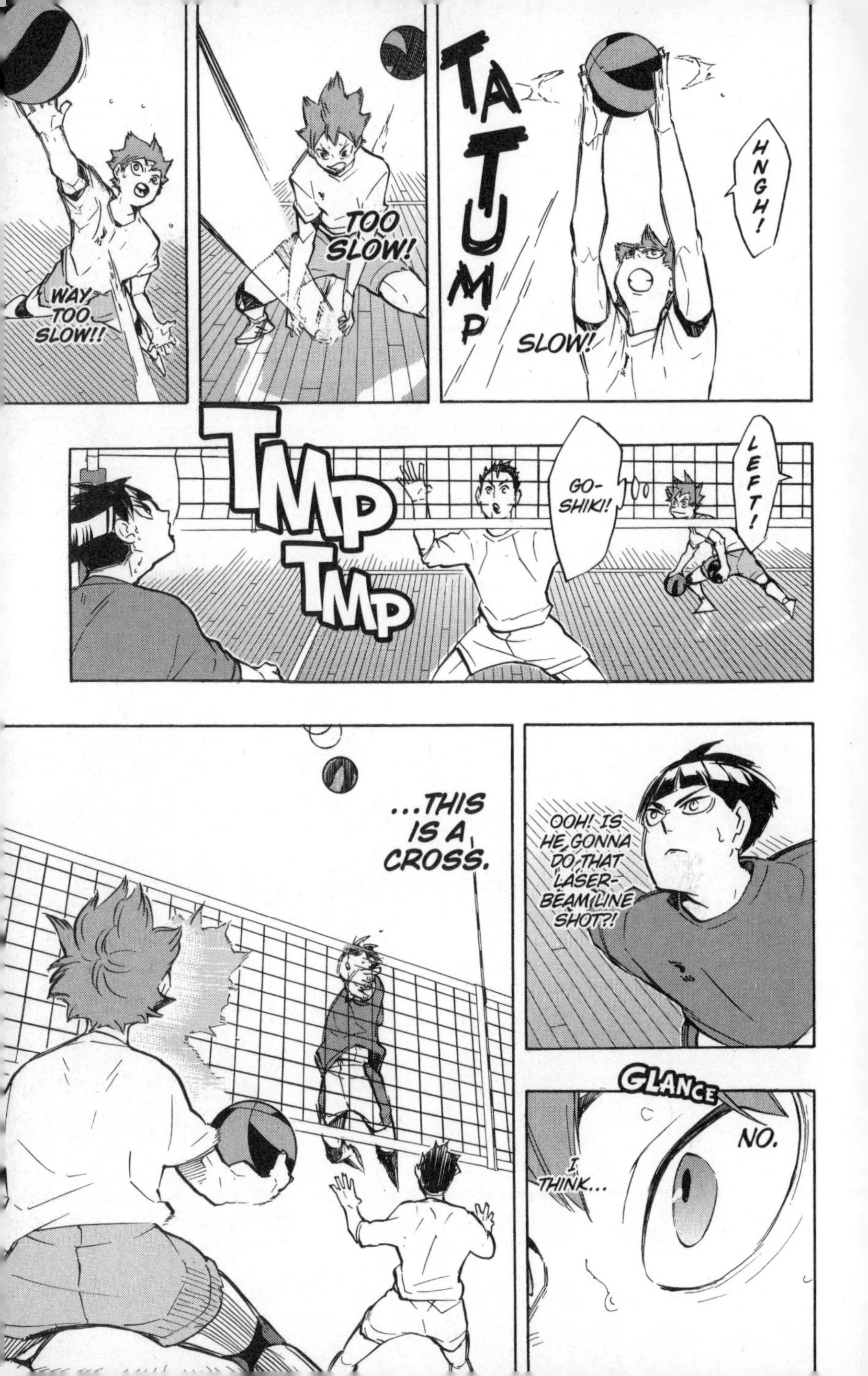
HNGH!
SLOW!
TA JUMP
TOO SLOW!
WAY TOO SLOW!!
LEFT!
GO-SHIKI!
TMP TMP
OOH! IS HE GONNA DO THAT LASER-BEAM LINE SHOT?!
GLANCE
NO.
I THINK...
...THIS IS A CROSS.

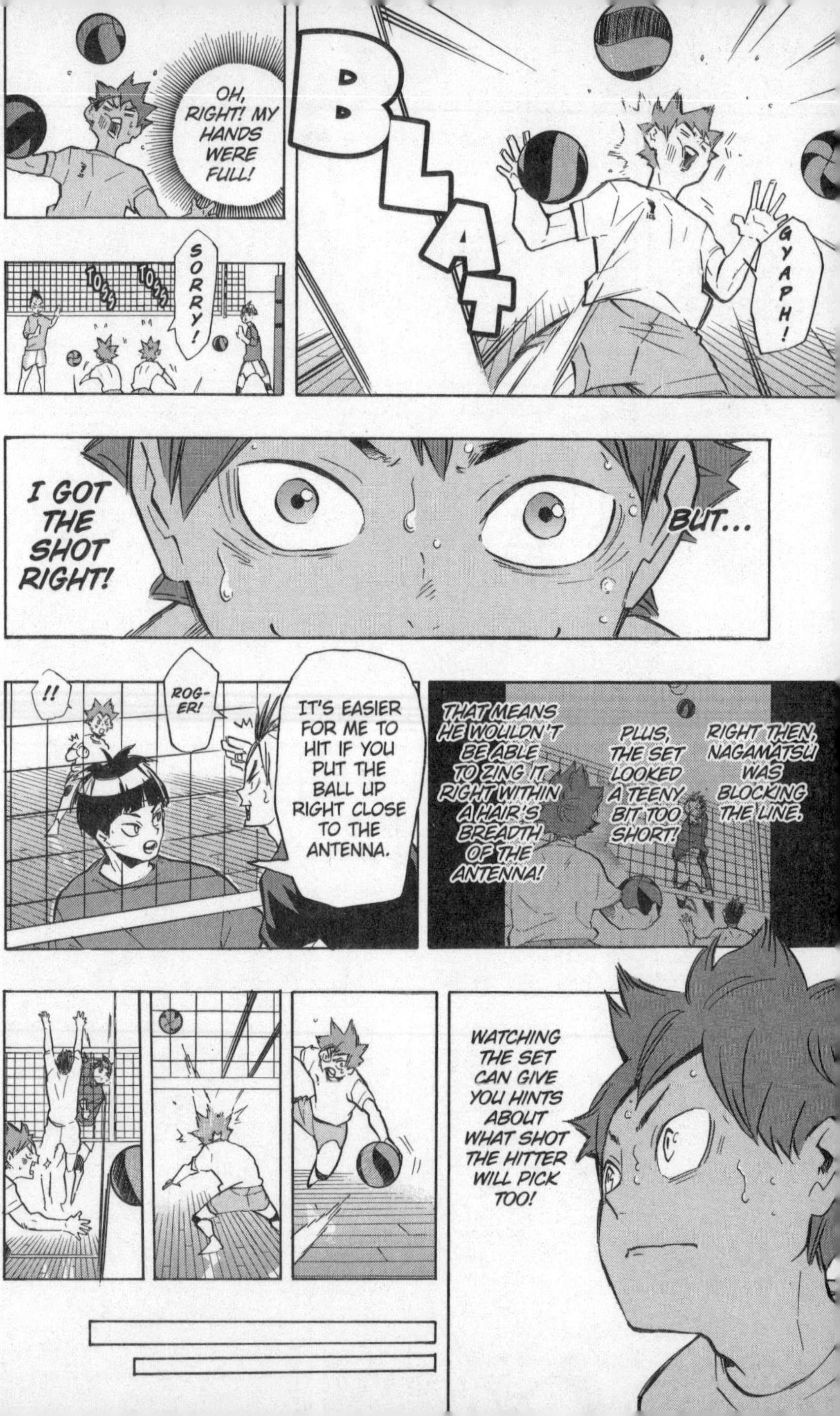
BLAT
GYAPH!
OH, RIGHT! MY HANDS WERE FULL!
TOSS
TOSS
SORRY!
I GOT THE SHOT RIGHT!
BUT...
RIGHT THEN, NAGAMATSU WAS BLOCKING THE LINE.
PLUS, THE SET LOOKED A TEENY BIT TOO SHORT!
THAT MEANS HE WOULDN'T BE ABLE TO ZING IT RIGHT WITHIN A HAIR'S BREADTH OF THE ANTENNA!
IT'S EASIER FOR ME TO HIT IF YOU PUT THE BALL UP RIGHT CLOSE TO THE ANTENNA.
ROG-ER!
!!
WATCHING THE SET CAN GIVE YOU HINTS ABOUT WHAT SHOT THE HITTER WILL PICK TOO!

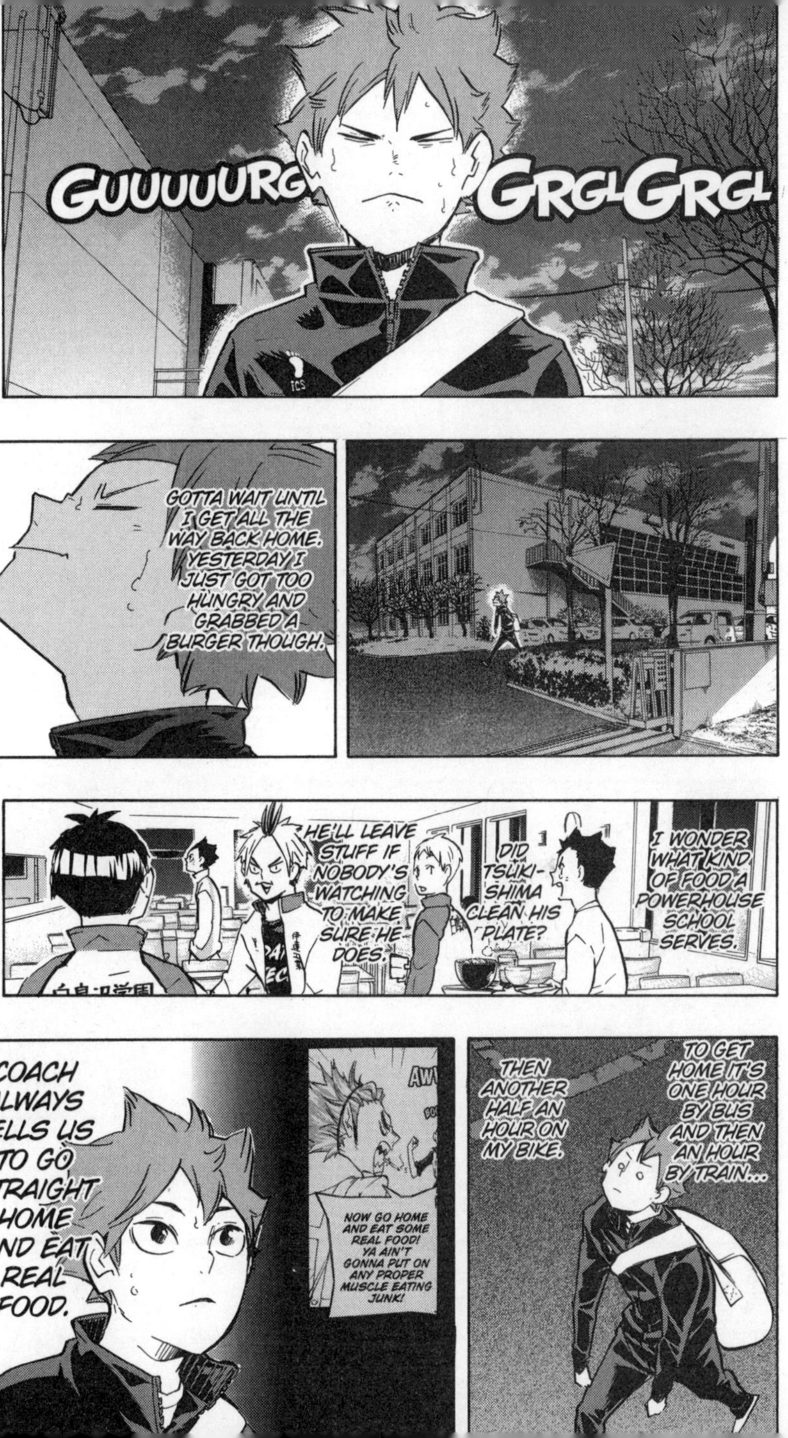
GRGL GRGL
GUUUUURG
GOTTA WAIT UNTIL I GET ALL THE WAY BACK HOME. YESTERDAY I JUST GOT TOO HUNGRY AND GRABBED A BURGER THOUGH.
I WONDER WHAT KIND OF FOOD A POWERHOUSE SCHOOL SERVES.
DID TSUKISHIMA CLEAN HIS PLATE?
HE'LL LEAVE STUFF IF NOBODY'S WATCHING TO MAKE SURE HE DOES.
TO GET HOME IT'S ONE HOUR BY BUS AND THEN AN HOUR BY TRAIN...
THEN ANOTHER HALF AN HOUR ON MY BIKE.
COACH ALWAYS TELLS US TO GO STRAIGHT HOME AND EAT REAL FOOD.
NOW GO HOME AND EAT SOME REAL FOOD! YA AIN'T GONNA PUT ON ANY PROPER MUSCLE EATING JUNK!

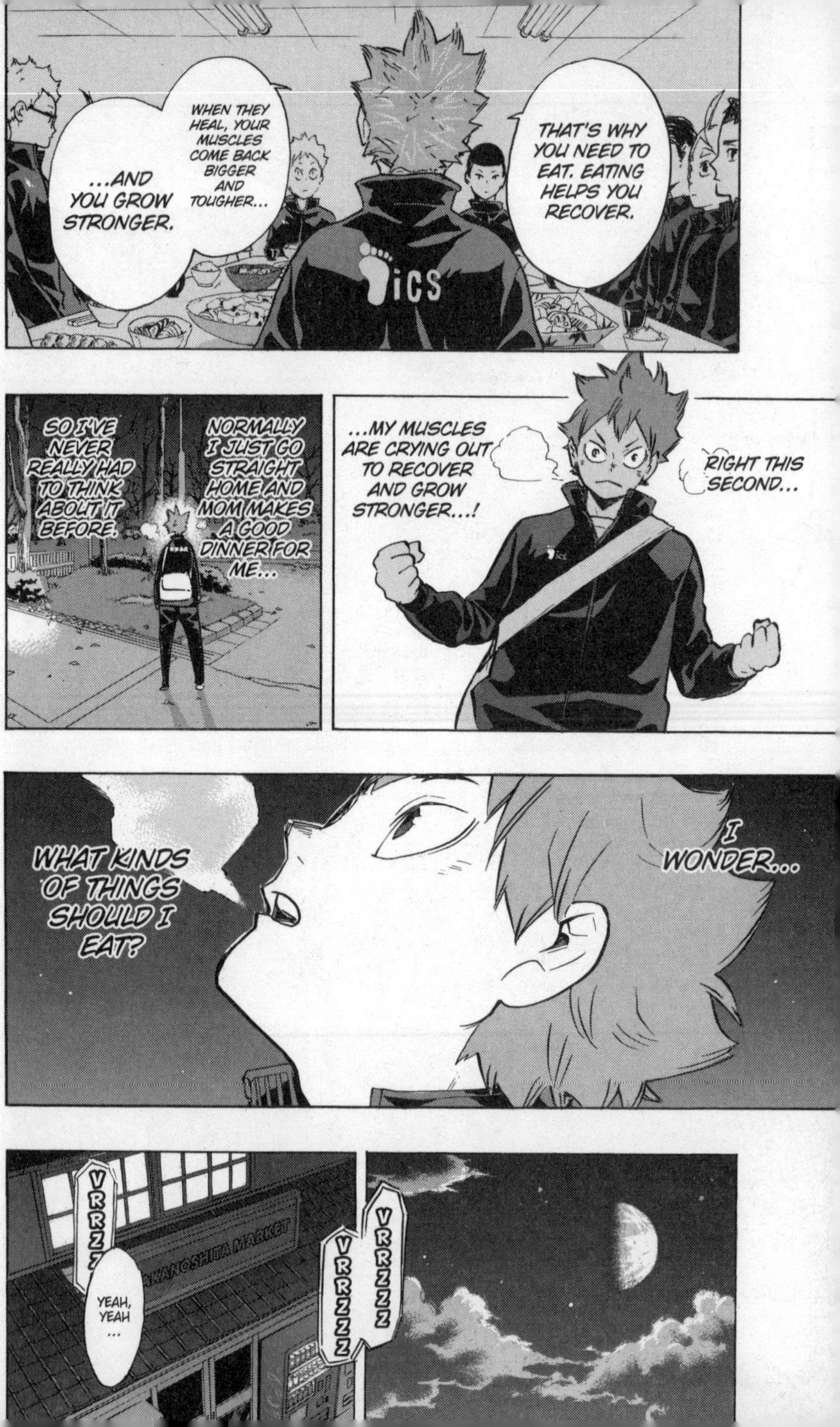
THAT'S WHY YOU NEED TO EAT. EATING HELPS YOU RECOVER.
WHEN THEY HEAL, YOUR MUSCLES COME BACK BIGGER AND TOUGHER...
...AND YOU GROW STRONGER.
RIGHT THIS SECOND...
...MY MUSCLES ARE CRYING OUT TO RECOVER AND GROW STRONGER...!
NORMALLY I JUST GO STRAIGHT HOME AND MOM MAKES A GOOD DINNER FOR ME...
SO I'VE NEVER REALLY HAD TO THINK ABOUT IT BEFORE.
I WONDER...
WHAT KINDS OF THINGS SHOULD I EAT?
VRRZZZ
VRRZZZ
VRRZZ
KANOSHITA MARKET
YEAH, YEAH ...

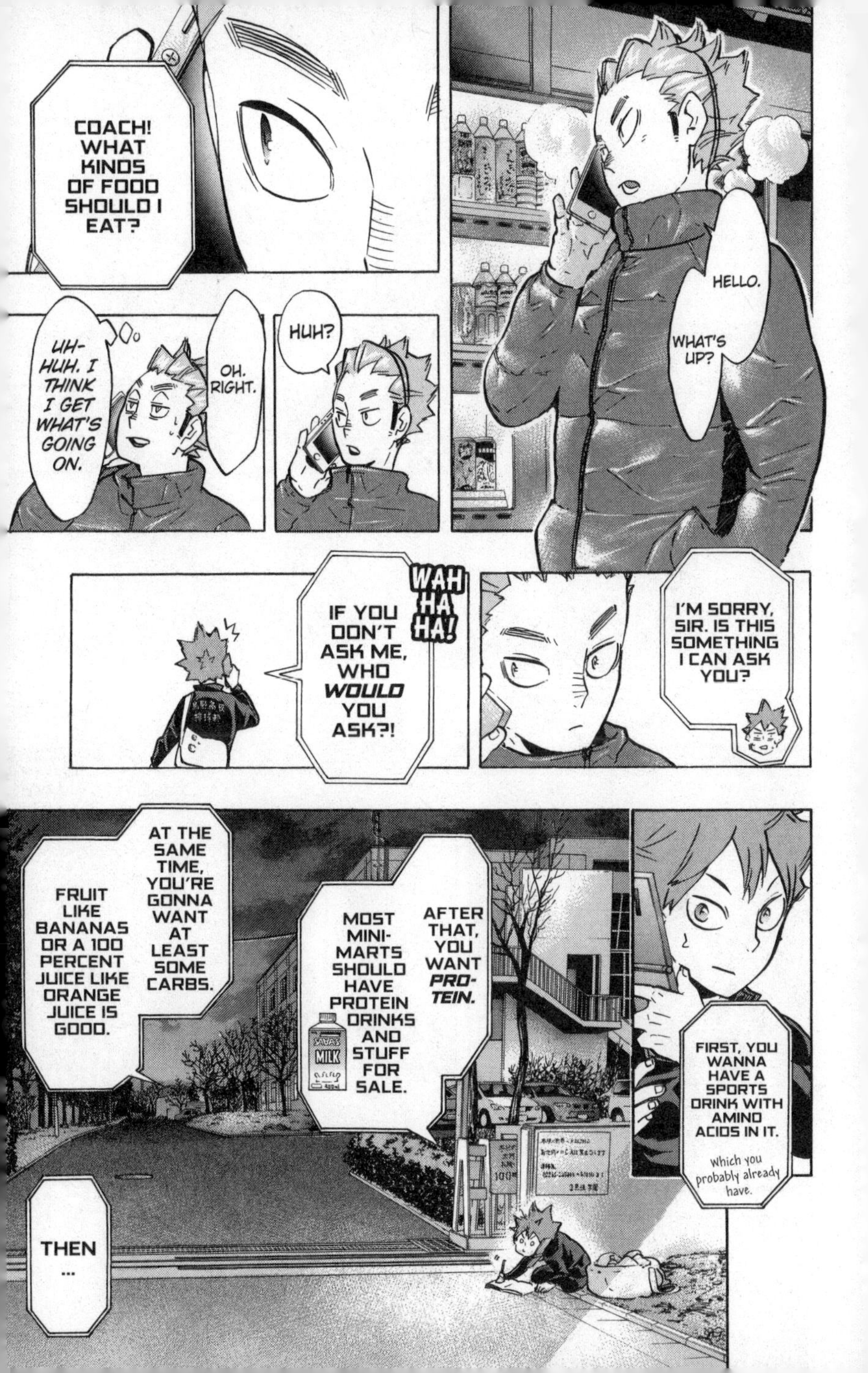
HELLO.
WHAT'S UP?
COACH! WHAT KINDS OF FOOD SHOULD I EAT?
HUH?
OH. RIGHT.
UH-HUH. I THINK I GET WHAT'S GOING ON.
I'M SORRY, SIR. IS THIS SOMETHING I CAN ASK YOU?
WAH HA HA!
IF YOU DON'T ASK ME, WHO *WOULD* YOU ASK?!
FIRST, YOU WANNA HAVE A SPORTS DRINK WITH AMINO ACIDS IN IT.
Which you probably already have.
AFTER THAT, YOU WANT *PROTEIN.*
MOST MINI-MARTS SHOULD HAVE PROTEIN DRINKS AND STUFF FOR SALE.
SAVAS
MILK
AT THE SAME TIME, YOU'RE GONNA WANT AT LEAST SOME CARBS.
FRUIT LIKE BANANAS OR A 100 PERCENT JUICE LIKE ORANGE JUICE IS GOOD.
THEN...

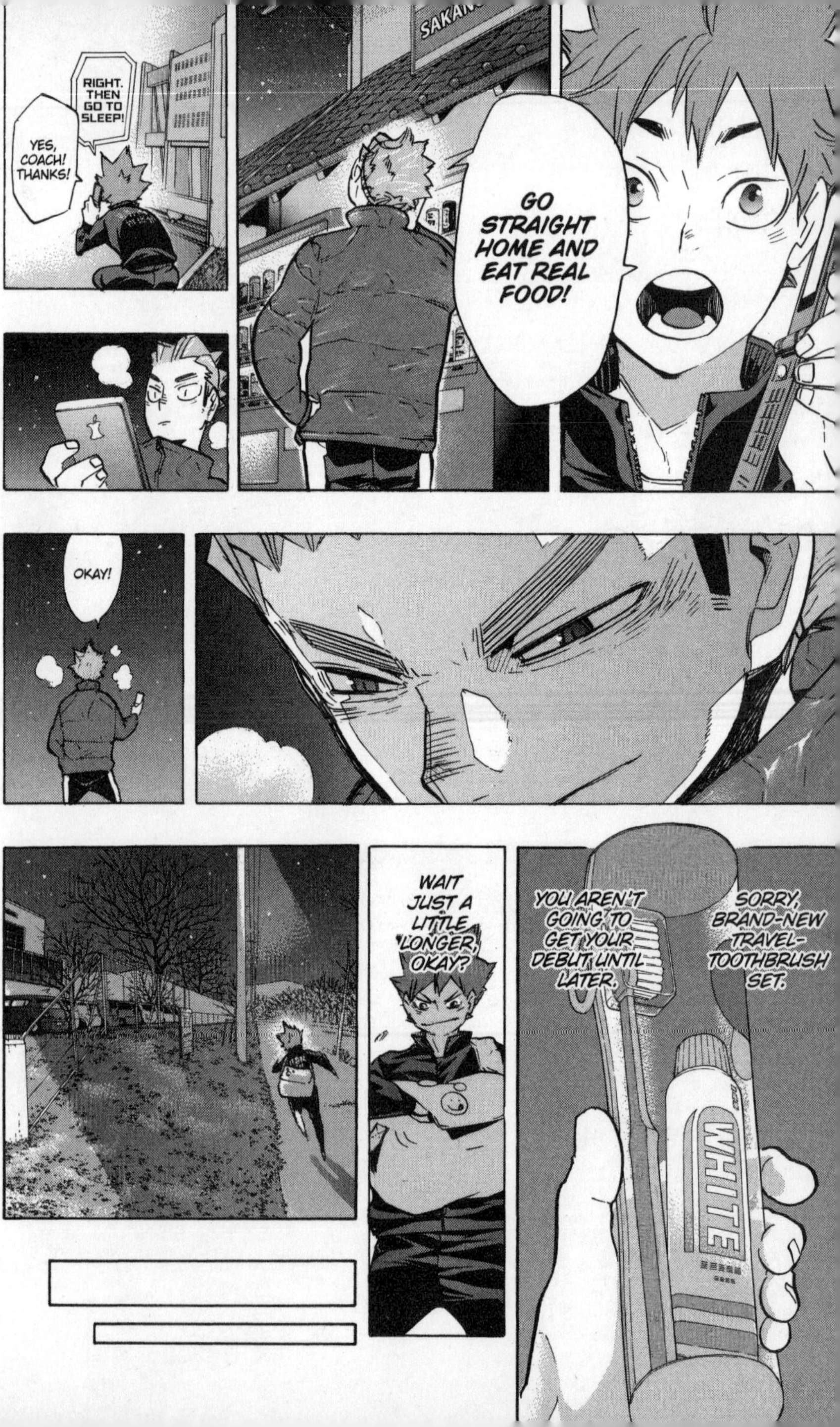
GO STRAIGHT HOME AND EAT REAL FOOD!
RIGHT. THEN GO TO SLEEP!
YES, COACH! THANKS!
OKAY!
SORRY, BRAND-NEW TRAVEL-TOOTHBRUSH SET.
YOU AREN'T GOING TO GET YOUR DEBUT UNTIL LATER.
WHITE
WAIT JUST A LITTLE LONGER, OKAY?

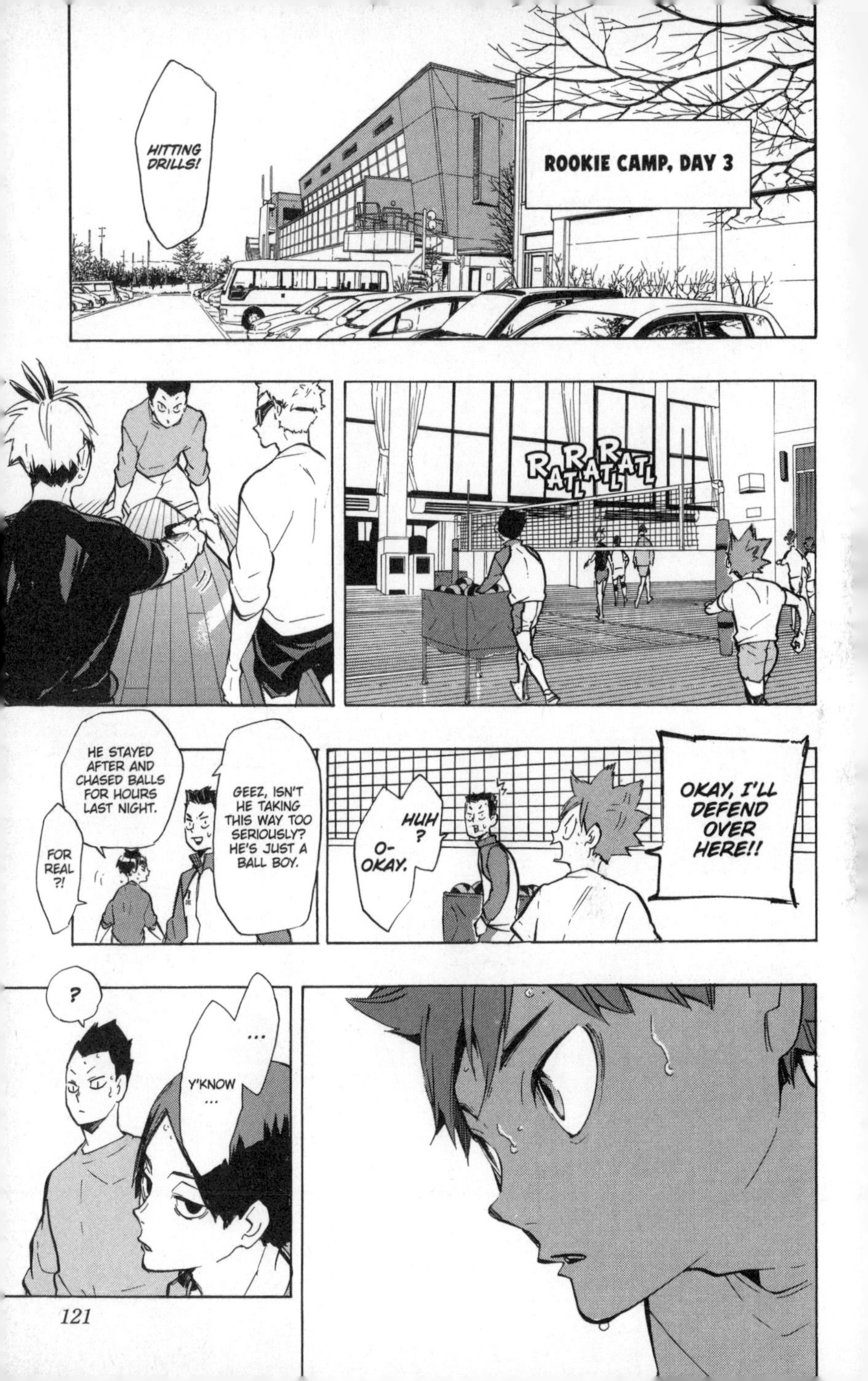
ROOKIE CAMP, DAY 3
HITTING DRILLS!
RATLRATLRATL
OKAY, I'LL DEFEND OVER HERE!!
HUH?
O-OKAY.
GEEZ, ISN'T HE TAKING THIS WAY TOO SERIOUSLY? HE'S JUST A BALL BOY.
HE STAYED AFTER AND CHASED BALLS FOR HOURS LAST NIGHT.
FOR REAL?!
...
Y'KNOW ...
?

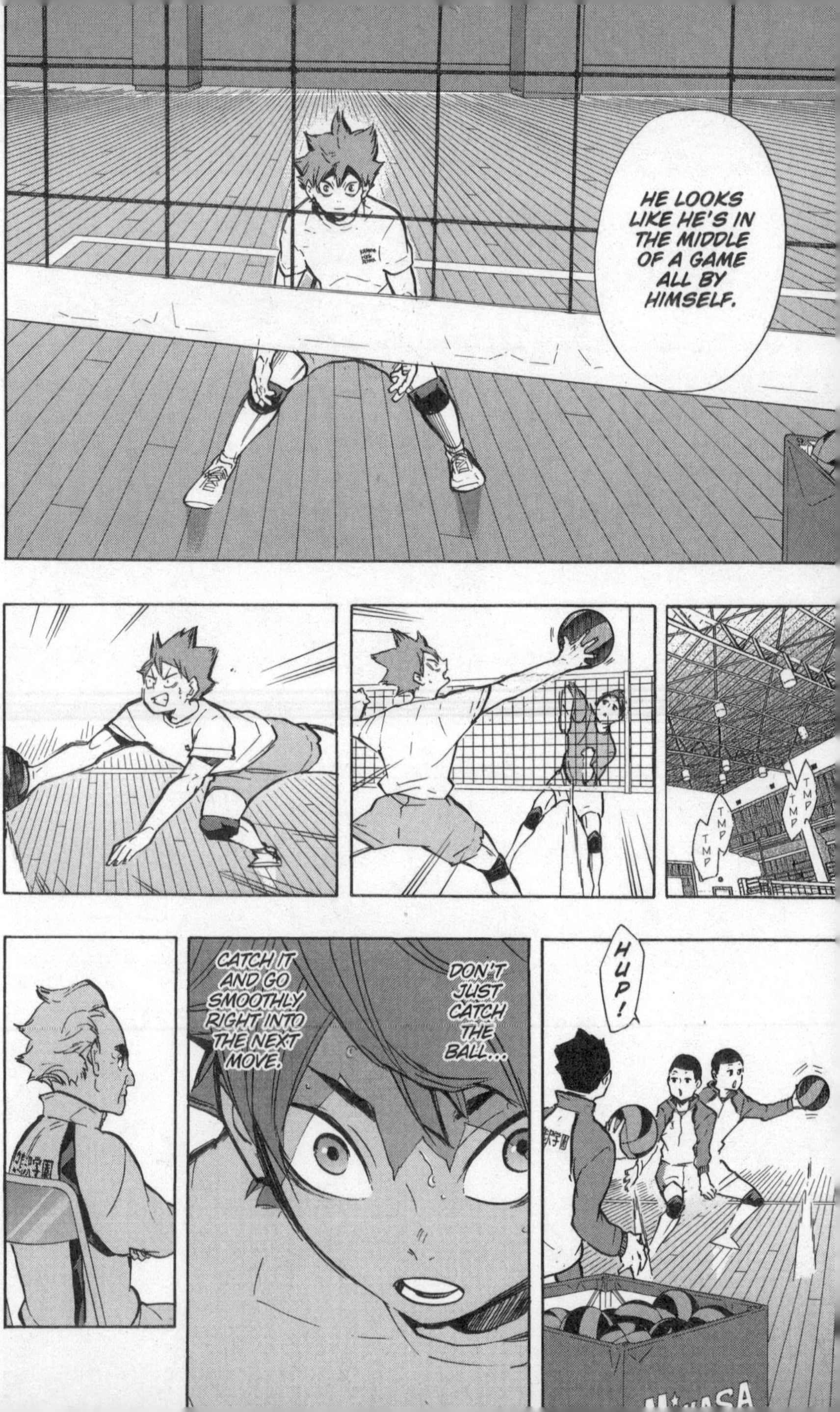
HE LOOKS LIKE HE'S IN THE MIDDLE OF A GAME ALL BY HIMSELF.
TMP TMP
TMP TMP
HUP!
DON'T JUST CATCH THE BALL...
CATCH IT AND GO SMOOTHLY RIGHT INTO THE NEXT MOVE.

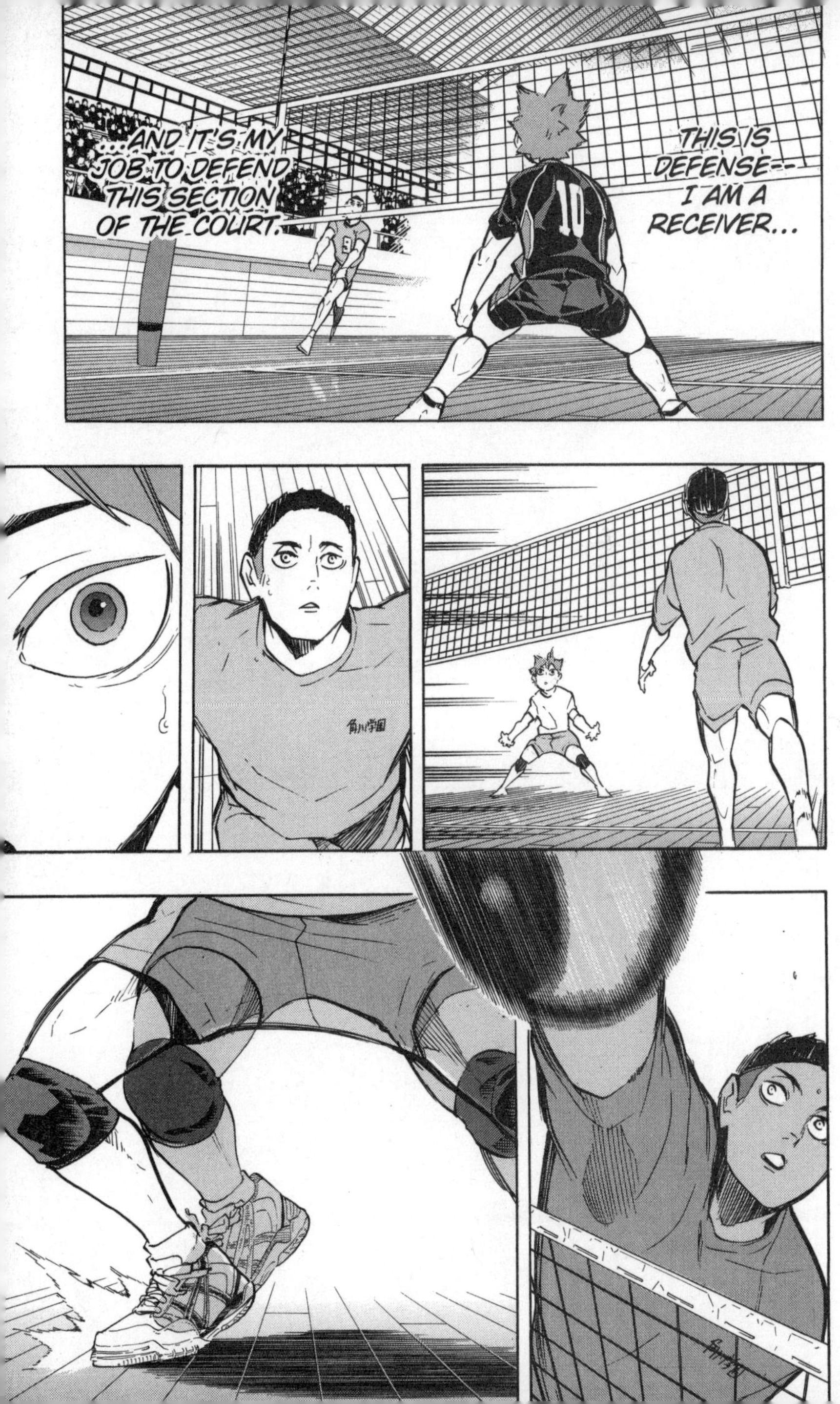
THIS IS DEFENSE-- I AM A RECEIVER...
...AND IT'S MY JOB TO DEFEND THIS SECTION OF THE COURT.

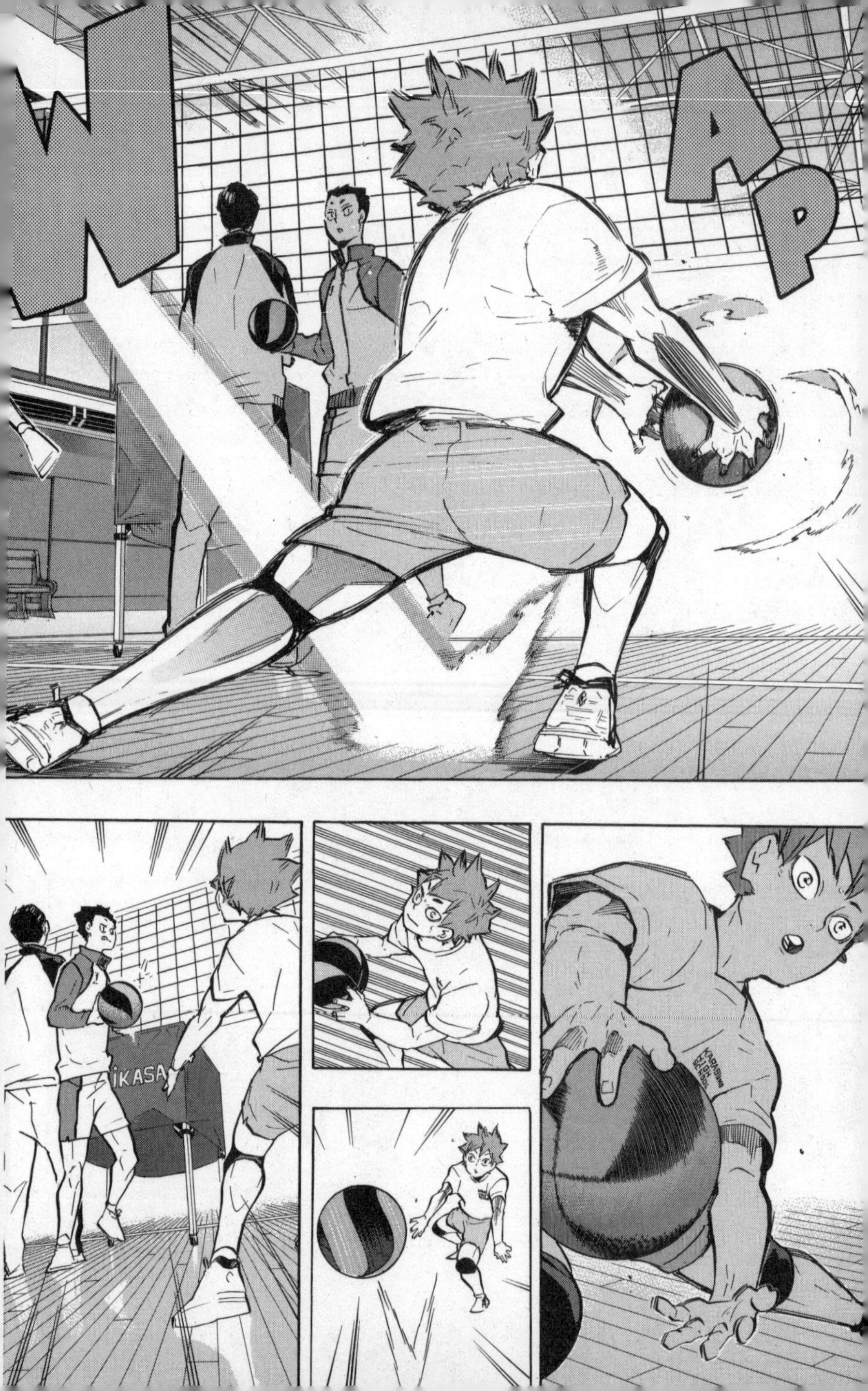
WAP
IKASA

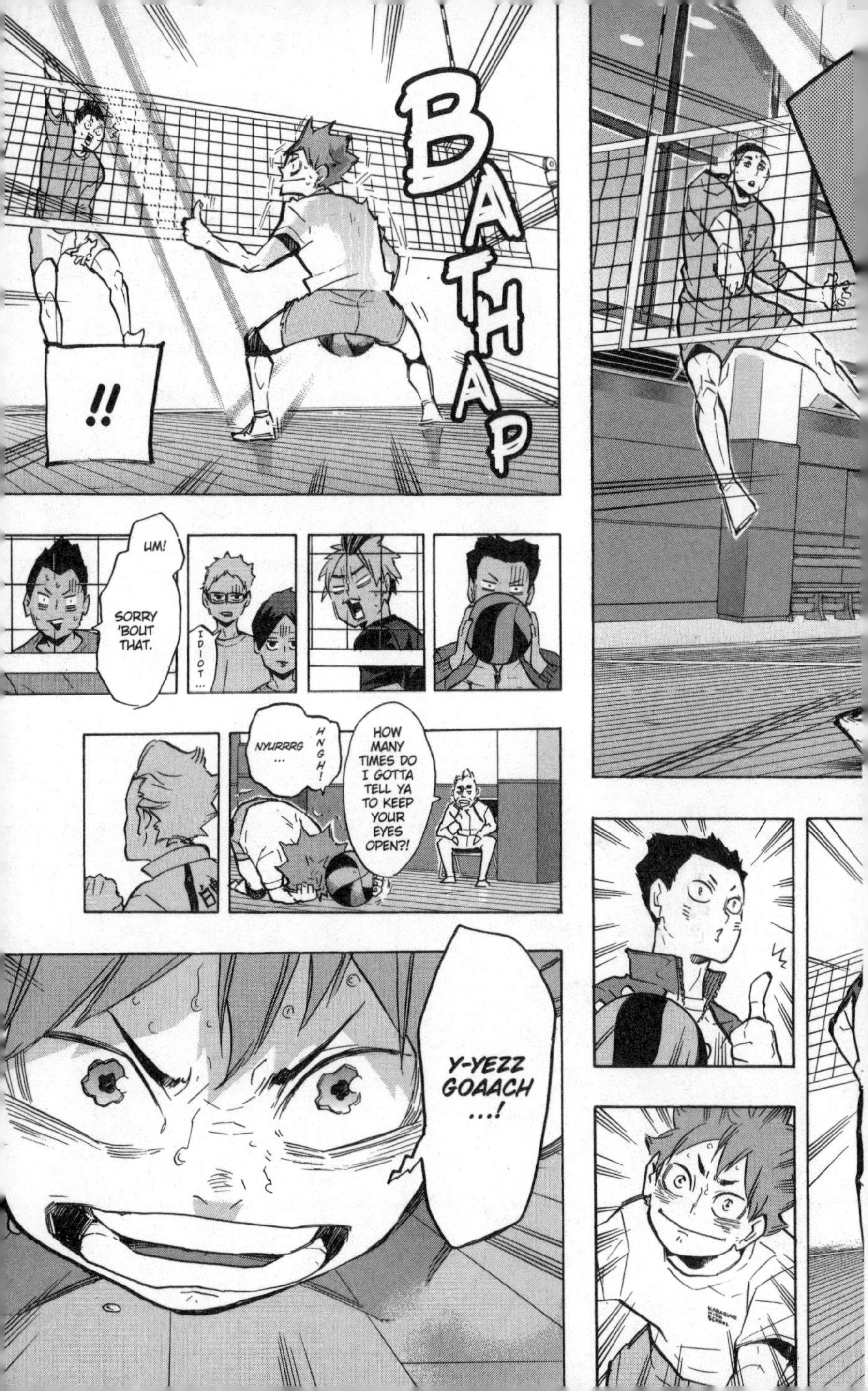

BATHAP
!!
IDIOT...
UM!
SORRY 'BOUT THAT.
HOW MANY TIMES DO I GOTTA TELL YA TO KEEP YOUR EYES OPEN?!
HNGH!
NYURRRG...
Y-YEZZ GOAACH...!

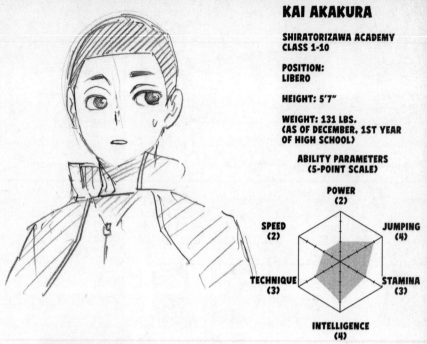

KAI AKAKURA

**SHIRATORIZAWA ACADEMY
CLASS 1-10**

**POSITION:
LIBERO**

HEIGHT: 5'7"

**WEIGHT: 131 LBS.
(AS OF DECEMBER, 1ST YEAR
OF HIGH SCHOOL)**

**ABILITY PARAMETERS
(5-POINT SCALE)**

POWER
(2)

SPEED
(2)

JUMPING
(4)

TECHNIQUE
(3)

STAMINA
(3)

INTELLIGENCE
(4)

YUSHO SAGAE

**SHIRATORIZAWA ACADEMY
CLASS 1-4**

**POSITION:
WING SPIKER**

HEIGHT: 5'10"

**WEIGHT: 139 LBS.
(AS OF DECEMBER, 1ST YEAR
OF HIGH SCHOOL)**

**ABILITY PARAMETERS
(5-POINT SCALE)**

POWER
(3)

SPEED
(3)

JUMPING
(3)

TECHNIQUE
(3)

STAMINA
(2)

INTELLIGENCE
(2)

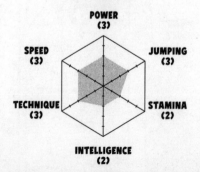

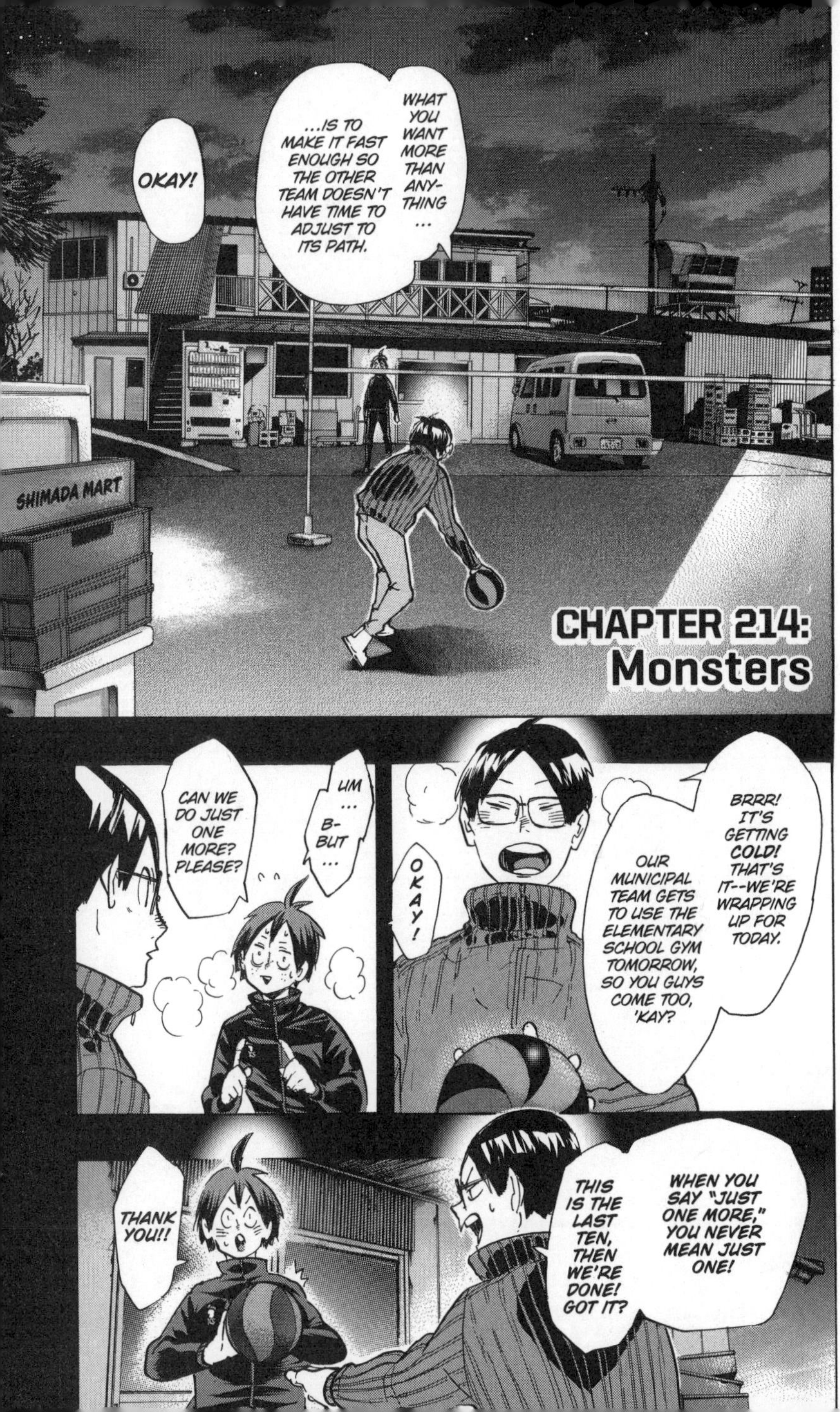
WHAT YOU WANT MORE THAN ANYTHING...
...IS TO MAKE IT FAST ENOUGH SO THE OTHER TEAM DOESN'T HAVE TIME TO ADJUST TO ITS PATH.
OKAY!
SHIMADA MART
CHAPTER 214: Monsters
BRRR! IT'S GETTING COLD! THAT'S IT--WE'RE WRAPPING UP FOR TODAY.
OUR MUNICIPAL TEAM GETS TO USE THE ELEMENTARY SCHOOL GYM TOMORROW, SO YOU GUYS COME TOO, 'KAY?
OKAY!
UM... B-BUT...
CAN WE DO JUST ONE MORE? PLEASE?
WHEN YOU SAY "JUST ONE MORE," YOU NEVER MEAN JUST ONE!
THIS IS THE LAST TEN, THEN WE'RE DONE! GOT IT?
THANK YOU!!

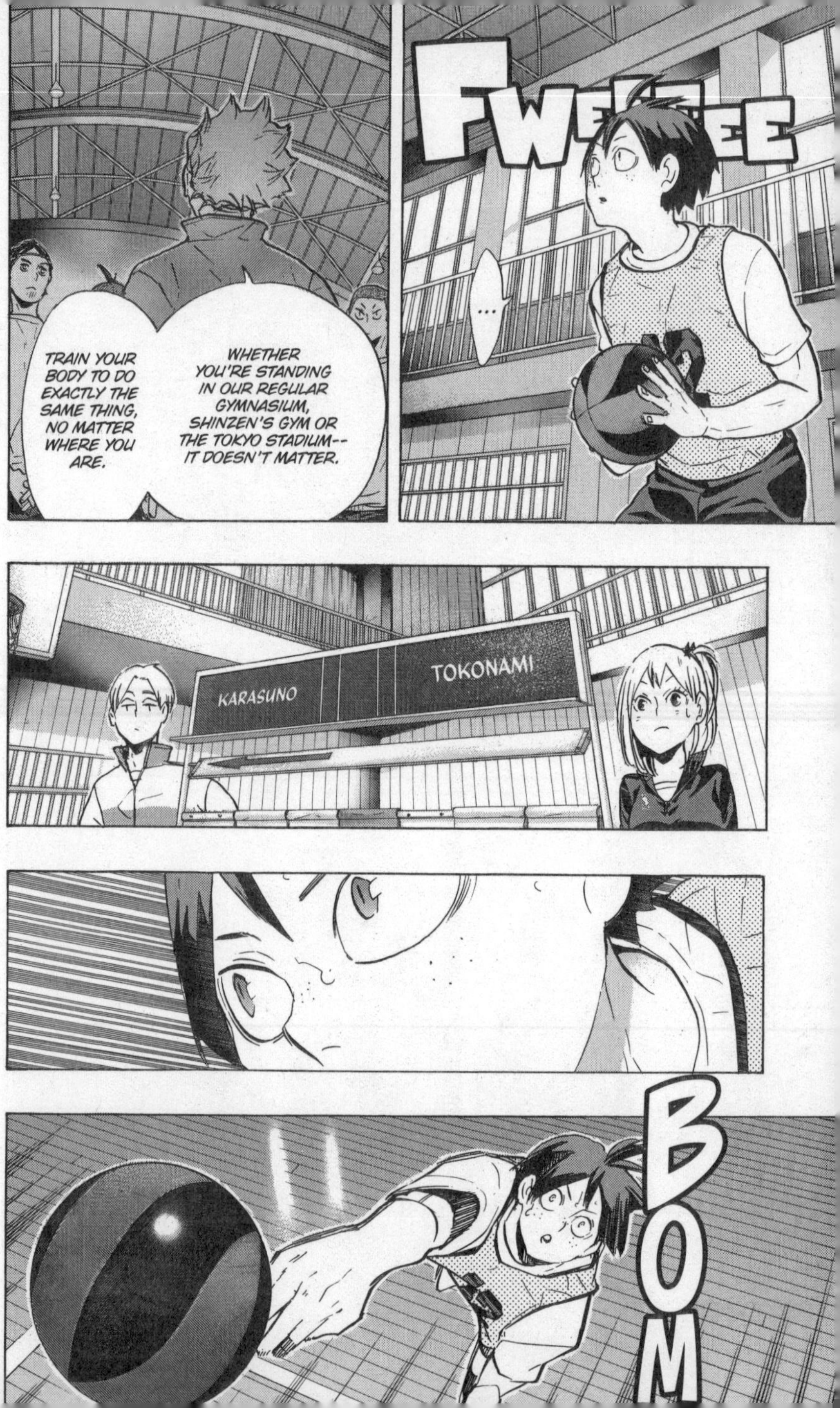
FWEEEE
...
WHETHER YOU'RE STANDING IN OUR REGULAR GYMNASIUM, SHINZEN'S GYM OR THE TOKYO STADIUM-- IT DOESN'T MATTER.
TRAIN YOUR BODY TO DO EXACTLY THE SAME THING, NO MATTER WHERE YOU ARE.
TOKONAMI
KARASUNO
BOOM

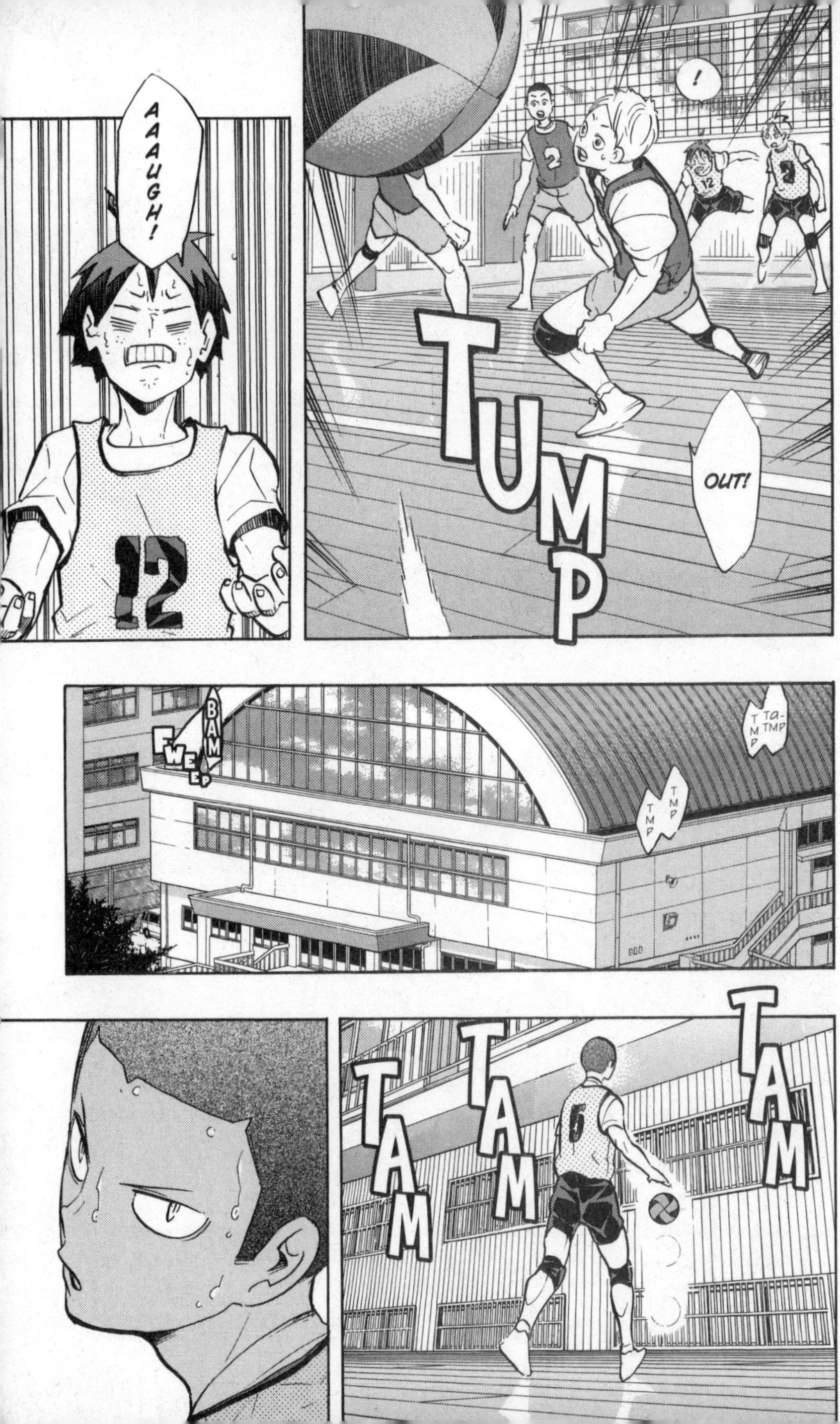
!
TUMP
OUT!
AAAUGH!
TMP TA-TMP
TMP TMP
FWEEP
BAM
TAM TAM TAM

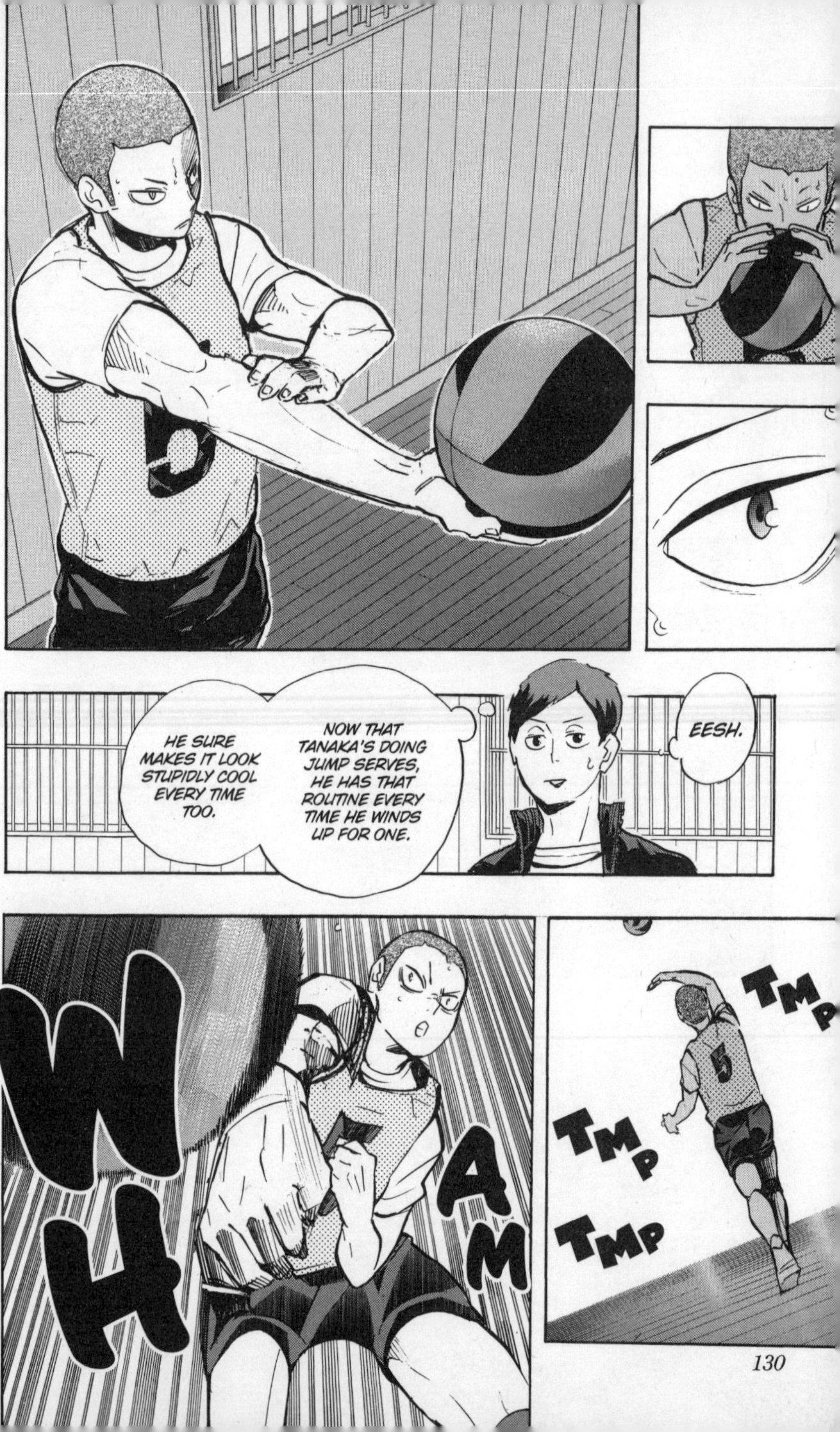
EESH.
NOW THAT TANAKA'S DOING JUMP SERVES, HE HAS THAT ROUTINE EVERY TIME HE WINDS UP FOR ONE.
HE SURE MAKES IT LOOK STUPIDLY COOL EVERY TIME TOO.
TMP
TMP
TMP
WHAM

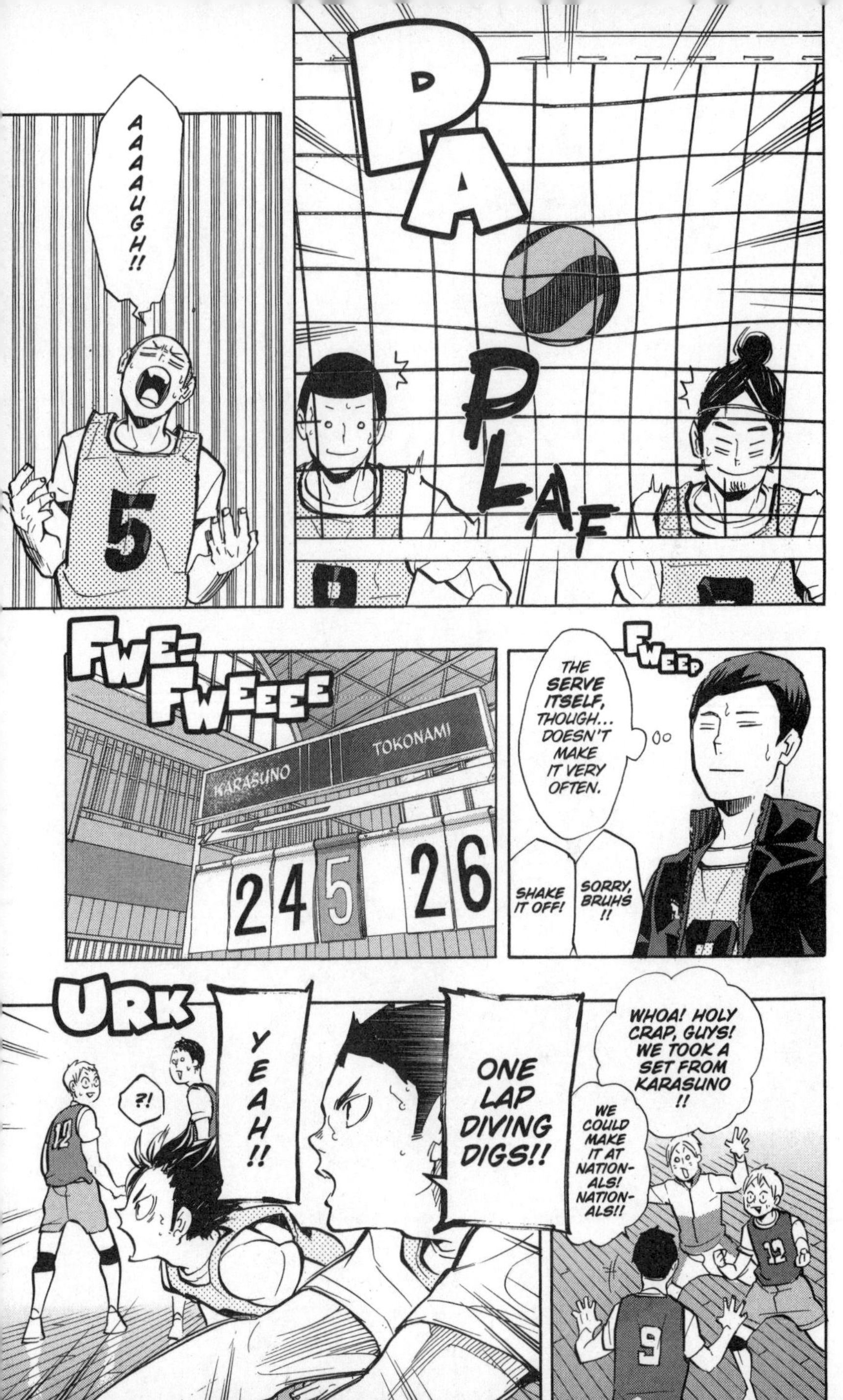
PA
PLAF
AAAAAUGH!!
FWEEP
THE SERVE ITSELF, THOUGH... DOESN'T MAKE IT VERY OFTEN.
SORRY, BRUHS !!
SHAKE IT OFF!
FWE-FWEEEE
TOKONAMI
KARASUNO
24 5 26
WHOA! HOLY CRAP, GUYS! WE TOOK A SET FROM KARASUNO !!
WE COULD MAKE IT AT NATION-ALS! NATION-ALS!!
ONE LAP DIVING DIGS!!
YEAH!!
URK
?!

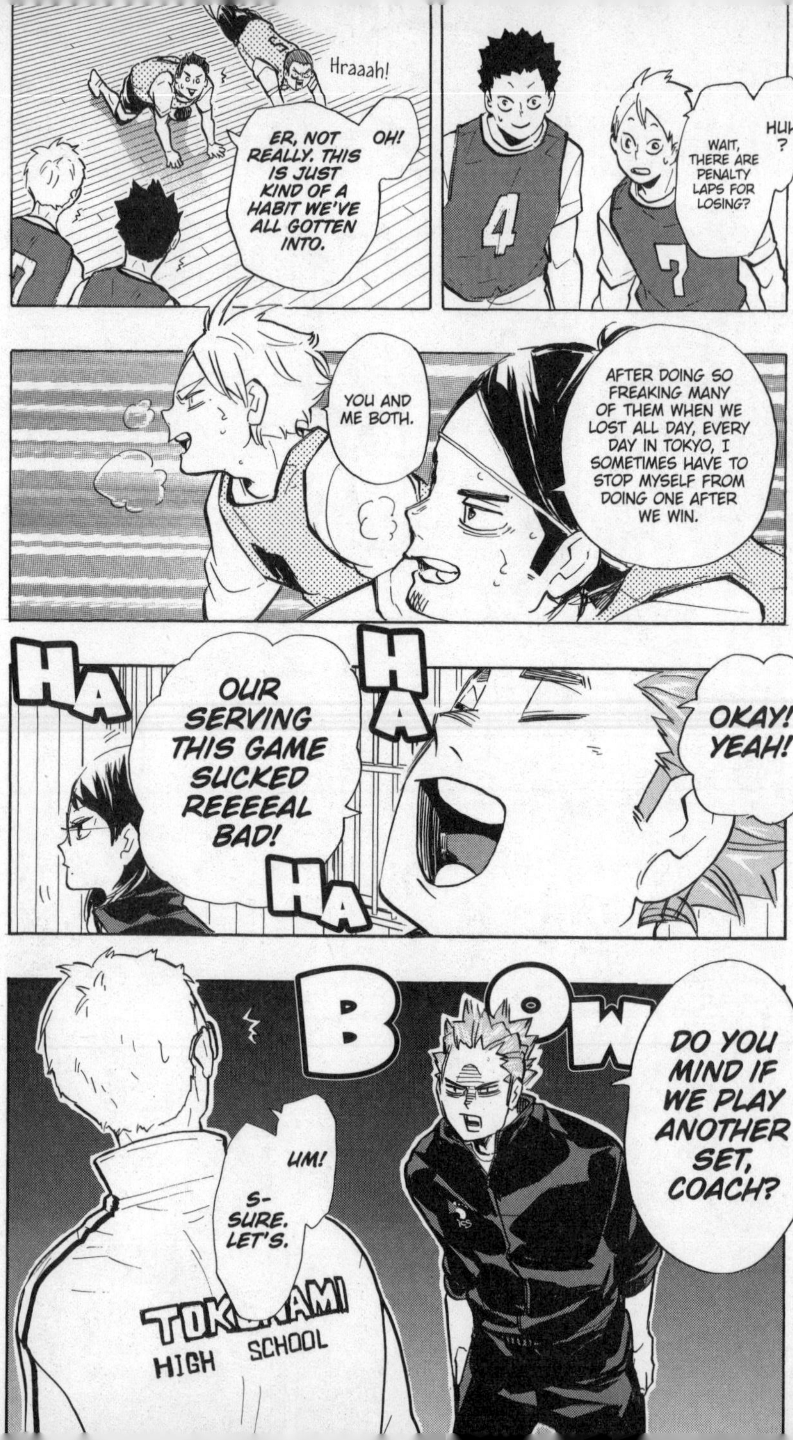
HUH?
WAIT, THERE ARE PENALTY LAPS FOR LOSING?
Hraaah!
OH!
ER, NOT REALLY. THIS IS JUST KIND OF A HABIT WE'VE ALL GOTTEN INTO.
AFTER DOING SO FREAKING MANY OF THEM WHEN WE LOST ALL DAY, EVERY DAY IN TOKYO, I SOMETIMES HAVE TO STOP MYSELF FROM DOING ONE AFTER WE WIN.
YOU AND ME BOTH.
OKAY! YEAH!
HA
HA
OUR SERVING THIS GAME SUCKED REEEEAL BAD!
HA
BOW
DO YOU MIND IF WE PLAY ANOTHER SET, COACH?
UM!
S-SURE. LET'S.
HIGH SCHOOL

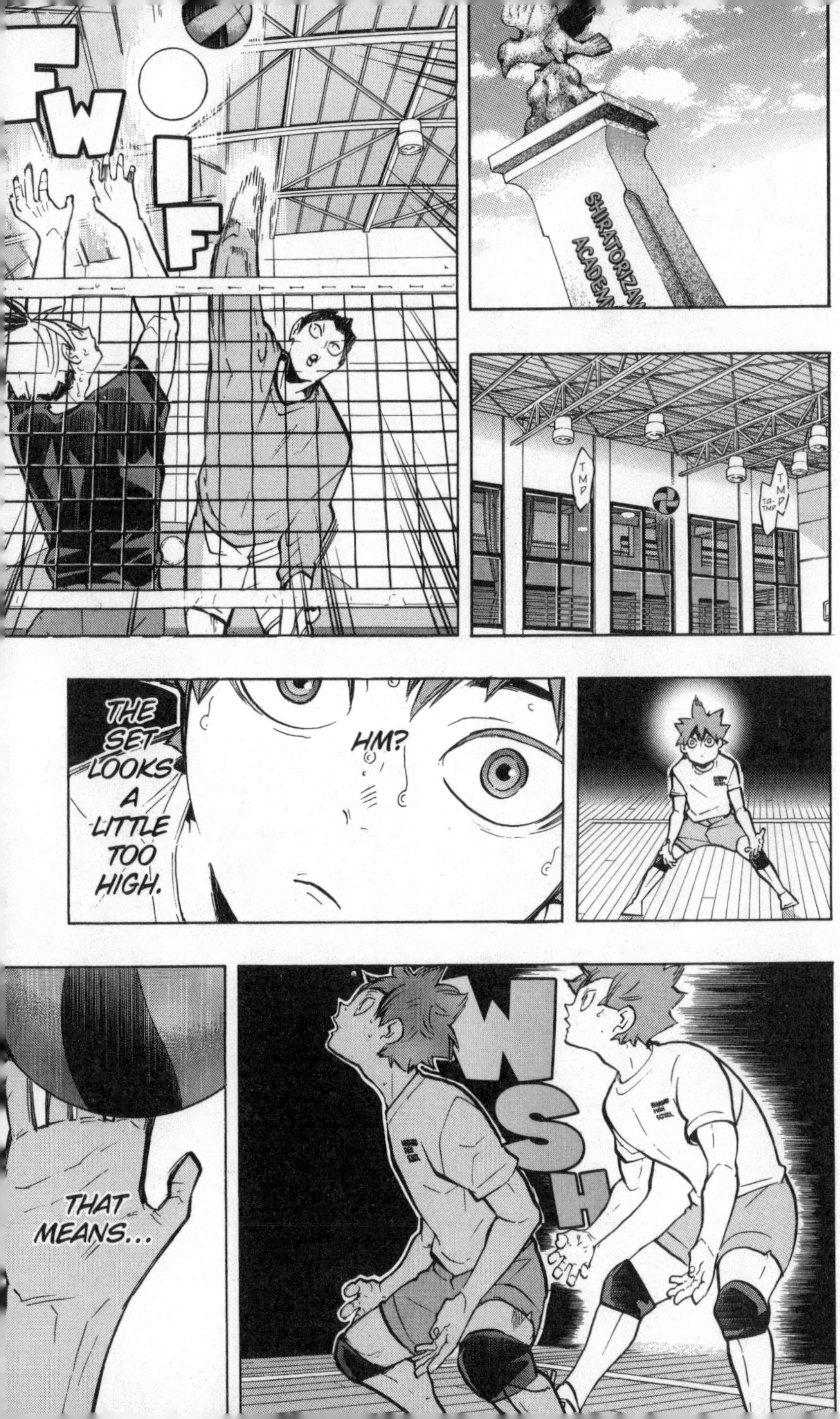
SHIRATORIZAW
ACADEM
TMP
TA-TMP TMP
FWIF
HM?
THE SET LOOKS A LITTLE TOO HIGH.
WSH
THAT MEANS...

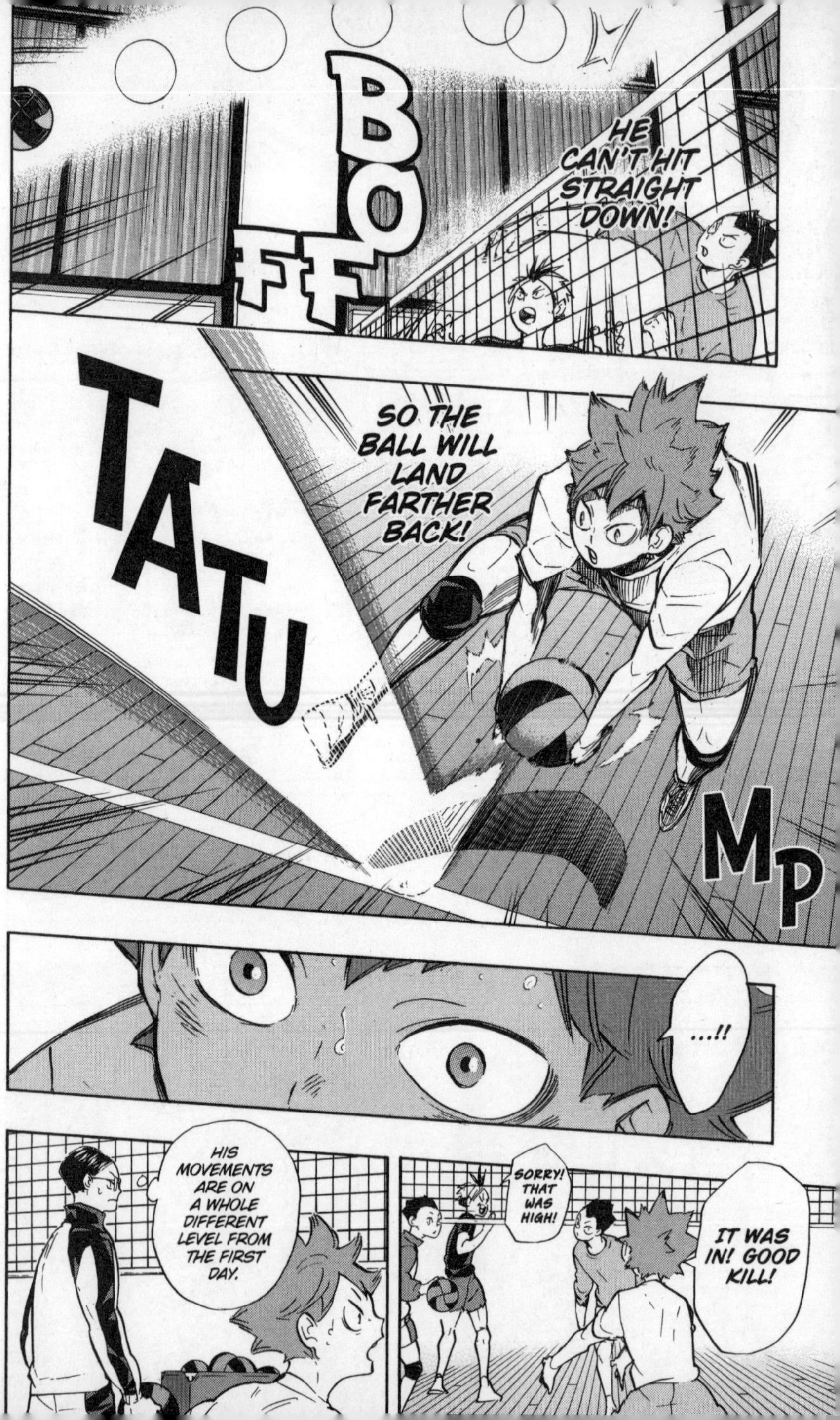
BOFF
HE CAN'T HIT STRAIGHT DOWN!
SO THE BALL WILL LAND FARTHER BACK!
TATUMP
...!!
SORRY! THAT WAS HIGH!
IT WAS IN! GOOD KILL!
HIS MOVEMENTS ARE ON A WHOLE DIFFERENT LEVEL FROM THE FIRST DAY.

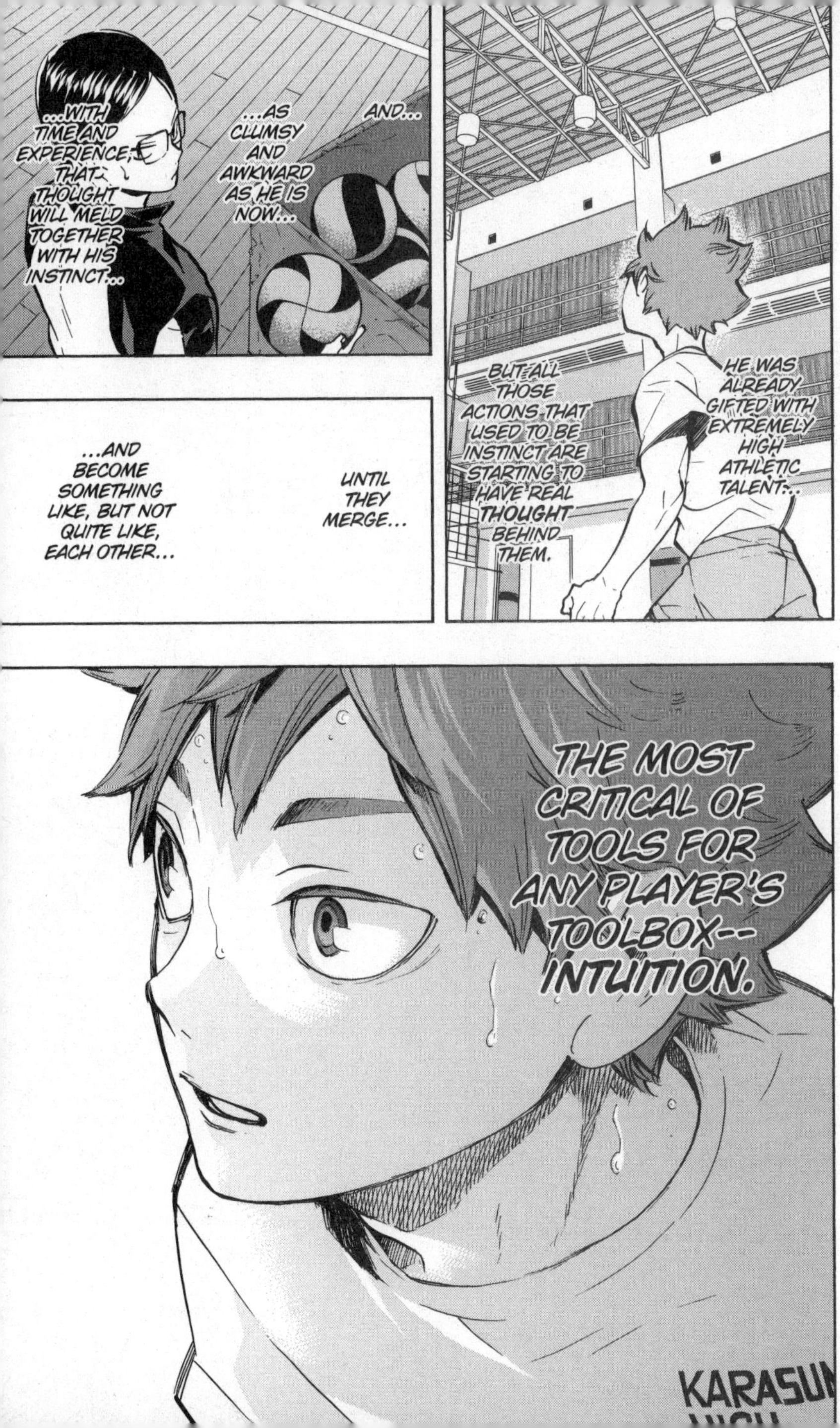
HE WAS ALREADY GIFTED WITH EXTREMELY HIGH ATHLETIC TALENT...
BUT ALL THOSE ACTIONS THAT USED TO BE INSTINCT ARE STARTING TO HAVE REAL THOUGHT BEHIND THEM.
AND...
...AS CLUMSY AND AWKWARD AS HE IS NOW...
...WITH TIME AND EXPERIENCE, THAT THOUGHT WILL MELD TOGETHER WITH HIS INSTINCT...
UNTIL THEY MERGE...
...AND BECOME SOMETHING LIKE, BUT NOT QUITE LIKE, EACH OTHER...
THE MOST CRITICAL OF TOOLS FOR ANY PLAYER'S TOOLBOX-- INTUITION.
KARASUN

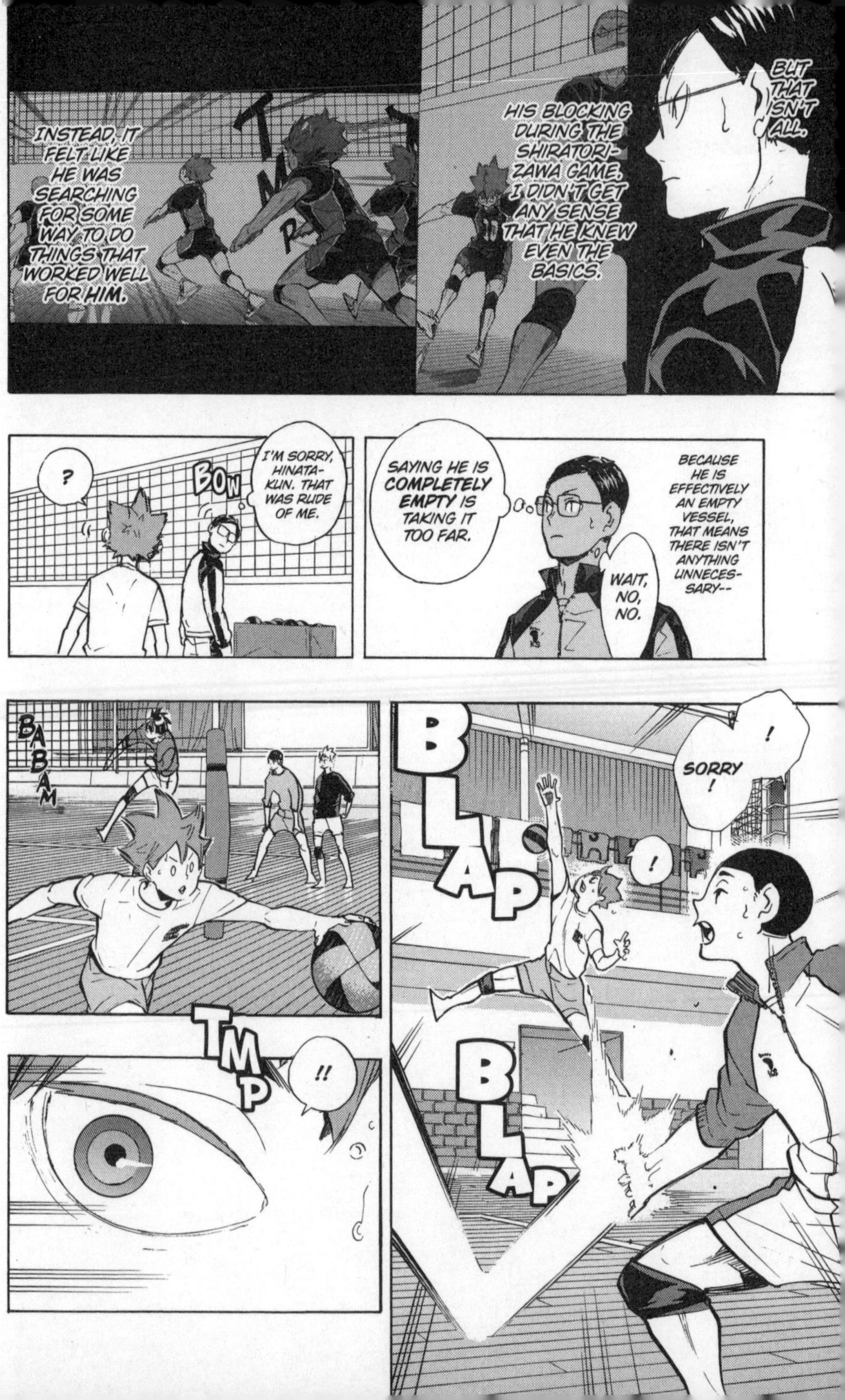
BUT THAT ISN'T ALL.
HIS BLOCKING DURING THE SHIRATORI-ZAWA GAME, I DIDN'T GET ANY SENSE THAT HE KNEW EVEN THE BASICS.
INSTEAD, IT FELT LIKE HE WAS SEARCHING FOR SOME WAY TO DO THINGS THAT WORKED WELL FOR HIM.
BECAUSE HE IS EFFECTIVELY AN EMPTY VESSEL, THAT MEANS THERE ISN'T ANYTHING UNNECES-SARY--
WAIT, NO, NO.
SAYING HE IS COMPLETELY EMPTY IS TAKING IT TOO FAR.
I'M SORRY, HINATA-KUN. THAT WAS RUDE OF ME.
BOW
?
!
SORRY!
BLAP
!
BLAP
BABAM
TMP
!!

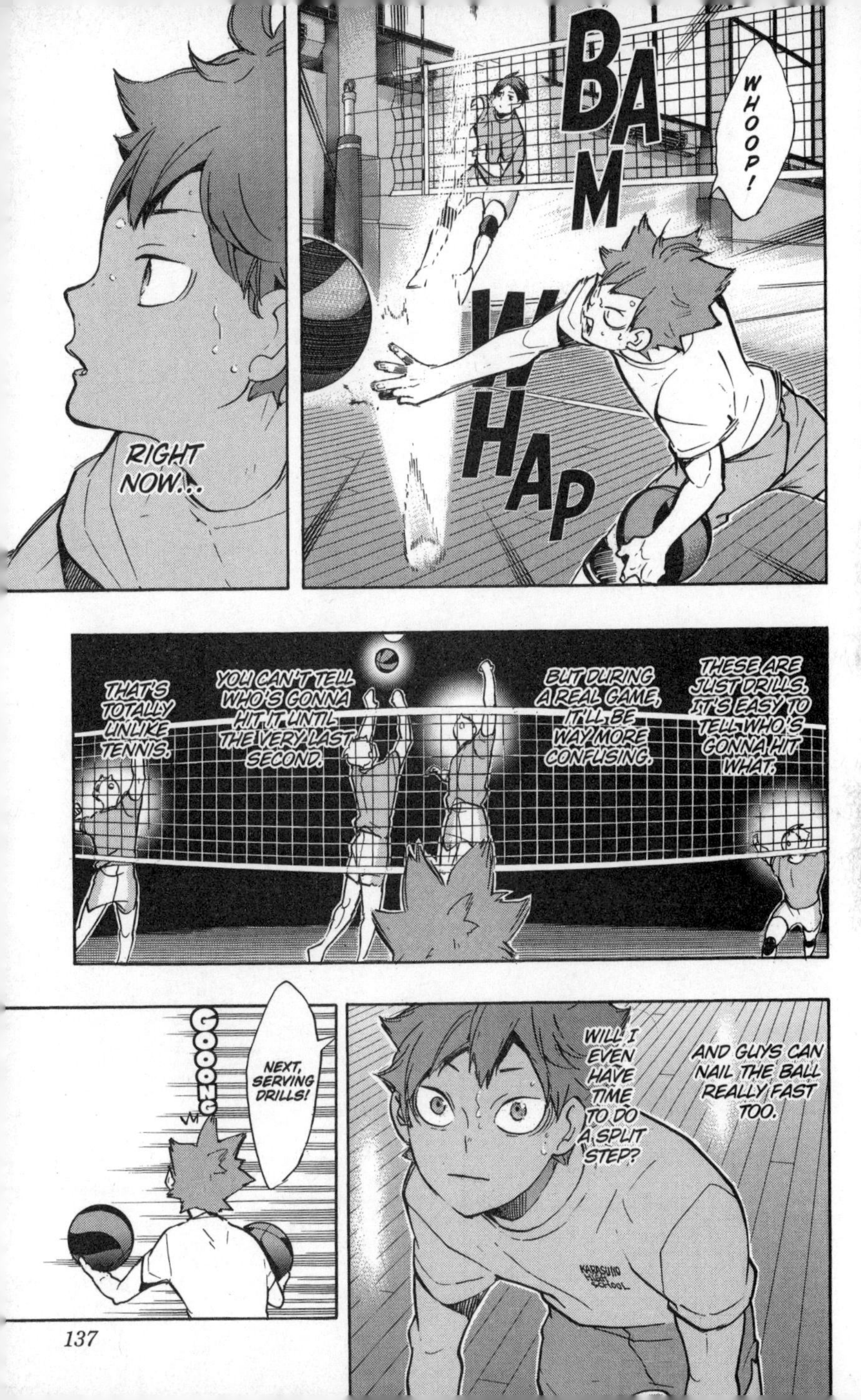
BAM
WHOOP!
WHAP
RIGHT NOW...
THESE ARE JUST DRILLS. IT'S EASY TO TELL WHO'S GONNA HIT WHAT.
BUT DURING A REAL GAME, IT'LL BE WAY MORE CONFUSING.
YOU CAN'T TELL WHO'S GONNA HIT IT UNTIL THE VERY LAST SECOND.
THAT'S TOTALLY UNLIKE TENNIS.
AND GUYS CAN NAIL THE BALL REALLY FAST TOO.
WILL I EVEN HAVE TIME TO DO A SPLIT STEP?
KARASUNO HIGH SCHOOL
NEXT, SERVING DRILLS!
GOOOONG

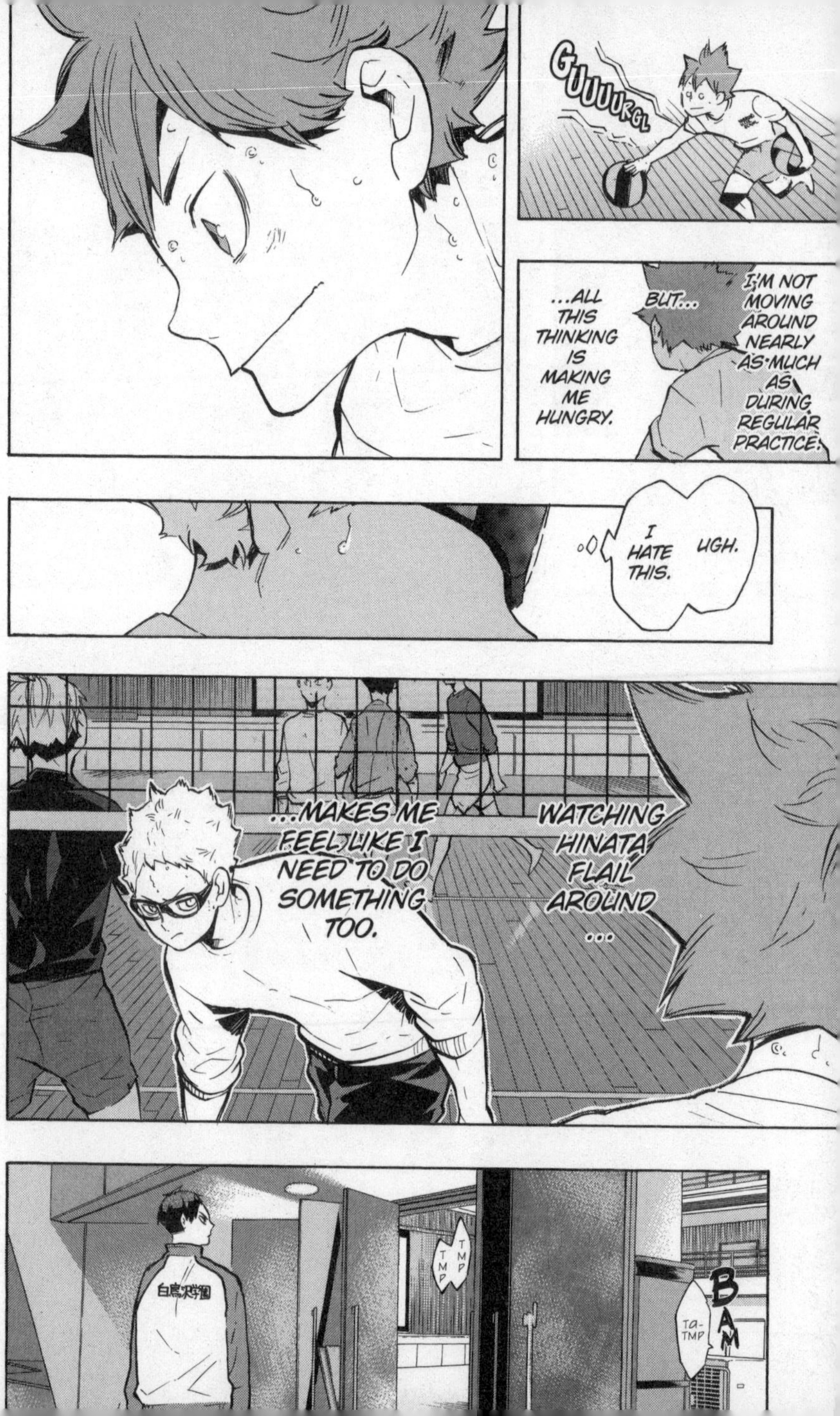
GUUUURGL
I'M NOT MOVING AROUND NEARLY AS MUCH AS DURING REGULAR PRACTICE.
BUT...
...ALL THIS THINKING IS MAKING ME HUNGRY.
UGH.
I HATE THIS.
WATCHING HINATA FLAIL AROUND...
...MAKES ME FEEL LIKE I NEED TO DO SOMETHING TOO.
BAM
TA-TMP
TMP TMP
白鳥沢学園

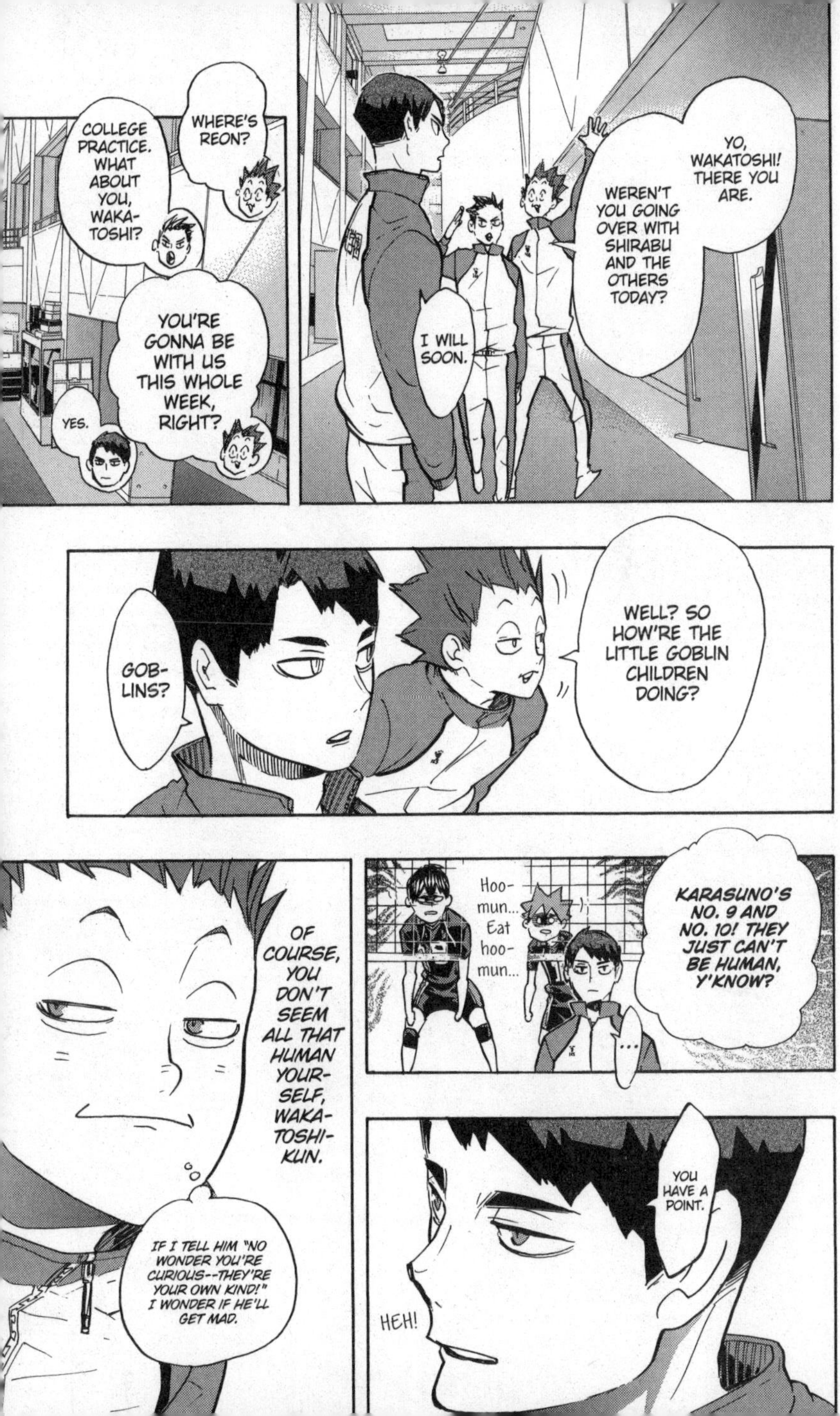
YO, WAKATOSHI! THERE YOU ARE.
WEREN'T YOU GOING OVER WITH SHIRABU AND THE OTHERS TODAY?
I WILL SOON.
WHERE'S REON?
COLLEGE PRACTICE. WHAT ABOUT YOU, WAKATOSHI?
YOU'RE GONNA BE WITH US THIS WHOLE WEEK, RIGHT?
YES.
WELL? SO HOW'RE THE LITTLE GOBLIN CHILDREN DOING?
GOB-LINS?
KARASUNO'S NO. 9 AND NO. 10! THEY JUST CAN'T BE HUMAN, Y'KNOW?
Hoo-mun... Eat hoo-mun...
...
YOU HAVE A POINT.
HEH!
OF COURSE, YOU DON'T SEEM ALL THAT HUMAN YOURSELF, WAKATOSHI-KUN.
IF I TELL HIM "NO WONDER YOU'RE CURIOUS--THEY'RE YOUR OWN KIND!" I WONDER IF HE'LL GET MAD.

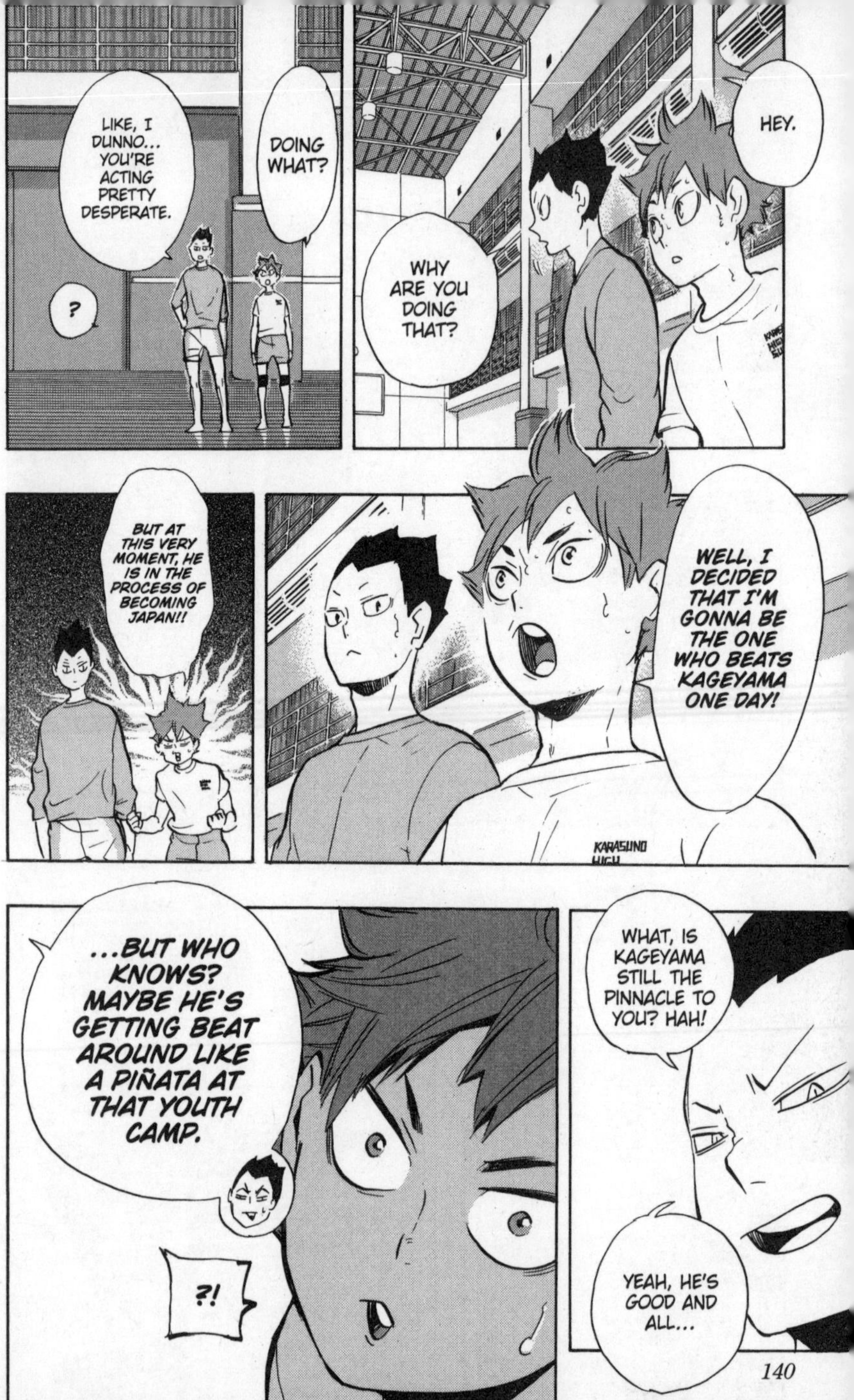
HEY.
WHY ARE YOU DOING THAT?
DOING WHAT?
LIKE, I DUNNO... YOU'RE ACTING PRETTY DESPERATE.
?
WELL, I DECIDED THAT I'M GONNA BE THE ONE WHO BEATS KAGEYAMA ONE DAY!
BUT AT THIS VERY MOMENT, HE IS IN THE PROCESS OF BECOMING JAPAN!!
WHAT, IS KAGEYAMA STILL THE PINNACLE TO YOU? HAH!
YEAH, HE'S GOOD AND ALL...
...BUT WHO KNOWS? MAYBE HE'S GETTING BEAT AROUND LIKE A PIÑATA AT THAT YOUTH CAMP.
?!

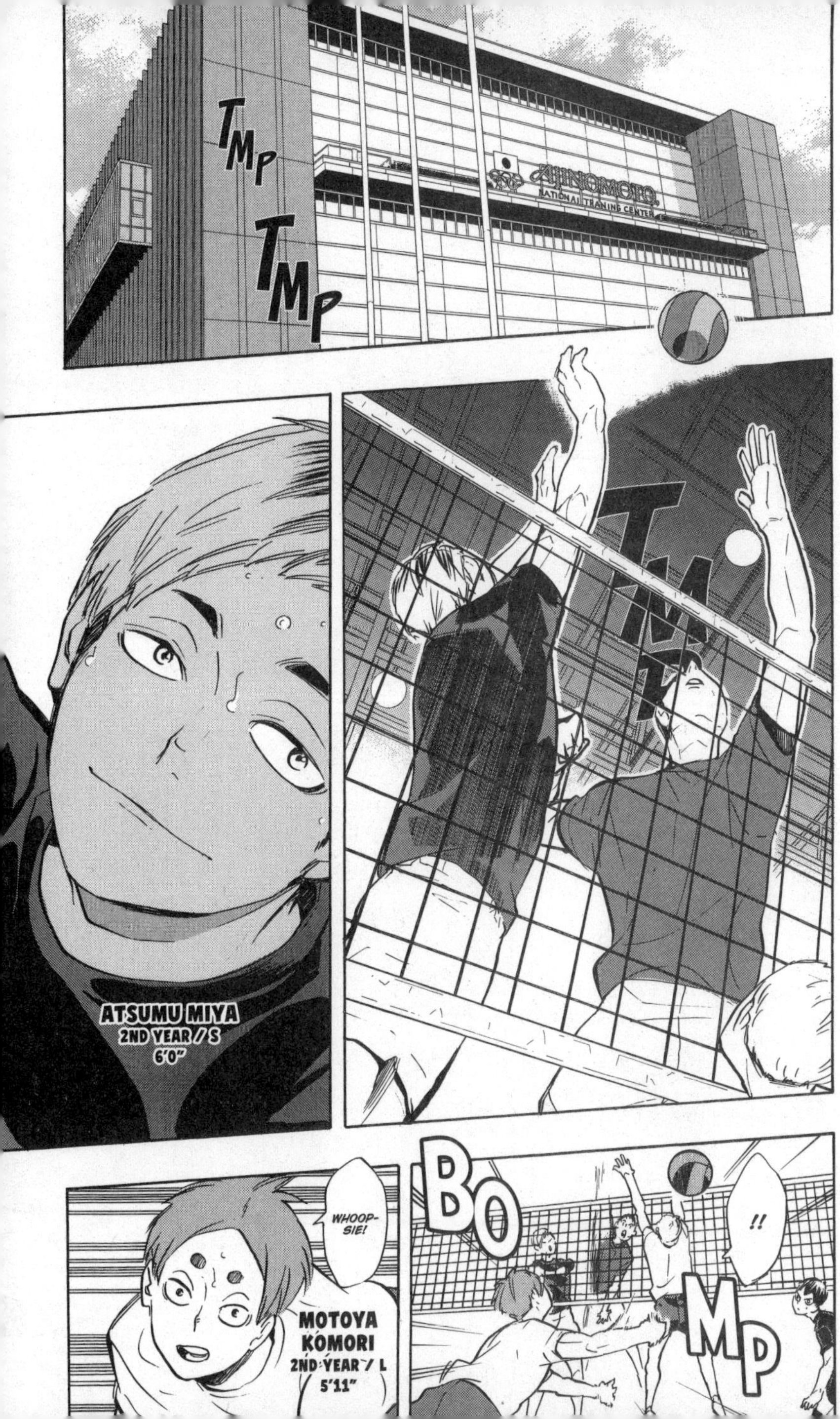
TMP TMP
AJINOMOTO
NATIONAL TRANING CENTER
TMP
ATSUMU MIYA
2ND YEAR / S
6'0"
BOMP
!!
WHOOP-SIE!
MOTOYA KOMORI
2ND YEAR / L
5'11"

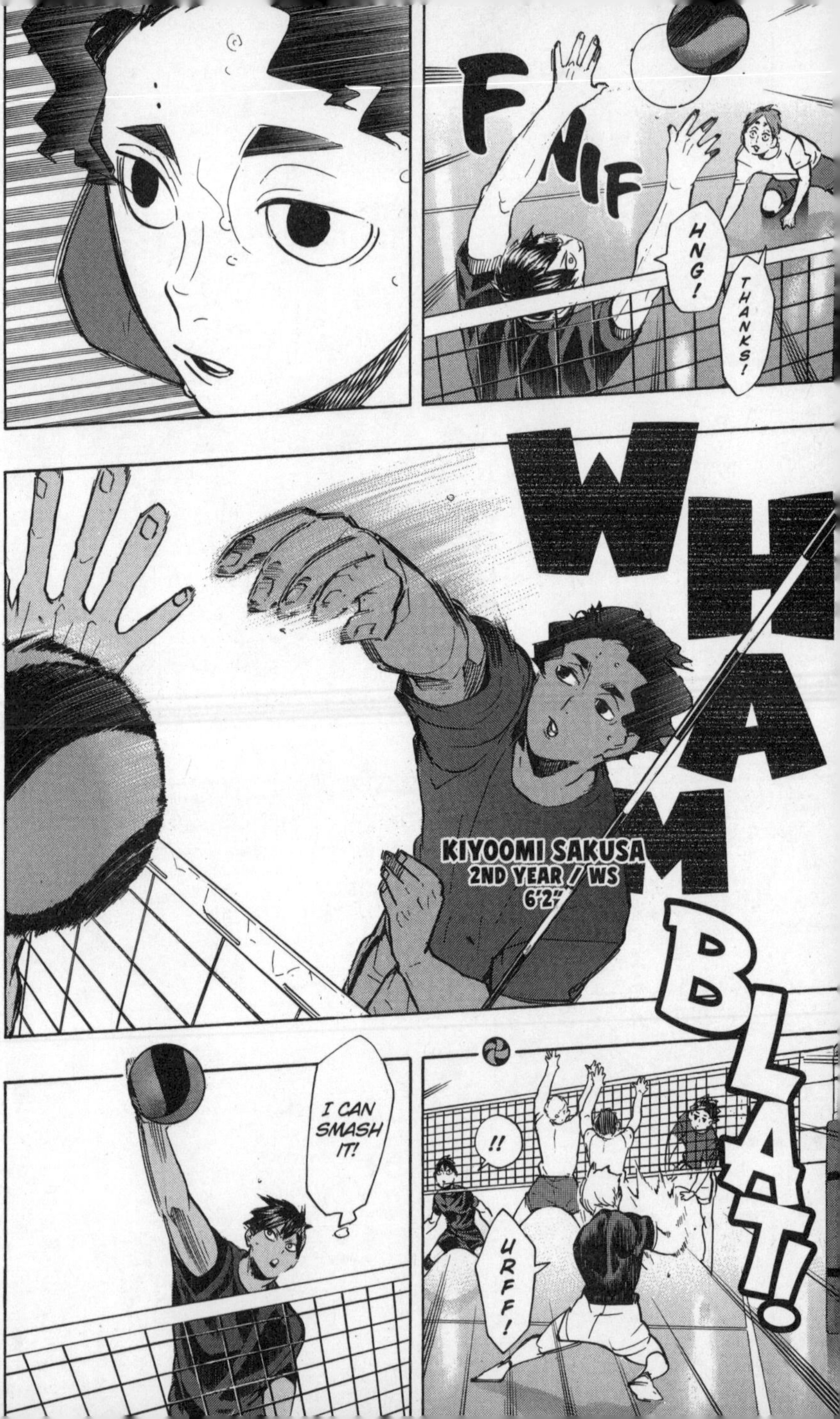
FNIF
HNG!
THANKS!
WHAM
KIYOOMI SAKUSA
2ND YEAR / WS
6'2"
!!
URFF!
BLAT!
I CAN SMASH IT!

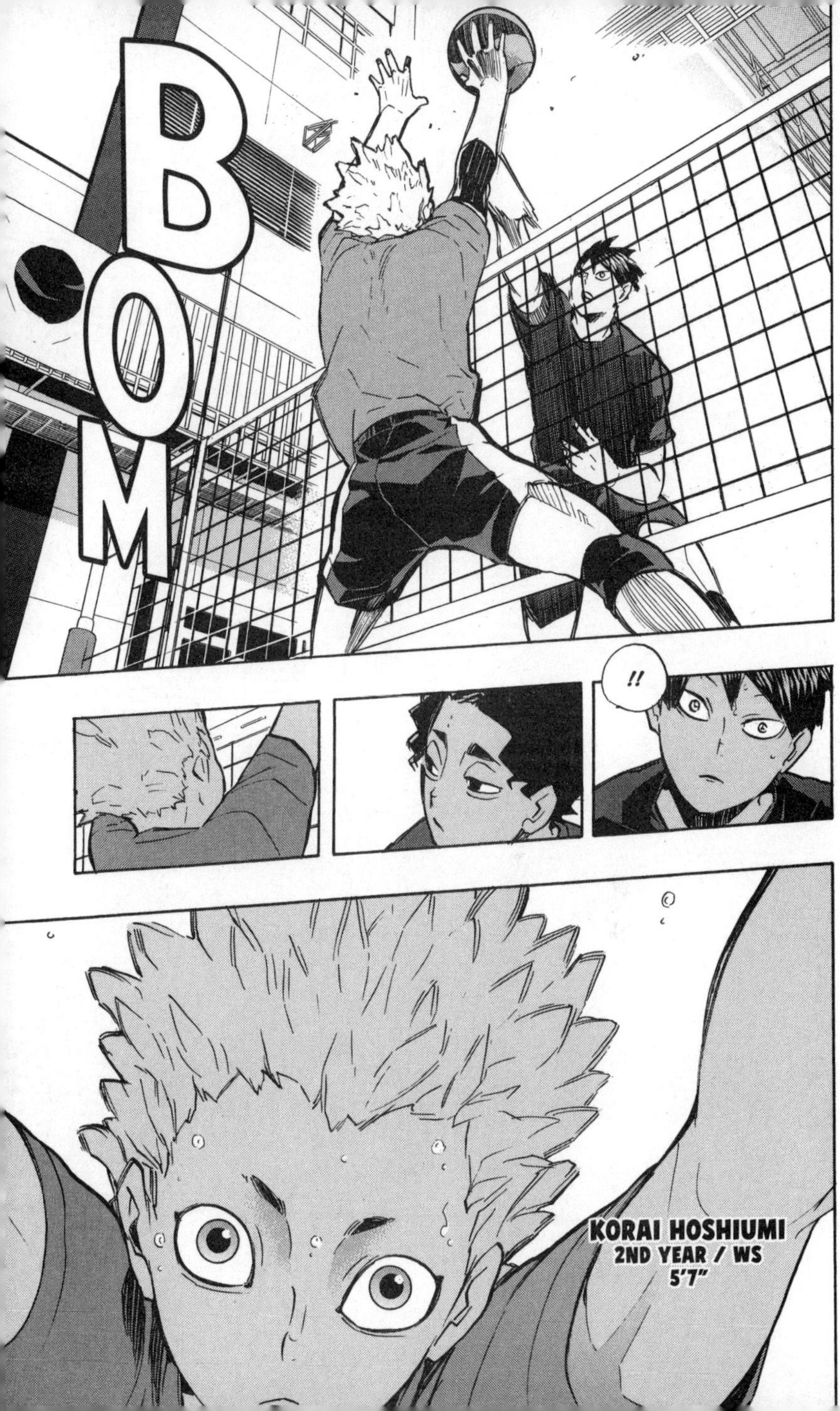
BOOM
!!
KORAI HOSHIUMI
2ND YEAR / WS
5'7"

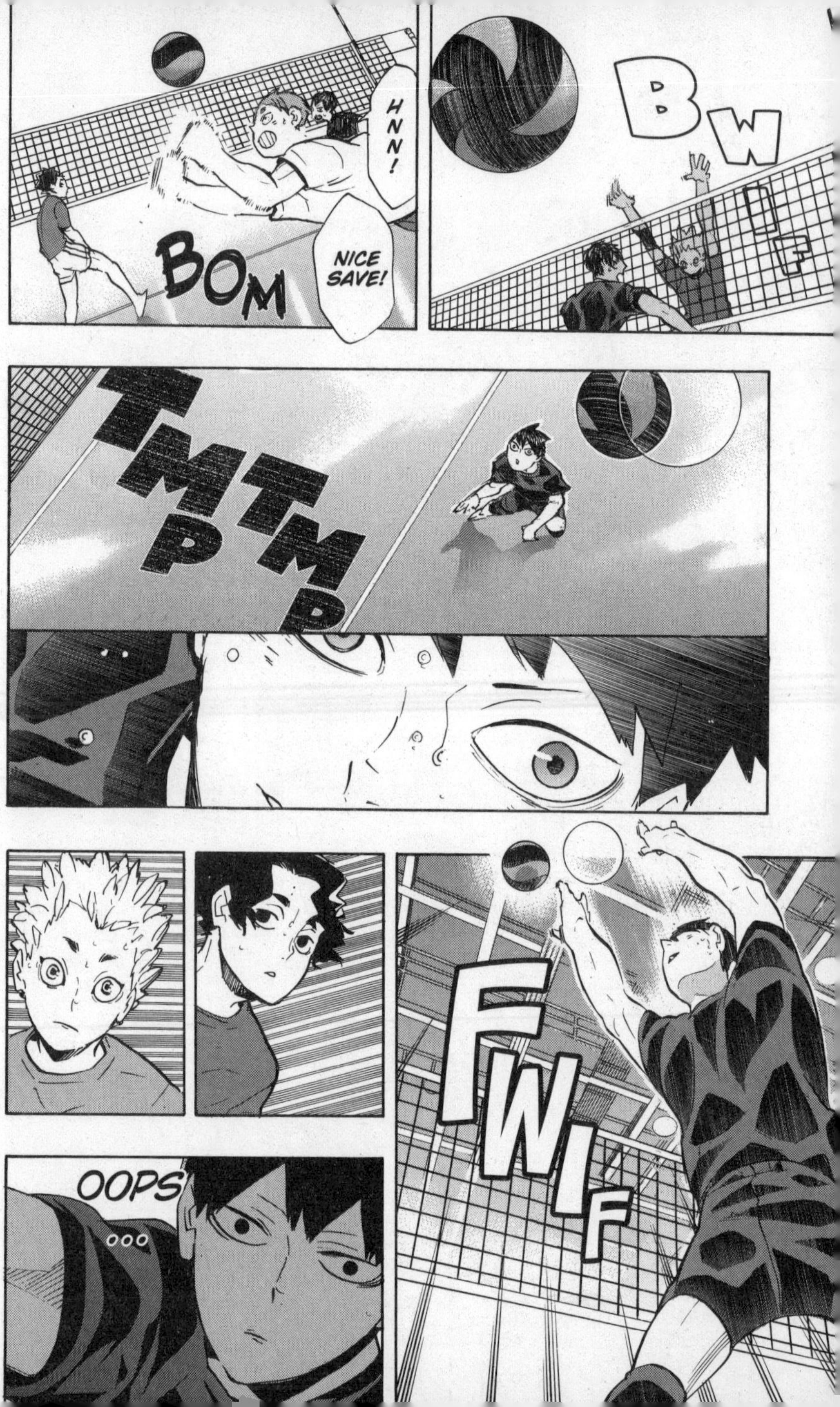
HNN!
NICE SAVE!
BOM
FWIF
OOPS
ooo

WELL, UH, THIS *IS* THE FIRST TIME WE'RE PLAYING TOGETHER.

TO NK

HABIT.

SORRY.

I GOT CARRIED AWAY AND LET AUTOPILOT TAKE OVER.

NICE...

...IS *HABIT* TO HIM?

A SET THAT SCREAMED "OF COURSE YOU'RE THIS FAR INTO YOUR APPROACH ALREADY, RIGHT?"...

TWITCH

OHO...

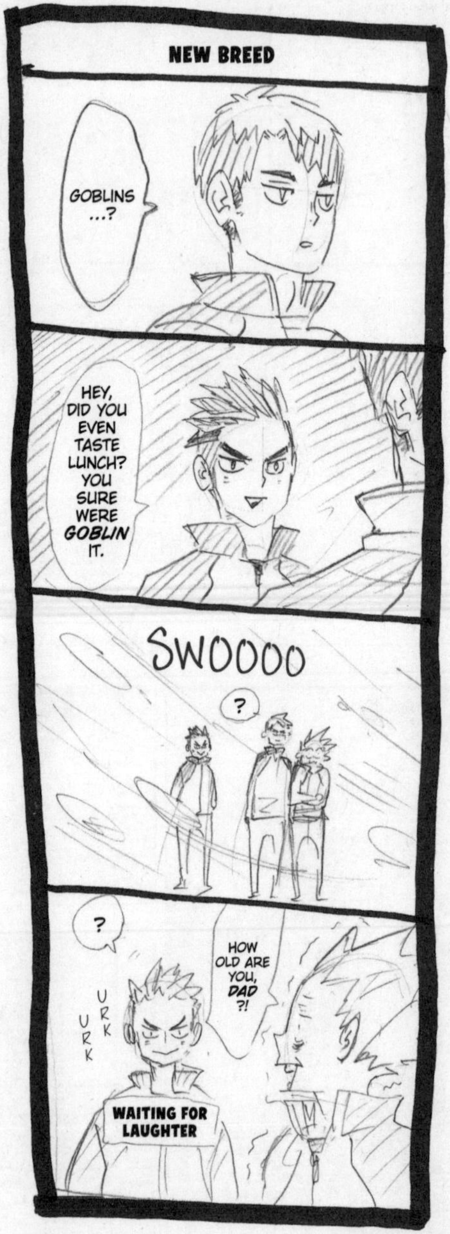
NEW BREED
GOBLINS ...?
HEY, DID YOU EVEN TASTE LUNCH? YOU SURE WERE GOBLIN IT.
SWOOOO
?
HOW OLD ARE YOU, DAD?!
?
URK URK
WAITING FOR LAUGHTER

CHAPTER 215: Sound

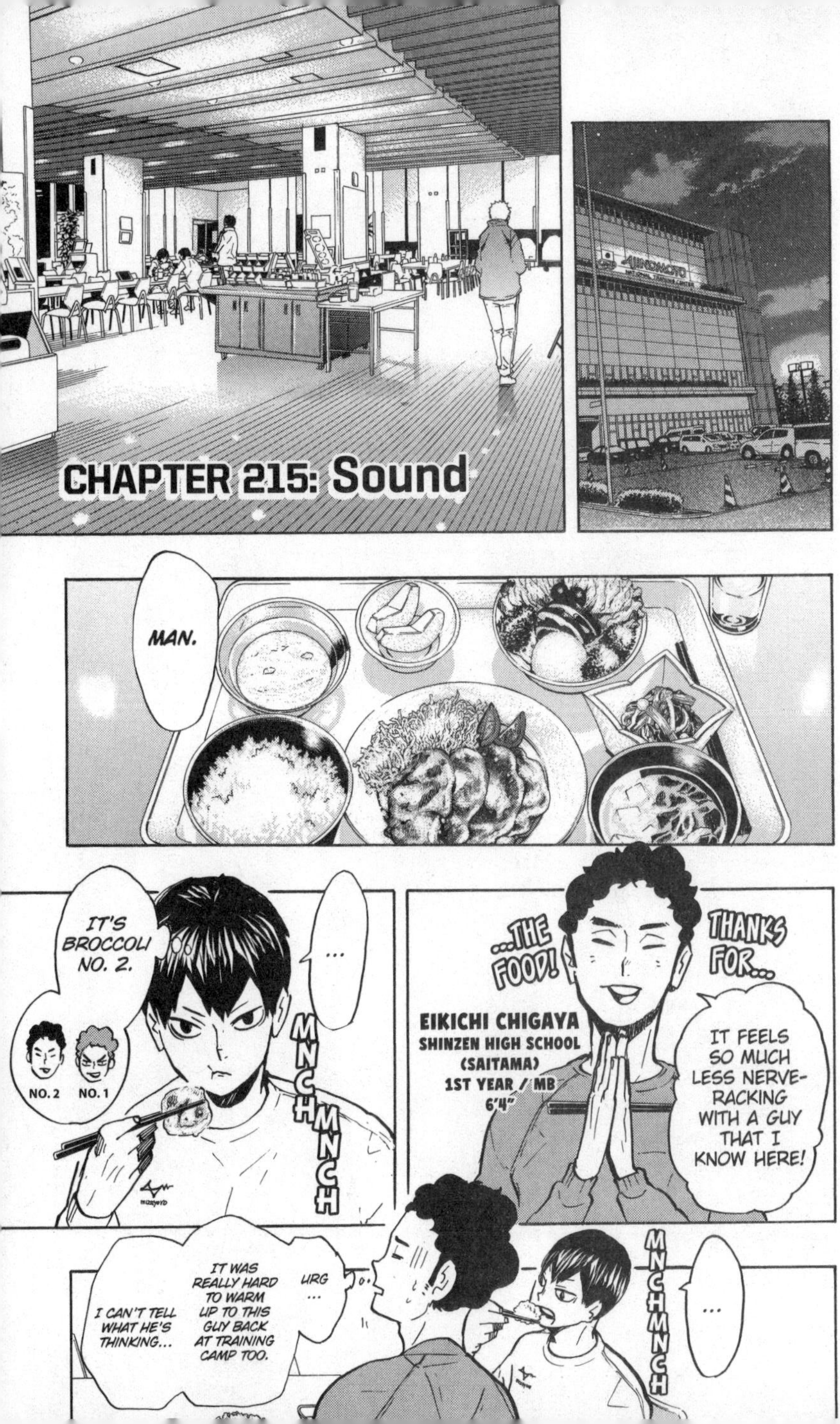

MAN.
THANKS FOR... ...THE FOOD!
EIKICHI CHIGAYA
SHINZEN HIGH SCHOOL
(SAITAMA)
1ST YEAR / MB
6'4"
IT FEELS SO MUCH LESS NERVE-RACKING WITH A GUY THAT I KNOW HERE!
...
IT'S BROCCOLI NO. 2.
NO. 2
NO. 1
MNCH MNCH
...
MNCHMNCH
URG ...
IT WAS REALLY HARD TO WARM UP TO THIS GUY BACK AT TRAINING CAMP TOO.
I CAN'T TELL WHAT HE'S THINKING...

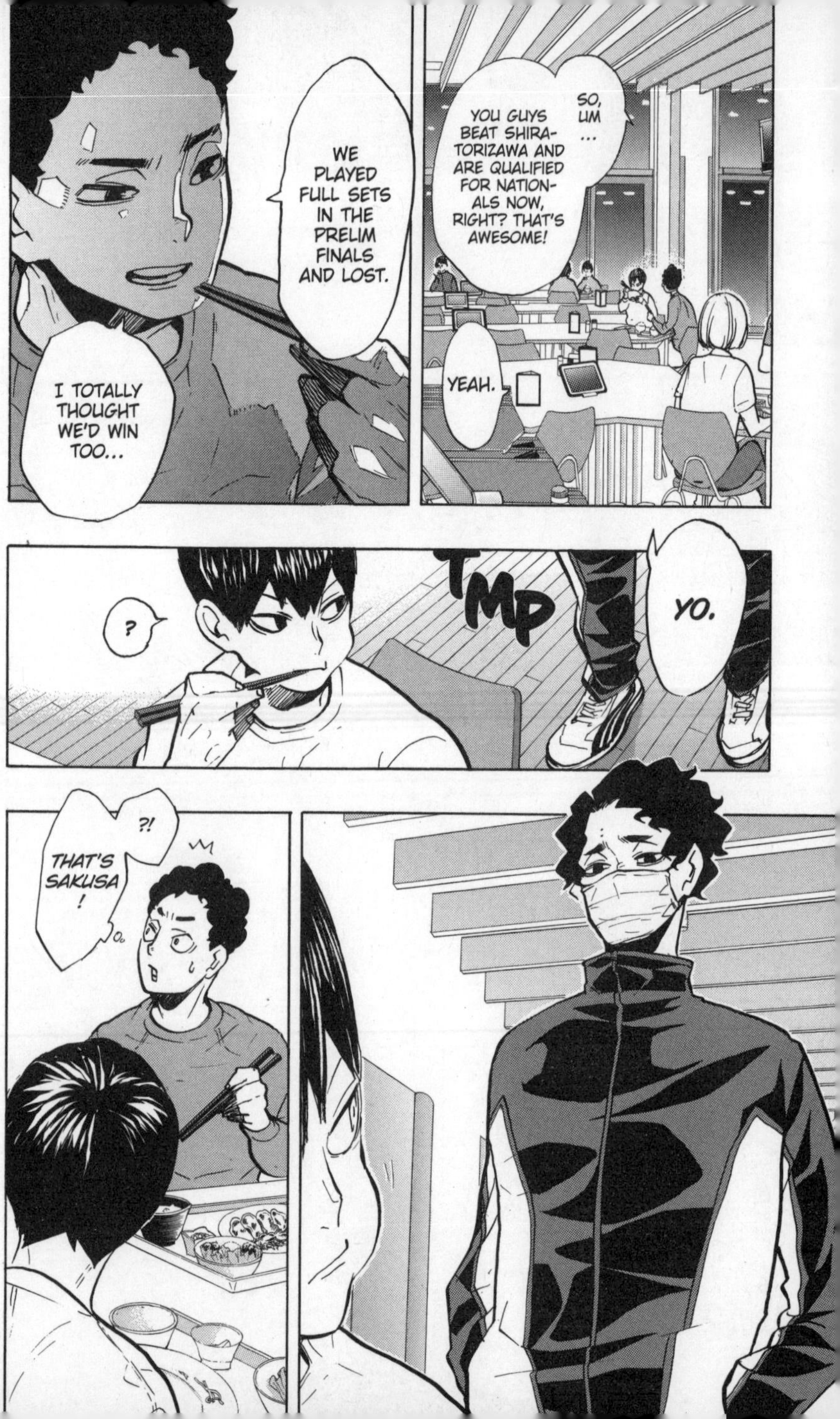
SO, UM ...
YOU GUYS BEAT SHIRATORIZAWA AND ARE QUALIFIED FOR NATIONALS NOW, RIGHT? THAT'S AWESOME!
YEAH.
WE PLAYED FULL SETS IN THE PRELIM FINALS AND LOST.
I TOTALLY THOUGHT WE'D WIN TOO...
YO.
TMP
?
?!
THAT'S SAKUSA!

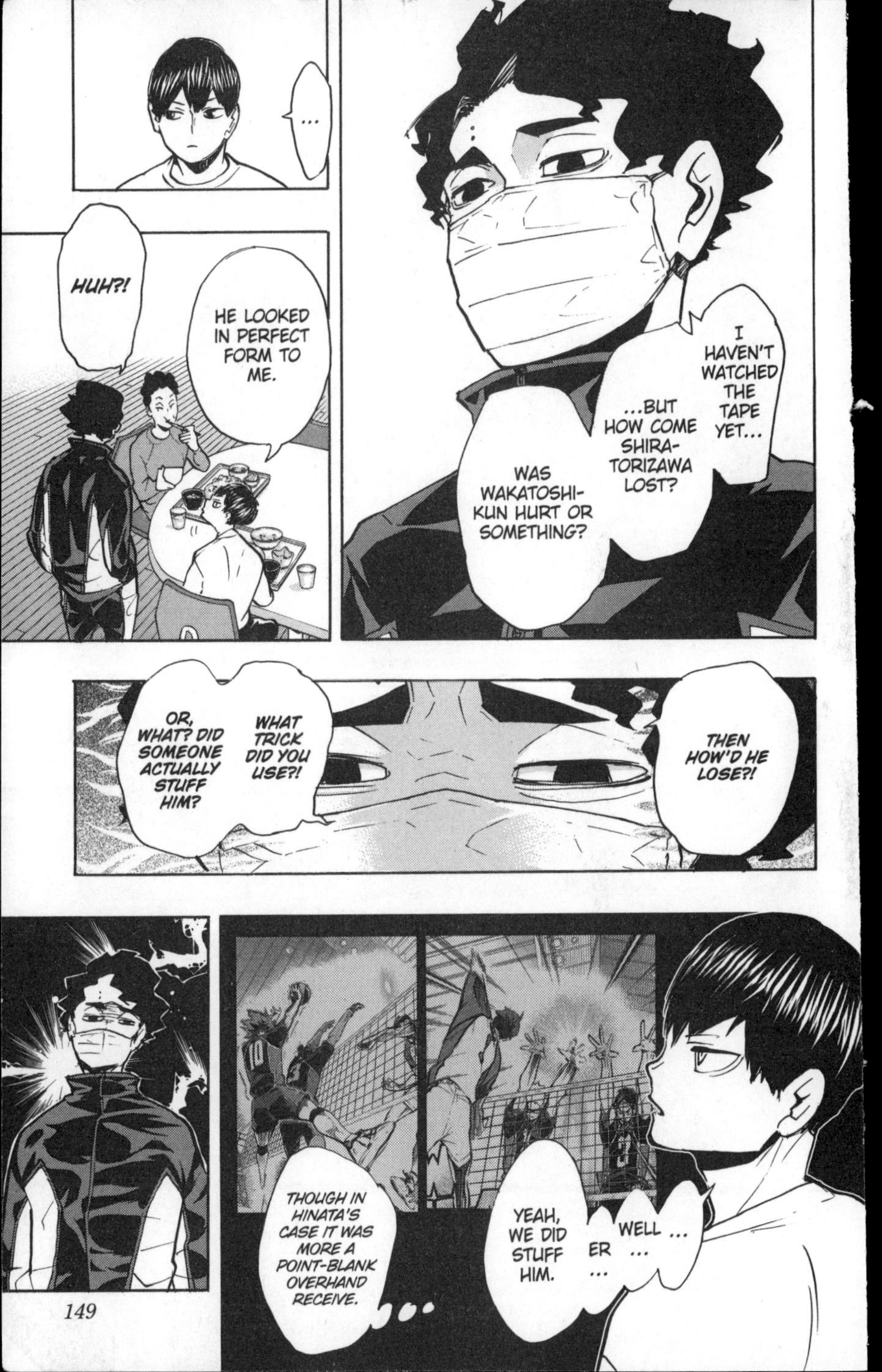
I HAVEN'T WATCHED THE TAPE YET...
...BUT HOW COME SHIRA-TORIZAWA LOST?
WAS WAKATOSHI-KUN HURT OR SOMETHING?
...
HE LOOKED IN PERFECT FORM TO ME.
HUH?!
THEN HOW'D HE LOSE?!
WHAT TRICK DID YOU USE?!
OR, WHAT? DID SOMEONE ACTUALLY STUFF HIM?
WELL ...
ER ...
YEAH, WE DID STUFF HIM.
THOUGH IN HINATA'S CASE IT WAS MORE A POINT-BLANK OVERHAND RECEIVE.
...

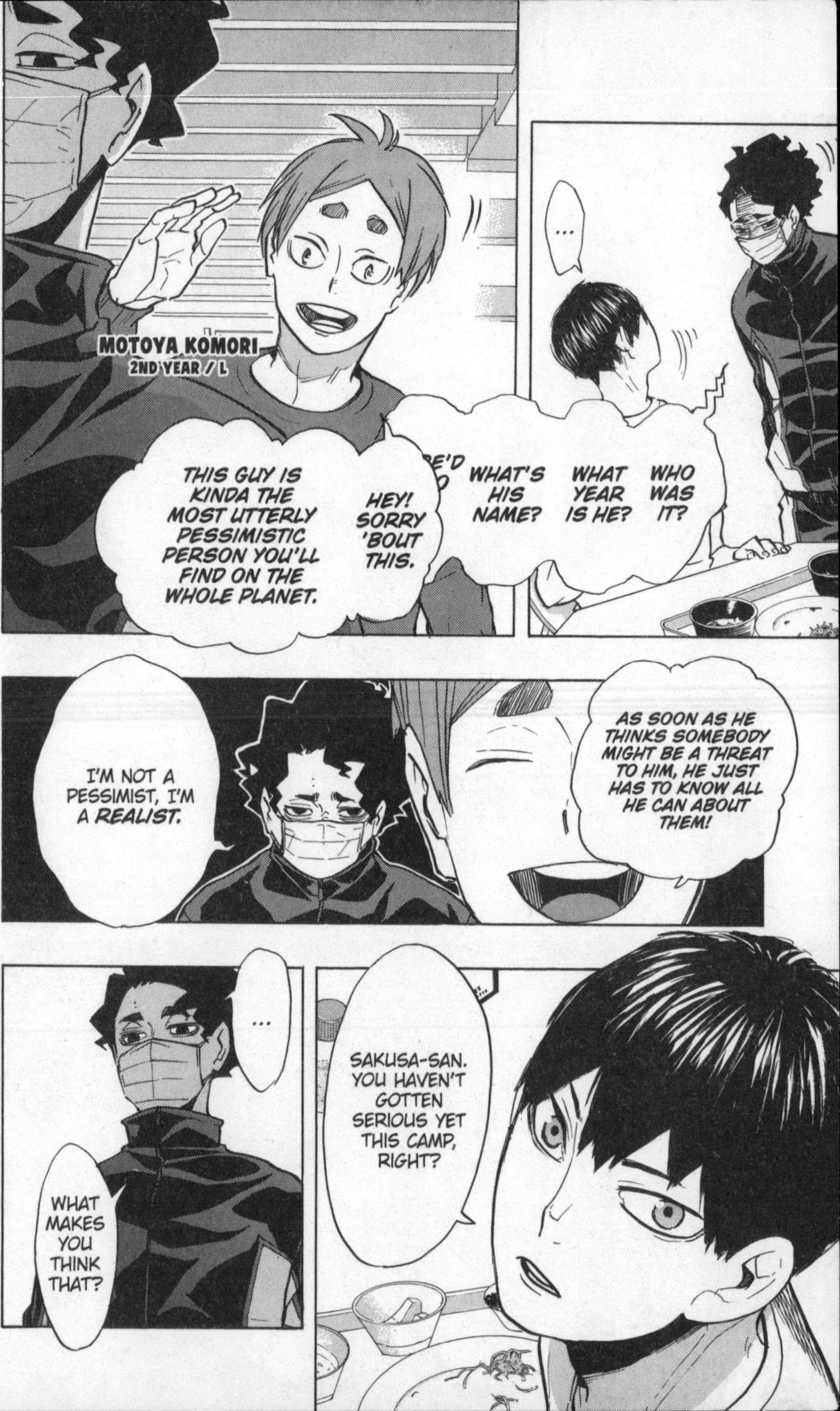
...
WHO WAS IT?
WHAT YEAR IS HE?
WHAT'S HIS NAME?
MOTOYA KOMORI
2ND YEAR / L
HEY! SORRY 'BOUT THIS.
THIS GUY IS KINDA THE MOST UTTERLY PESSIMISTIC PERSON YOU'LL FIND ON THE WHOLE PLANET.
AS SOON AS HE THINKS SOMEBODY MIGHT BE A THREAT TO HIM, HE JUST HAS TO KNOW ALL HE CAN ABOUT THEM!
I'M NOT A PESSIMIST, I'M A REALIST.
SAKUSA-SAN. YOU HAVEN'T GOTTEN SERIOUS YET THIS CAMP, RIGHT?
...
WHAT MAKES YOU THINK THAT?

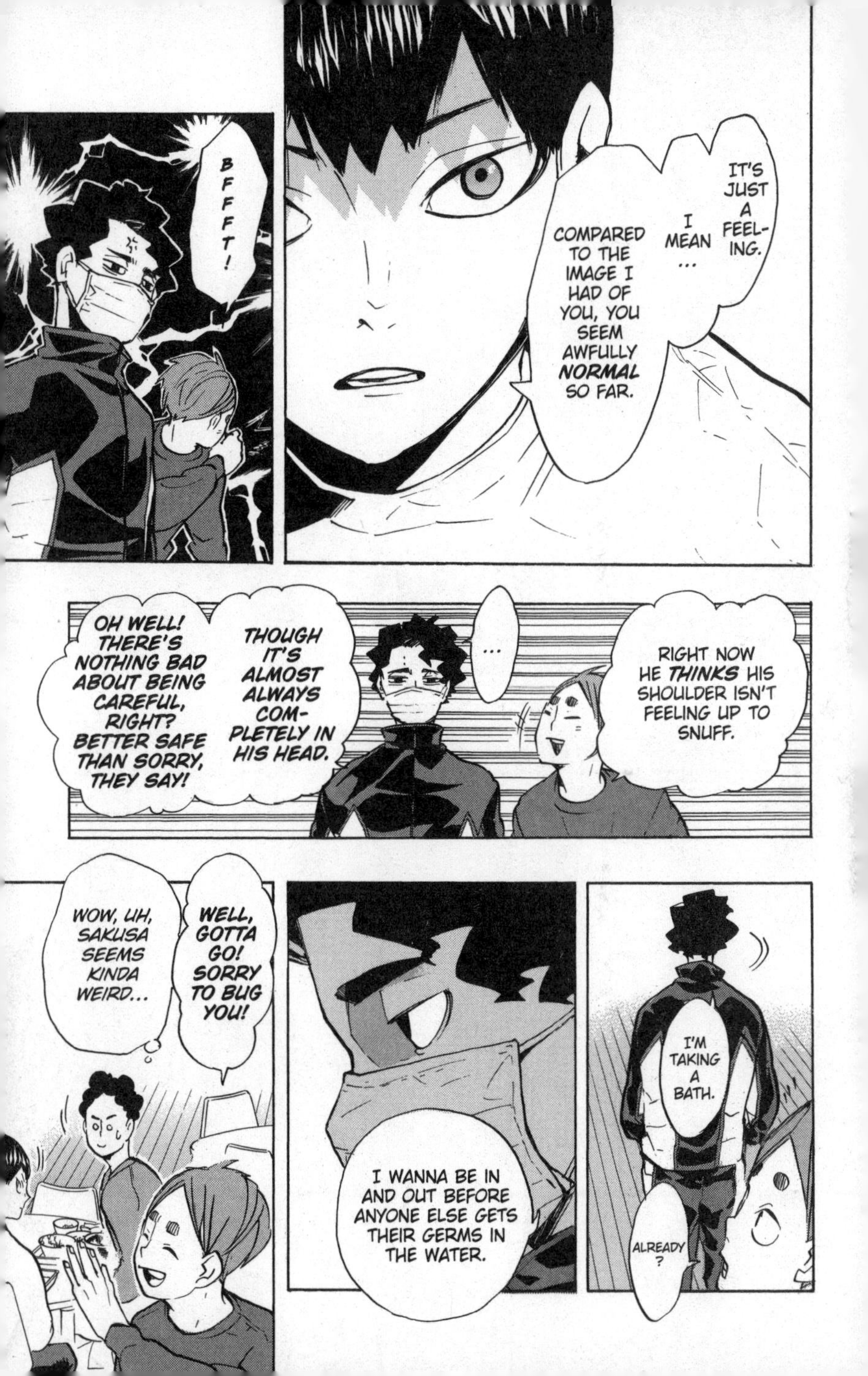
IT'S JUST A FEEL-ING.
I MEAN...
COMPARED TO THE IMAGE I HAD OF YOU, YOU SEEM AWFULLY NORMAL SO FAR.
BFFFT!
RIGHT NOW HE THINKS HIS SHOULDER ISN'T FEELING UP TO SNUFF.
...
THOUGH IT'S ALMOST ALWAYS COM-PLETELY IN HIS HEAD.
OH WELL! THERE'S NOTHING BAD ABOUT BEING CAREFUL, RIGHT? BETTER SAFE THAN SORRY, THEY SAY!
I'M TAKING A BATH.
ALREADY?
I WANNA BE IN AND OUT BEFORE ANYONE ELSE GETS THEIR GERMS IN THE WATER.
WELL, GOTTA GO! SORRY TO BUG YOU!
WOW, UH, SAKUSA SEEMS KINDA WEIRD...

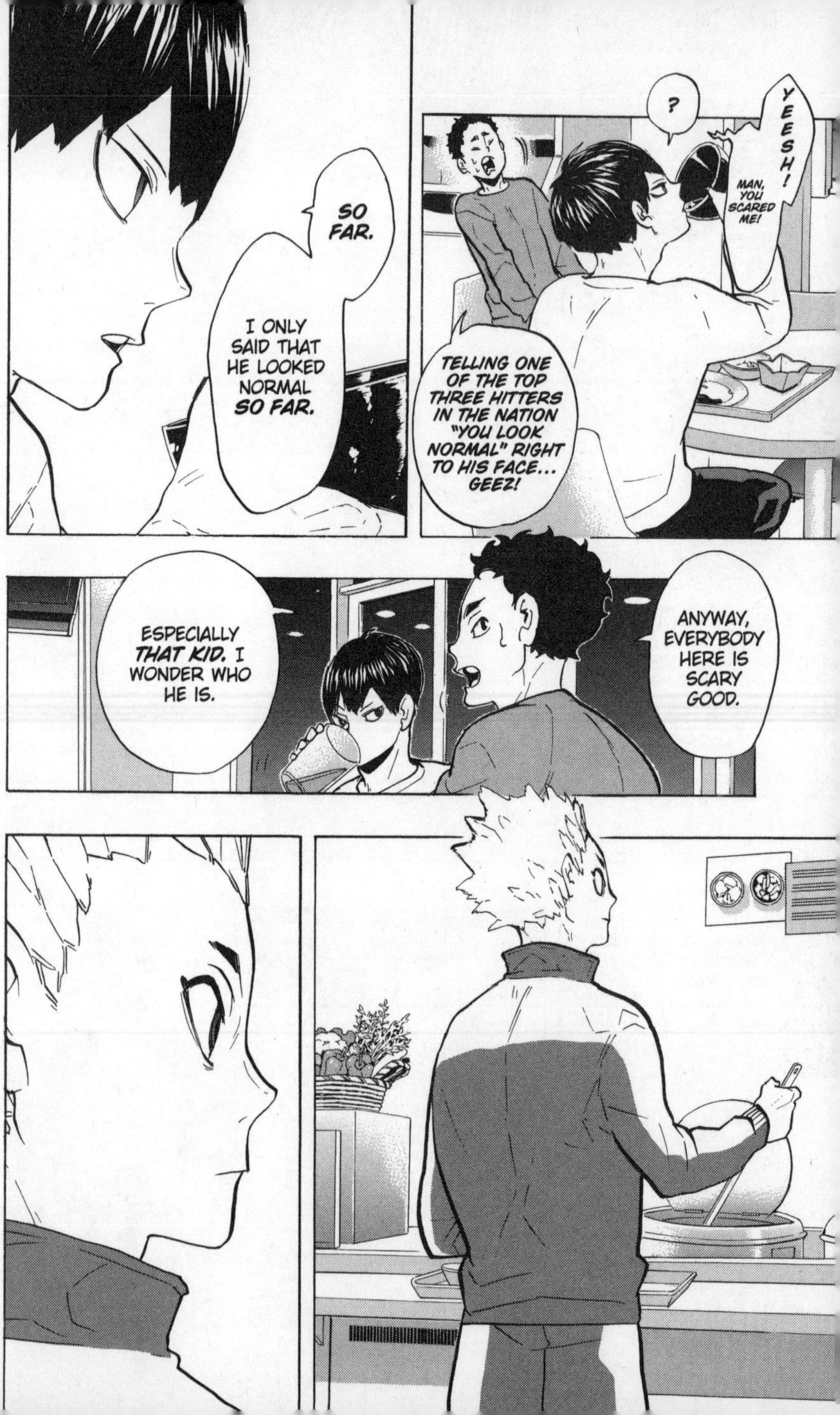
YEESH!
MAN, YOU SCARED ME!
?
TELLING ONE OF THE TOP THREE HITTERS IN THE NATION "YOU LOOK NORMAL" RIGHT TO HIS FACE... GEEZ!
SO FAR.
I ONLY SAID THAT HE LOOKED NORMAL SO FAR.
ANYWAY, EVERYBODY HERE IS SCARY GOOD.
ESPECIALLY THAT KID. I WONDER WHO HE IS.

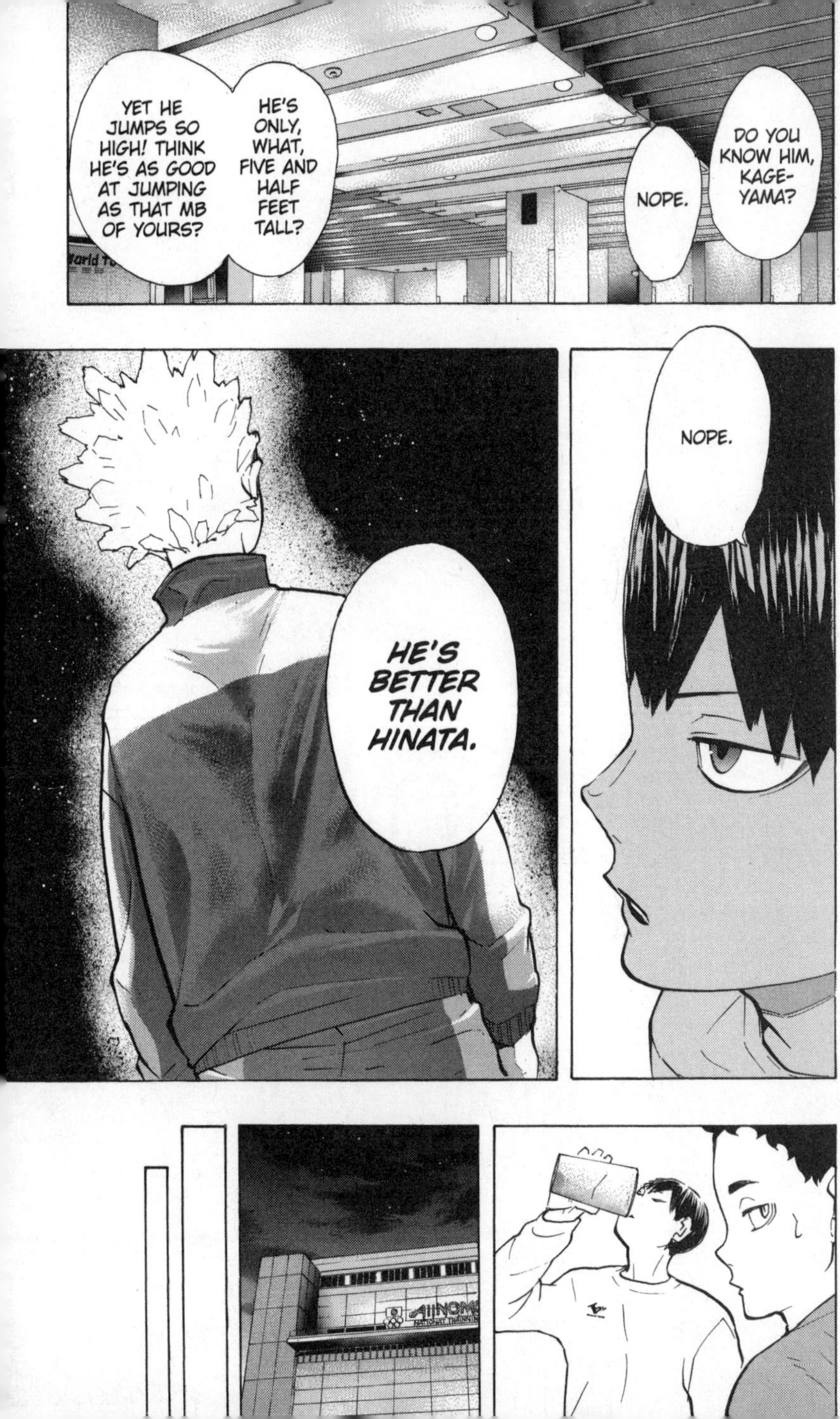
DO YOU KNOW HIM, KAGE-YAMA?
NOPE.
HE'S ONLY, WHAT, FIVE AND HALF FEET TALL?
YET HE JUMPS SO HIGH! THINK HE'S AS GOOD AT JUMPING AS THAT MB OF YOURS?
NOPE.
HE'S BETTER THAN HINATA.

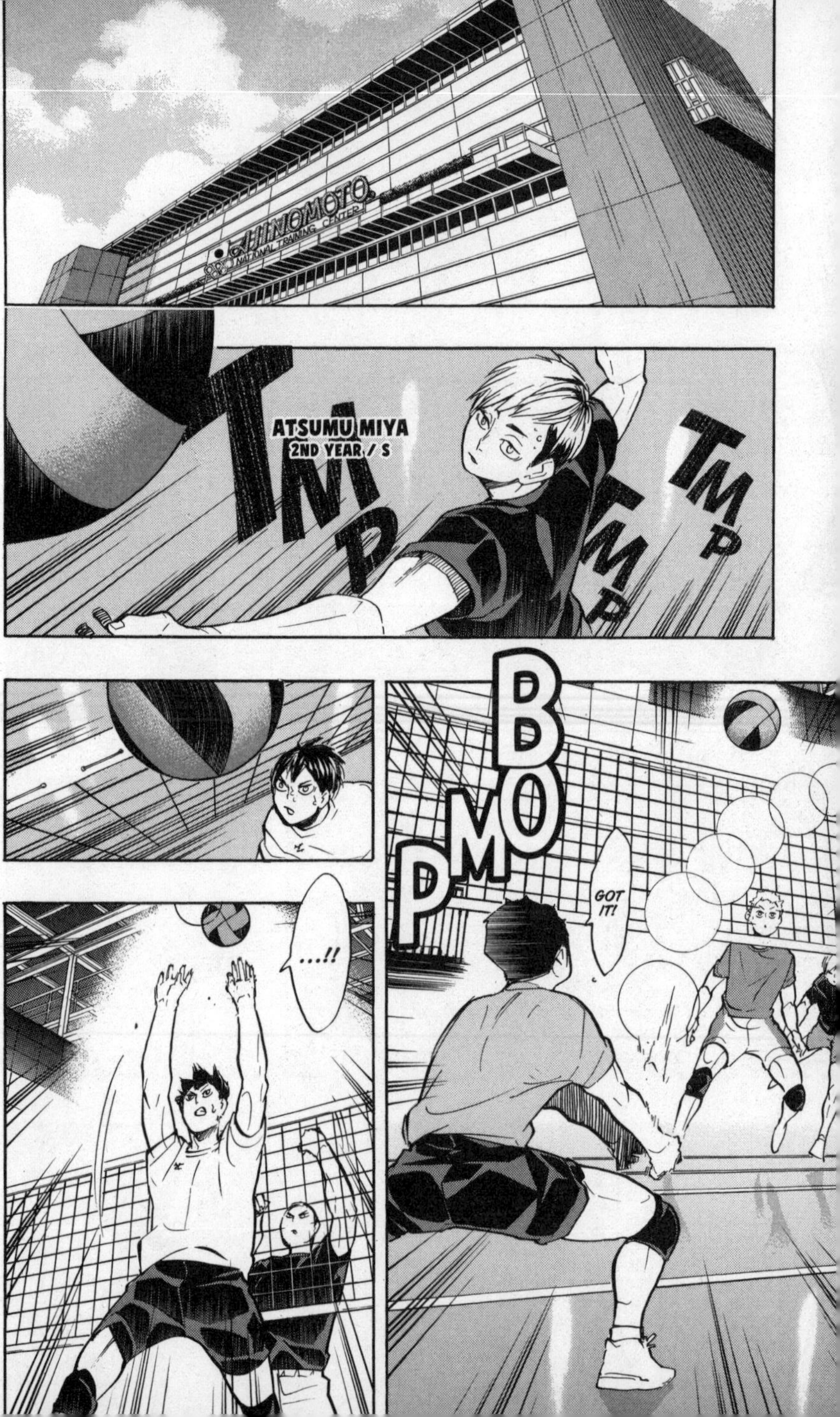
AJINOMOTO
NATIONAL TRAINING CENTER
TMP
TMP
ATSUMU MIYA
2ND YEAR / S
TMP
BOMP
GOT IT!
...!!

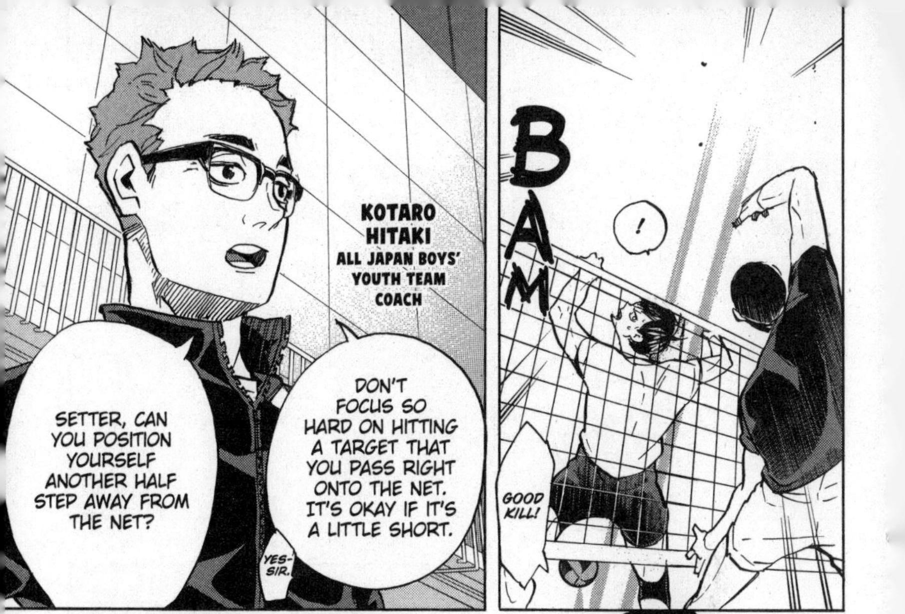
BAM
!
GOOD KILL!
KOTARO HITAKI ALL JAPAN BOYS' YOUTH TEAM COACH
DON'T FOCUS SO HARD ON HITTING A TARGET THAT YOU PASS RIGHT ONTO THE NET. IT'S OKAY IF IT'S A LITTLE SHORT.
SETTER, CAN YOU POSITION YOURSELF ANOTHER HALF STEP AWAY FROM THE NET?
YES-SIR.

*TARGET: THE RIGHT FRONT AREA OF THE COURT WHERE THE SETTER IS USUALLY POSITIONED.

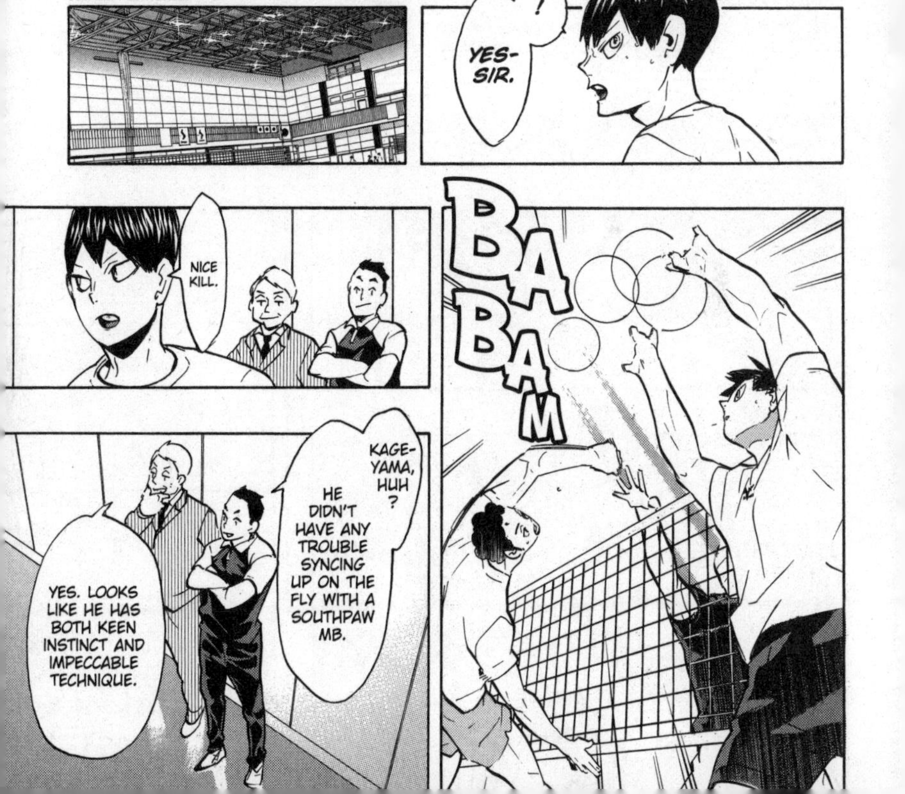
!
YES-SIR.
BABABAM
NICE KILL.
KAGE-YAMA, HUH?
HE DIDN'T HAVE ANY TROUBLE SYNCING UP ON THE FLY WITH A SOUTHPAW MB.
YES. LOOKS LIKE HE HAS BOTH KEEN INSTINCT AND IMPECCABLE TECHNIQUE.

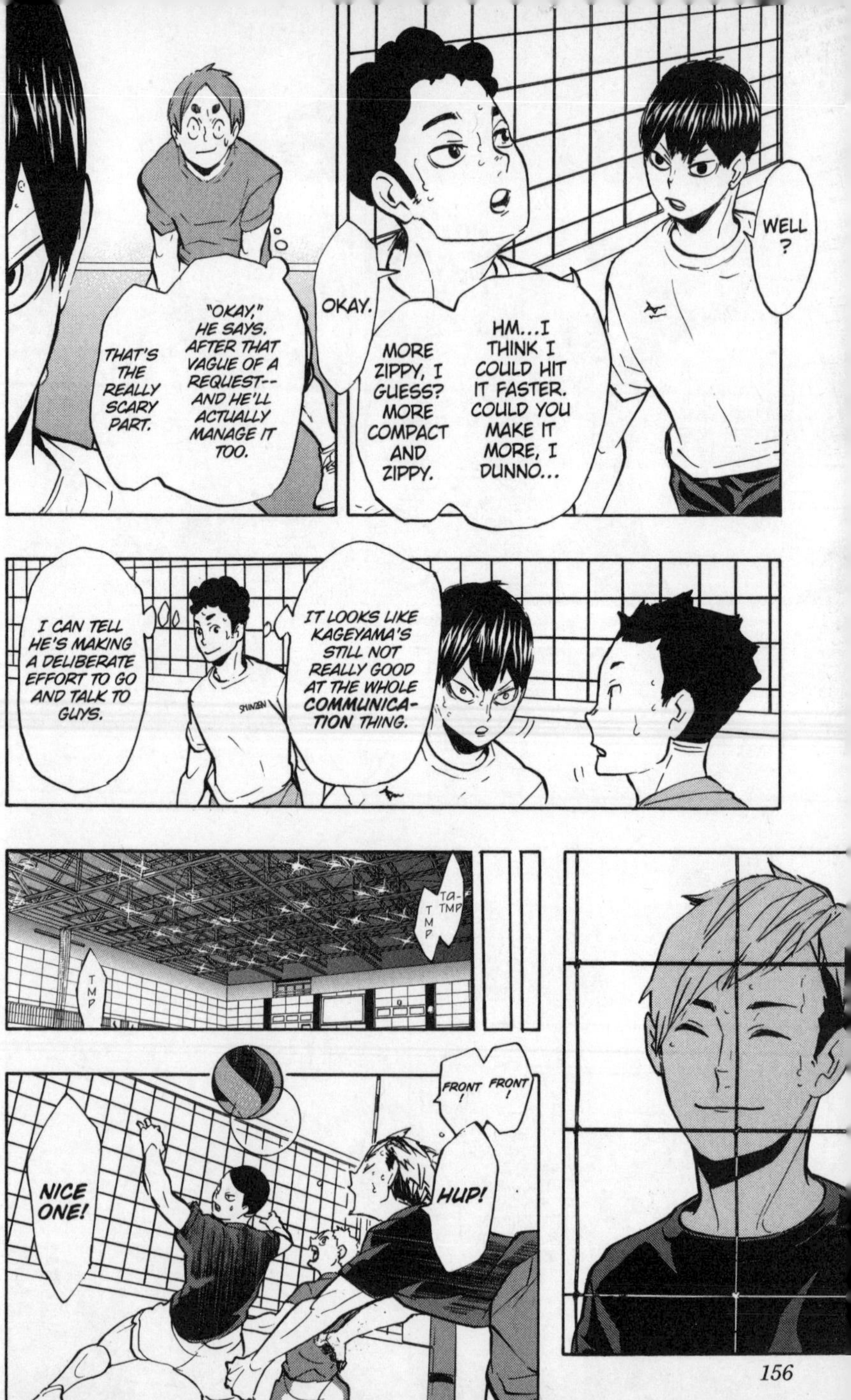
WELL?
HM...I THINK I COULD HIT IT FASTER. COULD YOU MAKE IT MORE, I DUNNO...
MORE ZIPPY, I GUESS? MORE COMPACT AND ZIPPY.
OKAY.
"OKAY," HE SAYS. AFTER THAT VAGUE OF A REQUEST--AND HE'LL ACTUALLY MANAGE IT TOO.
THAT'S THE REALLY SCARY PART.
IT LOOKS LIKE KAGEYAMA'S STILL NOT REALLY GOOD AT THE WHOLE COMMUNICATION THING.
I CAN TELL HE'S MAKING A DELIBERATE EFFORT TO GO AND TALK TO GUYS.
TA-TMP
TMP
TMP
FRONT!
FRONT!
HUP!
NICE ONE!

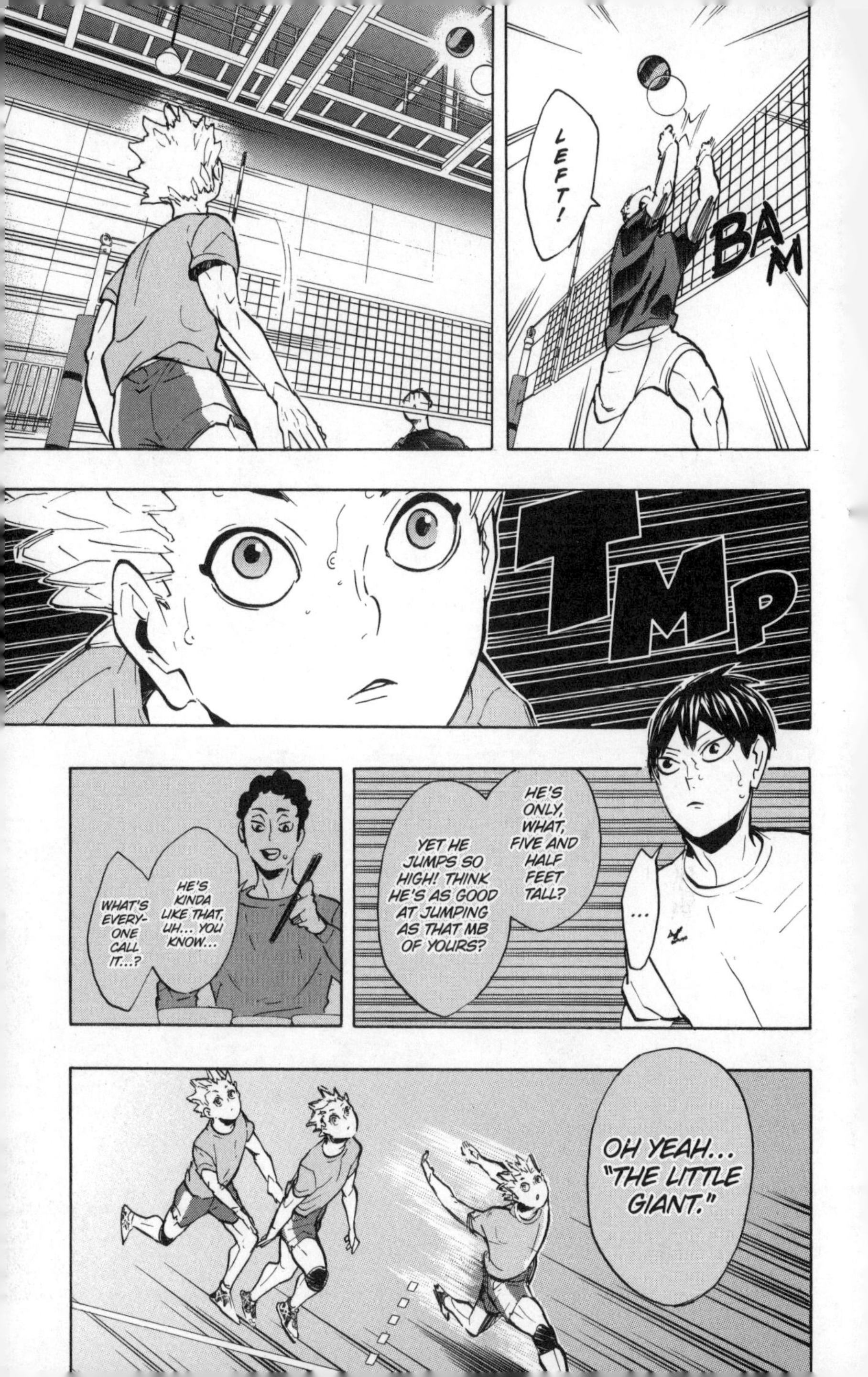
LEFT!
BAM
TMP
HE'S ONLY, WHAT, FIVE AND HALF FEET TALL?
YET HE JUMPS SO HIGH! THINK HE'S AS GOOD AT JUMPING AS THAT MB OF YOURS?
...
HE'S KINDA LIKE THAT, UH... YOU KNOW...
WHAT'S EVERY-ONE CALL IT...?
OH YEAH... "THE LITTLE GIANT."

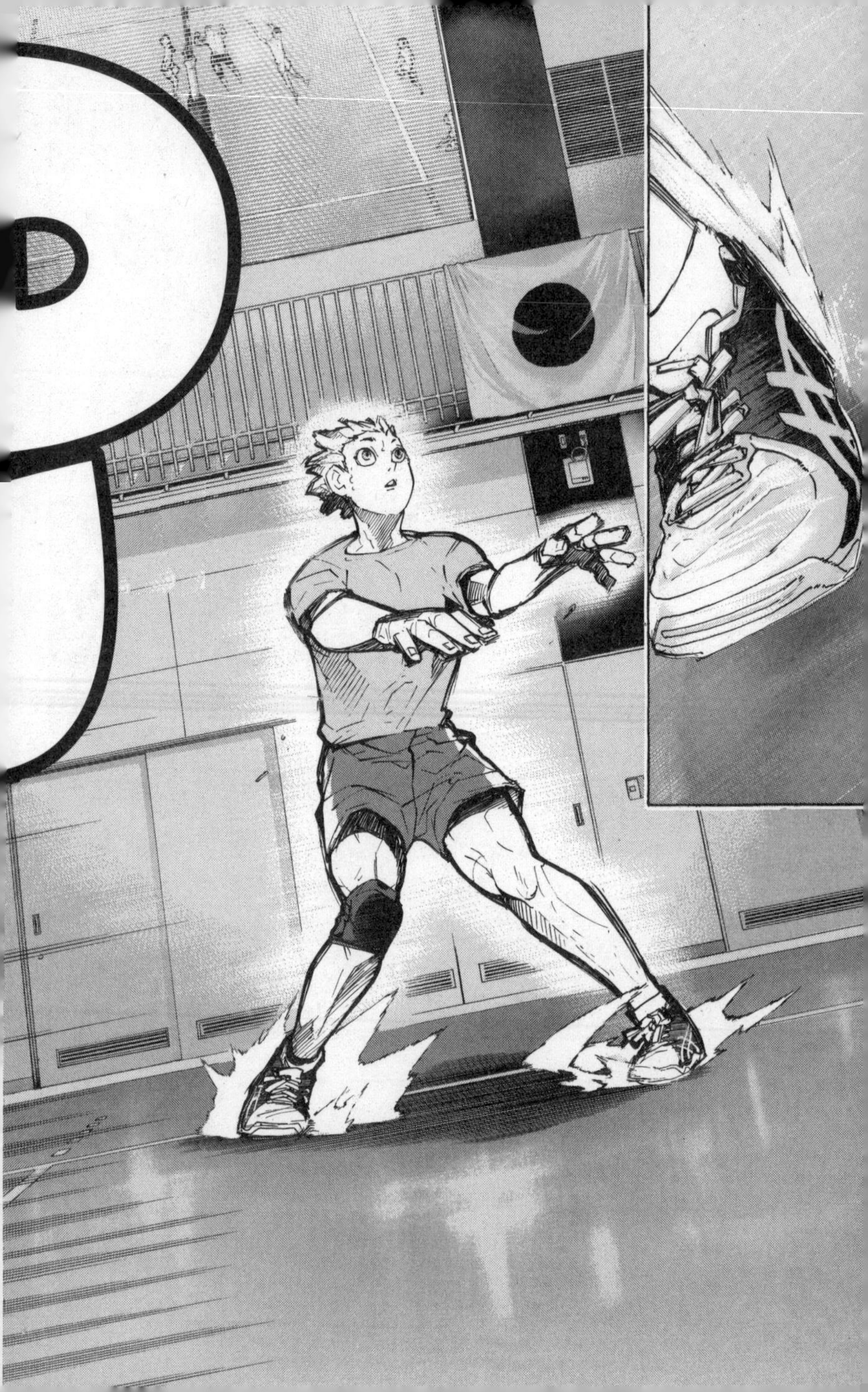

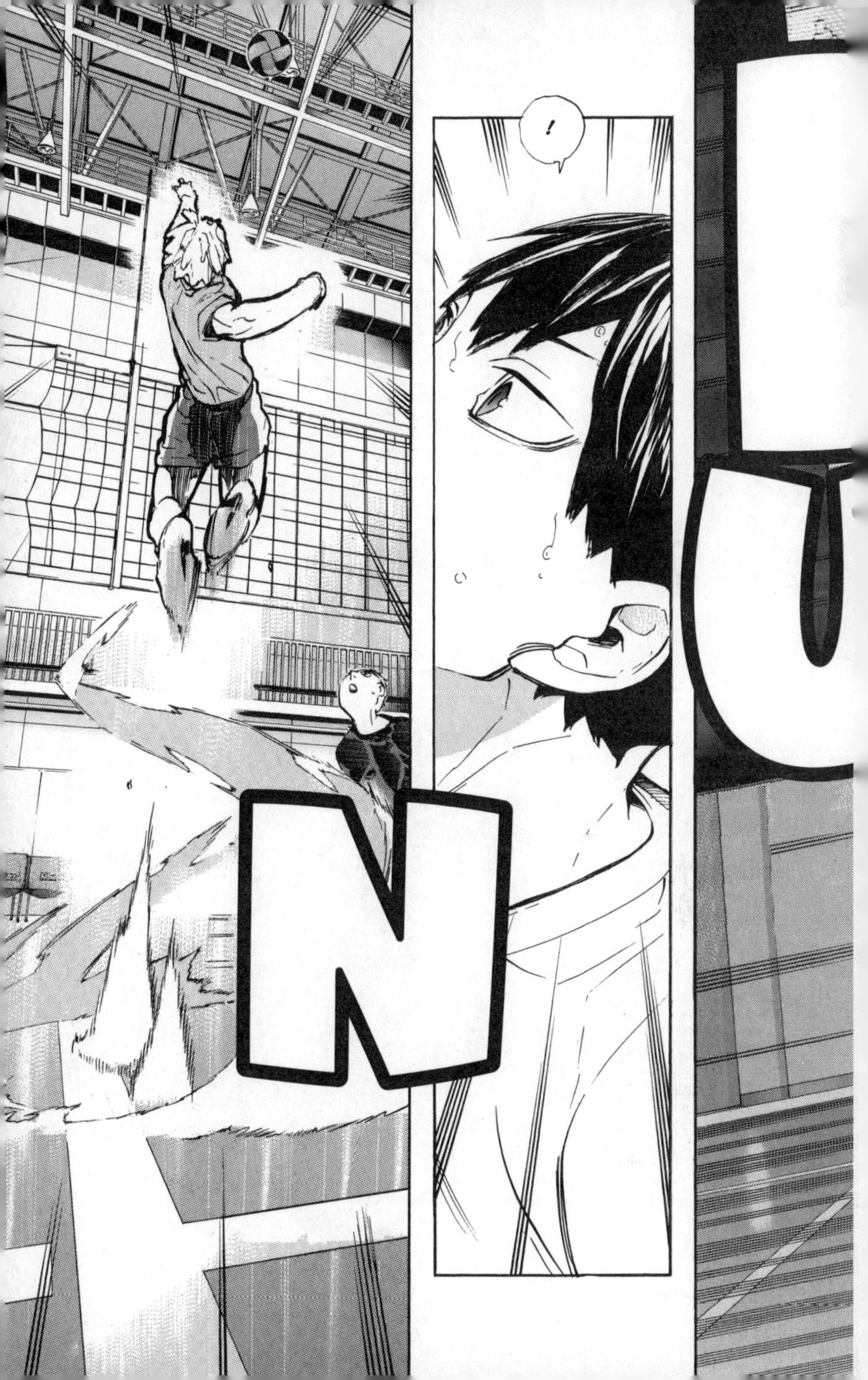
!
N

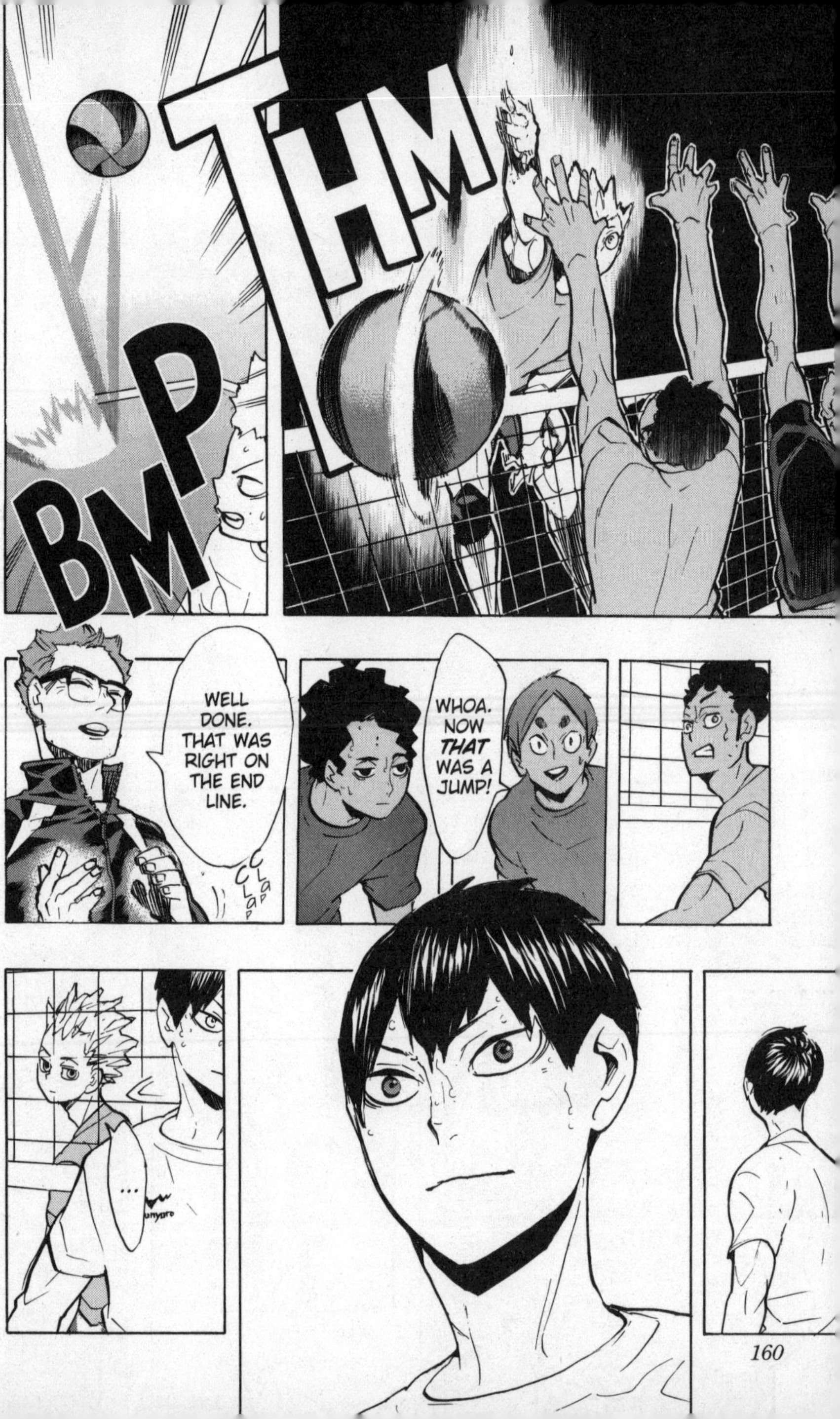
THM
BMP
WHOA. NOW *THAT* WAS A JUMP!
WELL DONE. THAT WAS RIGHT ON THE END LINE.
CLAP CLAP
...

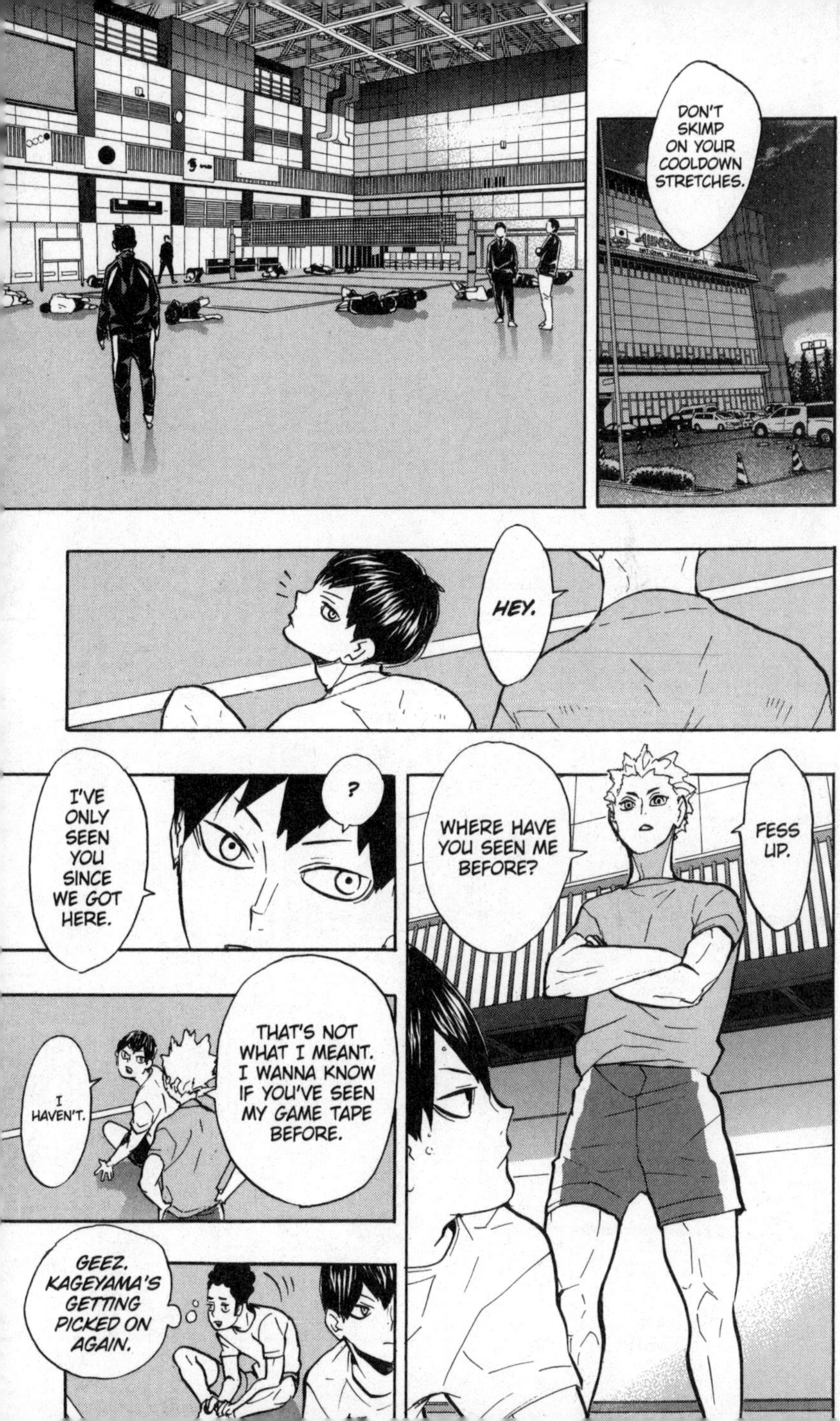
DON'T SKIMP ON YOUR COOLDOWN STRETCHES.
HEY.
FESS UP.
WHERE HAVE YOU SEEN ME BEFORE?
?
I'VE ONLY SEEN YOU SINCE WE GOT HERE.
THAT'S NOT WHAT I MEANT. I WANNA KNOW IF YOU'VE SEEN MY GAME TAPE BEFORE.
I HAVEN'T.
GEEZ. KAGEYAMA'S GETTING PICKED ON AGAIN.

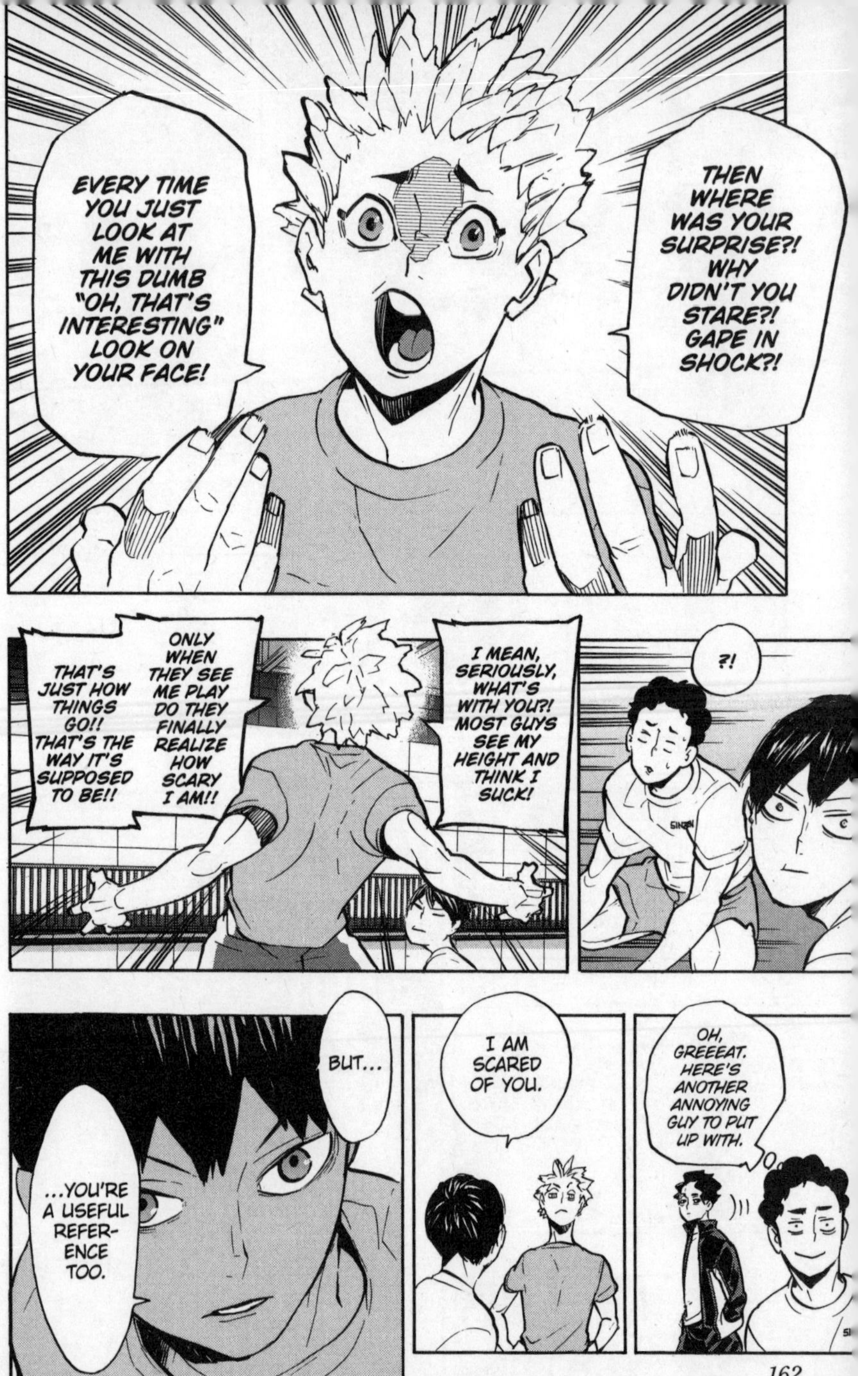
THEN WHERE WAS YOUR SURPRISE?! WHY DIDN'T YOU STARE?! GAPE IN SHOCK?!
EVERY TIME YOU JUST LOOK AT ME WITH THIS DUMB "OH, THAT'S INTERESTING" LOOK ON YOUR FACE!
?!
I MEAN, SERIOUSLY, WHAT'S WITH YOU?! MOST GUYS SEE MY HEIGHT AND THINK I SUCK!
ONLY WHEN THEY SEE ME PLAY DO THEY FINALLY REALIZE HOW SCARY I AM!!
THAT'S JUST HOW THINGS GO!! THAT'S THE WAY IT'S SUPPOSED TO BE!!
OH, GREEEAT. HERE'S ANOTHER ANNOYING GUY TO PUT UP WITH.
I AM SCARED OF YOU.
BUT...
...YOU'RE A USEFUL REFER-ENCE TOO.

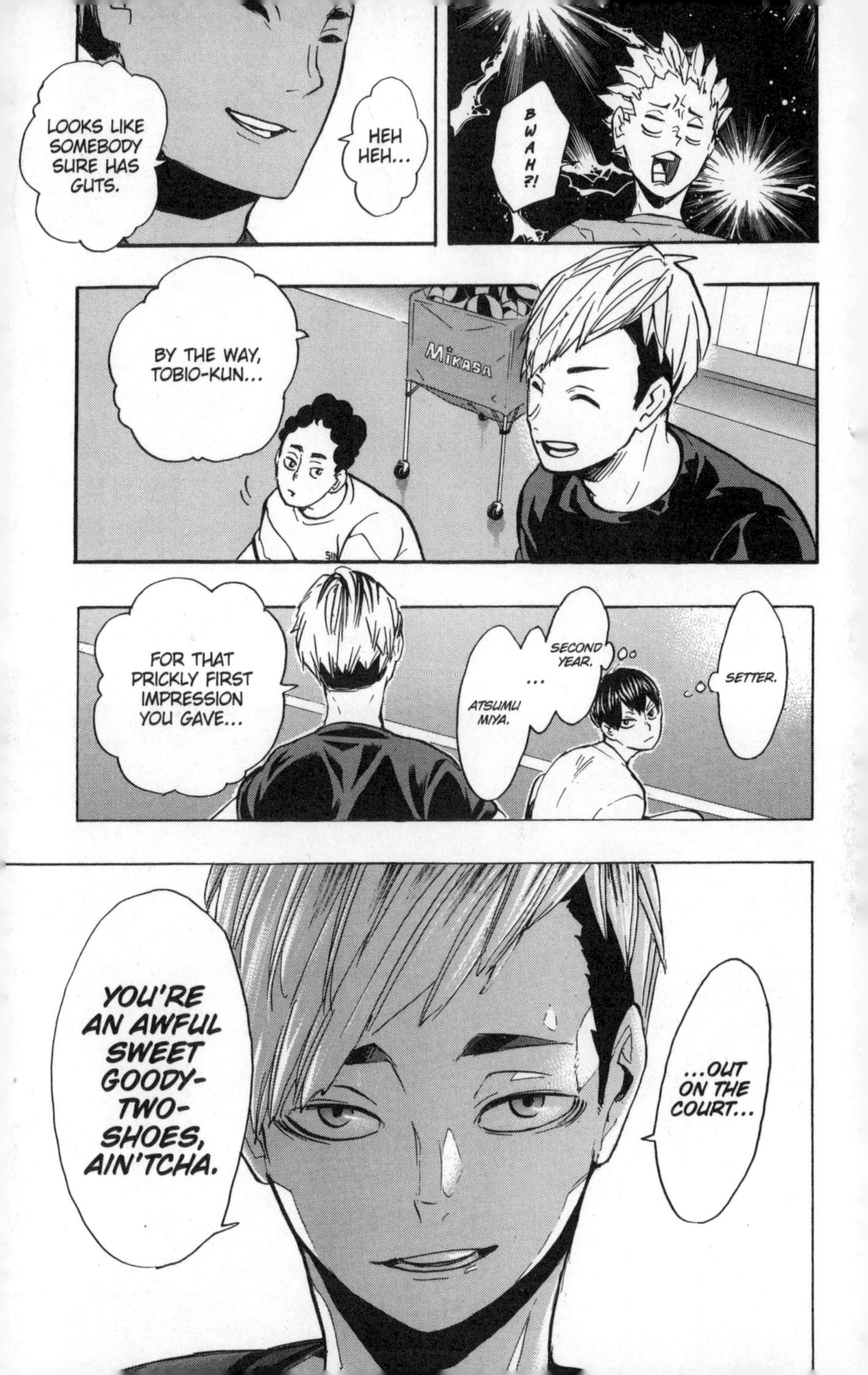
BWAH?!
HEH HEH...
LOOKS LIKE SOMEBODY SURE HAS GUTS.
BY THE WAY, TOBIO-KUN...
MIKASA
ATSUMU MIYA.
...
SECOND YEAR.
SETTER.
FOR THAT PRICKLY FIRST IMPRESSION YOU GAVE...
...OUT ON THE COURT...
YOU'RE AN AWFUL SWEET GOODY-TWO-SHOES, AIN'TCHA.

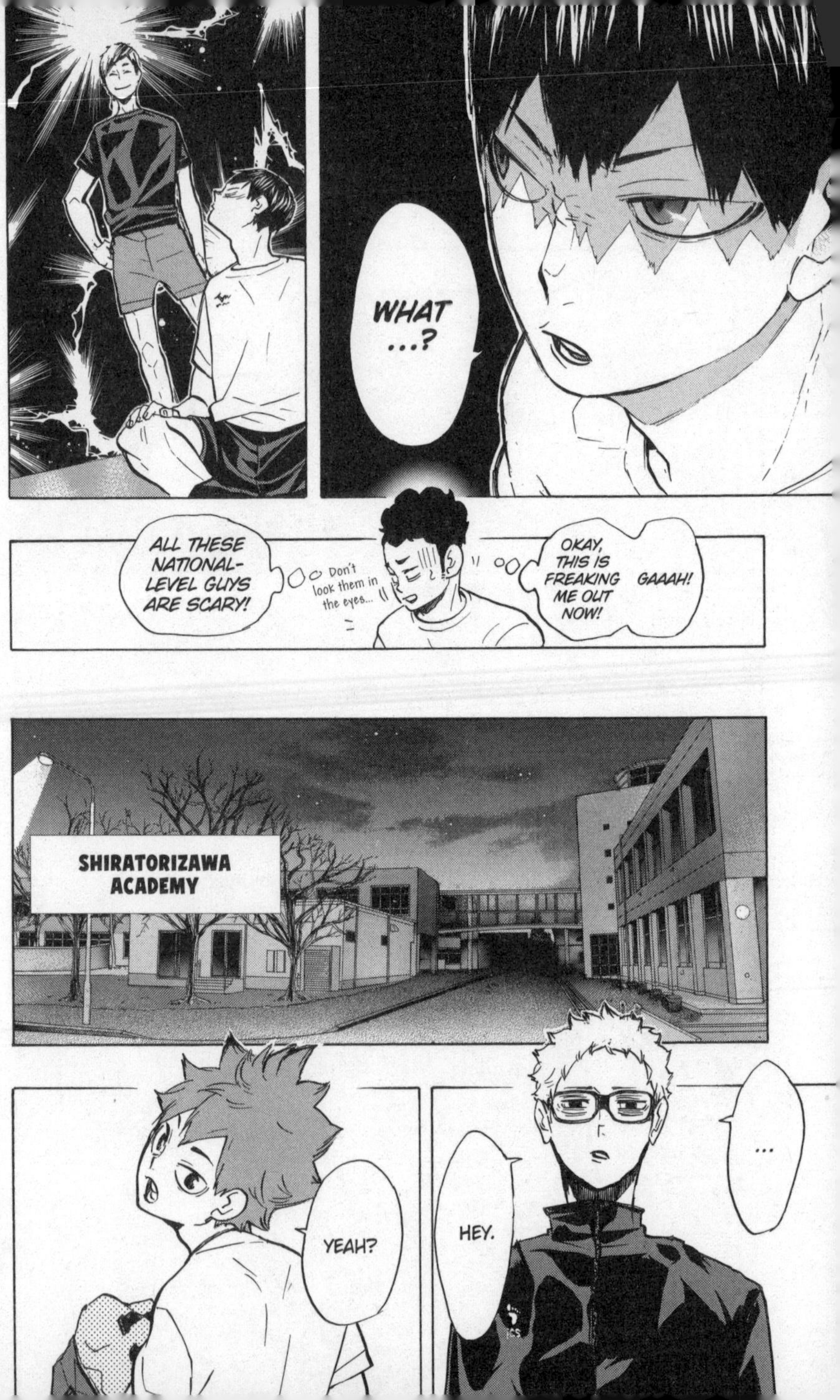
WHAT ...?
GAAAH!
OKAY, THIS IS FREAKING ME OUT NOW!
Don't look them in the eyes...
ALL THESE NATIONAL-LEVEL GUYS ARE SCARY!
SHIRATORIZAWA ACADEMY
...
HEY.
YEAH?

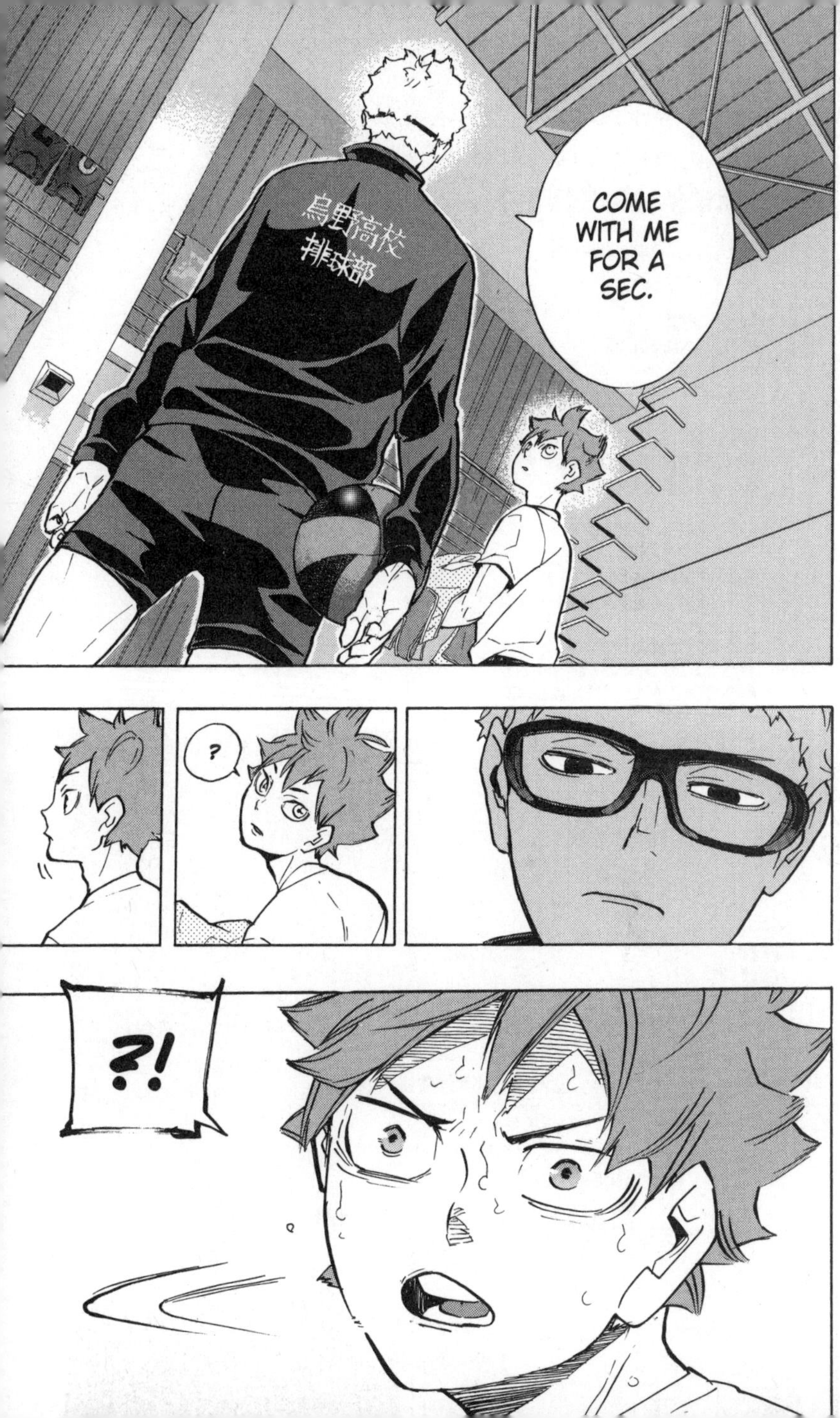
COME WITH ME FOR A SEC.
烏野高校
排球部
?
?!

EIKICHI CHIGAYA

SHINZEN HIGH SCHOOL
CLASS 1-5

POSITION:
MIDDLE BLOCKER

HEIGHT: 6'4"

WEIGHT: 173 LBS.
(AS OF DECEMBER, 1ST YEAR OF HIGH SCHOOL)

BIRTHDAY: OCTOBER 19

FAVORITE FOOD:
GRILLED *TARAKO* RICE BALLS

CURRENT WORRY:
THE TEAM MANAGER LOVES RED BEAN RICE AND MAKES IT FOR THE TEAM A LOT, BUT HE DOESN'T REALLY LIKE THE STUFF...

ABILITY PARAMETERS
(5-POINT SCALE)

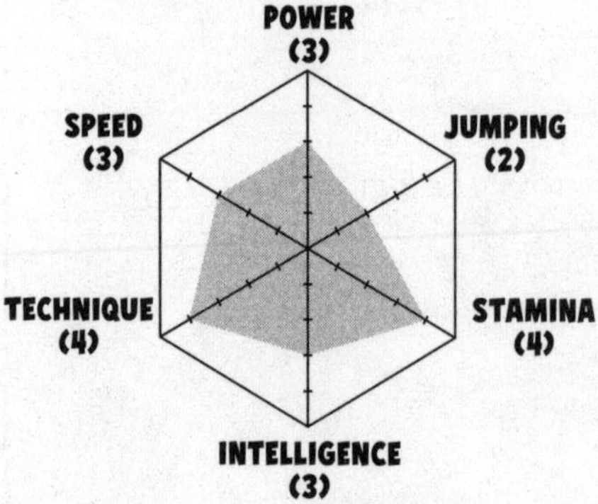
POWER (3)
JUMPING (2)
STAMINA (4)
INTELLIGENCE (3)
TECHNIQUE (4)
SPEED (3)

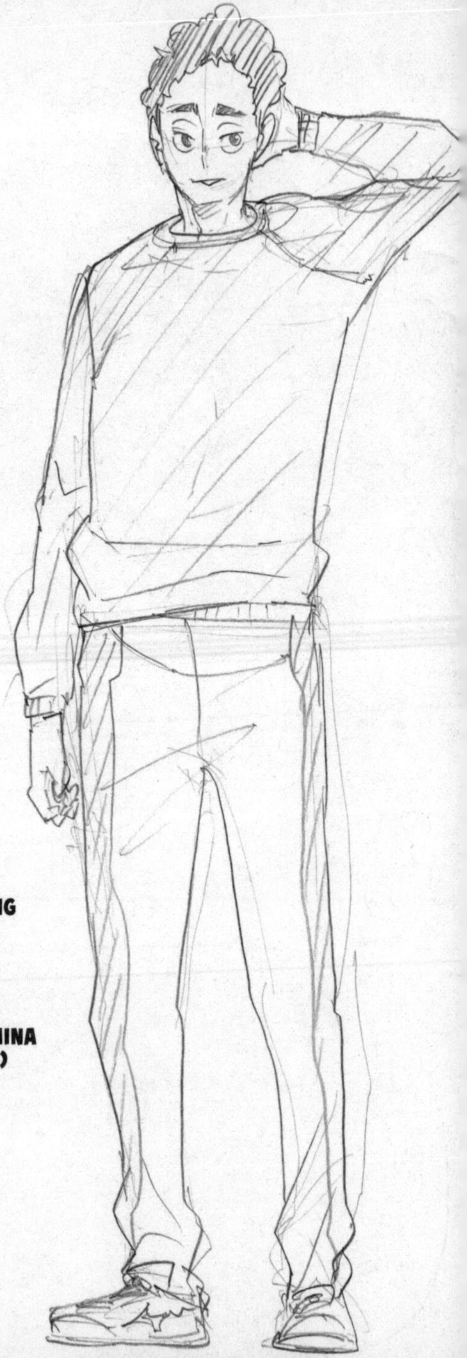

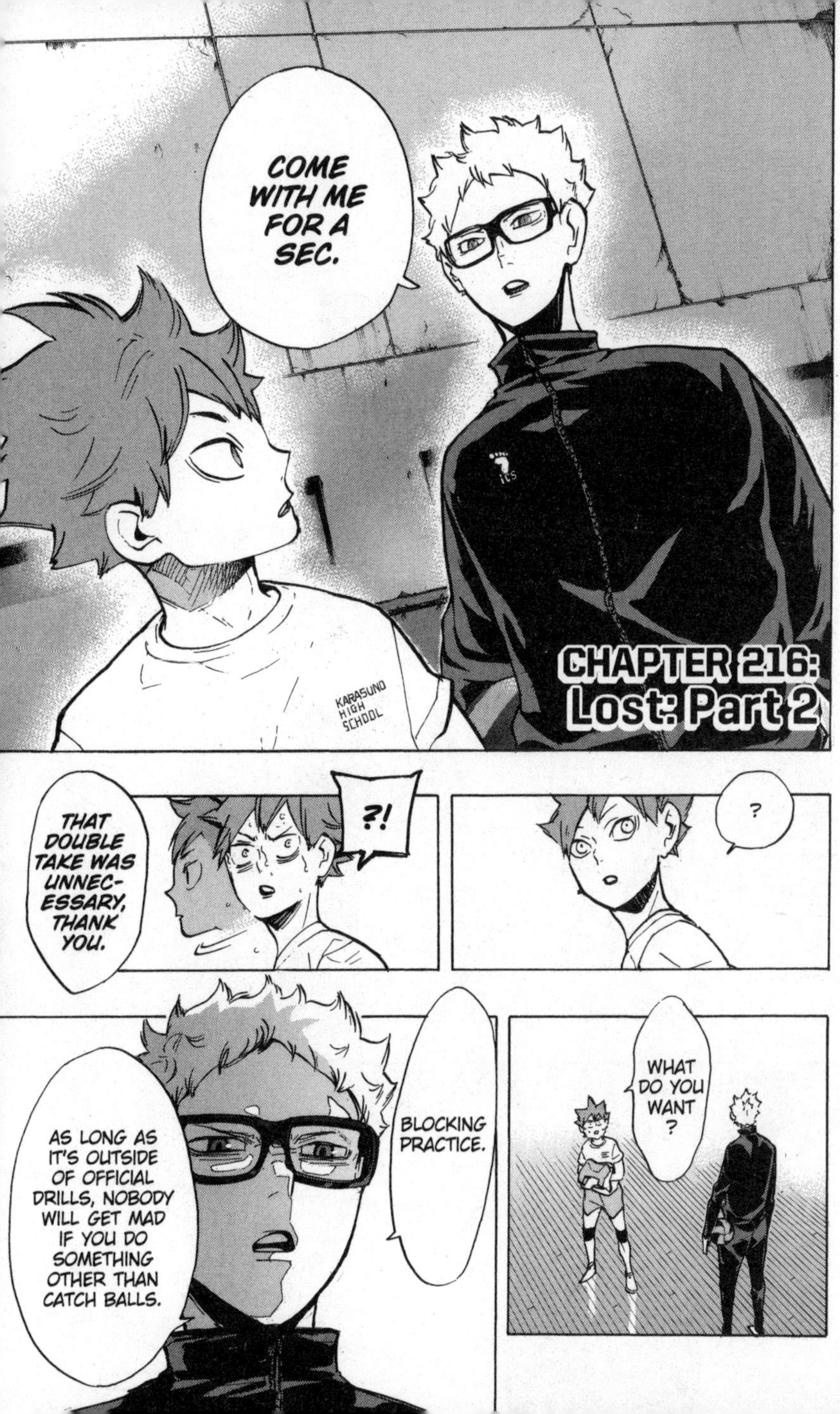
COME WITH ME FOR A SEC.
CHAPTER 216: Lost: Part 2
?
?!
THAT DOUBLE TAKE WAS UNNEC- ESSARY, THANK YOU.
WHAT DO YOU WANT ?
BLOCKING PRACTICE.
AS LONG AS IT'S OUTSIDE OF OFFICIAL DRILLS, NOBODY WILL GET MAD IF YOU DO SOMETHING OTHER THAN CATCH BALLS.
KARASUNO HIGH SCHOOL

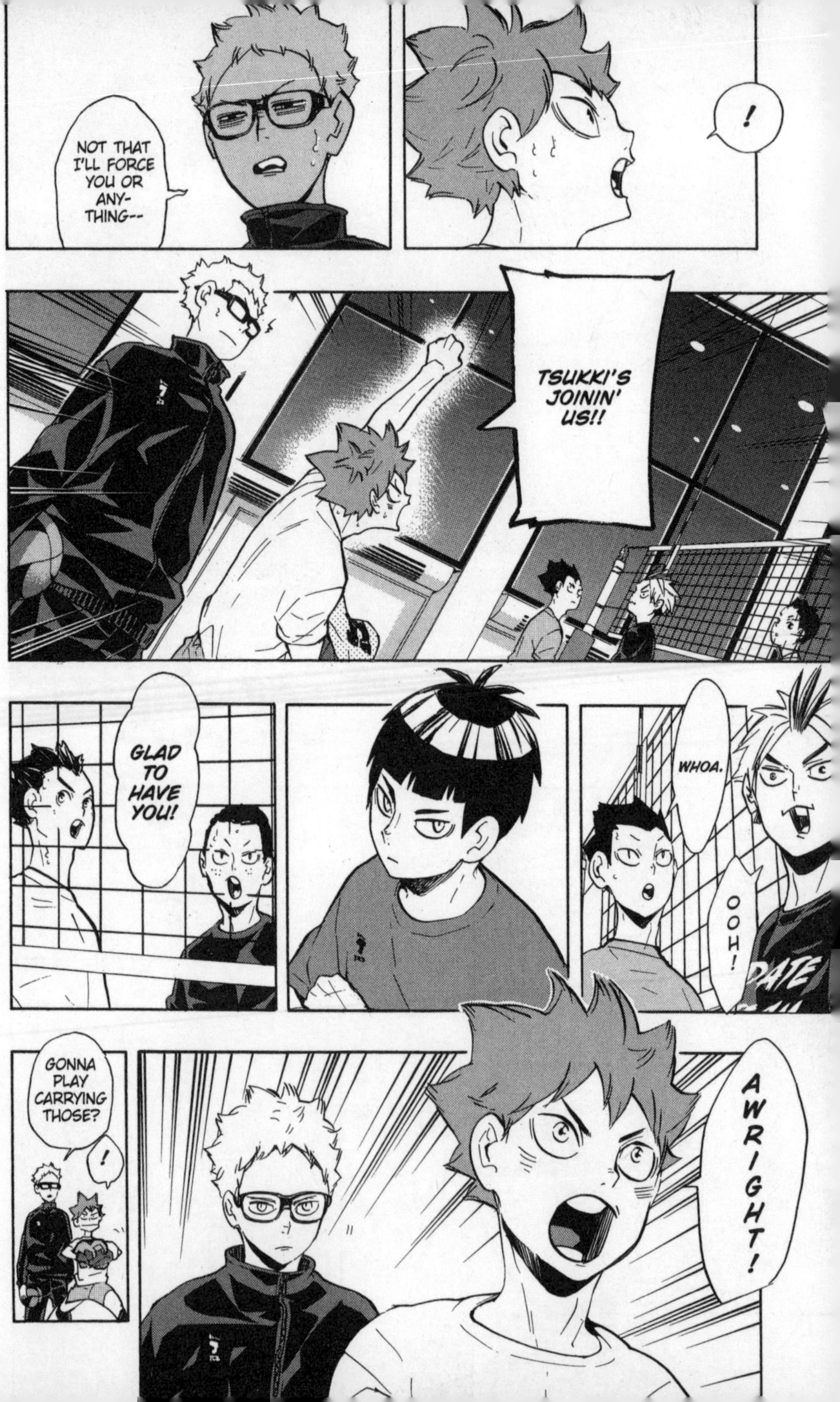
!
NOT THAT I'LL FORCE YOU OR ANY-THING--
TSUKKI'S JOININ' US!!
WHOA.
OOH!
GLAD TO HAVE YOU!
AWRIGHT!
GONNA PLAY CARRYING THOSE?
!

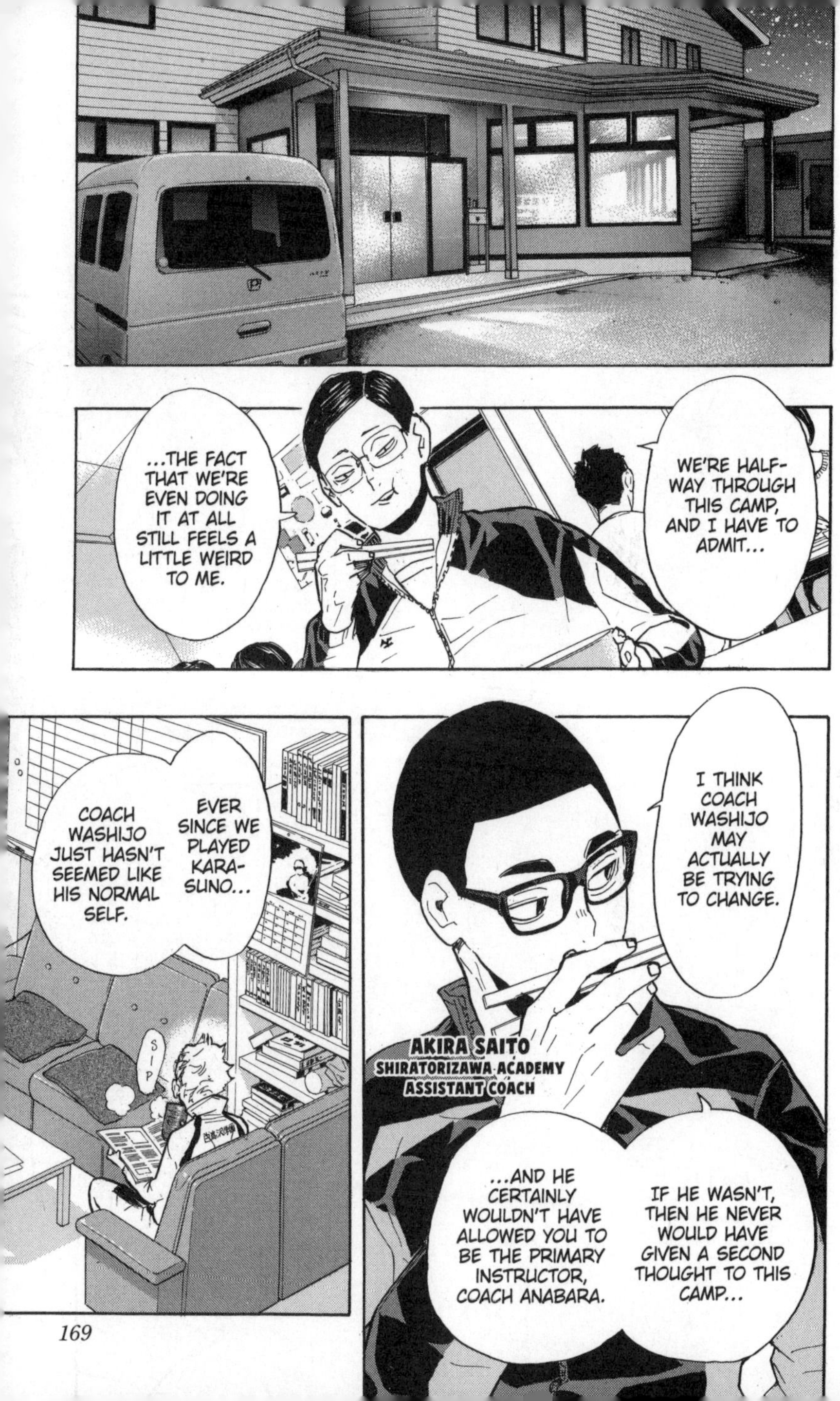
WE'RE HALF-WAY THROUGH THIS CAMP, AND I HAVE TO ADMIT...
...THE FACT THAT WE'RE EVEN DOING IT AT ALL STILL FEELS A LITTLE WEIRD TO ME.
I THINK COACH WASHIJO MAY ACTUALLY BE TRYING TO CHANGE.
AKIRA SAITO
SHIRATORIZAWA ACADEMY ASSISTANT COACH
IF HE WASN'T, THEN HE NEVER WOULD HAVE GIVEN A SECOND THOUGHT TO THIS CAMP...
...AND HE CERTAINLY WOULDN'T HAVE ALLOWED YOU TO BE THE PRIMARY INSTRUCTOR, COACH ANABARA.
EVER SINCE WE PLAYED KARA-SUNO...
COACH WASHIJO JUST HASN'T SEEMED LIKE HIS NORMAL SELF.
SIP

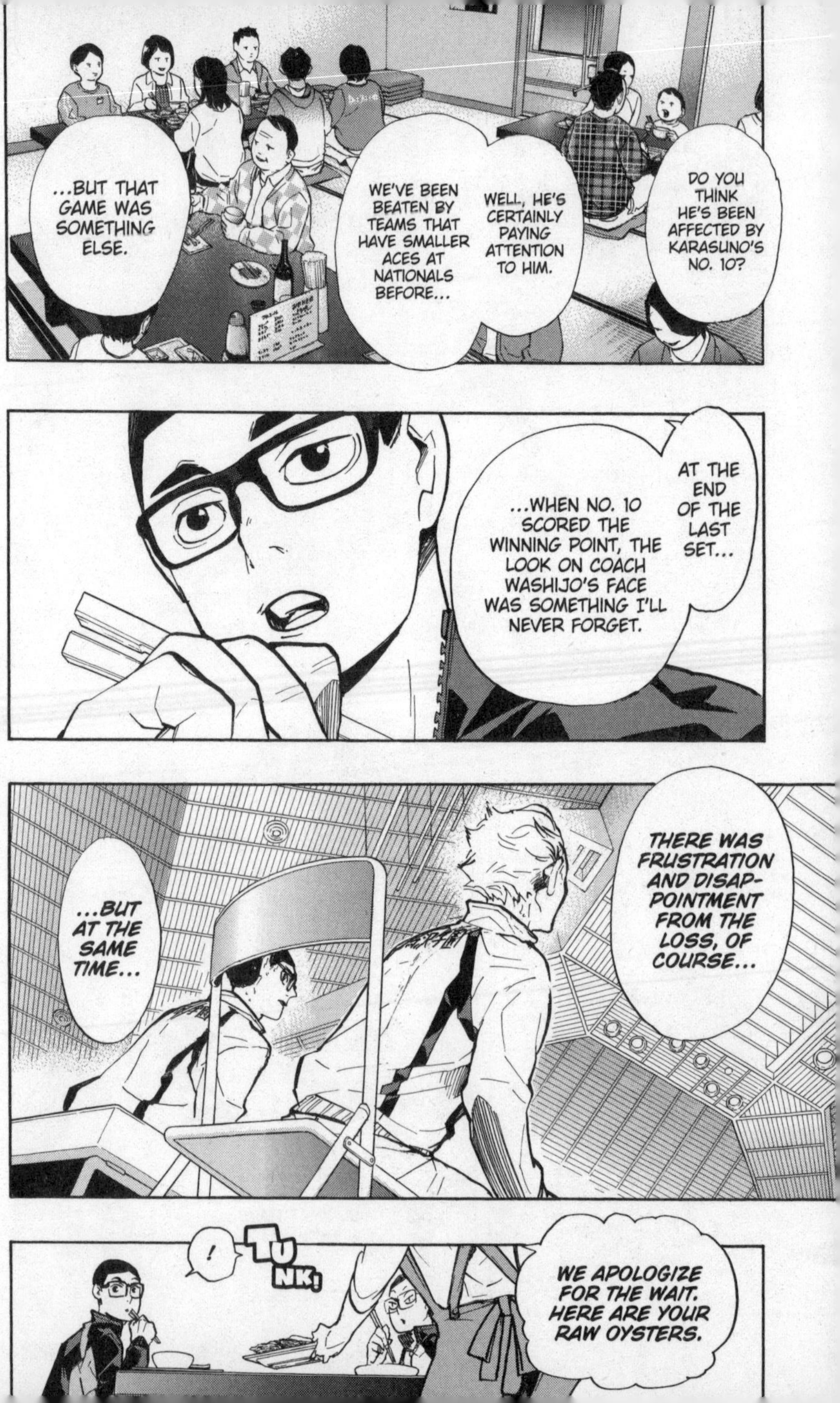
DO YOU THINK HE'S BEEN AFFECTED BY KARASUNO'S NO. 10?
WELL, HE'S CERTAINLY PAYING ATTENTION TO HIM.
WE'VE BEEN BEATEN BY TEAMS THAT HAVE SMALLER ACES AT NATIONALS BEFORE...
...BUT THAT GAME WAS SOMETHING ELSE.
AT THE END OF THE LAST SET...
...WHEN NO. 10 SCORED THE WINNING POINT, THE LOOK ON COACH WASHIJO'S FACE WAS SOMETHING I'LL NEVER FORGET.
THERE WAS FRUSTRATION AND DISAP-POINTMENT FROM THE LOSS, OF COURSE...
...BUT AT THE SAME TIME...
WE APOLOGIZE FOR THE WAIT. HERE ARE YOUR RAW OYSTERS.
TUNK!
!

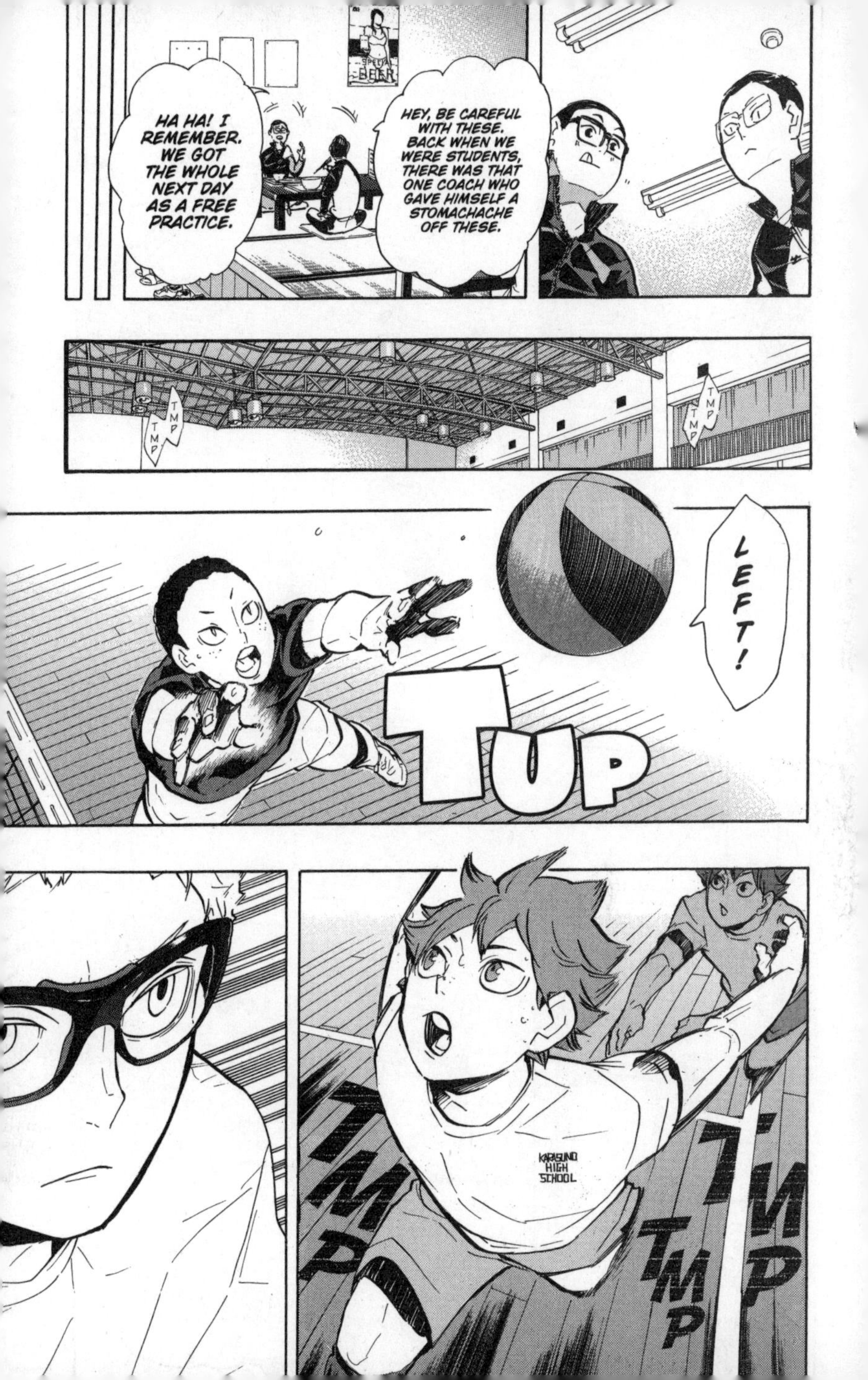
HEY, BE CAREFUL WITH THESE. BACK WHEN WE WERE STUDENTS, THERE WAS THAT ONE COACH WHO GAVE HIMSELF A STOMACHACHE OFF THESE.
HA HA! I REMEMBER. WE GOT THE WHOLE NEXT DAY AS A FREE PRACTICE.
TMP TMP
TMP TMP
LEFT!
TUP
KARASUNO HIGH SCHOOL
TMP TMP
TMP
TMP

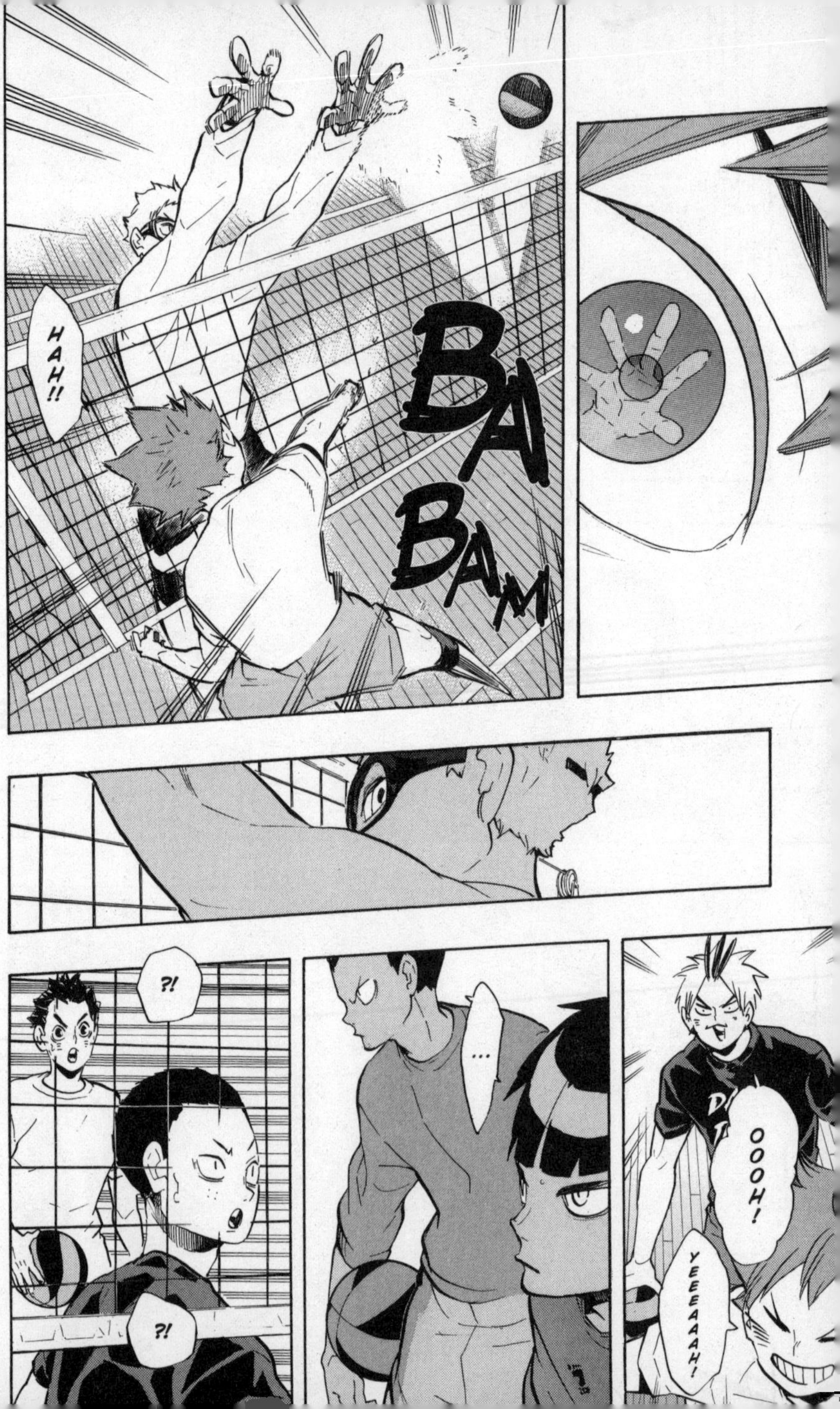
BA BAM
HAH!!
OOOOH!
YEEEAAAAH!
...
?!
?!

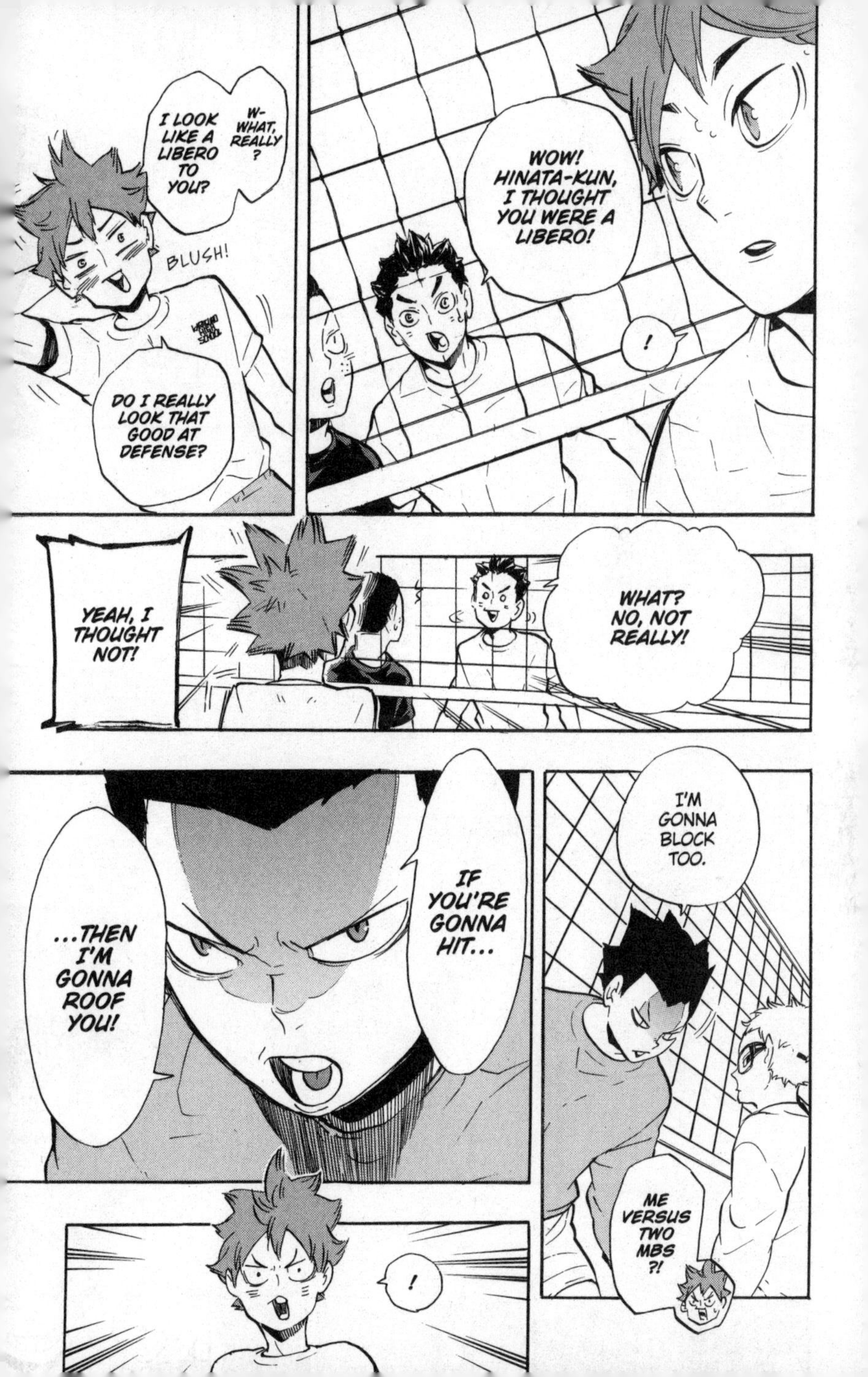
WOW! HINATA-KUN, I THOUGHT YOU WERE A LIBERO!
!
W-WHAT, REALLY?
I LOOK LIKE A LIBERO TO YOU?
BLUSH!
DO I REALLY LOOK THAT GOOD AT DEFENSE?
WHAT? NO, NOT REALLY!
YEAH, I THOUGHT NOT!
I'M GONNA BLOCK TOO.
ME VERSUS TWO MBS?!
IF YOU'RE GONNA HIT...
...THEN I'M GONNA ROOF YOU!
!

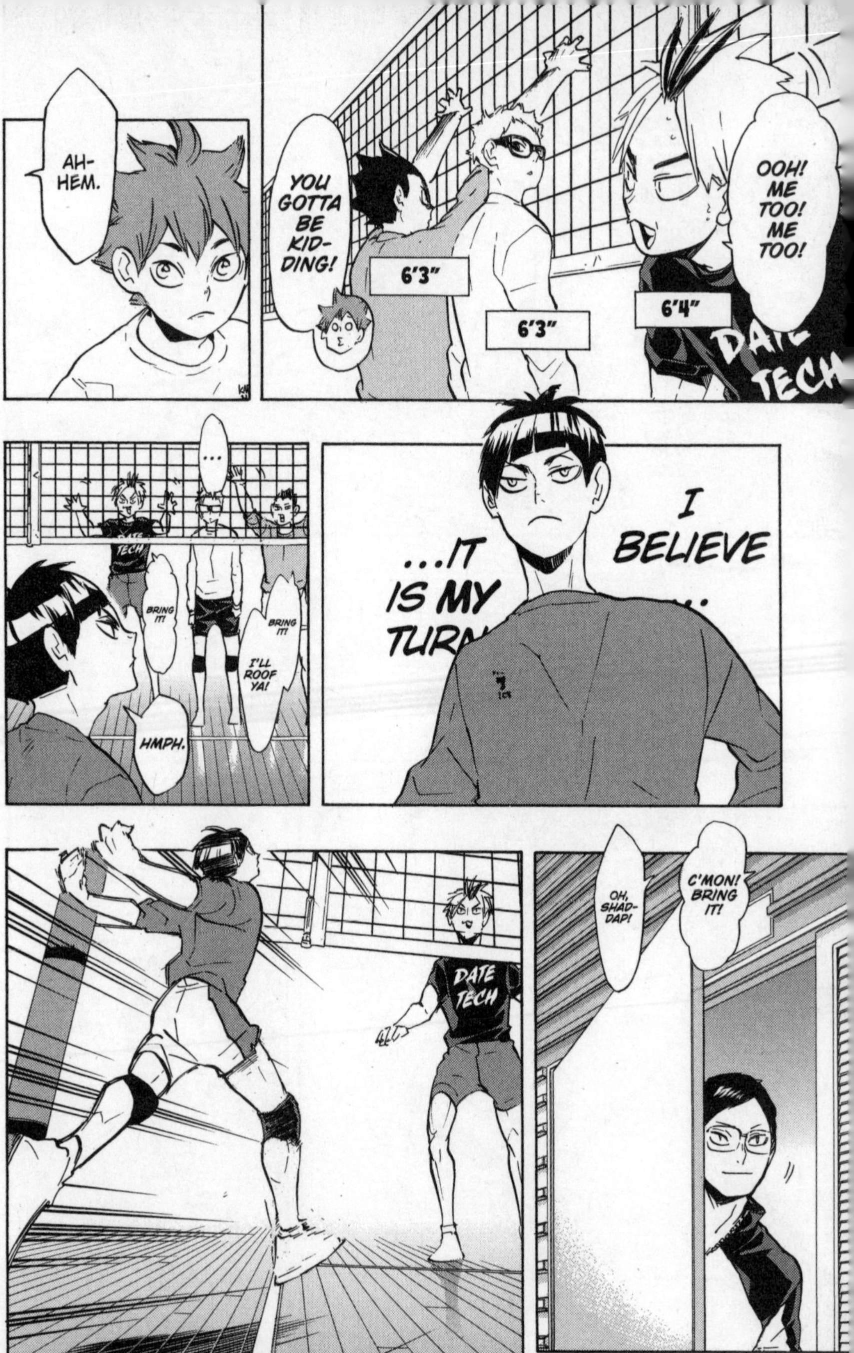
OOH! ME TOO! ME TOO!
6'4"
DATE TECH
6'3"
6'3"
YOU GOTTA BE KID-DING!
AH-HEM.
I BELIEVE...
...IT IS MY TURN.
...
BRING IT!
BRING IT!
I'LL ROOF YA!
HMPH.
C'MON! BRING IT!
OH, SHAD-DAP!
DATE TECH

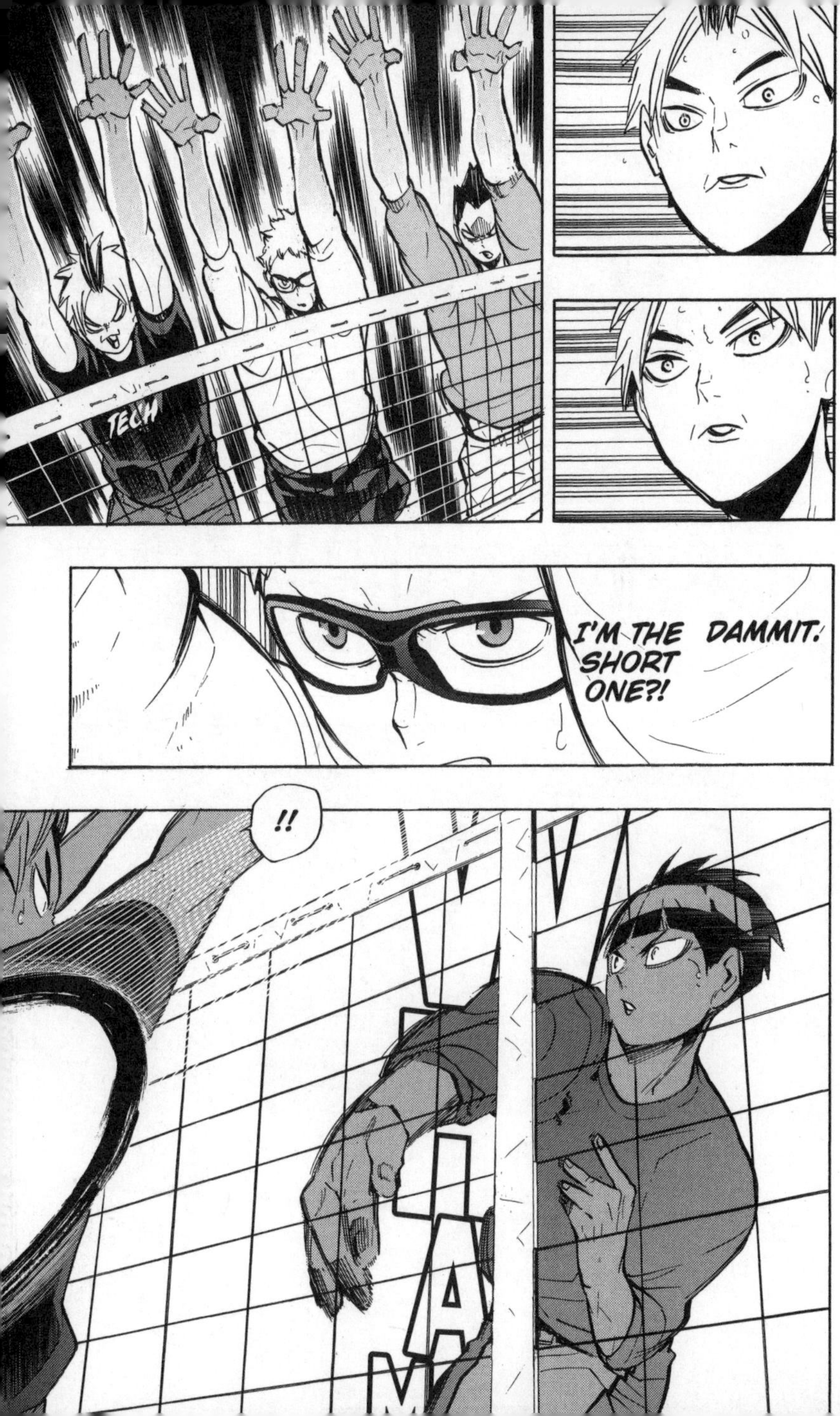
DAMMIT.
I'M THE SHORT ONE?!
!!

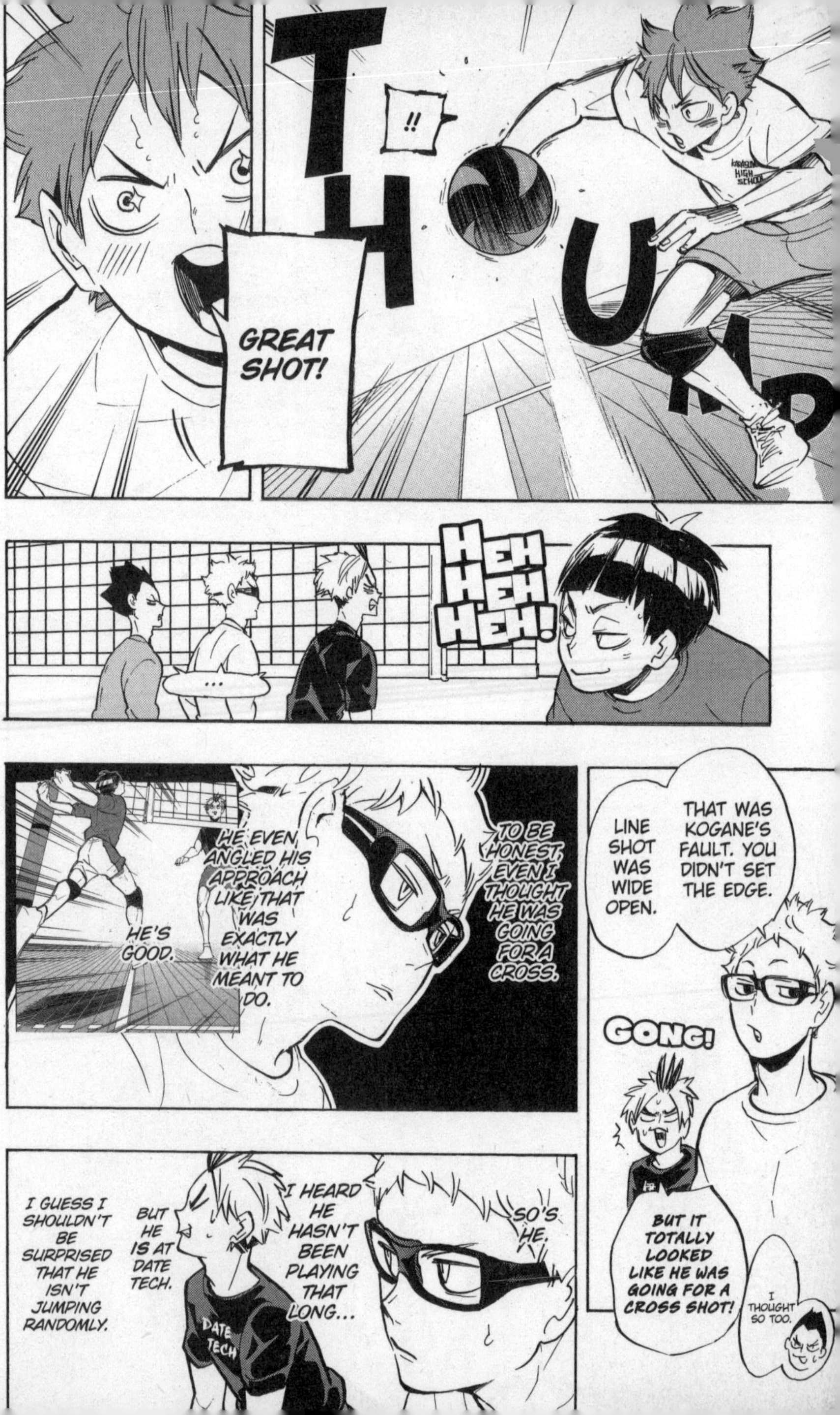
THUMP
!!
GREAT SHOT!
HEH HEH HEH!
...
LINE SHOT WAS WIDE OPEN. THAT WAS KOGANE'S FAULT. YOU DIDN'T SET THE EDGE.
GONG!
BUT IT TOTALLY LOOKED LIKE HE WAS GOING FOR A CROSS SHOT!
I THOUGHT SO TOO.
TO BE HONEST, EVEN I THOUGHT HE WAS GOING FOR A CROSS.
HE EVEN ANGLED HIS APPROACH LIKE THAT WAS EXACTLY WHAT HE MEANT TO DO.
HE'S GOOD.
SO'S HE.
I HEARD HE HASN'T BEEN PLAYING THAT LONG...
BUT HE IS AT DATE TECH.
I GUESS I SHOULDN'T BE SURPRISED THAT HE ISN'T JUMPING RANDOMLY.

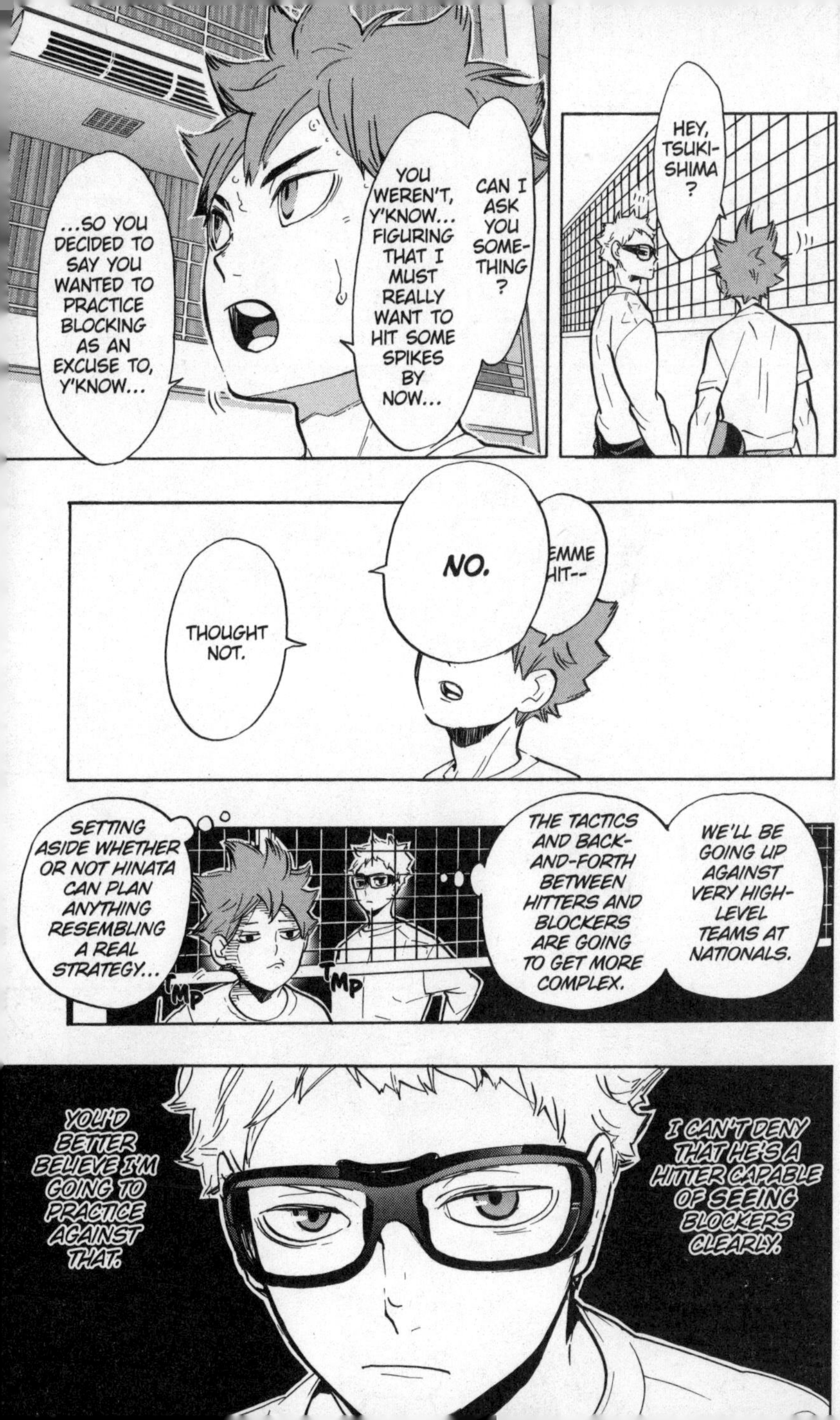
HEY, TSUKISHIMA?
CAN I ASK YOU SOMETHING?
YOU WEREN'T, Y'KNOW... FIGURING THAT I MUST REALLY WANT TO HIT SOME SPIKES BY NOW...
...SO YOU DECIDED TO SAY YOU WANTED TO PRACTICE BLOCKING AS AN EXCUSE TO, Y'KNOW...
EMME HIT--
NO.
THOUGHT NOT.
WE'LL BE GOING UP AGAINST VERY HIGH-LEVEL TEAMS AT NATIONALS.
THE TACTICS AND BACK-AND-FORTH BETWEEN HITTERS AND BLOCKERS ARE GOING TO GET MORE COMPLEX.
SETTING ASIDE WHETHER OR NOT HINATA CAN PLAN ANYTHING RESEMBLING A REAL STRATEGY...
TMP
TMP
I CAN'T DENY THAT HE'S A HITTER CAPABLE OF SEEING BLOCKERS CLEARLY.
YOU'D BETTER BELIEVE I'M GOING TO PRACTICE AGAINST THAT.

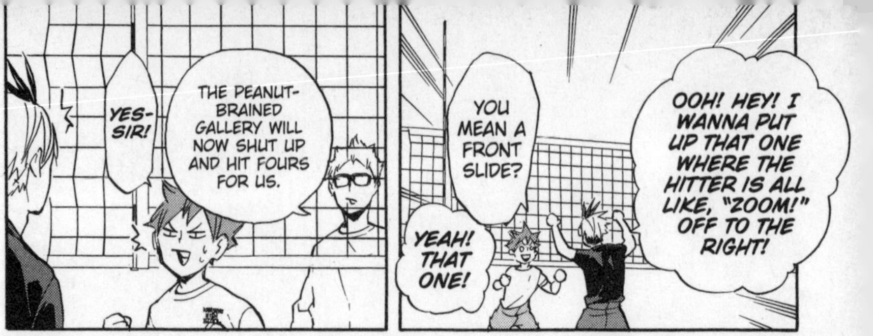
OOH! HEY! I WANNA PUT UP THAT ONE WHERE THE HITTER IS ALL LIKE, "ZOOM!" OFF TO THE RIGHT!
YOU MEAN A FRONT SLIDE?
YEAH! THAT ONE!
THE PEANUT-BRAINED GALLERY WILL NOW SHUT UP AND HIT FOURS FOR US.
YES-SIR!

*A FOUR SET IS A SET WHERE THE BALL IS PUT UP IN A HIGH ARC TO EITHER THE LEFT OR THE RIGHT. IT IS A BASIC, SIMPLE SET.

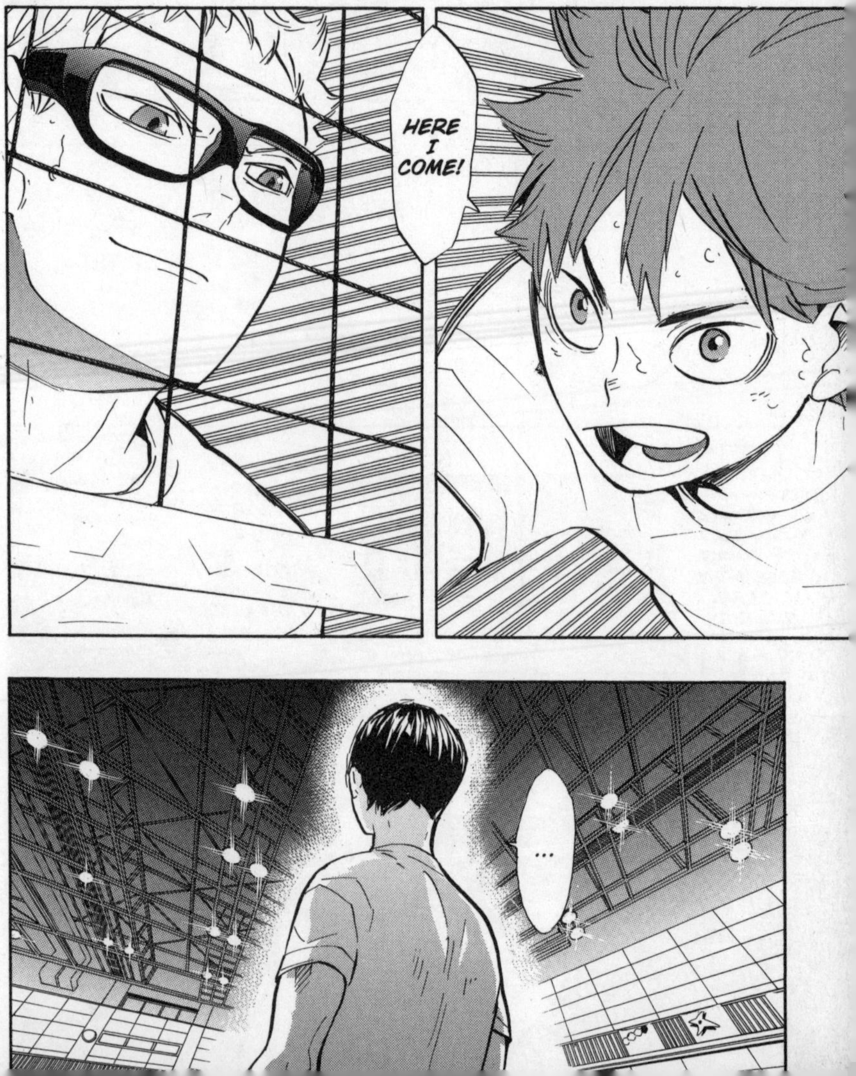
HERE I COME!
...

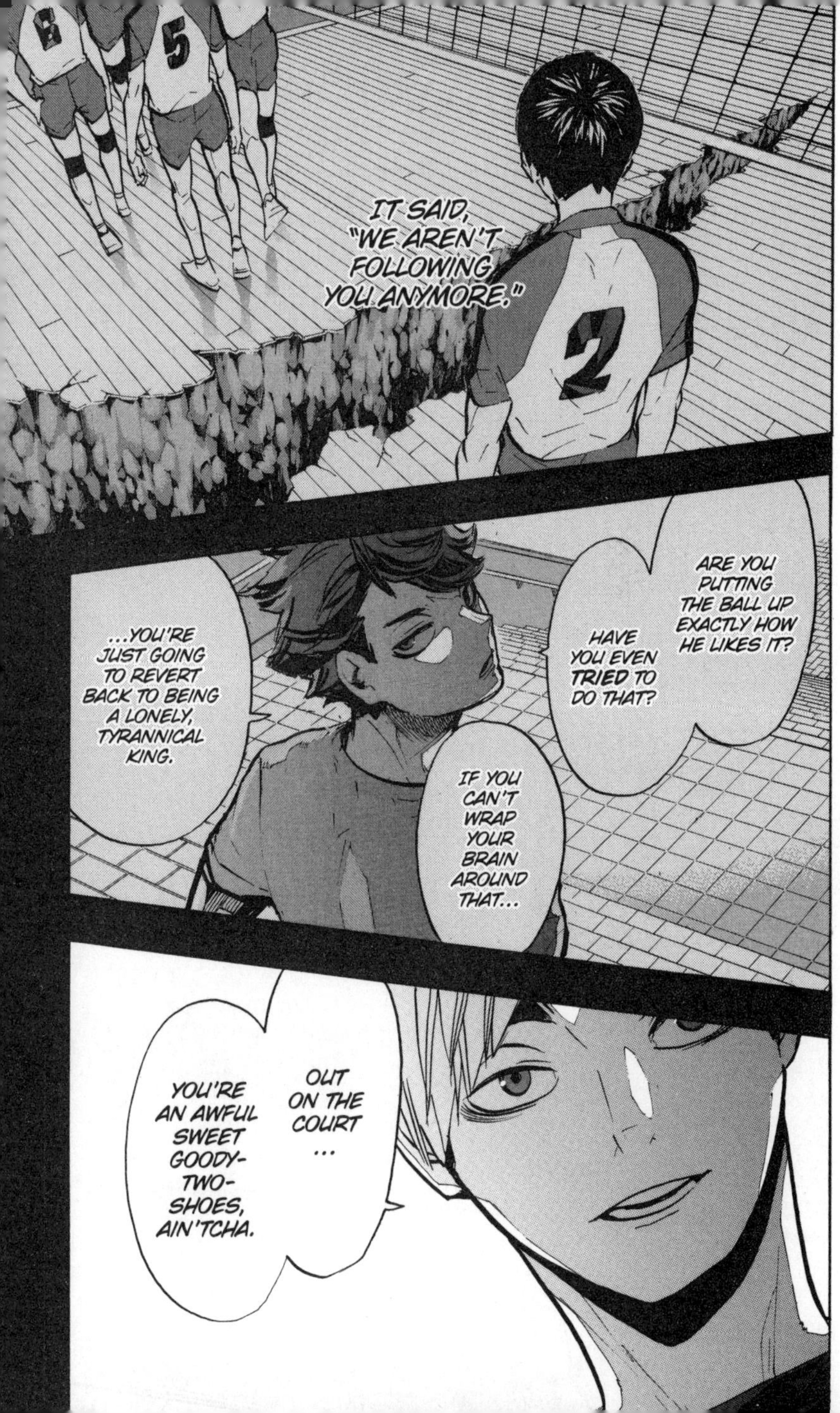
IT SAID, "WE AREN'T FOLLOWING YOU ANYMORE."
ARE YOU PUTTING THE BALL UP EXACTLY HOW HE LIKES IT?
HAVE YOU EVEN **TRIED** TO DO THAT?
IF YOU CAN'T WRAP YOUR BRAIN AROUND THAT...
...YOU'RE JUST GOING TO REVERT BACK TO BEING A LONELY, TYRANNICAL KING.
OUT ON THE COURT...
YOU'RE AN AWFUL SWEET GOODY-TWO-SHOES, AIN'TCHA.

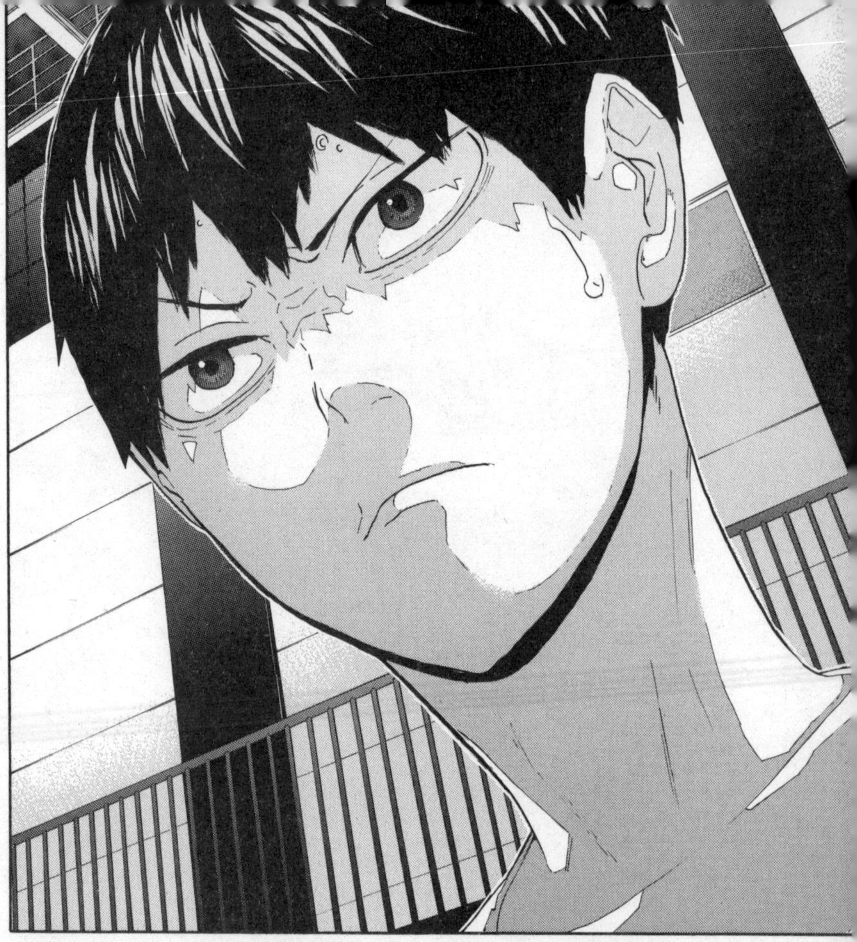

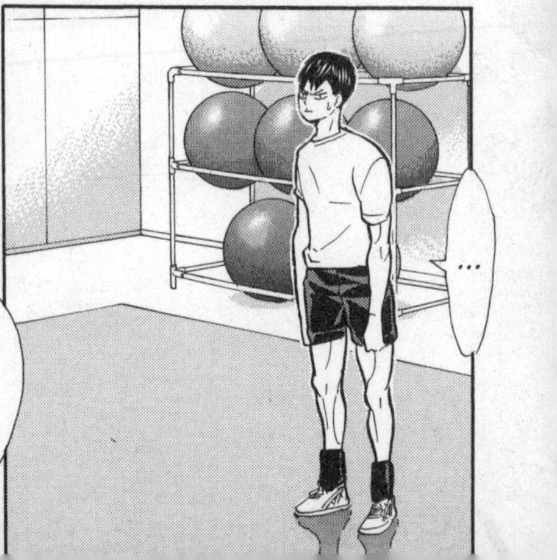
...

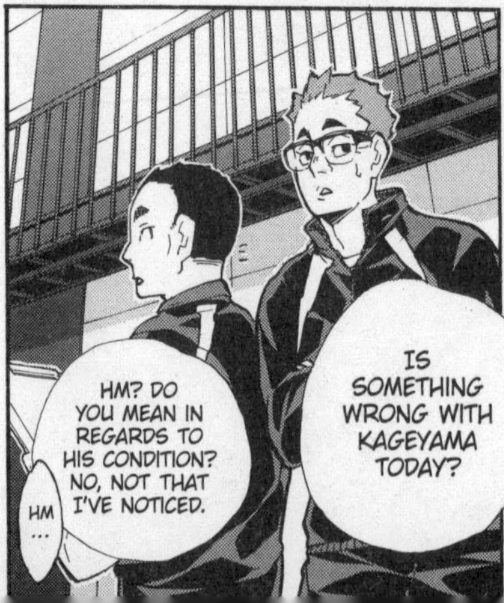
IS SOMETHING WRONG WITH KAGEYAMA TODAY?
HM? DO YOU MEAN IN REGARDS TO HIS CONDITION? NO, NOT THAT I'VE NOTICED.
HM ...

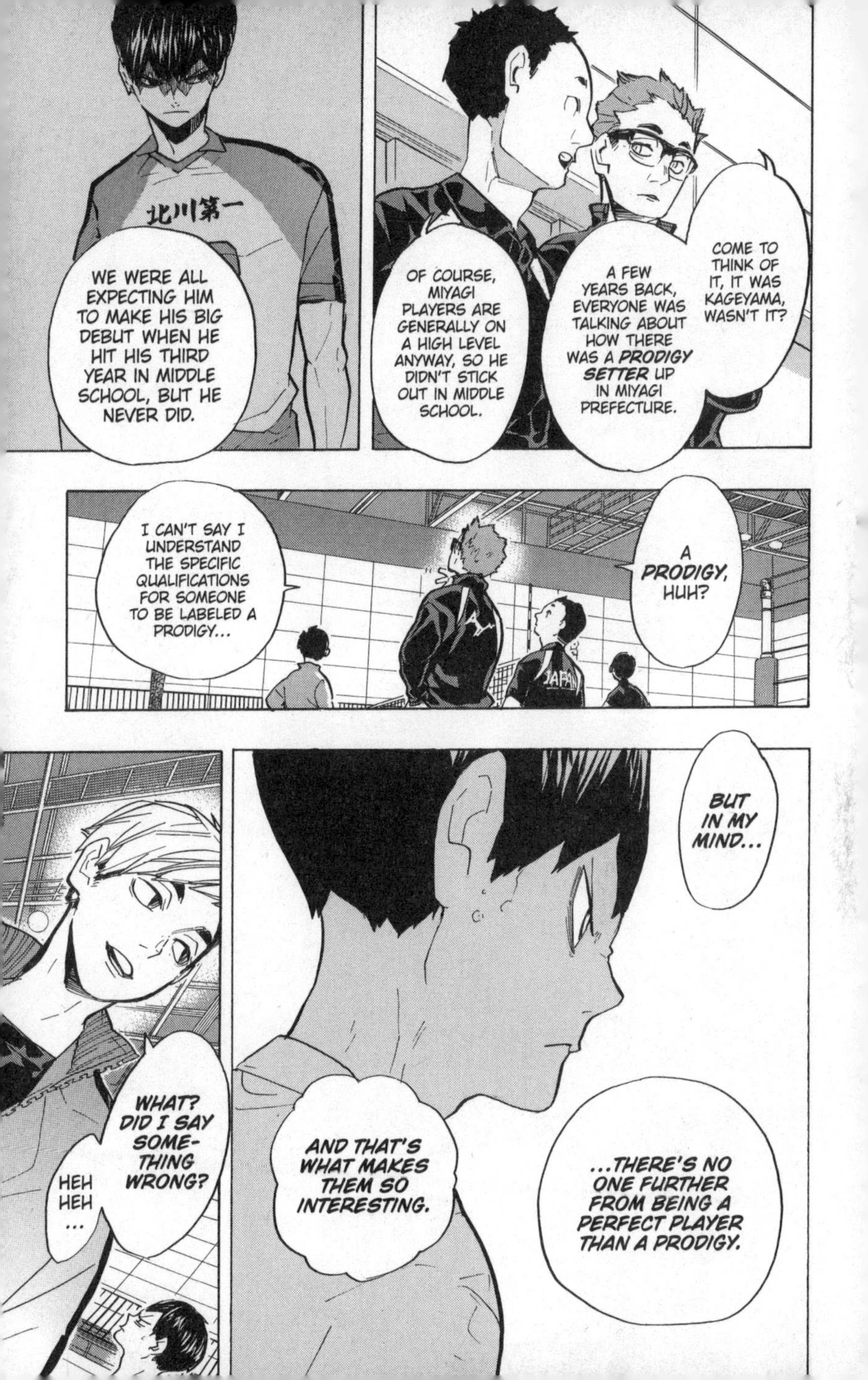
COME TO THINK OF IT, IT WAS KAGEYAMA, WASN'T IT?
A FEW YEARS BACK, EVERYONE WAS TALKING ABOUT HOW THERE WAS A *PRODIGY SETTER* UP IN MIYAGI PREFECTURE.
OF COURSE, MIYAGI PLAYERS ARE GENERALLY ON A HIGH LEVEL ANYWAY, SO HE DIDN'T STICK OUT IN MIDDLE SCHOOL.
北川第一
WE WERE ALL EXPECTING HIM TO MAKE HIS BIG DEBUT WHEN HE HIT HIS THIRD YEAR IN MIDDLE SCHOOL, BUT HE NEVER DID.
A *PRODIGY,* HUH?
I CAN'T SAY I UNDERSTAND THE SPECIFIC QUALIFICATIONS FOR SOMEONE TO BE LABELED A PRODIGY...
JAPAN
BUT IN MY MIND...
...THERE'S NO ONE FURTHER FROM BEING A PERFECT PLAYER THAN A PRODIGY.
AND THAT'S WHAT MAKES THEM SO INTERESTING.
WHAT? DID I SAY SOME-THING WRONG?
HEH HEH...

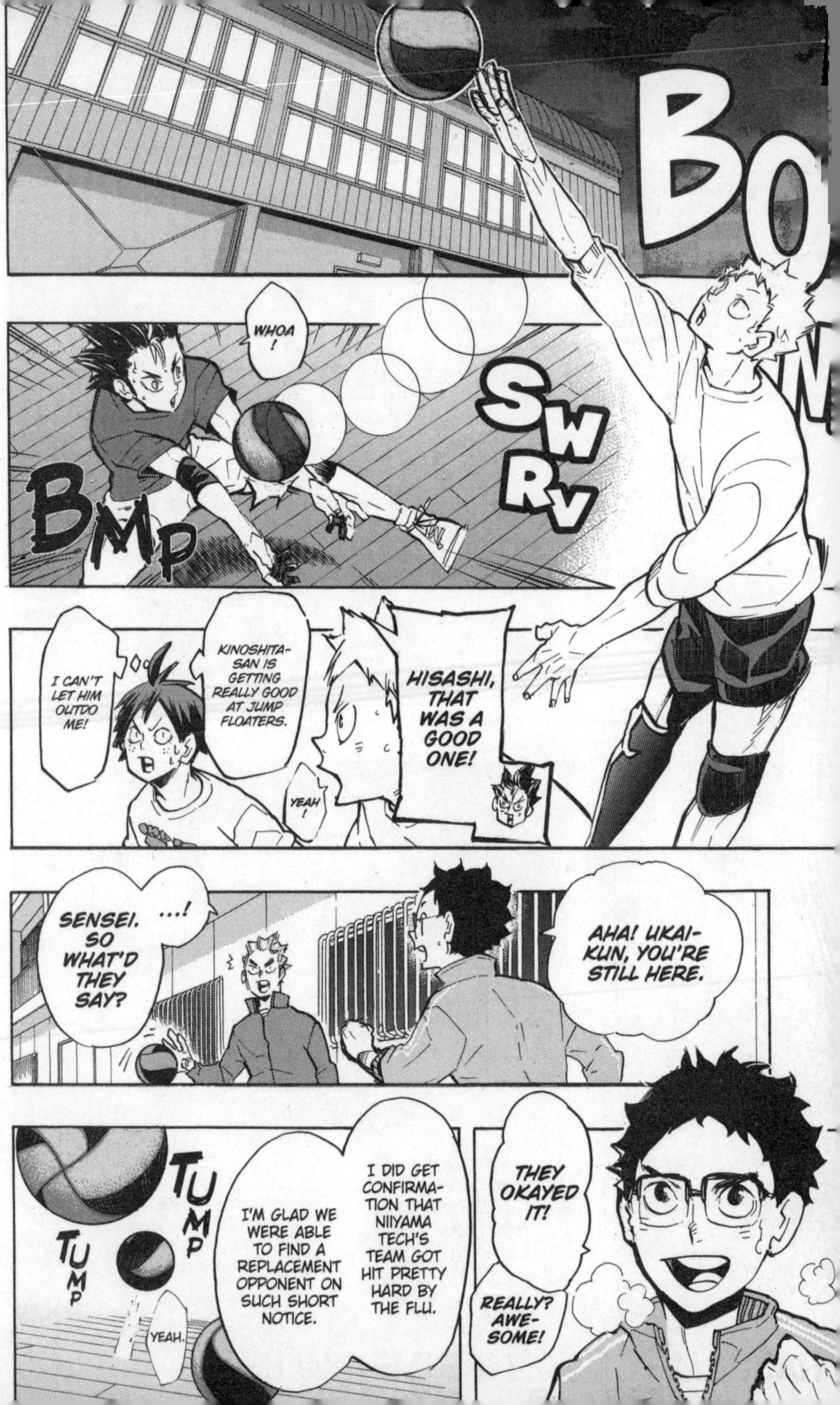
BO
WHOA!
SWRV
BMP
HISASHI, THAT WAS A GOOD ONE!
KINOSHITA-SAN IS GETTING REALLY GOOD AT JUMP FLOATERS.
YEAH!
I CAN'T LET HIM OUTDO ME!
AHA! UKAI-KUN, YOU'RE STILL HERE.
...!
SENSEI. SO WHAT'D THEY SAY?
THEY OKAYED IT!
REALLY? AWESOME!
I DID GET CONFIRMATION THAT NIIYAMA TECH'S TEAM GOT HIT PRETTY HARD BY THE FLU.
I'M GLAD WE WERE ABLE TO FIND A REPLACEMENT OPPONENT ON SUCH SHORT NOTICE.
TUMP
TUMP
YEAH.

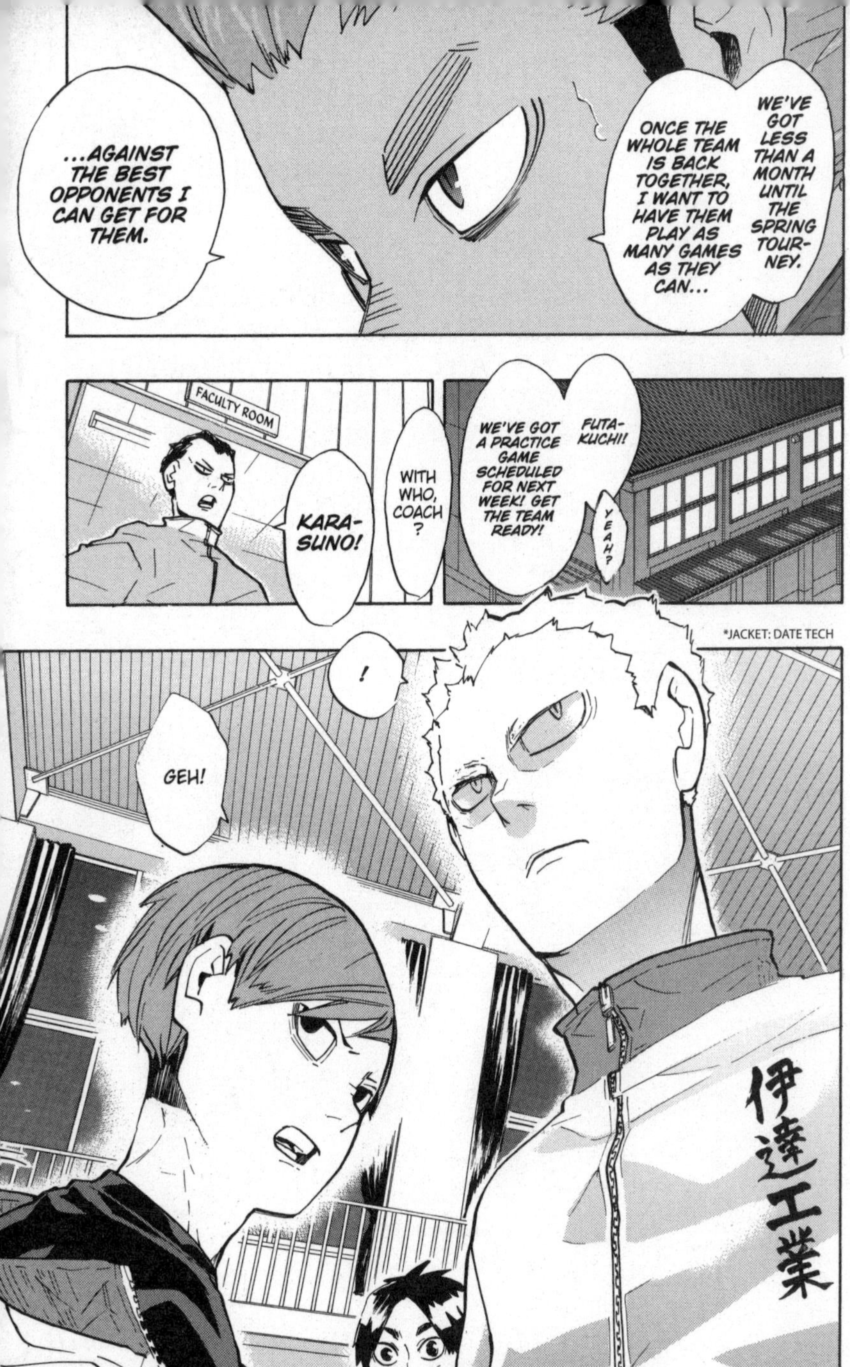
WE'VE GOT LESS THAN A MONTH UNTIL THE SPRING TOURNEY.
ONCE THE WHOLE TEAM IS BACK TOGETHER, I WANT TO HAVE THEM PLAY AS MANY GAMES AS THEY CAN...
...AGAINST THE BEST OPPONENTS I CAN GET FOR THEM.
FUTA-KUCHI!
WE'VE GOT A PRACTICE GAME SCHEDULED FOR NEXT WEEK! GET THE TEAM READY!
YEAH?
FACULTY ROOM
WITH WHO, COACH?
KARA-SUNO!
*JACKET: DATE TECH
!
GEH!
伊達工業

HAIKYU!! VOL 24: FIRST SNOW (END)

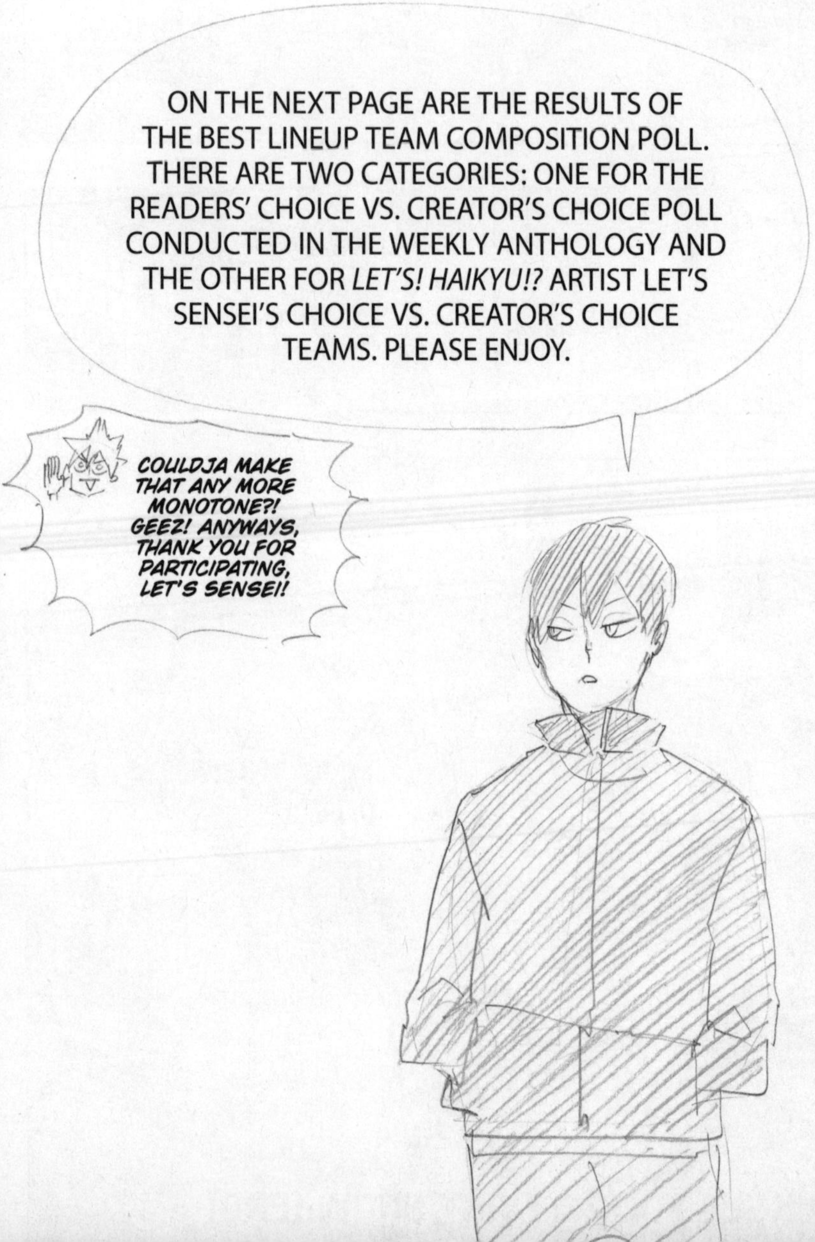
ON THE NEXT PAGE ARE THE RESULTS OF THE BEST LINEUP TEAM COMPOSITION POLL. THERE ARE TWO CATEGORIES: ONE FOR THE READERS' CHOICE VS. CREATOR'S CHOICE POLL CONDUCTED IN THE WEEKLY ANTHOLOGY AND THE OTHER FOR *LET'S! HAIKYU!?* ARTIST LET'S SENSEI'S CHOICE VS. CREATOR'S CHOICE TEAMS. PLEASE ENJOY.
COULDJA MAKE THAT ANY MORE MONOTONE?! GEEZ! ANYWAYS, THANK YOU FOR PARTICIPATING, LET'S SENSEI!

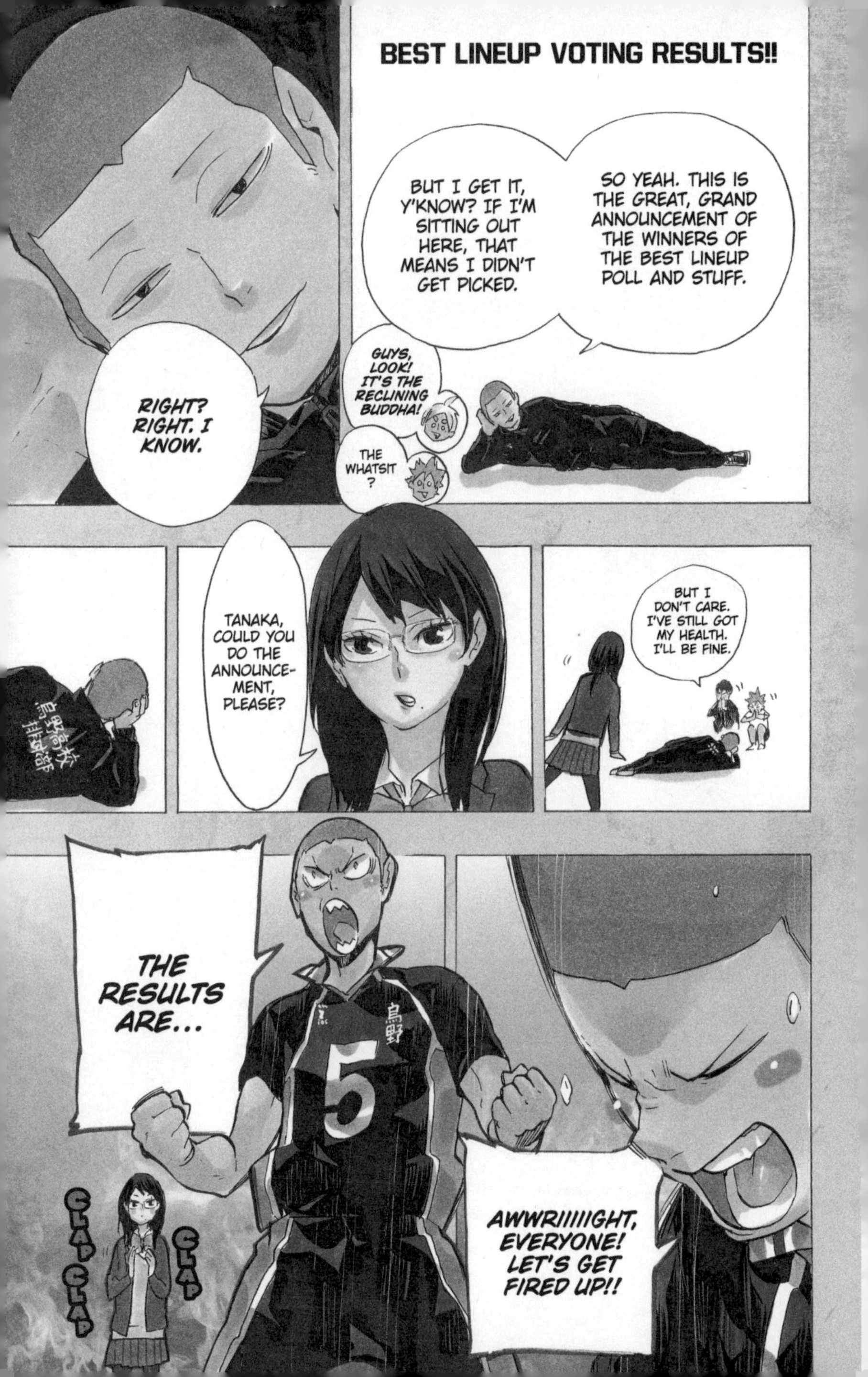
BEST LINEUP VOTING RESULTS!!
SO YEAH. THIS IS THE GREAT, GRAND ANNOUNCEMENT OF THE WINNERS OF THE BEST LINEUP POLL AND STUFF.
BUT I GET IT, Y'KNOW? IF I'M SITTING OUT HERE, THAT MEANS I DIDN'T GET PICKED.
GUYS, LOOK! IT'S THE RECLINING BUDDHA!
THE WHATSIT?
RIGHT? RIGHT. I KNOW.
BUT I DON'T CARE. I'VE STILL GOT MY HEALTH. I'LL BE FINE.
TANAKA, COULD YOU DO THE ANNOUNCEMENT, PLEASE?
AWWRIIIIIGHT, EVERYONE! LET'S GET FIRED UP!!
THE RESULTS ARE...
CLAP
CLAP CLAP

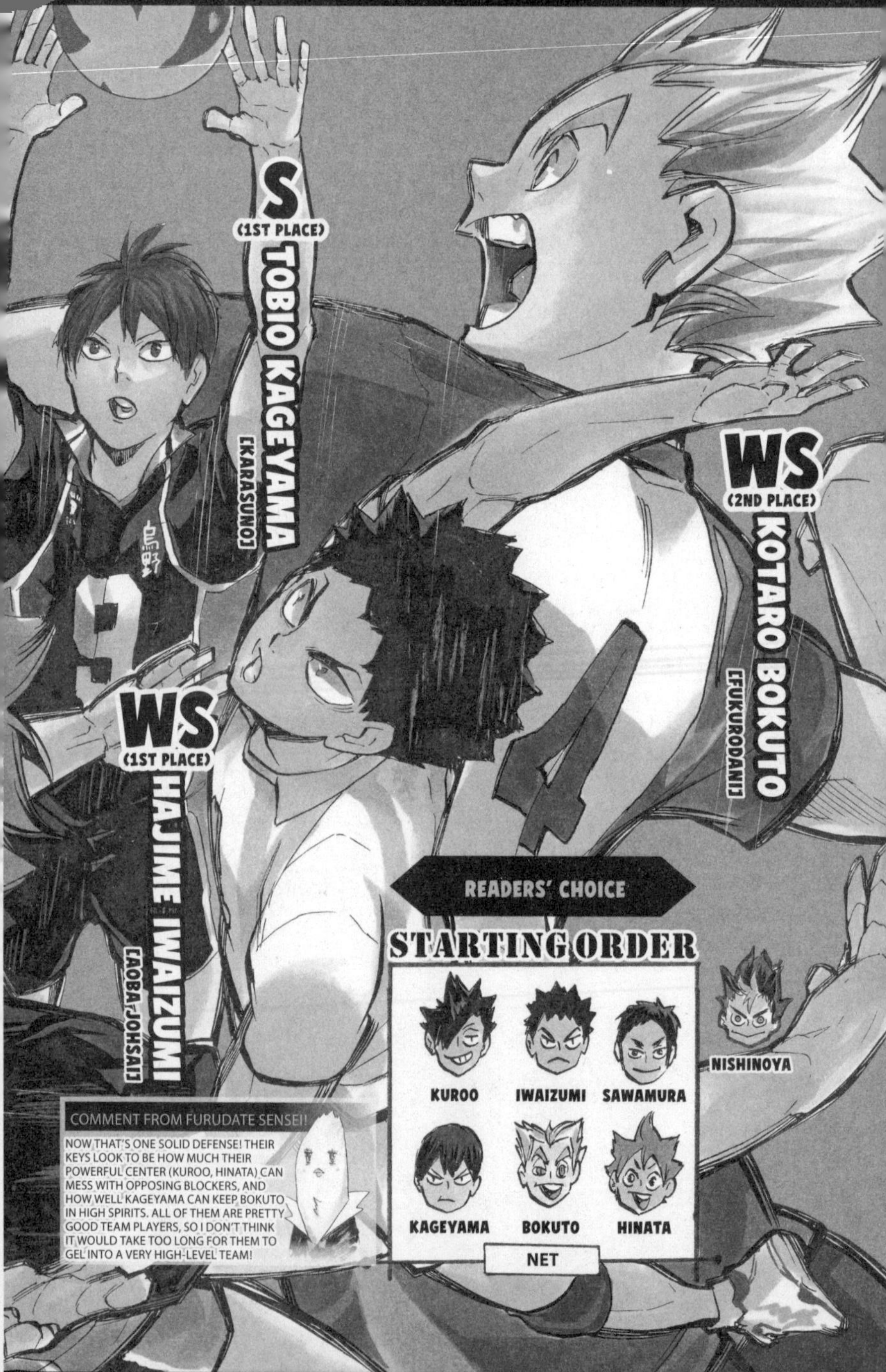
WS
(2ND PLACE)
KOTARO BOKUTO
[FUKURODANI]
S
(1ST PLACE)
TOBIO KAGEYAMA
[KARASUNO]
WS
(1ST PLACE)
HAJIME IWAIZUMI
[AOBA JOHSAI]
READERS' CHOICE
STARTING ORDER
KUROO
IWAIZUMI
SAWAMURA
NISHINOYA
KAGEYAMA
BOKUTO
HINATA
NET
COMMENT FROM FURUDATE SENSEI!
NOW THAT'S ONE SOLID DEFENSE! THEIR KEYS LOOK TO BE HOW MUCH THEIR POWERFUL CENTER (KUROO, HINATA) CAN MESS WITH OPPOSING BLOCKERS, AND HOW WELL KAGEYAMA CAN KEEP BOKUTO IN HIGH SPIRITS. ALL OF THEM ARE PRETTY GOOD TEAM PLAYERS, SO I DON'T THINK IT WOULD TAKE TOO LONG FOR THEM TO GEL INTO A VERY HIGH-LEVEL TEAM!

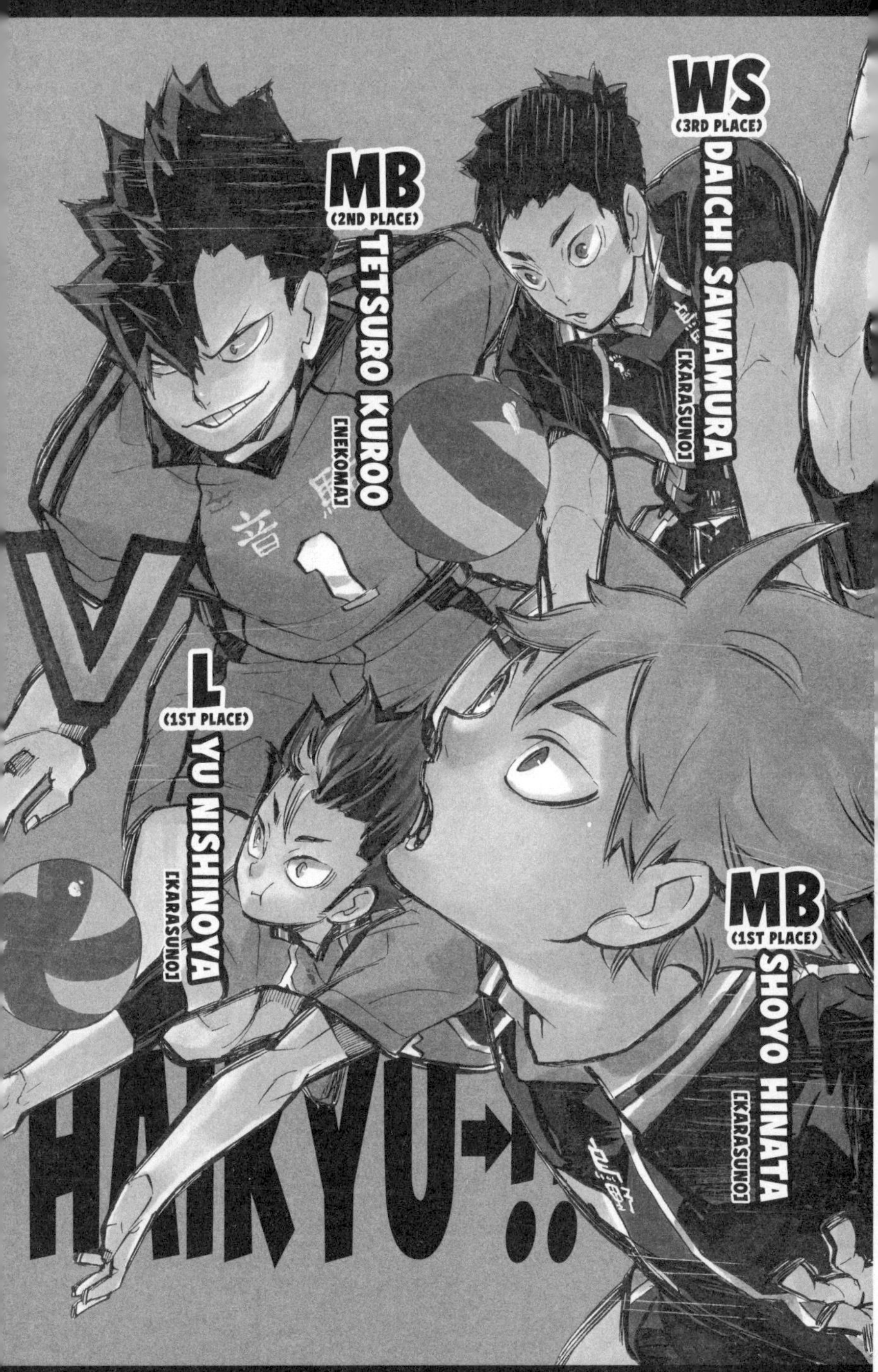
WS
(3RD PLACE)
DAICHI SAWAMURA
[KARASUNO]
MB
(2ND PLACE)
TETSURO KUROO
[NEKOMA]
MB
(1ST PLACE)
SHOYO HINATA
[KARASUNO]
L
(1ST PLACE)
YU NISHINOYA
[KARASUNO]
HAIKYU!!

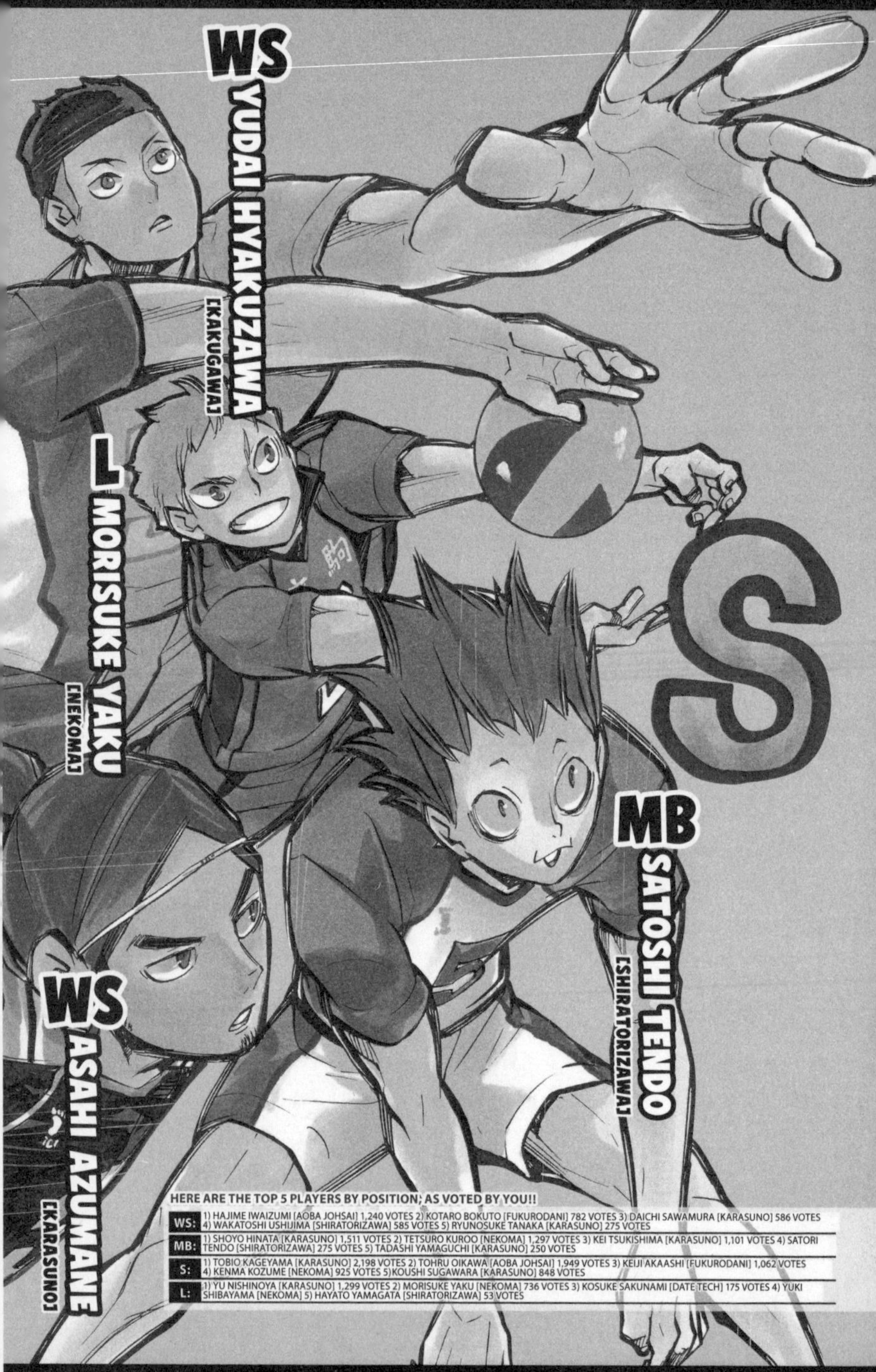
WS
YUDAI HYAKUZAWA
[KAKUGAWA]
L
MORISUKE YAKU
[NEKOMA]
S
MB
SATOSHI TENDO
[SHIRATORIZAWA]
WS
ASAHI AZUMANE
[KARASUNO]

HERE ARE THE TOP 5 PLAYERS BY POSITION; AS VOTED BY YOU!!

WS:	1) HAJIME IWAIZUMI [AOBA JOHSAI] 1,240 VOTES 2) KOTARO BOKUTO [FUKURODANI] 782 VOTES 3) DAICHI SAWAMURA [KARASUNO] 586 VOTES 4) WAKATOSHI USHIJIMA [SHIRATORIZAWA] 585 VOTES 5) RYUNOSUKE TANAKA [KARASUNO] 275 VOTES
MB:	1) SHOYO HINATA [KARASUNO] 1,511 VOTES 2) TETSURO KUROO [NEKOMA] 1,297 VOTES 3) KEI TSUKISHIMA [KARASUNO] 1,101 VOTES 4) SATORI TENDO [SHIRATORIZAWA] 275 VOTES 5) TADASHI YAMAGUCHI [KARASUNO] 250 VOTES
S:	1) TOBIO KAGEYAMA [KARASUNO] 2,198 VOTES 2) TOHRU OIKAWA [AOBA JOHSAI] 1,949 VOTES 3) KEIJI AKAASHI [FUKURODANI] 1,062 VOTES 4) KENMA KOZUME [NEKOMA] 925 VOTES 5)KOUSHI SUGAWARA [KARASUNO] 848 VOTES
L:	1) YU NISHINOYA [KARASUNO] 1,299 VOTES 2) MORISUKE YAKU [NEKOMA] 736 VOTES 3) KOSUKE SAKUNAMI [DATE TECH] 175 VOTES 4) YUKI SHIBAYAMA [NEKOMA] 5) HAYATO YAMAGATA [SHIRATORIZAWA] 53 VOTES

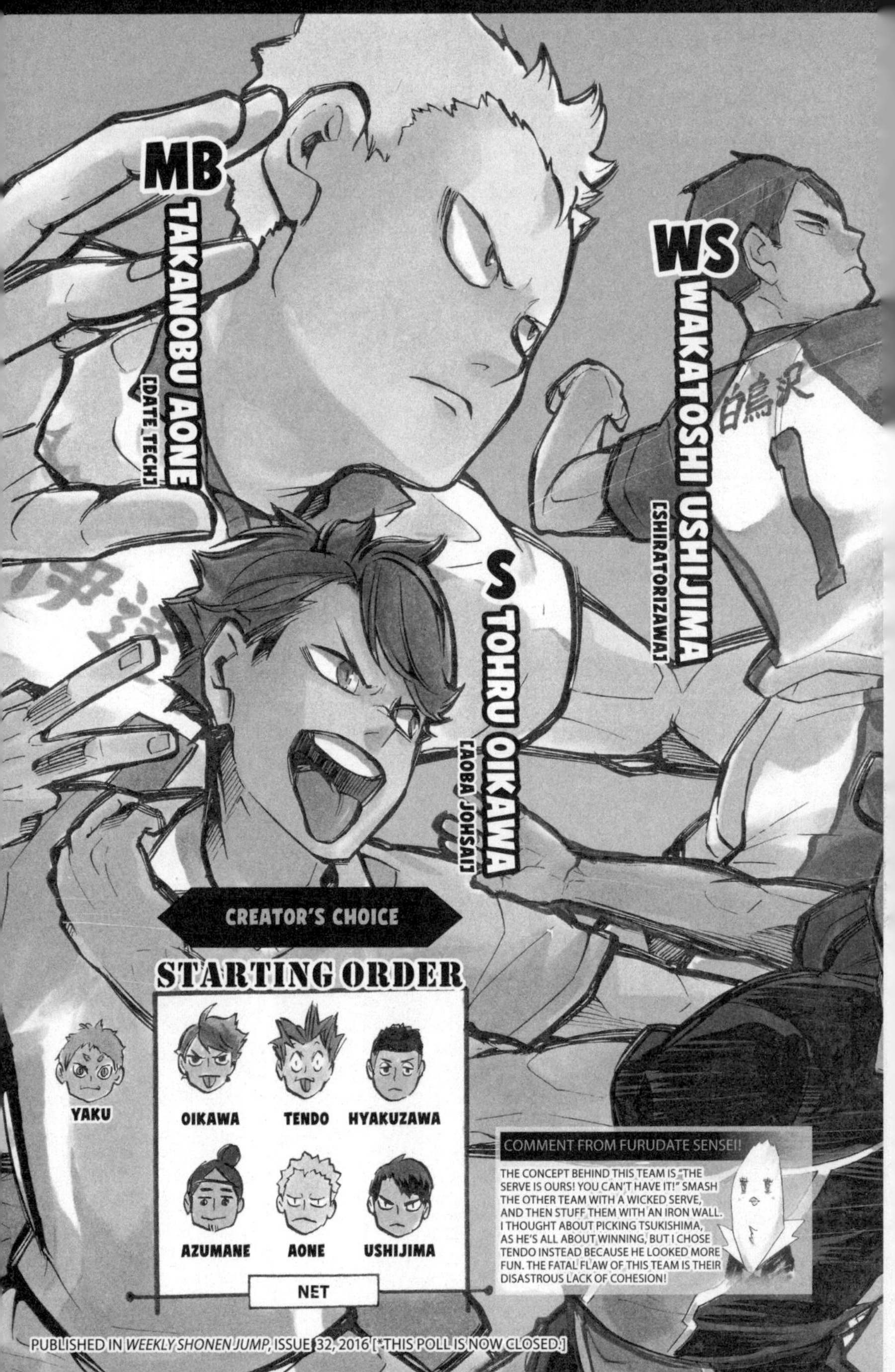
MB
TAKANOBU AONE
[DATE TECH]
WS
WAKATOSHI USHIJIMA
[SHIRATORIZAWA]
白鳥沢
S
TOHRU OIKAWA
[AOBA JOHSAI]
CREATOR'S CHOICE
STARTING ORDER
YAKU
OIKAWA
TENDO
HYAKUZAWA
AZUMANE
AONE
USHIJIMA
NET
COMMENT FROM FURUDATE SENSEI!
THE CONCEPT BEHIND THIS TEAM IS "THE SERVE IS OURS! YOU CAN'T HAVE IT!" SMASH THE OTHER TEAM WITH A WICKED SERVE, AND THEN STUFF THEM WITH AN IRON WALL. I THOUGHT ABOUT PICKING TSUKISHIMA, AS HE'S ALL ABOUT WINNING, BUT I CHOSE TENDO INSTEAD BECAUSE HE LOOKED MORE FUN. THE FATAL FLAW OF THIS TEAM IS THEIR DISASTROUS LACK OF COHESION!

PUBLISHED IN *WEEKLY SHONEN JUMP*, ISSUE 32, 2016 [*THIS POLL IS NOW CLOSED.]

JUMP+'S LET'S! HAIKYU!? VOLUMES 1–3 ON SALE NOW IN JAPAN! (AS OF DEC. 2016)

[LET'S SENSEI'S CHOSEN LINEUP!!]

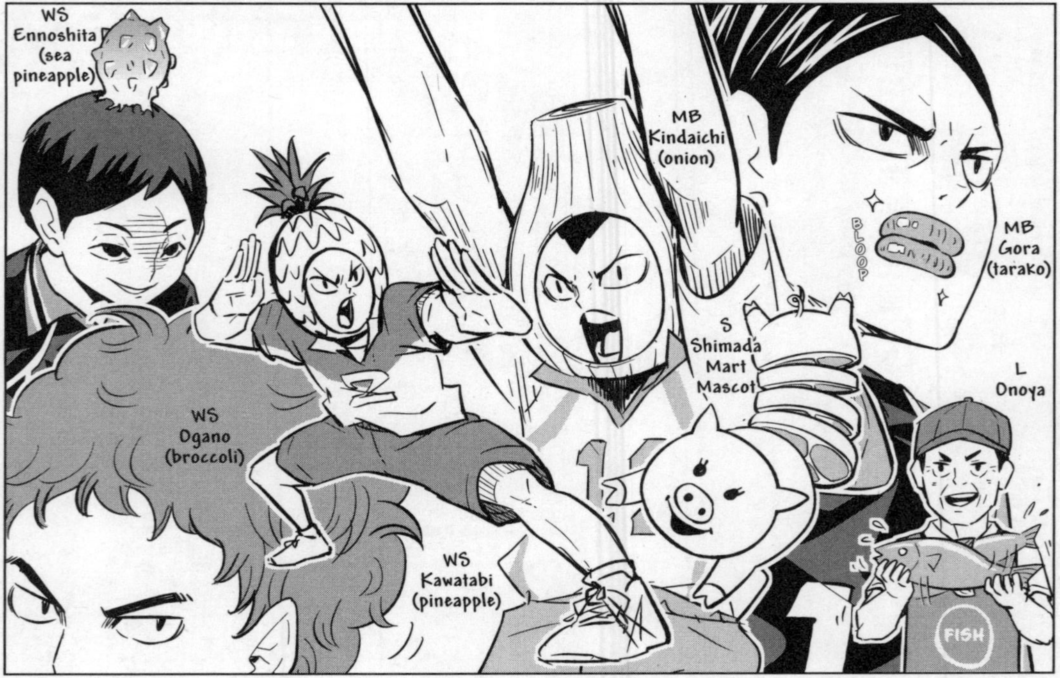
MB Gora (tarako)
BLOOP
MB Kindaichi (onion)
S Shimada Mart Mascot
L Onoya
FISH
WS Ennoshita (sea pineapple)
WS Ogano (broccoli)
WS Kawatabi (pineapple)

WOW! LOOK! I PUT TOGETHER A TEAM OF THE *LET'S! HAIKYU!?* CHARACTERS! THE CONCEPT WAS AN ALL-FOOD LINEUP. POSITIONS ARE JUST WHATEVER I FELT LIKE. I LIKE TO THINK IT'S A NUTRITIONALLY BALANCED TEAM WITH SEAFOOD, MEAT, VEGETABLES, FRUIT AND MORE! HECK, I THINK THE ONLY THING MISSING IS SOME CARBOHYDRATES?

[CREATOR'S CHOICE 2!!]

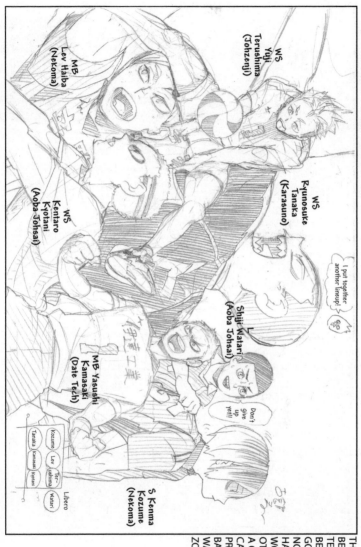

WS
Yuji
Terushima
(Johzenji)

MB
Lev Haiba
(Nekoma)

WS
Ryunosuke
Tanaka
(Karasuno)

WS
Kentaro
Kyotani
(Aoba Johsai)

I put together
another lineup!

L
Shuji Watari
(Aoba Johsai)

Don't
give
up
yet!!

MB Yasushi
Kamasaki
(Date Tech)

S Kenma
Kozume
(Nekoma)

Libero

Kozume		
Tanaka	Kamasaki	Kyotani

| Ter- |
| ushima |

| Lev |

| Watari |

THE CONCEPT
BEHIND THIS
TEAM IS "THE
BEST DEFENSE IS A
GOOD OFFENSE!"
NO MATTER WHAT
HAPPENS, THEY
WON'T LET THE
OTHER TEAM HAVE
A CHANCE BALL!
CAN KOZUME AND
PRACTICALLY-
BACKUP-SETTER
WATARI KEEP THIS
ZOO IN LINE?!

EDITOR'S NOTES

The English edition of Haikyu!! maintains the honorifics used in the original Japanese version. For those of you who are new to these terms, here's a brief explanation to help with your reading experience!

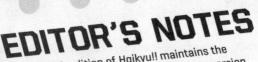

When saying someone's name in Japanese, a suffix is often attached to indicate how familiar the speaker is with the person. Some are more polite and respectful, while others are endearing.

1 *-kun* is often used for young men or boys, usually someone you are familiar with.

2 *-chan* is used for young children and can be used as a term of endearment.

3 *-san* is used for someone you respect or are not close to, or to be polite.

4 *Senpai* is used for someone who is older than you or in a higher position or grade in school.

5 *Kohai* is used for someone who is younger than you or in a lower position or grade in school.

6 *Sensei* means teacher.

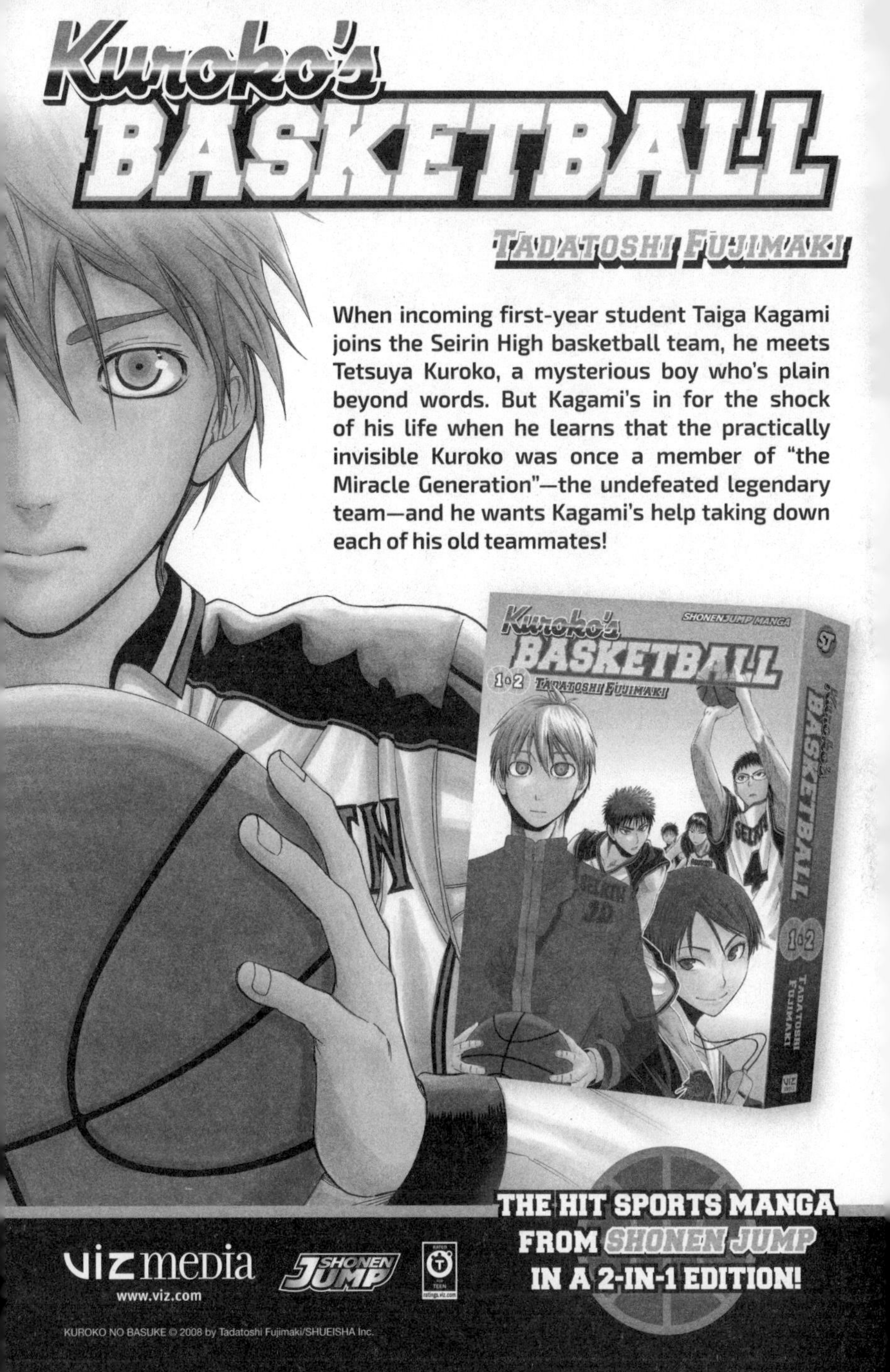

Kuroko's BASKETBALL
TADATOSHI FUJIMAKI
When incoming first-year student Taiga Kagami joins the Seirin High basketball team, he meets Tetsuya Kuroko, a mysterious boy who's plain beyond words. But Kagami's in for the shock of his life when he learns that the practically invisible Kuroko was once a member of "the Miracle Generation"—the undefeated legendary team—and he wants Kagami's help taking down each of his old teammates!
Kuroko's BASKETBALL
SHONENJUMP MANGA
1•2 TADATOSHI FUJIMAKI
THE HIT SPORTS MANGA FROM SHONEN JUMP IN A 2-IN-1 EDITION!
viz media
www.viz.com
SHONEN JUMP
RATED T TEEN
ratings.viz.com
KUROKO NO BASUKE © 2008 by Tadatoshi Fujimaki/SHUEISHA Inc.

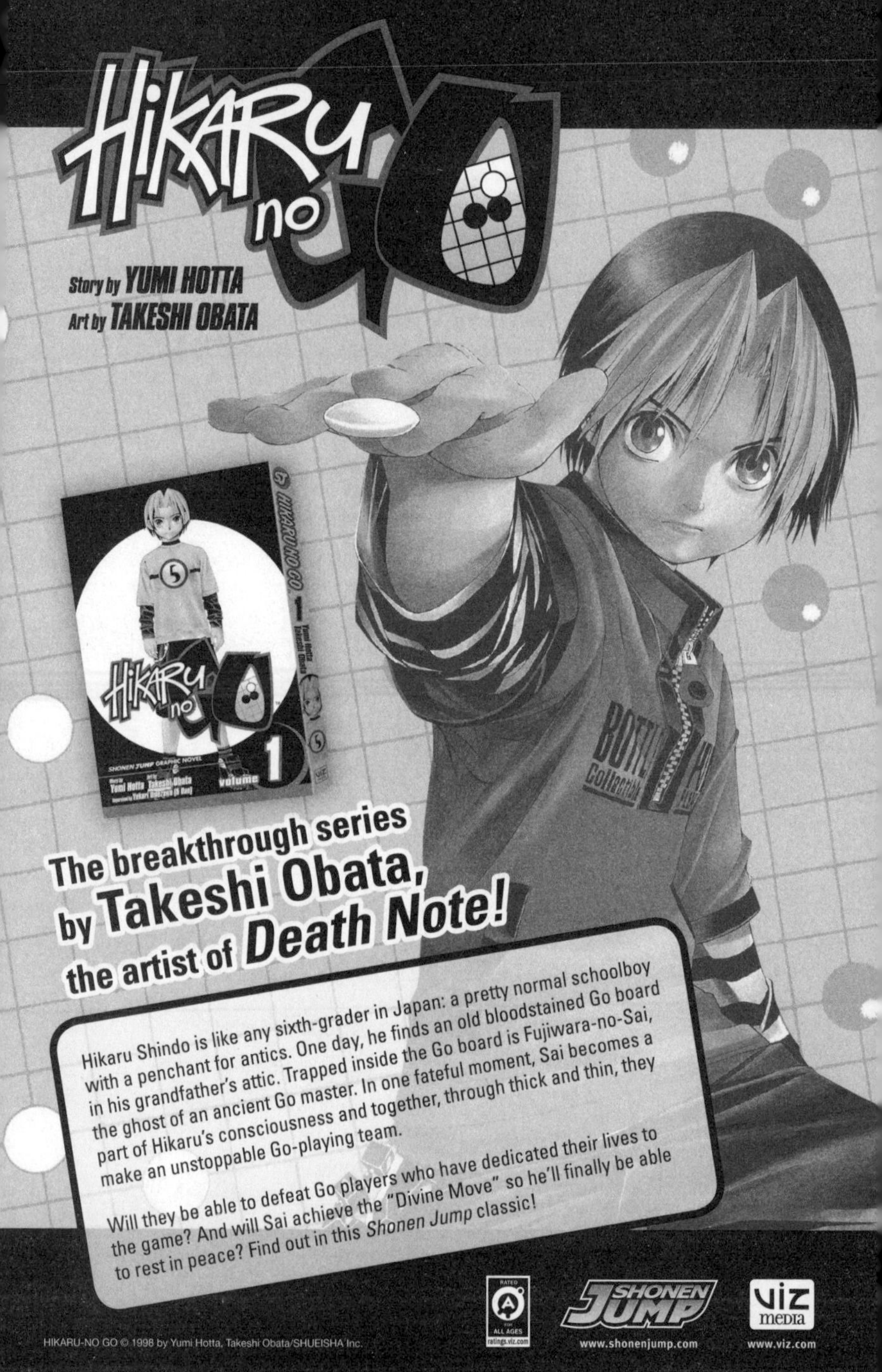
HIKARU no GO
Story by YUMI HOTTA
Art by TAKESHI OBATA
The breakthrough series by Takeshi Obata, the artist of Death Note!
Hikaru Shindo is like any sixth-grader in Japan: a pretty normal schoolboy with a penchant for antics. One day, he finds an old bloodstained Go board in his grandfather's attic. Trapped inside the Go board is Fujiwara-no-Sai, the ghost of an ancient Go master. In one fateful moment, Sai becomes a part of Hikaru's consciousness and together, through thick and thin, they make an unstoppable Go-playing team.
Will they be able to defeat Go players who have dedicated their lives to the game? And will Sai achieve the "Divine Move" so he'll finally be able to rest in peace? Find out in this Shonen Jump classic!
HIKARU-NO GO © 1998 by Yumi Hotta, Takeshi Obata/SHUEISHA Inc.
RATED A FOR ALL AGES ratings.viz.com
SHONEN JUMP
www.shonenjump.com
VIZ media
www.viz.com

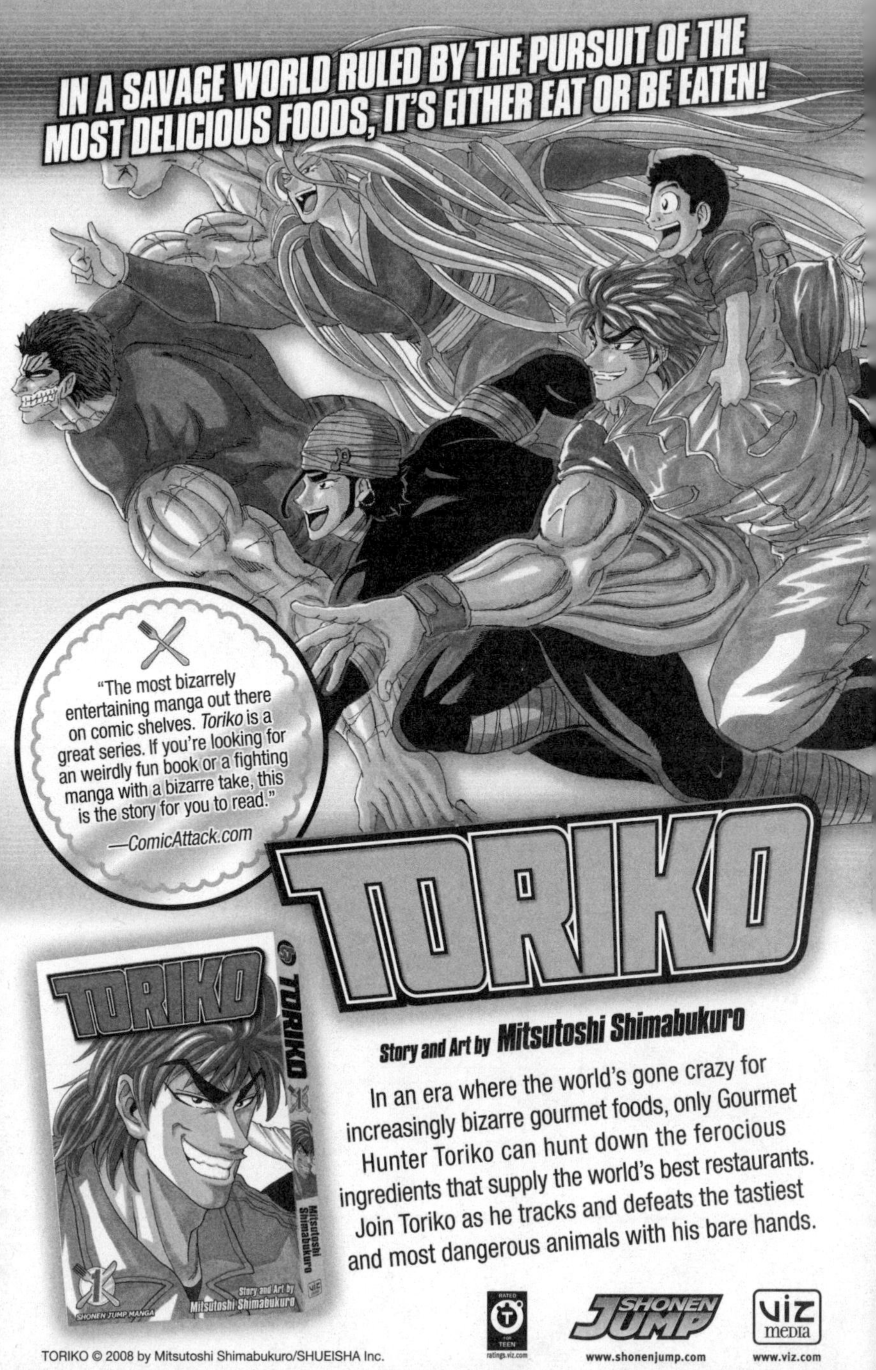
IN A SAVAGE WORLD RULED BY THE PURSUIT OF THE MOST DELICIOUS FOODS, IT'S EITHER EAT OR BE EATEN!
"The most bizarrely entertaining manga out there on comic shelves. Toriko is a great series. If you're looking for an weirdly fun book or a fighting manga with a bizarre take, this is the story for you to read."
—ComicAttack.com
TORIKO
Story and Art by Mitsutoshi Shimabukuro
In an era where the world's gone crazy for increasingly bizarre gourmet foods, only Gourmet Hunter Toriko can hunt down the ferocious ingredients that supply the world's best restaurants. Join Toriko as he tracks and defeats the tastiest and most dangerous animals with his bare hands.
TORIKO © 2008 by Mitsutoshi Shimabukuro/SHUEISHA Inc.
RATED T FOR TEEN
ratings.viz.com
SHONEN JUMP
www.shonenjump.com
VIZ media
www.viz.com

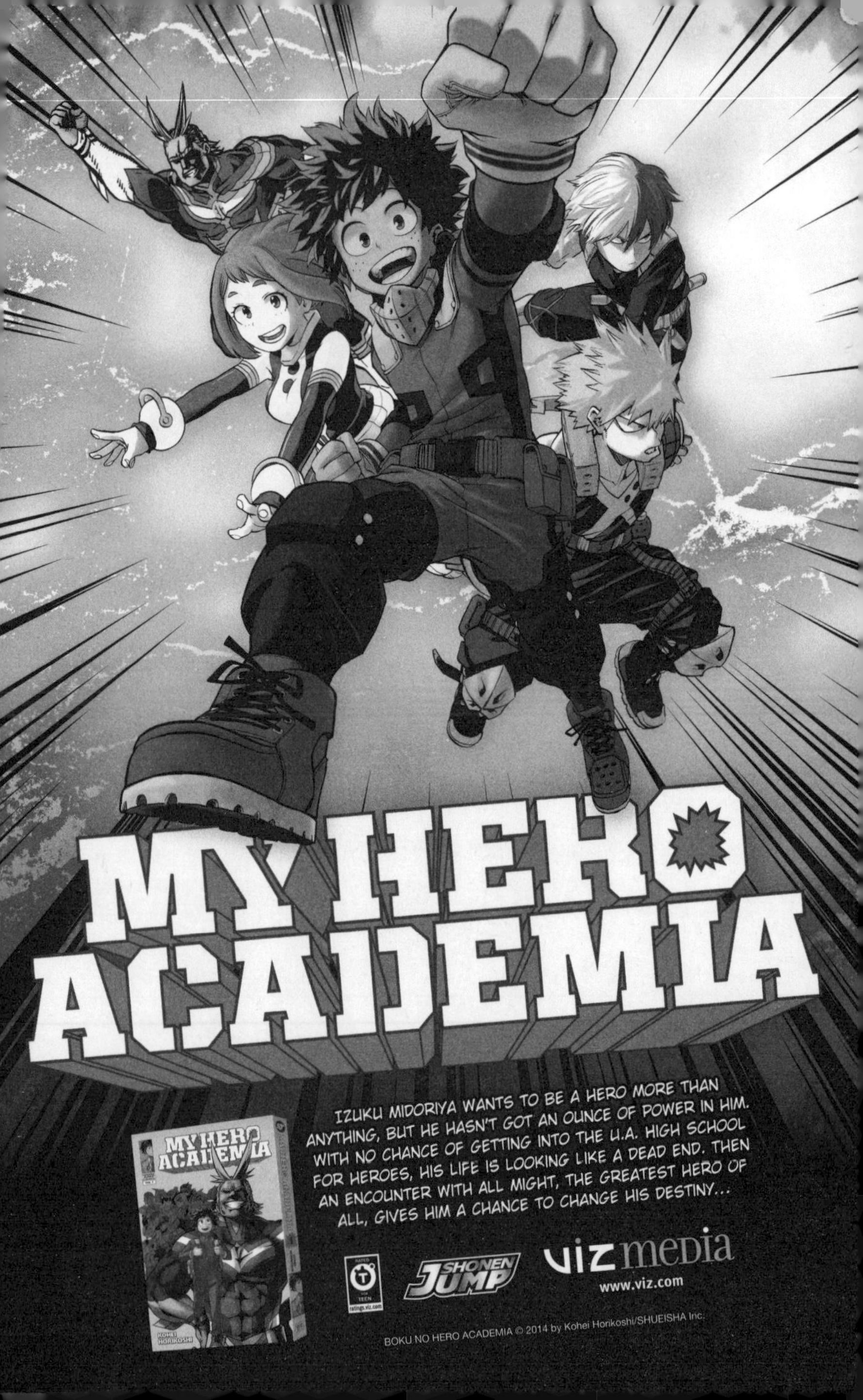
MY HERO ACADEMIA
IZUKU MIDORIYA WANTS TO BE A HERO MORE THAN ANYTHING, BUT HE HASN'T GOT AN OUNCE OF POWER IN HIM. WITH NO CHANCE OF GETTING INTO THE U.A. HIGH SCHOOL FOR HEROES, HIS LIFE IS LOOKING LIKE A DEAD END. THEN AN ENCOUNTER WITH ALL MIGHT, THE GREATEST HERO OF ALL, GIVES HIM A CHANCE TO CHANGE HIS DESTINY...
SHONEN JUMP
viz media
www.viz.com
BOKU NO HERO ACADEMIA © 2014 by Kohei Horikoshi/SHUEISHA Inc.

A PREMIUM BOX SET OF THE FIRST TWO STORY ARCS OF ONE PIECE!

A PIRATE'S TREASURE FOR ANY MANGA FAN!

STORY AND ART BY EIICHIRO ODA

Comes with
EXCLUSIVE POSTER
and the
ROMANCE DAWN
mini-comic!

As a child, Monkey D. Luffy dreamed of becoming King of the Pirates. But his life changed when he accidentally gained the power to stretch like rubber...at the cost of never being able to swim again! Years later, Luffy sets off in search of the "One Piece," said to be the greatest treasure in the world...

This box set includes VOLUMES 1-23, which comprise the EAST BLUE and BAROQUE WORKS story arcs.

EXCLUSIVE PREMIUMS and GREAT SAVINGS
over buying the individual volumes!

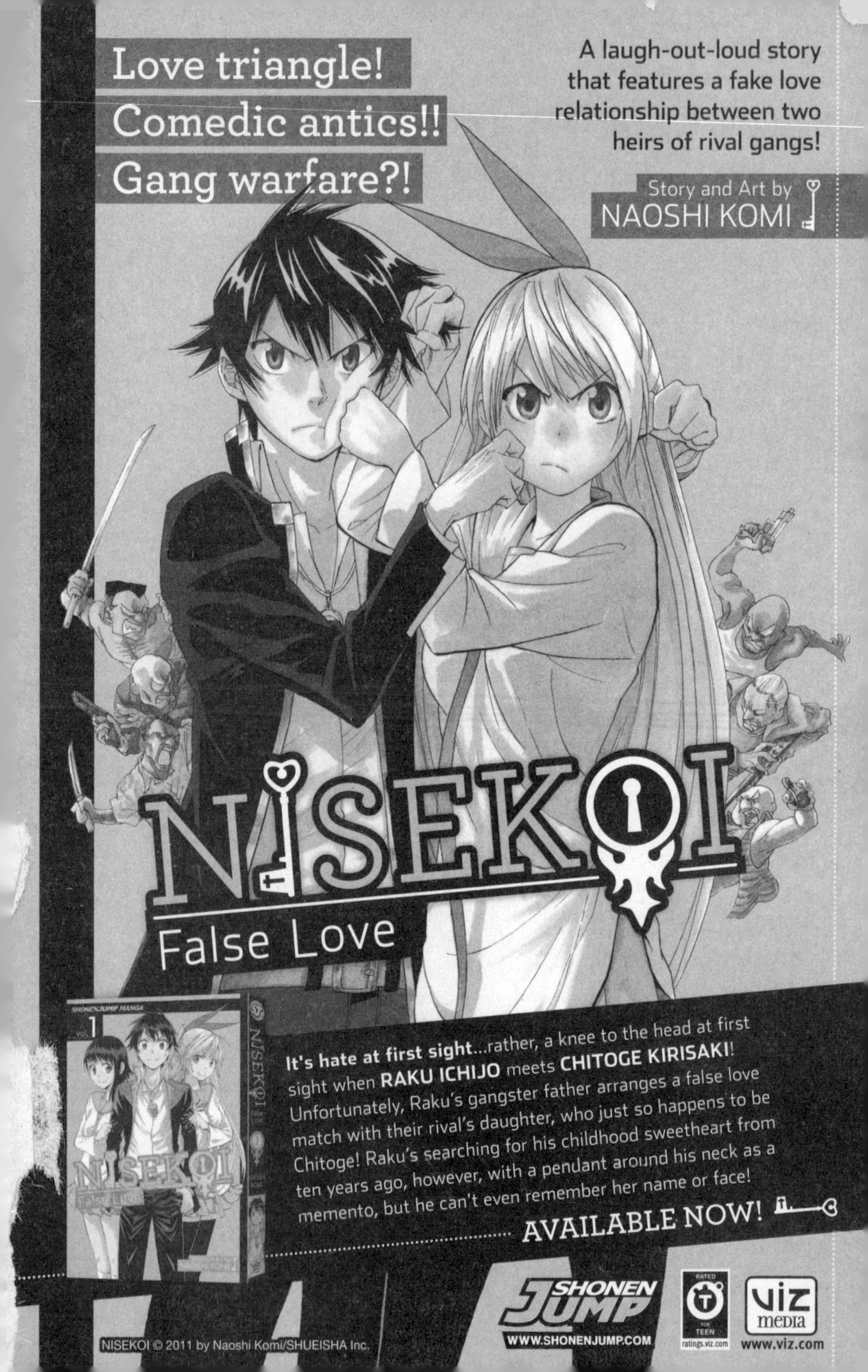

Love triangle!
Comedic antics!!
Gang warfare?!
A laugh-out-loud story that features a fake love relationship between two heirs of rival gangs!
Story and Art by
NAOSHI KOMI
NISEKOI
False Love
SHONENJUMP MANGA
VOL. 1
NISEKOI
False Love
It's hate at first sight...rather, a knee to the head at first sight when RAKU ICHIJO meets CHITOGE KIRISAKI! Unfortunately, Raku's gangster father arranges a false love match with their rival's daughter, who just so happens to be Chitoge! Raku's searching for his childhood sweetheart from ten years ago, however, with a pendant around his neck as a memento, but he can't even remember her name or face!
AVAILABLE NOW!
SHONEN JUMP
WWW.SHONENJUMP.COM
RATED T FOR TEEN
ratings.viz.com
VIZ media
www.viz.com
NISEKOI © 2011 by Naoshi Komi/SHUEISHA Inc.

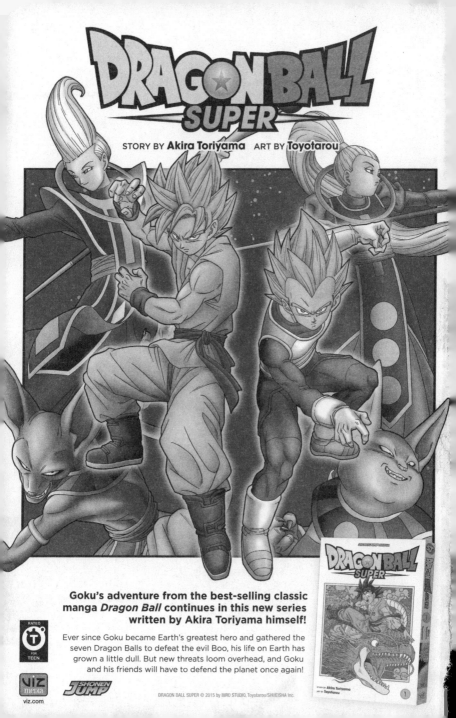

You're Reading the
WRONG WAY!

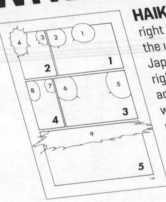

HAIKYU!! reads from right to left, starting in the upper-right corner. Japanese is read from right to left, meaning that action, sound effects and word-balloon order are completely reversed from English order.